THE STONES OF BALAZUC

ALSO BY JOHN MERRIMAN

A History of Modern Europe
The Margins of City Life: Explorations on the French Urban Frontier
The Red City: Limoges and the French Nineteenth Century
Agony of the Republic: The Repression of the Left in
Revolutionary France, 1848–1851

(AS EDITOR)

For Want of a Horse: Chance and Humor in History
French Cities in the Nineteenth Century
Consciousness and Class Experience in Nineteenth-Century Europe
1830 in France

(AS COEDITOR)

Edo and Paris: Urban Life and the State in the Early Modern Era

(AS COAUTHOR)

The Story of Mankind

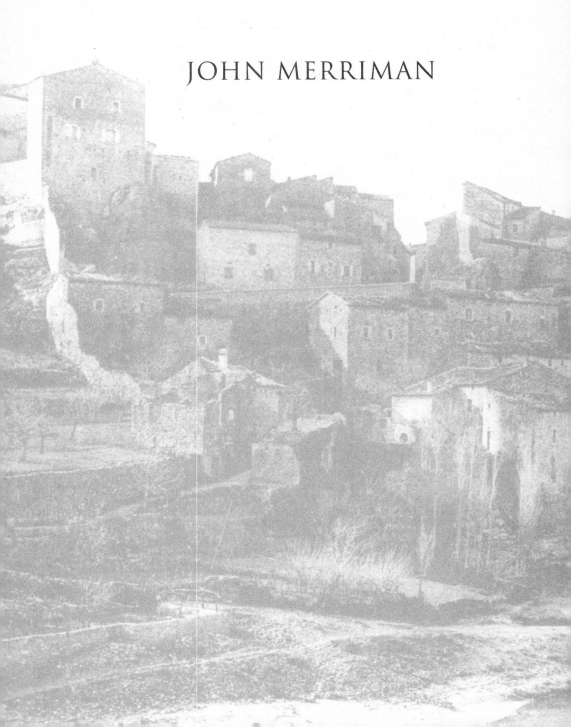

THE STONES OF

JOHN MERRIMAN

BALAZUC

A French Village in Time

W. W. Norton & Company
New York · London

For information about permission to reproduce selections from this book, write to Permissions,
W. W. Norton & Company, Inc., 500 Fifth Avenue, New York, NY 10110

The text of this book is composed in Garamond Three
with the display set in Trajan and Pouty
Composition by Gina Webster
Manufacturing by The Maple-Vail Book Manufacturing Group.
Book design by Charlotte Staub
Production manager: Andrew Marasia

Library of Congress Cataloging-in-Publication Data

Merriman, John M.
The stones of Balazuc : a French village in time / John Merriman.
p.   cm.
Includes bibiographical references and index.
ISBN 0-393-05113-7
1. Balazuc (France)—History. I. Title.
DC801.B15355 M47 2002
944'.589—dc21   2002000515

W. W. Norton & Company, Inc., 500 Fifth Avenue, New York, N.Y. 10110
www.wwnorton.com

W. W. Norton & Company Ltd., Castle House, 75/76 Wells Street, London W1T 3QT

1 2 3 4 5 6 7 8 9 0

Pour Eric et pour Mathieu

CONTENTS

PREFACE

UNLIKE SEVERAL NINETEENTH-CENTURY VISITORS, I did not first go to Balazuc in search of the Saracens popularly believed to have founded the village and certainly not with the intention of writing a book about that village or any village. It was 1987. After a year with our baby, Laura, in Paris, fatigued from carrying a baby carriage, groceries, and everything else up the stairs, we needed some room, fresh air, and sunshine. Having had the pleasure of spending many years exploring provincial France and its archives, I had been to the Ardèche several times before, and remembering its beauty, we decided to spend a couple of weeks in June in Les Vans, on the edge of the Cévennes. One day, Michelin guide in hand, alerted by a star, we came to Balazuc. Arriving from the other side of the Ardèche River, we were stunned by the beauty of the village perched high above the river. We walked about the village. It was just like that, a lightning bolt. Just like that, we had some connection, although at first only during summer and Christmas vacations, with a spectacu-

lar place. Our son, Christopher, came to Balazuc for the first time
when he was ten days old. We met some people, but our connection
to Balazuc was then unavoidably intermittent.

Our sense of the place changed in the early 1990s. We spent most
of 1991–93 in Balazuc, a combination of leaves of absence from Yale
University and teaching at Université Lumière—Lyon II, well more
than two hours to the north. Laura and Christopher began school, the
former in Balazuc's school, a *classe unique* (that is, one teacher for
grades one to five), Christopher in the nursery school in nearby
Vogüé, because Balazuc's village school did not normally accept children below the equivalent of American first grade (that has changed,
for reasons we shall later see). The year before our children's arrival,
the school had had only nine pupils, eight girls and one boy. One-
room schoolhouses were being closed all over France by the Ministry
of Education, particularly in regions, like the Ardèche, in which the
rural population, which had begun to drop steadily in the late nineteenth century, had continued to fall as well as to age. Periodic meetings of parents with Balazuc's teacher, Jacques Imbertèche, and
school activities formed friendships.

Yet the idea of writing a book about Balazuc had not yet occurred
to me. I admired a good many village studies, above all, Laurence
Wylie's splendid *Village in the Vaucluse*, a sociologist's analysis of a
changing village in the immediate postwar era, written in the very
early 1950s.[1] I knew of Peter Mayle's enormously popular *A Year in
Provence*. That kind of book simply did not interest me. In any case,
one year is nowhere near enough.

In the meantime I was in Balazuc working on two projects, one a
history of Europe since the Renaissance, the other a book on the margins of urban life in nineteenth-century France. Balazuc certainly
seemed a minuscule part of the former and very far away from the latter. During subsequent vacations and another semester in 1996, I
sometimes used to sit on our terrace, walk through the village on the
way to take the kids to school or pick them up, or run over the rocky,
arid, and rugged Jurassic plateau (the *gras*) that lies beyond and above
the Ardèche River and try to imagine how people managed to scrape
a living out of what people sometimes referred to as the "ungrateful"

soil. I also wondered what difference the "great events" that came and went—the wars of religion, the French Revolution, the Revolution of 1848, and, above all, the world wars—had made in Balazuc. Even though television and depopulation had killed off the *veillées* (evening gatherings around the fire to eat chestnuts, drink wine, and listen to stories), I had many occasions to hear about the past. Some stories had been about storms. Then, September 22, 1992, a tremendous storm began with lightning about three in the morning. It rained and rained. The river rose rapidly, coming within not many feet of the top of the bridge. It killed three people higher up the river (the same storm killed many people in the Vaucluse across the Rhône). From the bridge, we could see all sorts of things it had ripped away in its path. I was struck by the sense of inevitability with which the dramatic storm had been greeted and wanted to know how people whose lives had depended on extracting a living from rocky soil, some near the river, had managed to bounce back after catastrophes that were described as periodic but that were powerful enough to have left a mark on the collective memory.

I knew that the list of grievances (*cahier de doléances*) that had been drawn up in Balazuc during the spring of 1789 had been signed by those men who knew how to do so in the Romanesque church across the small rocky square below our terrace. I decided to go over the Col d'Escrinet to Privas (a somewhat grim administrative town, known for its enormous asylum) to read what they had to say about their isolation and poverty and of their hopes. I was amazed to find that of the twenty-eight men who signed the document, the families of seventeen of them still live in Balazuc, astonishing continuity in a village whose population had risen from four or five hundred in the eighteenth century to nine hundred in the mid-nineteenth century, before falling to barely two hundred following World War II. Many people had left, for reasons we shall explore, but many of the families who had owned and worked "thankless" land in Balazuc so long ago were still there. I found some of the same names, not surprisingly, etched on the monument outside the church honoring those killed in the bloodbath of World War I.

One evening the parents of the schoolchildren were asked to meet in the school. The topic to be discussed was the creation of a school lunchroom, to discourage mothers from putting their children in the school in the town in which they worked. This was a meeting like others in which we had participated, to discuss lessons in canoeing and kayaking or to plan fund-raising activities, including the school bingo on Sunday, or to plan for "Nature's Classroom," the *classe verte* (green class; when the kids went to Paris, we called it the *classe grise,* gray class), a stay for four or five days in another region. The mayor, whom we barely knew at all, was going to attend, and that lent an air of unusual formality to an occasion that invariably finished with a bottle of Armagnac. When we began to discuss ways of keeping our school going, the importance of which virtually everyone in the vil-lage—whatever disagreements they had had in the past—agreed upon, the mayor said something that struck me. It made me wonder if the relationship between the state and France as a whole and our small village and its one-room schoolhouse had not been reversed since the nineteenth century. I then began to go regularly to the Archives Départementales in Privas, and to return to my familiar haunts of the Archives Nationales and the Bibliothèque Nationale in Paris to see if it was possible to assess the continuities and changes across time and bring them to life in one of the more than thirty-six thousand towns, bourgs, and villages in France. Then I went up to the village hall to see what, if any, documents and censuses remained there. The news was good, and I set out on a long journey through the past. I wanted to know much more about the continuities among the very distant past, the nineteenth century, and more recent history. I also wanted to know about the changes that have shaped the pre-sent in Balazuc and to see if what documents I found could take me inside the small stone schoolhouses that became such an important, even defining presence in the village.

I have been struck by the ability of the people of Balazuc not only to survive (though many for not very long) but over the past two cen-turies to adapt to change, when opportunities presented themselves, and even to manipulate the state to their advantage. The peasants of Balazuc thus appear nothing like the frequent stereotype of the coun-trypersons locked in routine until they could be rescued by various agents of "modernization" and brought into the modern world. At the same time, I am interested in the way national politics helped shape local politics, particularly during the struggles in the decades before World War I over the role of the church and the laicization (secularization) of schools.

The lay of the land and indeed the very stones over which rough paths and roads were forged and with which houses and walls were built over the centuries are actors in this book. The role, if not primacy, of physical environment in the writing of history a century ago, underlined by two generations of French humanistic geographers, has been too often forgotten. Photographs and descriptions by older people portray a village in which there was astonishingly little greenery. This is no longer the case. I wanted to know why. This book gives a place to *la mémoire des pierres* (the memory of the stones) of Balazuc and to continuities and changes over a long time, even as national events intervened (and themselves were often shaped at the local level by ordinary people). Moreover, as no village can truly be studied in isolation, I gladly set Balazuc in the context of its fascinating region, as far back as the oldest cave drawings yet discovered to its considerably more recent annual discovery by thousands of summer tourists.

At first glance, Balazuc might seem to an outsider to be a village that has somehow failed. Its agricultural economy, after a half century of unprecedented prosperity, collapsed tragically. The village's population plunged, along with that not only of its region but of much of rural France.[2] But this is a story about resilience, often heroic, rooted in sturdy families attached to their land and their village, generation after generation. It is about a place to which I am very attached and that has become part of my life and the lives of my family.

The anthropologist Clifford Geertz once said that anthropologists do not write books about villages; they write them in villages. I am not an anthropologist, but the advice is well taken. Yet I certainly do not see Balazuc as any kind of laboratory or our friends and other residents as "informants" or samples. Peter Jones notes that a good many

French village studies have the title *Mon village.*[3] Moreover, this is not a book intended to plunge one into nostalgia for a time past, and, above all, not one intended to encourage further tourism. Since we were not born in Balazuc (although we did get our residency papers a good many years ago), it would be ridiculous in a place where many families can trace their origins back centuries to claim that Balazuc is "my village." Residents of the village who were not born there are still referred to, without malice, as *estrangers,* patois for *étrangers* (outsiders, and not at all necessarily foreigners). One is accepted as one participates in village events—above all, with the school. I remember when a friend of ours was discussing prices charged for work he did on houses: *"On ne peut pas prendre tout le monde pour des américains"* ("You can't take everyone for Americans"); they have a reputation of being naïve (*bon enfant*) and willing to pay large sums of money when they might not have to do so. Several sentences later he suddenly interjected, "Oops!," having forgotten that we are Americans (as inevitably, going back to our beginnings in the village, we first became known as the Americans). That this had slipped his mind pleased me no end. But we remain *estrangers,* as do our friends who came here from the north of France, yet we are integrated into village life. Balazuc is a place in which we have been fortunate enough to have spent a good part of every year and several years all the way through. Sometimes it is a little strange going back and forth so much. One evening last year I was invited to attend the meeting of the cell of the Communist party of Balazuc. The gathering was in a wonderful old stone house up in Audon on the other side of the river. Our host, who was ninety-two, had joined the Party in Paris in 1930. His wife had joined a little later and was even older. Ten days or so later I attended a kickoff meeting for the candidacy of a friend who was running for first selectperson in North Haven, Connecticut. The meeting was in an American Legion hall, decked out in red, white, and blue balloons. It had its own kind of quaintness.

Several years ago Laura, asked what she thought of Balazuc by a journalist from the United States come to write a story about our lives here, replied, "It's just a pile of rocks!" She could not understand why I had decided to write a book about it. "Daddy, how many people are

going to care how many goats there were in Balazuc in 1827?"
Sometimes she missed American malls. One day after she turned fifteen, she told me that she had changed her mind. When I asked why,
she replied, "I prefer France; there are hot guys there!" (*"Je préfère la
France; il y a des beaux mecs là!"*). Now one of the things Laura most
likes about Balazuc is that "It's how you are, not what kind of car you
have." For me, it has been a labor of love to dig into archives to recon-
struct and to evoke Balazuc's past and present, even as I worry about
its future. The last chapter, which looks at changes and continuities
in the village since World War II, draws on archival documents, to
be sure, but it also depends on countless conversations with people
from whom I have learned so much (including, I hasten to add, my
wife and children, who, having spent a good portion of the past fourteen years here, have their own views and have become part of the
story). On some subjects, people who are originally from Balazuc or
who have lived here for a long time may agree; on others, not at all.
A village is like that.

With this in mind, I should like to thank, among many others,
Thérèse Muller, Paulette Balazuc, Lucien and Catherine Mollier, Guy
and Marie-Renée Boyer, Guy Larochette and Marie-Élise Hilaire,
Ginette Gineys, Jean-Claude and Ginette Michalon, Patrick Socrate,
Jean-Marc and Edith Dupuy-Engberts, Hervé and Françoise Parain,
Catherine Husulmé, Georges Duffaud, Huguette Laroche (and in
memory of Jacques), Patrick and Françoise Constant, Raymond
Chevalier, Bernard Charousset, Paulette Mirabel, Janine Pinède, Max
and Doris Brioude, Clovis Hilaire, l'abbé Fortuné Rouveyrol, Pierre
Soares (an in memory of Danielle), Huguette (Sapède) Gamel,
Thierry Lachery, who shared his considerable knowledge of prehis-
tory with me, and Carole Lacherey.

When we initially came to Balazuc, Jean Boyer and his wife,
Suzanne, were two of the first people we got to know. A retired his-
tory teacher who had taught in the Paris region, Jean Boyer loved
Balazuc. He prepared an unpublished account of the village from the
Revolution on, one that is both history and, in part, memoir.
Walking by his house, frequently I heard him typing late at night.
His passion for his village inspired me, and still does. He concludes

his pages with a thought that should move anyone who has walked in and around Balazuc, evoking in "[t]hese painful pages children who died in their cribs, peasants who exhausted themselves struggling against such ungrateful soil, these young people chased from their villages by the poverty of resources."

I very much admire Jacques Imbertèche, our children's teacher and our friend. His long career as a teacher is ending, but not his influence on the children (and their families) who have been lucky enough to have been in his school. I also want to thank Dominique Dupraz, director of the Archives Départementales in Privas, and his unfailingly helpful staff; Yves Morel, who recently completed a doctoral dissertation on silk throwing in the Ardèche and provided one of the photos in this book; Ginette Michalon, Paulette Balazuc, and Numa Charousset, for providing photos; Peter Jones, for his superb studies of the lower Massif Central; Michael Sonenscher, for permission to cite his doctoral dissertation; Eric Darrieux, for providing information on the murder of Gilbert Serret in 1943; Julia Paolitto for expediting the manuscript through its final stages; Pearl Hanig for copyediting; and Yale University, for providing research funds and a generous amount of time on leave.

W. W. Norton is a wonderful and unique publisher. Don Lamm helped make it so. We first began to work together in 1984; Drake McFeely continues a great tradition. Steve Forman has been my talented and extraordinarily helpful editor for years, as well as a good friend. He and his family also made the trek to Balazuc. When I first went to Yale, my former colleague Edmund Morgan once gave me rather intimidating advice: "Got a minute? Write a line!" Steve has turned it around: "Got a minute? Cut a line!" But all for the better.

I want to thank other friends as well: Yves and Colette Lequin, Maurice and Marie-Claude Garden, Claude and Simone Mazaurik, Hans and Annemarie Schmidt, Alan Forrest and Rosemary Morris; Bob Schwartz and Marietta Clement, Ted and Joby Margadant, Chris and Lois Johnson, Pascal Dupuy, Philippe and Karine Mougey-Chamett, Philippe Calmus and Corinne Mouchard, Jean and Gila Serreau, André and Christianne Parent; Daniel, Dominique, and Faustine Chevet; and Jeanne and John Innes. Dick and Cindy

Brodhead and Ben Kiernan and Glenda Gilmore enlivened the celebration of the Feux St.-Jean in 2000, when Balazuc rocked. And of
course Victoria Johnson.

I have been lucky to have good friends who have read this book in
draft and made suggestions, many, if not most, of which I have followed. Robert Schwartz, Alan Forrest, and Paul Freedman contributed their expertise to the earlier chapters. Peter McPhee, Peter
Gay, Chris Johnson, David Bell, and Jay Winter read the whole manuscript with care and encouragement, as did Carol Merriman, yet
again.

Eric Fruleux and Mathieu Fruleux, who spent most of a year in
Connecticut as a freshman in North Haven Connecticut High School,
have helped make two worlds fully complementary.

Finally, thanks and so much love to Carol, Laura, and Christopher
Merriman, who have lived and thrived in both worlds for years.

Balazuc, August 3, 2001

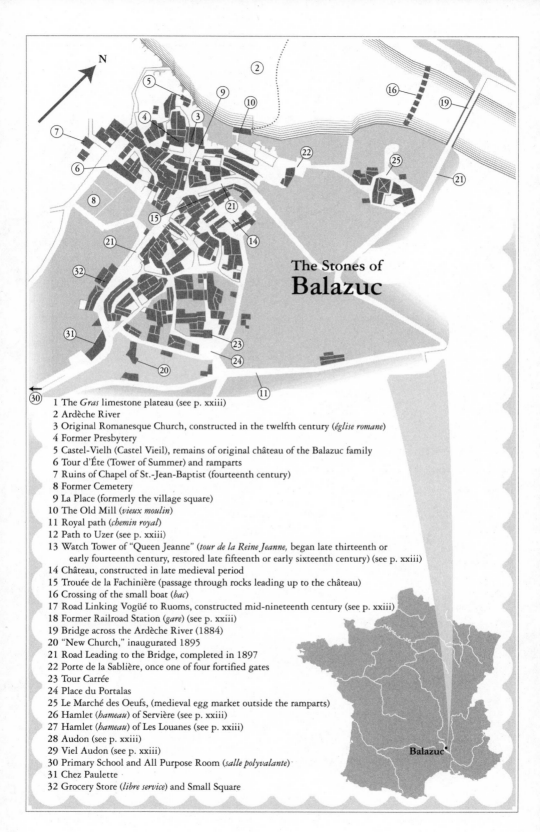

The Stones of
Balazuc

1 The *Gras* limestone plateau (see p. xxiii)
2 Ardèche River
3 Original Romanesque Church, constructed in the twelfth century (*église romane*)
4 Former Presbytery
5 Castel-Vielh (Castel Vieil), remains of original château of the Balazuc family
6 Tour d'Été (Tower of Summer) and ramparts
7 Ruins of Chapel of St.-Jean-Baptist (fourteenth century)
8 Former Cemetery
9 La Place (formerly the village square)
10 The Old Mill (*vieux moulin*)
11 Royal path (*chemin royal*)
12 Path to Uzer (see p. xxiii)
13 Watch Tower of "Queen Jeanne" (*tour de la Reine Jeanne,* began late thirteenth or
     early fourteenth century, restored late fifteenth or early sixteenth century) (see p. xxiii)
14 Château, constructed in late medieval period
15 Trouée de la Fachinière (passage through rocks leading up to the château)
16 Crossing of the small boat (*bac*)
17 Road Linking Vogüé to Ruoms, constructed mid-nineteenth century (see p. xxiii)
18 Former Railroad Station (*gare*) (see p. xxiii)
19 Bridge across the Ardèche River (1884)
20 "New Church," inaugurated 1895
21 Road Leading to the Bridge, completed in 1897
22 Porte de la Sablière, once one of four fortified gates
23 Tour Carrée
24 Place du Portalas
25 Le Marché des Oeufs, (medieval egg market outside the ramparts)
26 Hamlet (*hameau*) of Servière (see p. xxiii)
27 Hamlet (*hameau*) of Les Louanes (see p. xxiii)
28 Audon (see p. xxiii)
29 Viel Audon (see p. xxiii)
30 Primary School and All Purpose Room (*salle polyvalente*)
31 Chez Paulette
32 Grocery Store (*libre service*) and Small Square

Balazuc

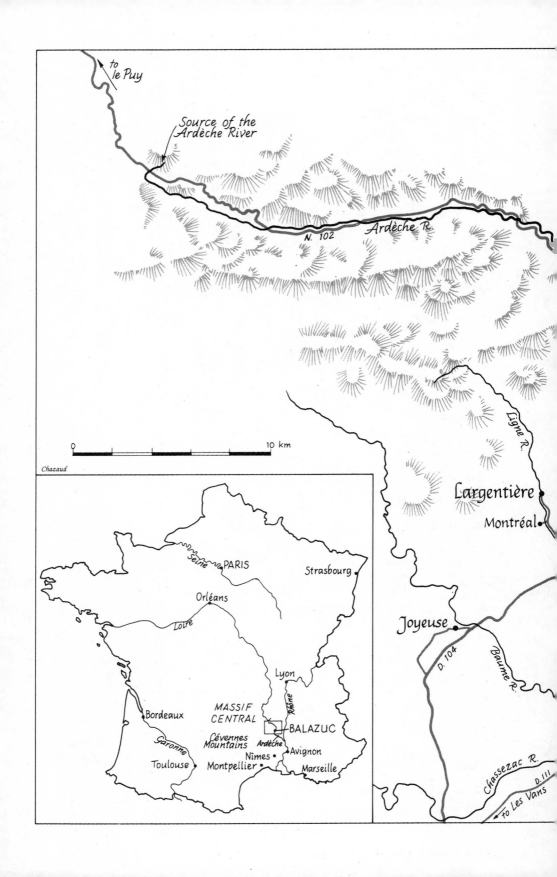

to
le Puy

Source of the
Ardèche River

N. 102   Ardèche R.

Ligne R.

10 km

Chazaud

Largentière

Montréal

Joyeuse

D. 104   Baume R.

Chassezac R.

D. 111

to Les Vans

Seine   PARIS

Strasbourg

Orléans

Loire

Lyon

Rhône

MASSIF
CENTRAL

Bordeaux

BALAZUC

Garonne

Cévennes
Mountains

Ardèche

Avignon

Toulouse

Nîmes

Montpellier

Marseille

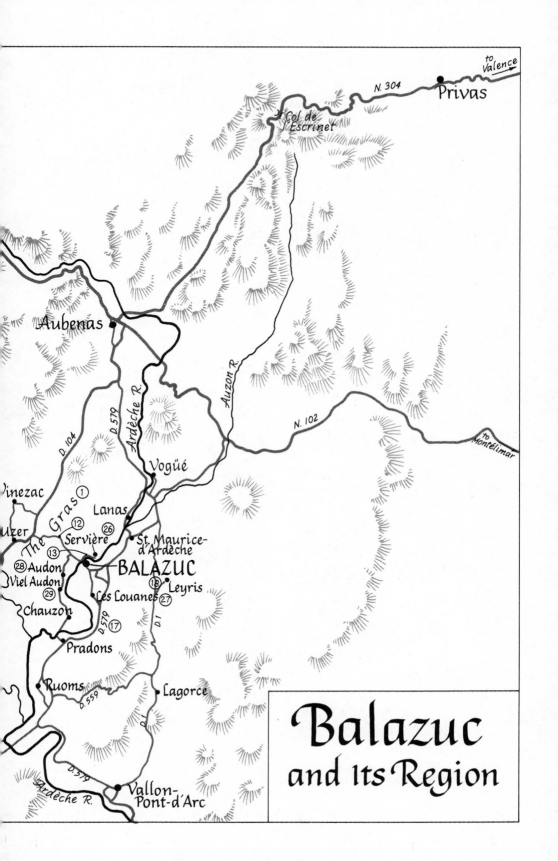

to Valence →

N. 304

Privas

Col de
Escrinet

Aubenas

Auzon R.

Ardèche R.

D.579

D.104

N. 102

to
Montélimar

Vogüé

Vinezac

①

The Gras

Lanas

Uzer

⑫

⑬

Servière

㉖

St. Maurice-
d'Ardèche

㉘ Audon

BALAZUC

Viel Audon

㉙

⑱ Leyris

Les Louanes

㉗

Chauzon

D.579

⑰

D.1

Pradons

Ruoms

D.559

Lagorce

D.1

Ardèche R.

D.579

Vallon-
Pont-d'Arc

Balazuc
and Its Region

THE STONES OF BALAZUC

ONE

A Village Set in Stone

The Ardèche offers first of all rock, nothing but rock. . . . There is nothing more arid, nor more harsh. You already sense the struggle of man, his persistent, prodigious battle against the constraints of nature. Between rock and more rock, schist and more schist, two or three sprigs of rye present their meager offerings.   —JULES MICHELET, 1844[1]

VIEWED FROM ACROSS THE RIVER, BALAZUC SEEMS PART of the huge limestone cliff that towers above the Ardèche River. Its houses and the remains of the old village walls seem welded to the immense stone cliff, "attached to the rock like a wasps' nest." Houses appear to stand on rock cubes in the form of half an amphitheater sloping rapidly down to the river. Most are built of limestone (held together by mortar made of crushed stone), the one gift of nature found in abundance in the Bas-Vivarais, the southern part of the region of the Vivarais and the *département* (department) of the Ardèche. Because of the notorious storms that can come in September or October, transforming the Ardèche, "which nature has made so dreadful," in Michelet's words, into a rampaging torrent destroying everything in its swollen path, it was out of the question to build too near the normal course of the river. A perched village, Balazuc's houses seem "piled against each other, stacked high on the hill either for reasons of defense or from lack of space, joined

3

together with the enormous rock, standing wedded as one by the passing of time."[2]

In 1893, Eugène-Melchoir de Vogüé, a writer and member of the Académie française, placed the village in the context of the Bas-Vivarais: "It is at Balazuc, along the deep fault through which the Ardèche River winds, that nature assumes all of its intensity. Rock is everywhere. Topsoil, reduced to a minimum, disappears in the fields under the enormous stone tablets; several shrubs and several twisted vine shoots desperately reach from the cracks of these slabs. This poor and noble soil, an Arab land, all bones and muscles, without any flesh. My driver put it very well: 'Ah! Monsieur, the land is so nervous here!' "[3]

In December 1994 three scientists entered a *grotte,* or cave, high above the Ardèche River near Vallon–Pont d'Arc, about eleven miles downstream from Balazuc. They crawled on their stomachs for about ten yards and then, lowering themselves down by rope, found themselves in the first of several large caverns. To their astonishment, they had entered a veritable prehistoric zoo: beautifully drawn animals in red or black, including bears, horses, stags, mammoths, reindeer, cats, ibex, aurochs, bison, and many lions and rhinoceroses, as well as a panther, a hyena, and an owl, and other beasts that cannot be identified. More than two hundred figures have now been counted and examined, and some of them have been dated by radiocarbon. The artists used precocious techniques, including perspective and stump drawing, to provide detail and to accentuate the relief, imparting a sense of action to the animals.

The cave drawings of the Grotte Chauvet, named after one of the scientists, are the oldest ever discovered. Not far from other prehistoric caves from later periods, the drawings of the Grotte Chauvet have been dated by carbon to about thirty-two thousand years ago. This places sophisticated drafting techniques at a much earlier time than was previously believed. The absence of daylight over the millennia and the isolation of the caves themselves preserved these remarkable figures.[4]

The prehistory of Balazuc and of the valley of the Ardèche is incredibly rich. Tribes of hunters found shelter in the caves that had been formed by erosion in the cliffs along the Ardèche and other rivers. Evidence of veritable camps on the Jurassic plateau (*table de gras*) across the river suggest that more than the caverns along the river were inhabited during the Paleolithic and Neolithic ages.[5] In 1967, bones of a stag, bear, and even a rhinoceros were found in one cave along the river in Balazuc. The limestone region of the Bas-Vivarais offers a remarkable concentration of dolmens, prehistoric monuments of stone. Many may be seen in the territory of Balazuc, some dating from 2500 B.C. Dotting the arid *gras* are prehistoric tombs, rather large stone slabs covered by smaller, loose stones, in some of which gifts had been placed in honor of respected warriors. The population of hunters (who today would join the hunters' club and feel at home in Balazuc) may have lived for the most part on and above the right bank of the Ardèche, probably in caves. Pastoral and agricultural peoples certainly lived on the *gras* between 2600 and 2200 B.C., and perhaps much earlier. Peasants and archaeologists in the nineteenth century discovered bracelets, copper tools, pottery, knives, and other weapons of war on the *gras* from the Bronze Age (1800–700 B.C.) on the right bank of the Ardèche River.

Legend has some of the peoples of prehistory worshiping the sun from a pagan temple on the high rocky cliff where the deconsecrated Romanesque church now stands. In the Bas-Vivarais, there is lots of sun to worship. A rectangular stone slab, bordered by grooves draining toward one of its corners, unearthed several decades ago, may have been used for sacrifices, human or animal. It now stands as part of an altar in the Romanesque church. In our day, summer visitors also worship the sun, lying on the small beach and on the large rocks along the Ardèche River.[6]

The Vivarais forms the eastern part of the southern edge of the Massif Central, France's central highlands. Lying to the west of the Rhône River, the Vivarais is a region of transition between the mountains of the center and the Midi and offers a remarkable geographic variety. The climate of the Vivarais ranges from its mountainous high plateau that can resemble Norway, or at least the Massif Central, to the Mediterranean temperatures, vegetation, and open-air life of the Bas-Vivarais.[7]

The northwestern part of the Vivarais is mountainous, culminating at Mont Mézenc, more than forty-five hundred feet high. Between the latter and the Tanargue to the south, at forty-two hundred feet, stands the Plateau Ardéchois. Here, in the subregion known as the Mountain (*la Montagne*), winter seems interminable. Stone houses, with thick walls of granite or basalt, facing south, crouch low to the ground or even half sunk into it for protection against the elements, some roofs exposed to the north almost reaching the ground.[8] The Coiron, a subregion, extends the Mountain perpendicularly, but at lower altitude, from the Massif Central leaning into the Bas-Vivarais toward the Rhône. The inhabitants of the Coiron, like those of the Mountain, raised cattle and what crops they could.[9] A long rivalry and mutual suspicion, reflected in song and cruel jokes, existed between the people of the mountains, the *pagel*, more conservative and fatalist, and those of the slopes, the *rayol*, less accepting and more contentious.

The Haut-Vivarais lies between the Mountain and the Rhône River that it parallels. Always relatively densely populated, it forms a triangle of fairly prosperous agriculture, its valley bourgs maintaining commercial links to St.-Etienne and Lyon to the north. This subregion begins in the gray climate of Lyon and ends in the southern sunshine of the Mediterranean.[10]

The Cévennes, "country of slopes, country of chestnut trees," stands as the southeastern flank of the Massif Central, opening up like a fan. The forested slopes of the Cévennes thus, in particular, serve as the point of transition, a sort of a vestibule, between the Massif Central and the Mediterranean. Many readers of English in the late nineteenth century learned about the Cévennes through Robert Louis Stevenson's *Travels with a Donkey*. Thousands of acres of chestnut trees, standing at nine hundred to twenty-four hundred feet in altitude, provided the bread of the poor. Peasants began gathering chestnuts in early October. After carrying the chestnuts down the paths that crisscrossed the slopes, peasants dried and stored them in small stone structures (*clèdes*) not far from their houses.

The Bas-Vivarais, including about a sixth of the Ardèche and its southernmost region, is a relatively low-lying plateau, much of it below nine hundred feet in altitude. An area of limestone (*pays de cal-caire*) over millions of years rivers cut through the rock to leave remarkably rugged, beautiful valleys. The Ardèche River is, to be sure, "one of the most temperamental in France, even in the entire world."[11] With its source far above Aubenas at La Chavade, in the forest of Bauzon, four thousand feet high, it runs seventy miles until it reaches the Rhône. Michel Carlat describes its course: "From the balcony of the Mountain, [the Ardèche River] tumbles rapidly down the steep ravines of the Cévennes . . . reaching the rugged lowlands and limestone plateaus of the Bas-Vivarais . . . blending with the charms of its canyons before dying under the sun in the arms of the Rhône River. . . . [T]he mountains spawn streams, rivers, and cascades that sing, mirror, and reflect the colors of the seasons. Nature here seems to have given free rein to all of its caprices."[12] It picks up its tributaries—the Lignon, Beaume, Drobie, and the Chassezac—along the way.

The Ardèche weaves through the magnificent limestone rock formations. Below Aubenas, at Vogüé, dramatic rock formations begin to loom above and are reflected in the river. As one approaches Balazuc, the limestone on first one and then the other side of the river becomes massive and increasingly white. The middle valley of the Ardèche cuts through a desert of rock and *garrigues,* or scrublands. The most spectacular rock formations are the three-star Gorges of the Ardèche, which begin at Vallon–Pont-d'Arc. The permeable limestone quickly absorbs water and heat, which it releases at night, contributing to the warm climate.[13]

Although Mediterranean in climate and vegetation, the Bas-Vivarais can have dramatic autumn storms and hot summers, with periodic droughts ("In July or August, drink has a good taste" goes one adage[14]). On several occasions in the past ten years, the sparse vegetation on the *gras* has burst into flames, necessitating the dramatic arrival of Canadairs firefighting planes. With mild winters, and snow rare at the lower elevations, the Bas-Vivarais is often described as *Midi moins le quart*—almost the south of the Mediterranean.[15]

Whether one arrives by passing over the majestic Col d'Escrinet or by negotiating the long descent from Le Puy to Aubenas, the high

plateau of sheep and cattle and forests of chestnut trees gives way to
the vineyards, mulberry and olive trees, and vegetation of the Midi.
The skies take on the deep blue of Provence, the scent of lavender,
thyme, and other plants adapted to the dry heat of the summer
abounds, the smell of garlic is near, and the temptations of pastis are
strong, amid the clack of *boules,* that quintessential southern French
game played with steel balls and invariably followed by pastis or rosé
wine, all accompanied by the southern French symphony of the *cigale*
(cicada). [16]

As the topography changes, so does the accent. It too bespeaks the
south, influenced by Occitan (the langue d'oc), which shaped the spoken language for the vast majority of the population through the
beginning of the twentieth century. The division between the upper
reaches of the Ardèche and the Bas-Vivarais has been described as representing the line between two Europes, two Frances, indeed two civ-
ilizations. The France of butter gives way to that of olive oil. [17] Here
are the most essential elements of the Bas-Vivarais, "the subordina-
tion of all elements of the landscape to rock, polished white by the
water, its scraggy, gleaming vegetation standing on a powder of red
ochre." [18]

If anything, centuries of deforestation accomplished by villagers
and goats had by the end of the eighteenth century accentuated the
character of the limestone lower regions of the Bas-Vivarais. [19]
Deforestation also contributed to the periodic devastating floods generated by torrential rains swelling the small streams and rivers that
flow into the volatile Ardèche River.

To see Balazuc today plunges one into its past. Seen from across the
river, its houses seem huddled together for protection. Such indeed
was the origin of villages like Balazuc. Until well into the nineteenth
century, most houses in Balazuc were grouped in the nucleated village—that is, within its old walls. The original choice of the imposing cliff for a settlement stemmed from that most compelling of
medieval needs, that of safety. The Tower of "Queen Jeanne," built in
the middle ages and restored in the late fifteenth or early sixteenth
century, served as a watchtower against *malfaiteurs* (evildoers)
approaching from the other side of the river.

Houses merge with caverns, caves, and cellars and narrow stone paths and passages cut between groups of houses. The Trouée de la Fachinière (of the sorcerer, who could cast a bad spell [*la fachine*]) still leads from the road into the upper village through and under a considerable rock formation. The Passage de l'Échoppe (of the store) plunges one into a dark cave. Fig trees stand here and there. Sun passes through them in the winter, and their leaves offer some protection from the hot summer sun. Small fields and gardens lie just beyond the old ramparts, and a few within them. Most plots of land are far from any habitation.

Building houses huddled together reduced the surface directly exposed to summer sun and the cold winter wind. Limestone, a porous stone that can be shaped with relative ease, constituted thick walls sometimes more than three feet deep. With such minimal comfort, as well as security and taxes in mind, the number and size of windows were limited.[20]

One did not have to dig deep for foundations: "[W]ith the single sweep of a broom could be found rock on which to build."[21] Mules carried lime and clay, which often replaced mortar. The result was houses that could resist wind, storms, and the years. The oldest houses of the village have stones cut in a more rectangular shape and closest to the ground, a sign of their very early construction. Over the centuries, peasants began to add sloping tiles of red clay, another sign of the Midi. In order to stand up to the pounding of the autumnal storms, some were shaped around the calf of a very large man. The passage from straw to tile roofs was in itself an indication of movement from total poverty to mere misery. After the Hundred Years War, which stretched across the fourteenth and fifteenth centuries, "as soldiers went away and epidemics disappeared, life began again, children were born, and tile replaced the straw that had covered houses." The tile roofs usually extended somewhat beyond the walls of the house because of the violent rainstorms; deep cisterns stood ready to catch the rainwater.[22] The red tile roofs accented the unity of the ensemble, both of a single structure and of the village itself.

Characteristic of the Bas-Vivarais, Balazuc has for centuries had three *hameaux* (hamlets), each relatively isolated from the village itself by distance, poor, unreliable paths, and, in two cases, the river. Servière, the largest, was upstream and across the Ardèche River and to the northeast. Downstream, the residents of Audon lived dangerously close to the river, but some residents, thinking better of it after several floods, moved early in the nineteenth century above and beyond the cliff. This put them even farther from the village, and a trek there with a wagon took them on a detour of five tough miles. Finally, a good walk to the south of the nucleated village leads to the *hameau* of Louanes.

The physical structure of the village, with houses standing next to one another suggests a strong tradition of interdependence, solidarity, and *entraide* (mutual assistance). The hamlets of Louanes and Servière too resembled tiny villages, their houses packed closely together. Moreover, Balazuc's relative isolation encouraged frequent intermarriage between families, affirming links of solidarity manifested during crises, harvests, and life's major events. The birth of a child brought gifts, however modest, carried by the mothers of other families; entire villages celebrated marriages, usually with a meal, as permitted by the resources of the families; deaths too gathered the entire community, with another meal offered by the bereaving family. Sunday Mass, the annual votive festival in July, carnival, and other events of the calendar brought villagers together, reinforcing a sense of community, even if considerable tensions and even hatred between individuals and families have remained endemic to village life. Local traditions reinforced collective identity and solidarity, facilitating the struggle—sometimes hopeless—against nature and for existence. Of course, through centuries of every conceivable kind of natural disaster, disease, epidemics, and war, Balazuciens have been able to fall back on the family, the center on which life has always been organized.[23]

Viewing houses in the Bas-Vivarais today reminds us not only of the daunting challenges of the agricultural economy but also of the willingness of peasants to adapt to the constraints imposed by nature as well as of the opportunities, however modest, of a changing agricultural economy. These changes, as we shall see, brought telling additions to the structure of houses. Everywhere families and animals lived together, the former profiting from the heat the latter generated (such close proximity gave rise to the dubious, to our eyes or noses, saying that "the smell of animals purifies").[24] The *rez-de-chaussée* (ground floor) included a stable that housed sheep, goats, an occasional horse or ox, and that proud king of the Vivarais animal world, the pig, while chickens dashed around the small *basse-cour* (farmyard). The pig was the "providential animal," referred to with a certain degree of respect, if not near reverence. Many a family fortunate enough to own a pig slaughtered it around Christmas (depending on the weather). After celebrating the bloody event, the slaughter (*lo tua* [the kill], in patois), by eating some of the late beast and rewarding neighbors who helped out during the year with some of its meat, the family then prepared sausages, to be stored and eaten over the year.

But because the Bas-Vivarais was poor in animals, as in almost everything else, visitors observed that the *cave,* or cellar, with a hard earthen floor, took precedence over the stable. Its location on the ground floor stems from the omnipresence of limestone. The *cave* was designed to serve as a storage area for wine in casks, the cistern, the winepress, and tools for maintaining the vineyards. With its form perhaps having come from crypts, it offered space for storing potatoes, sausages, and chestnuts. The ground floor of the *cave* was usually vaulted and thus similar in appearance to the natural caverns that had provided shelter to prehistoric peoples. Some *caves* protruded outdoors, providing a sheltered structure or shed for storage and work.[25]

Many of the stone houses of the Bas-Vivarais have a unique characteristic: exterior staircases leading to a covered balcony (*couradou*) on the second floor. This balcony increasingly served as an outdoor room, cooler during the summer heat, but warmer than inside during the afternoon sun of winter. With the advent of the production of raw silk, the covered balcony became a key "room" of the household. The house itself became an instrument or tool of work.[26]

The covered balcony led to the kitchen, the center of the household. Centuries earlier Olivier de Serres, the agronomist, stated that to build any house in the Bas-Vivarais, one started with the kitchen. The English word "kitchen" does not do justice to the importance and sometimes the size of this center of the Ardéchois house. The presence of a high, deep fireplace, with a chimney hook hanging from a wooden beam across it, made the kitchen by far the most important room in any house. Providing the only source of heat during the winter (in many parts of the Vivarais, and other regions as well, the oversize room therefore also served as the bedroom, with boards or straw serving as beds), the kitchen was essential for survival. "To start a fire," goes a saying, "was the sign of life and without doubt also of eternity." The last cinders were carefully kept, "in order to chase away isolation or distress." It was considered bad luck to let the embers die, as well as a waste of matches.[27] The chimney symbolized a refuge, where one had a "sense of security" with wind howling outside. A man remembers childhood evenings near the fire: "[T]he fantastical flame dances through the shadows and paints the shower of its blaze on the beams . . . figures seemed to surge forward, a moving tapestry, a procession of all those who gathered exactly like this in the glow of this hearth. . . . Twenty generations of peasants have come to sit here in silence before the hearth rediscovered but already lost." It was in the kitchen near the chimney during the long winter months that family, relatives, and friends once came together in the evening for *veillées*, gathering for the telling of the stories that shaped the collective memory of families and entire villages. A twentieth-century writer recalled stories told by his grandparents, who had been born during the Second Empire, passed down "without help of a written text, the memory transmitted by tradition via *veillées* already more than two centuries before the preoccupations of the present." In this way, "a year of drought" could come to occupy the same place in the collective memory as a war.[28]

Because of the torrential autumnal rains, a cap of tiles covered the chimney as it protruded from the roof. The kitchen was almost constantly busy with the preparation of at least four meals, however modest, from breakfast to a light supper at nightfall.[29] A small alcove contiguous to the kitchen once served to store milk, cheese, and other food, cold air provided when needed by a small window. If the patriarch was the master of the fields and the family, an authoritarian presence whose word was the law (a fact unchanged by cohabitation with his son and his family or with unmarried aunts and uncles), his wife, "the soul of the house," ruled the kitchen. She acquired what had to be purchased or traded for, preparing on the hearth and serving the thick soup and potatoes at the meals that fueled work in the fields. Yet it remained common through the nineteenth century for the woman of the house to eat standing up while the men and the rest of the family sat at a massive wooden table (around which before-meal rounds of drinks—*apéros*—are still served). *"Souvèn quaou viro l'hasto, Noun tasto"* ("Often the person who turns the skewer never tastes the roast") went one expression. The woman of the house also managed the population of goats, chickens, and pigs. In addition, as we shall see, her role in the production of raw silk was essential. She stood among chestnut benches and eventually wardrobes of oak or pine.[30]

From the kitchen a doorway or, in some cases, an interior staircase led in larger, more prosperous houses to other rooms and to the attic. After the eighteenth century, a tall clock stood in the kitchen, at least in houses whose families could afford one, reaffirming the centrality of that room; it was made of walnut or pine and often had designs painted on it, with a copper pendulum, ticking "in monotone, the elongated shape of the clock recalling that of a casket . . . placed in the brightest corner of the room."[31]

To live in Balazuc, like most of the Midi, one needed protection against the winds. The mistral comes from the north. Peasants often called it the *bise* (which also means "a kiss"), the name for the northern direction. A wind of good weather, it can chase away clouds but also intensify drought and heat. On the high plateau, the mistral can unleash in winter the *burle*, a swirling, blinding snowstorm propelled almost horizontally.[32] The mistral whistles down the valley of the Rhône, slamming shutters against stone walls. It is popularly believed to come in cycles of three days. The west wind is generally warm and humid but is feared for sudden hail that can in a matter of minutes destroy vineyards. The slight east wind usually comes during periods of good weather in the morning. The south wind—*lou ven* (the wind)—especially the southeast wind, brings rain, sometimes welcome relief from drought, or, more immediately, the end of a game of boules. Yet its rapidly moving dark clouds also notoriously bring the violent, devastating storms of autumn whose lightning

strikes transform day into night and with incredible speed drive the
Ardèche and other rivers, and modest streams as well, far beyond
their banks. The flood of 1846 came so rapidly that the women of
Vogüé, with small baskets on their heads for carrying laundry, did
not even have time to save the clothes they were washing before running for their lives.[33] Lesser winds from the south can dry harvests
and plants to a crisp or in the spring can bring rain. The wind's force
is such that once in a great while one awakens to find almost everything covered with a reddish sand the wind has carried across the
Mediterranean from North Africa.

Houses were therefore built to protect their residents against the
wind. When possible, they were set to face south. Few had windows
or other openings toward the north. Openings faced south to attract
"the good wind" that dried and brought a bit of needed freshness to
stables and the farm courtyard.[34]

Above the right bank of the Ardèche and beyond its steep cliffs lies
the *gras*, the desolate stone desert of gray limestone. It was formed
millions of years ago before the river dug its present course. It is still
easy to find fossils in the layers of limestone uncovered by erosion as
the plateau of *gras* rose. On seeing it in 1805, a geologist could only
admire "the horror" of it all, "a countryside of moor of greater or less
thickness, interspersed with juniper trees, wild fig trees, and brush,
where thyme, lavender, and cade give off scents like burning incense
distilled by heat of summer."[35] When Albin Mazon, a prolific local
writer, visited Balazuc in 1884 while undertaking a study of the ravages of cholera in the region, he described the rugged limestone landscape dotted by boxwood and lavender, trees appearing here and
there, and "a vine protected by a scarecrow holding his arm in the
air—one can find only scarecrows in the poor world of the *gras*."[36]

The imposing rocky landscape in and around Balazuc evokes an
astonishing agricultural society of which very little remains.[37]
Survival depended on the energy of peasants to extract, break, carry,
and build with stone and rock. Low walls of rocks piled one on
another to separate rocky fields or pastureland formed into fences still
stand, or just piles of stones, and here and there the remnants of
cabanes (stone huts) in which shepherds took shelter or tools were

stored. Stone was used to build most everything. Peasants loaded rocks into a *saccol*, a padded cloth sack borne on the shoulders, and carried up to 130 pounds at a time.

Agricultural production continued on the *gras* into the 1950s. *Épierrement* (clearing fields of stones), piling them up or building fences with them (*empierrement*), was the only way that these remarkable "makers of soil" could have soil on which anything could be grown. Having created partially arable land out of wilderness, they enriched the rocky soil by adding fertilizer, provided for the most part by boxwood collected from nearby pastures. If all went well (at least this land far above the river could not be swept away by the storms that swelled up the river below), then peasants working with their hands could grow potatoes, chickpeas, and even some grain. Peasants went up to the *gras* in the early morning with their pockets full of seeds for planting. At best, there were a few fruit trees, particularly almond trees, mulberry trees, and perhaps a few fig trees. Now all this is hard even to imagine, on this desolate land, returned to its savage state.[38]

Such challenges were commonplace in the Bas-Vivarais. In order to survive, the peasants of the Cévennes, in particular, had to build terraces with dry stones on the slopes of their invariably tiny parcels of land (so small that during the Ancien Régime minuscule units of measures were used). Fertilizer had to be carried up the same way. It took about two days of hard work to put up a wall about ten feet long and three high. These terraces, reached by paths, had to be rebuilt time and time again with care (and attention to dangerous slides). A study of the Vivarais written in the early 1760s notes that peasants "continually are obliged to rebuild the soil that the rains have carried down with them; such soil can only be held up by an enormous quantity of walls forming terraces. . . . [T]he best land is continually subject to floods or water pouring down from higher elevations, necessitating continual attention by the beaten-down peasant."[39]

When Jules Michelet traveled from Nîmes to Le Puy in 1844, he described with awe the endless struggle of the inhabitants of the Bas-Vivarais to overcome the daunting disadvantages of "thankless" soil and harsh, arid climate. About the same time, an observer praised the inhabitants of the southern part of the Vivarais, who "have acquired a remarkable talent for the construction of walls of dry rock, using every kind of material, here of limestone, there of schist, further on, of granite." Now abandoned terraces in village after village remind us not only of the daunting courage, ingenuity, and hard work of the peasants of the Ancien Régime and the nineteenth century but also of the subsequent dramatic depopulation of the Bas-Vivarais.[40]

Relative isolation contributed to the lasting impression of the weight of tradition and suspicion of what seems new. Indeed the heartless soil and temperamental climate of the Bas-Vivarais have often been given an explanatory power in shaping the character of those trying to grow on it anything to eat, drink, or sell. Writing a hundred years ago, another knowledgeable observer insisted that the difficult nature of the land shaped the way that the Ardéchois peasant reflected on virtually every decision with extraordinary care: "[H]e will be careful not to jump into anything and nothing will change a decision that has been taken." Above all, he was tenacious. "The nature of the region forms character. The soil is poor, difficult to work, and floods come often to destroy the results of such difficult labor. It doesn't matter! He must keep his family going. He begins the most difficult task again, because he must do so, no matter what the price." Not having much and knowing the value of work, the Ardéchois was usually described as being thrifty, sometimes excessively so.[41]

Indeed one can today understand how "the tormented landscape, the poverty of the soil, and the harshness of rural life combined to create common features" in the people of the Bas-Vivarais.[42] A writer in the early nineteenth century depicted the peasant of the Ardèche as "patient and laborious, and heroically so; no fatigue can break his indomitable energy, no setback can break his courage."[43] Local sayings celebrated the hard work necessary to survive in such conditions: "[T]he land is to work as the wife is to the husband." Thus, when one said of a man, "he is poor, but a hard worker, this latter description redeems and ennobles his poverty."[44]

The daunting task of extracting a living from the rocky soil of the Vivarais helped shape the intensity with which peasants held on to their land. This contributed to the reputation of the peasants of the Vivarais as being extremely quarrelsome, routinely litigious over the fate of the smallest slice of land, rocks and all. The peasants of the Ardèche were a proud, dignified people: "Never ask something of anybody (they say) . . . no doubt to not have to depend on anyone else." Someone compared the peasant of the Ardèche with a bee: "[H]e amasses, he transforms, he constructs."[45] And when all went wrong—"God wills it" (*"Dieu le voulait"*)—he started to rebuild yet again.

Charles Ambroise Caffarelli, the first prefect of the Ardèche, at the very beginning of the nineteenth century wrote about the department to which he had been assigned. His reports became an ethnography of what seemed a strange land. "If," he insisted, "to be a farmer means to deliver oneself over to the most difficult work imaginable, to expose oneself to the most cruel fatigue in order to extract from the soil what the land refuses to yield easily, to cut steep hillsides into terraces, to put up wall after wall, carrying the rocks for their construction up to great heights . . . then there are few farmers more clever than the peasants of the Ardèche. There are certainly none who work harder."[46] Less than a quarter of the land could be cultivated, and only then with incredible energy and persistence. It had been that way from the very beginning.

TWO

Continuities

BALAZUC IS A VILLAGE WHERE ROUTINE SURVIVAL TOOK on heroic dimensions across the ages. The harsh, volatile climate of the Bas-Vivarais, its rocky soil, relative isolation, and domination by kings and powerful nobles combined to shape the lives of inhabitants for centuries. The agricultural and religious calendars were the only ones that mattered. Peasants planted, tended their plots, awaited harvest, and hoped that their prayers would be answered. Much of the time they were not. From the time Balazuc was settled in the eleventh century until the mid-eighteenth century, very little about this changed. Together these factors have provided some of the fascinating continuities that have defined the village and, to some extent, continued to do so until the early 1950s.

In the second century B.C. the Romans, whose slaves hauled goods up the Rhône River, conquered what was to become the Vivarais, the southern part of which was then known as the *pays des Helviens*, the tribe that the Romans found there. Roman legions marched on a road linking their stronghold at Uzès (Ucetium) to Alba, another Roman administrative center, and the Rhône River. The road, as it paralleled the Ardèche River, passed near what was to become Balazuc. In the third century A.D. St. Andéol preached Christianity in the vicinity; Alba and then Viviers on the Rhône became bishoprics. In the sixteenth century, peasants found a sarcophagus of white marble near what had been the Roman road.[1] Showing St. Peter seated on a throne, among fourteen personages drawn from the Old and New Testaments, it was somehow attributed to a late-third-century "bishop of Balazuc" but was probably carved for one of the first bishops of Alba in the late fourth or early fifth century.

Following the onslaught of the Vandals in the fifth century and the arrival of the Visigoths, in the eighth century, the Saracens took their turn, sacking Viviers three years after their defeat near Poitiers at the hands of Charles Martel in 732. Legend has Saracens, chased from Nîmes or arriving from the valley of the Rhône, taking refuge on the cliffs above the Ardèche, founding a hunting and fishing colony in Balazuc two years later.[2] Yet although various nineteenth-century savants were convinced that some Balazuciens they encountered offered physical characteristics that made them the distant descendants of the Saracens, no architectural trace of such exotic origins can truly be documented.[3]

During the time that Charlemagne, grandson of Charles Martel, imposed an administrative structure on his empire, the Vivarais began to develop an identity as a region. In the ninth century the diocese of Viviers gained considerable administrative autonomy and authority.[4] The Vivarais then passed, in succession, under the nominal control of the kings of Provence (879 to 933) and of Burgundy (933 to 1032). The absorption of the kingdom of Burgundy in 1039 into the Germanic empire, with its rulers so far away, served to reinforce the power of the bishops of Viviers, even as conquerors came and went. In a time of relentless insecurity, peasants sought protection by grouping themselves in villages near the imposing residences of local lords, in some cases exchanging use of land for dependence on and payments to nobles.[5]

The village of Balazuc probably was first settled shortly before

A.D. 1000 or very early in the eleventh century. "Baladunum" appears on the first-known document mentioning the beautiful spot in 1077. *Baladunum* comes from the Celtic words *Belen* and *Dun* (elevated), or, in Latin, *Belenus Dunum* ("Le Rocher de Belenus") as Belenus, or Baal, was the sun-god. Thus Balazuc means *Rocher de Baal*, or "rock of the sun," or even simply *roche haute*, the high rock.[6]

Balazuc was a fortified village in a region divided into thousands of fiefs large and small. Its peasants worked fields outside the ramparts that were constructed in the late twelfth or early thirteenth century or perhaps even earlier. By the High Middle Ages (twelfth and thirteenth centuries), the essential aspects of the peasant subsistence economy in the Bas-Vivarais had been established, and it was to change very little until the late eighteenth century. Chestnuts, gathered on the slopes of the Cévennes, and wine already played an important role in the family economy.[7] Rudimentary trade routes, most barely mule paths, led from the major route down the Rhône Valley that linked Lyon to Beaucaire, Provence, and the Mediterranean. Amid expansion of the agricultural economy, the population of the Vivarais slowly rose.

Powerful Outsiders: Seigneurs and Royal Authority

Whether or not Saracens were ever in Balazuc, in the eleventh century Gérard de Balazuc, in all likelihood its first seigneur, and his son, Pons de Balazuc, lived in a modest château, the Castel-Vielh (a small part of which stands as a house today), which stood on the giant cliff above the river. Pons de Balazuc left Balazuc to join the First Crusade and put Balazuc on the medieval map by being killed by a huge stone thrown in 1099 at the siege of Arcos, near Jerusalem.[8]

Attested by the homage paid to them by other local nobles, the seigneurs of Balazuc extended their authority in the region. In the twelfth century a timely marriage added to their domains the nearby seigneury of Montréal. Guillaume de Balazuc, the grandson of Pons, became a well-known troubadour at the court of Count Raymond of Toulouse, whose own family had extended its own influence into the Bas-Vivarais. However, Guillaume, so smitten with his love for an elegant lady for whom he composed songs that he once ripped out one of his fingernails to present to her as a token of his love, let the family fortunes slide. High above the Ardèche River, the Balazucs, intermarrying with other powerful families in the region, surrounded themselves with a small court.[9]

During the eleventh and twelfth centuries, relatively powerful seigneurs like the Balazuc emerged within the context of a feudal society. The barony of Balazuc, which included the villages of Pradons and Chauzon, was but one piece of the mosaic of seigneurial jurisdictions.[10] A document from late in the thirteenth century, in which Guillaume, seigneur of Balazuc, granted the right to fish and hunt rabbits to a faithful squire in exchange for his services, indicates the enforcement by arms of "justice" rendered in the name of the seigneur of Balazuc. The Balazucs built a somber donjon with walls well more than a meter thick toward the end of the twelfth century or early in the thirteenth and in the fourteenth century added a small stone funeral chapel of St.-Jean-Baptiste below their château, the ruins of which retain the etched sign of the sparrow hawk, symbol of Guillaume de Balazuc. The Balazucs received homage from the nobles of nearby Vogüé, Lanas, St.-Maurice, among other places in the thirteenth and fourteenth centuries. The medieval village of Balazuc thus remained under the domination of its seigneurs, sources of effective lay authority, and the bishop of Viviers.[11]

With the gradual growth of a money economy and agricultural development, albeit on a very limited scale, in the thirteenth century, seigneurs began to free their peasants from serfdom in order to collect fixed payments in money, as well as in kind and in labor. Onerous obligations to the powerful, including being subject to the whims of seigneurial justice, remained part of life for peasants. Seigneur Guillaume de Balazuc owned the right to charge anyone who crossed the Ardèche River in the *bac* (small boat) that linked the two sides.[12]

France was a precocious state whose kings consolidated and gradually expanded their territory amid the territorial fragmentation of medieval Europe. In the thirteenth century, the kings of France extended their effective authority from the north, particularly the region around Paris, into the south, including the Vivarais, inter-

vening in local disputes. The Vivarais became part of France, attached
to the province of Languedoc. Late in the thirteenth century Philip
IV (the Fair, 1284–1314) received the homage of the principal
seigneurs of the Vivarais and in 1308 the bishop of Viviers recognized
royal authority, consenting to substitute the arms of France for those
of the Germanic empire.[13]

However, the continued expansion of royal power in the fourteenth
century was the least of the concerns of people in Balazuc. The four
horsemen of the Apocalypse devastated the Vivarais, as they would
time and time again. The Black Death, a murderous plague, arrived
via the Rhône Valley in 1348–50, killing off at least a third of the
population, leaving behind indebted nobles, abandoned fields, and
miserable, starving peasants. Later in the century, violent struggles
between seigneurs, fought out by their armed retainers, added to the
misery of ordinary people, compounded by marauding bandits.
Villages built ramparts or added to or reinforced those that already
stood. It was probably at this time that the church of Balazuc was fortified, serving as a place of hope but also, necessarily, as a place that
could offer protection. In some places, peasants, weighed down by the
taille (tax) owed the king and the dîme (tithe) that went to the
Church, rose against nobles, resenting what they had to pay them.[14]

Increased royal levies in these hard times sparked revolts against
royal authority in the Vivarais in 1378–80. The struggle between the
kings of France and the papacy, with Avignon not far away, brought
more devastation. The Hundred Years War fought between France
and England in the fourteenth and fifteenth centuries (during which
French armies expelled their rivals, who had held much of the west,
from France) too inflicted considerable hardship, damaging the
watchtower on the other side of the river from the village. It was subsequently restored by Jeanne de Balazuc, then titular head of the
barony of Balazuc, and for that reason known as the Tower of "Queen
Jeanne." In 1422, the États du Vivarais, an assembly of nobles, the
bishop, and representatives from the largest towns, met for the first
time, in Villeneuve-de-Berg, the judicial center of the bailliage (bailiwick), to "approve" royal exactions. This contributed to the development of some regional identity among elites, even if the Vivarais

never became an independent province, while confirming the region's identity as part of France.[15]

Late Medieval Balazuc

In 1464, the États of Languedoc agreed that the province be assessed the royal taille, the tax on property owed the king. This in itself was a sign of expanded royal authority. Louis XI then ordered a survey (*estimes*) of land in order to make possible its efficient collection. Most land owned by nobles and the Church was exempt (nobles had only the obligation to follow the king into war, though such undertakings were expensive and ruined some of them). The *estimes* offer a glimpse into Balazuc in the late fifteenth century, even if we can only imagine the lives of impoverished, landless day laborers struggling to survive. The survey suggests that if all those who had no property at all were counted, Balazuc at the end of the fifteenth century may have had as many as five hundred people.[16]

Those carrying out the survey in August of that year entered Balazuc through the Portail d'Été above the river, the Porte de la Sablière at the far end of the village, the village's main street running between them, or the Portail Neuf beyond the Tour Carrée in the upper village. Visitors would have noticed their small château on the cliff and the bell tower of the church and perhaps glanced a bit nervously at the dungeon higher up in the village. Balazuc was large enough then to have had a market, suggested by the centuries-old name of the small place du Marché des Oeufs, which had been outside the ramparts below the Porte de la Sablière. Near this were grouped the houses of the quartier du Mercadio.

With the exception of several seigneurs, a merchant, a blacksmith, an ironsmith, and a draper, several of whose shopfronts may still be seen in the village, Balazuc was a community of peasants, almost all of whom lived in the *castrum*, the fortified village. The workshop of a cabinetmaker was in part in a *beaume*, a shelter provided by the structure of rock. The *estimes* confirm that some families can trace their presence in Balazuc back five hundred years. They include the Tastevins and Ranchins, as well two laborers called Rieu, working for the seigneurs. On the *gras* stood the fortified *mas* (large stone house) of Dame Margareta de Fabregalis. A member of the Fabregoule family still lives there.

The survey affirmed the "little fertility" of the lands of Balazuc, justifying the seemingly modest assessment of the taxable value of property. Much of the territory of Balazuc lay uncultivated or, like parts of the *gras*, was used for pasture. However, the village produced some grain, vegetables, and wine. Peasants thus owed obligations (*cens*) to the seigneur of Balazuc, among other nobles. They paid in kind—wheat, barley, rye, oats, and dry vegetables or sometimes wine or a capon. The fragmentation of the land into extremely small and dispersed plots already characterized Balazuc. This may in part account for the fact that there were 134 separately named parts of Balazuc. Guillaume Tastevin, whose house and garden stood on a village street, owned property in eight locations scattered throughout Balazuc (some of his descendants still do). Nicolas Tastevin owned several houses and ten plots of land, including vineyards, as well as several small gardens, for which he owed a seigneur annually "a bushel of oats well filled," about twelve to fifteen liters, and "still a measure more, likewise completely filled."

Jean Alègre lived near the river, where he had an enclosed garden and a stone hut that served as a small barn. He had another shed leaning up against part of the village wall, the upkeep of which he had to contribute. Alègre owned five small parcels of land in different locations in Balazuc. These added up to about six acres, and he almost certainly leased other plots. His land yielded some wine and wheat, and he carried olives from his trees to the mill of the seigneur, whom he paid to have them squeezed into olive oil. At the time of the *estimes,* he owned two oxen, one mule, seven pigs, and about thirty sheep. His animals were worth far more than his houses and tools, both deemed "of little value." He also owed wheat each year to seigneurs. However, Alègre was a relatively prosperous peasant. The destitute, who do not turn up in the *estimes,* fell far short of this, as they always would.

The very measures used to assess the size of plots of land reflected the struggle for survival. One *jornale* was the equivalent that a pair of oxen were able to *piocher* (to plow, though peasants had to use pickaxes because of the difficulty of the terrain) in one workday. Among others, a *muid* was six loads of liquid, about 900 liters—of wine—that could be carried by a mule, each load consisting of between 140 and 160 liters. Pierre Sabatier, who had come to Balazuc to marry, produced this much wine; it too was denigrated in the survey as "of little value."[17]

Most villages had a shepherd or two who were fed and paid by families whose goats they herded. Widely regarded as "being apart"— and by some as even something of a sorcerer—shepherds had a sixth sense about coming changes in the weather.[18] Balazuc's shepherds organized the transhumance (moving herds to grazing grounds in the mountains), leading, with German shepherd dogs, goats and sheep up into the Tanargue in the spring. On the *gras*, they met up with the shepherds and animals of Chauzon and other nearby villages. Then about two thousand animals followed a ram with a bell around its neck, accompanied by the shepherds and mules carrying food and drink. They retraced their path in the fall.[19]

Isolated or not, enough visitors passed through Balazuc (many to see the seigneurs) by the royal road (*chemin royal*) that passed near the village walls that La Terrasse, the name of one of the houses, probably referred to an auberge. The hamlet of Servière across and up the river offered the best pasture in Balazuc, interspersed by white oak trees. There the prosperous Borry brothers had fifteen cattle, eight pigs "beyond their needs," and a herd of six hundred sheep and goats.

By the late fifteenth century the members of the Balazuc family were no longer the direct descendants of Pons de Balazuc. The château stood in ruins on top of the cliff.[20] One of the now two branches of the family had constructed a larger, fortress-like château on the hill above the village. The other main branch of the family had moved into the Château de La Borie in Pradons. In 1638 the cadet family of the Balazucs, their holdings everywhere diminished, moved to the Château de Montréal, near Largentière.[21]

The Church

Every Holy Friday, children went through the village shaking rattles or castanets because bells could not be rung on that solemn day.

Religion provided the principal means of communal expression in
Balazuc and other villages. Social and religious life in Balazuc
remained in some ways virtually indistinguishable and continued so
for centuries.[22] Several Masses had to be held to accommodate the
faithful, and there may have even been a small convent near the old
Roman road at Salles and perhaps a chapel there as well. Religious
practice merged with sociability. Carnival, preceding the prescribed
asceticism of the sacrifice of Lent, allowed the faithful three days of
celebration. Festivities included a procession during which ordinary
people could playfully (often with barely disguised contempt) mock
through disguises, gestures, and even words seigneurs, churchmen,
and other powerful or well-known figures. The Church's imprint on
daily life was enormous, above all, on the *rites de passage*, or birth, marriage, and death. The latter was omnipresent, almost permeating
daily life, a constant reminder of the fragility of existence. It was not
unusual to see the sign of the cross traced on the top of bread. The
cult of the saints, marked by pious devotion to relics and pilgrimages, permeated religious life.[23] The Confraternity of St.-Antoine
probably dated from the fifteenth century. Most male peasants who
owned property belonged to it and probably contributed some grain
to it each year, for distribution to the poorest, along with meat from
a cow they slaughtered during carnival.

Balazuc's Romanesque church, dedicated to Ste.-Madeleine, dates
from the twelfth century. Built with shaped limestone blocks, with
a nave of three bays leading to a semicircular, rounded apse, the small
church is elegant in its simplicity, without columns or capitals. Its
bell tower is in the form of a *fenestré* (windowed) bell tower with three
openings, above which another three smaller openings stood, with
only one still standing. This form can be found elsewhere in the Bas-
Vivarais. The church is small, no more than fifty feet long, and its
original nave (another was added in the late seventeenth century to
accommodate an expanding population) was only about twenty-five
feet across.[24]

Balazuc's seigneurs helped shape the religious heritage of the village. When Antoine de Balazuc signed his will in 1480, he left
money for the lamp of Notre-Dame-de-Balazuc, a twelfth-century

statue of the Virgin Mary and Child, and for the parishes of Pradons and Chauzon as well. Pierre Brunier, seigneur of the barony of Balazuc signed his will in 1496 "in full possession of his mind, although feeble and crippled in body, knowing that the days of mankind pass as do the shadows." He asked to be buried alongside the other seigneurs of Balazuc. A veritable detachment of priests, fifty, in Aubenas and Largentière were to say a Mass for the repose of his soul. He also left money to Balazuc's new confraternity and to pay for a Mass to be said "by the priest to be chosen by the magnificent and powerful seigneur of Balazuc." In 1505, Pierre de Balazuc declared his wish to be buried at the gate of the cemetery, near the tomb of his brother, in order that "all those who enter the cemetery will walk over his poor body." He left money for Masses to be said for his soul, and sums for the poor and to the servants of the seigneurs of Balazuc.[25]

The Protestant Reformation, the schism that bitterly divided Christianity beginning in the second decade of the sixteenth century, spread south from Lyon starting in 1528. It challenged the strong hold of Catholicism on the Vivarais. From its base in Geneva, Calvinism, above all, found many followers, particularly in the Cévennes but also in several villages very near Balazuc. Like other Protestants, Calvinists rejected papal authority and denounced clerical abuses (particularly the sale of indulgences). In particular they rejected belief in the necessity of good works and the sacrament of penance in the quest for eternal salvation, while emphasizing predestination and Christian discipline. Calvinist preachers followed the paths taken by merchants, peddlers, and their mules through the Cévennes and into the villages of the Bas-Vivarais. They brought with them Bibles, chapbooks, and pamphlets reflecting the dramatic emergence of print culture.

The wars of religion brought savage fighting, enormous hardship, and lasting bitterness between Catholics and Protestants and threatened the stability of the monarchy. Against a backdrop of economic stagnation and following King Henry II's launching of a brutal repression in the 1550s against Huguenots (Protestants), religious division led to civil war. Full-scale fighting and destruction, marked by the desecration of churches, began in 1562 and raged off and on. Balazuc itself was obliged to host a small garrison for four years. The most powerful noble families of the Vivarais led the Catholic forces against those "of the new opinion," and the seigneurs of Balazuc earned the gratitude of the king.[26]

In February 1576, thirty Protestant and thirty Catholic delegates signed a peace treaty in the Château de La Borie, in Pradons near Balazuc. The signatories agreed that the people of the Vivarais "can no longer survive the exactions and expenses they endure, having nothing to live on for the rest of this year as a result of the ravaging, pillages, ransoming, and other hostile acts daily committed in the said province." Peace was short-lived. Three years later "the poor people of the third estate of Your Majesty's barren and desolated countryside of Vivarais—poor, miserable, martyred and abandoned men"—petitioned the king. They described the horrendous atrocities on both sides, including being garroted, buried alive in heaps of manure, and nailed in boxes without any air, that men, women, and children had suffered at the hands of "the insolence, authority, and power of the noblemen, captains, and soldiers." Ever respectful of royal authority and their seigneurs, they asked for reform of the system of justice in order "to purge the country of this vermin." The establishment of a special court helped troops restore order.[27] However, that particular peace lasted only until 1585. At the time of Henry IV's Edict of Nantes in 1598, which granted Protestants religious toleration, major Protestant enclaves remained in the Cévennes and in the center of the Vivarais, as well as in a number of villages in the southern part of the Bas-Vivarais. But unlike Lagorce and some other nearby villages, Balazuc remained staunchly Catholic, perhaps because of the military presence of some of its seigneurs, who remained Catholic (unlike the seigneurs of some villages in the region who helped shift inhabitants to Protestantism) and perhaps also because of its relative isolation.[28]

Religious warfare erupted again in 1620, beginning with a revolt by Huguenot nobles in western and southwestern France. In 1629, Louis XIII, Cardinal Richelieu (fresh from his blockade of La Rochelle and the surrender of Protestant forces there), and twenty thousand troops laid siege to Privas, which had been among the 150 fortified towns the monarchy had allowed Protestants to maintain. After a bloody struggle, royal troops burned and pillaged the town. They hung fifty men and sent the remainder of the rebels to the galleys. The previous year the *consuls* (the name for syndics or parish officials in the Midi) of Balazuc had furnished two loaves of bread (which must have been of considerable size), a jug of wine, and some beef— probably every day—to the ninety soldiers who stayed in Balazuc that April.[29]

The confessional geography of the Vivarais was thus largely established, combining, in uneasy proximity, strong Catholic allegiance to the Church with defiant enclaves of Protestantism, including those in the southern Bas-Vivarais, that emphasized simple services and reading the Bible.[30] Subsequent waves of fighting followed Louis XIV's revocation in 1685 of the Edict of Nantes. Almost 10 percent of the Protestants of the Vivarais (about 3,000 Protestants of 37,500) fled, and the remainder were forced to practice their religion in virtual secrecy.[31] Signs of the Catholic Reformation, a partially successful attempt to rekindle Catholic orthodoxy, may still be seen in stone crosses, or, in places, only their bases, that were erected following missions, several days of dramatic fire-and-brimstone sermons and flamboyantly theatrical religious services that swept across much of France. One at the Portail Neuf dates from 1689. At the same time, the Catholic hierarchy suppressed some popular festivals and forms of dance and worked hard to reestablish the authority of the Church hierarchy, imposing more order and discipline on religious orders and confraternities.

The Vivarais has always been a region of Catholic religiosity. Illegitimate births and unmarried couples were rare (only about 3 percent from 1771 to 1789), a small but telling sign of the strength of organized religion.[32] In Catholic towns and villages, the parish, defining a spiritual and cultural community, provided a sense of belonging, structure, and calendar. Priests were at the heart of the parish, maintaining registers of births, marriages, and deaths, listing the dates and witnesses of each of life's great events. Most priests were literate (in the Vivarais 78.7 percent could sign their names in 1734).

In response to official surveys, they were called upon to list the "rich" and the "poor" of their parishes, such assessments easily determined by their intimate knowledge of their parishioners.[33]

As they stood in a small, modest stone church in a village like Balazuc, priests as the interpreters of God's will on earth walked tall. The power of the pulpit was considerable, no matter how many parishioners ignored, did not understand, or slept through what the priests had to say. They led the community through the ecclesiastical calendar, toward Christmas, and, above all, to Easter. Generations of them watched over the cemetery, assuring that it was properly enclosed by walls, and fully respected—thus, no hanging laundry there to dry, flaying hay, pasturing animals, playing boules or other village games, or frolicking improperly during festive moments, the only witnesses to certain acts being the dead. Village priests arbitrated in innumerable disputes, (supposedly) neutral voices standing above local interests and long histories of mistrust. Priests said prayers for the harvest and supervised the confraternities, in the case of Balazuc only one. They also kept the pitifully small accounts of the parish.

The village priest's control over the ringing of the church bells was essential to his authority. The bell ringer also dug graves. He rang the appropriate cadence slowly, when his two tasks would be combined into one. He also sounded the Angelus three times a day and, in case of emergencies, rang the bells rapidly to signal alarm (the tocsin). The boundaries between the sacred and the profane were thin or indeterminate. Priests were asked to bless new houses, a rite that may have been closer to an exorcism of possible evil spirits, and to help preserve them during storms by sprinkling them with holy water or by reciting certain prayers.[34]

The fact that the parish and *communauté* were often not coterminous (as in the case of Balazuc) provided a source of some tension between the curé, named by the bishop (invariably someone from the region), and the *consul(s)*, lay officials with only minimal authority.[35] Such resentment could of course also be quietly directed toward the seigneurs, whether they lived in the *communauté* or not (as by then in the case of Balazuc), if they exerted their domination in ways that seemed to circumscribe or push aside the curé.

Disputes could rise over the choice of a schoolteacher or a midwife or over repairs to the church. Most priests enjoyed a slightly higher standard of living than did most of their parishioners. About a third of the ecclesiastical tax of the *dîme* went toward their support. Balazuc's priest in 1776 was assessed more than one pound, which made him slightly better off than most of his parishioners, most of whom were assessed less than a single pound.[36] The *dîme* was also intended to assist the poorest of the poor, as the village priest oversaw the small reach of charity.[37] Yet these responsibilities, along with the fact that priests could read and write, could be a source of resentment and grumbling.

In 1712, Balazuc's church and its priest received a visit from Chabert, the priest of the town of Largentière, five miles away, who presumably reported to the bishop of Viviers. While grousing that the church had never been properly consecrated, he described it as consisting of two naves ten long paces in length, (mistakenly) the same across, its vaulted (barely) tile roof held up by two pillars. The altar stood on steps of oak, with its tabernacle resting on gilded wood, leaving space for the exposition of the Holy Sacrament. The lamp intended to provide light for the Holy Sacrament did not always burn "because the parishioners lack oil." The heavy wooden door to the church was, as now, on the south side of the church, across the stone walkway from the presbytery. An old and peeling painting portrayed Christ on the cross, with the Virgin Mary, Ste.-Magdeleine and St.-Antoine, the hermit, overseen by the Eternal Father. There may even have been a statue, reputed to be the oldest of its kind in the Vivarais, an appropriately "poor Virgin for poor people . . . her stocky body in the form of a column, her face without traits, but carrying a crown, and her child sleeps in her arms. And more would be required to depict the consoling queen to whom for centuries were directed the prayers of despairing generations."[38] The sacristy was just a wooden wardrobe. Yet the priest saying Mass had at his disposal a chalice, a silver vase for communion hosts, and a silver container for the Eucharist in the classic form of the sun, as well as a number of tattered ecclesiastical robes, reminding us that even in villages as poor as Balazuc, resources such as they were, found their way into churches. There were four windows in the nave and a stone pulpit from which the priest gave his sermons. Some sort of small chapel, certainly only a lateral altar, stood on the Bible side of the main altar. The bell tower, only part of which remains but which has become the symbol of Balazuc, had "three good bells." The presbytery had one main room, a floorless kitchen, a small office, and a *grenier* (attic). The village priest had a small garden at his disposal—it still stands behind the deconsecrated church today—and a stable on the square below. Three hundred steps down through the village stood the Chapel of St.-Jean-Baptiste, which still belonged to the seigneur of Balazuc, now the marquis de La Fare. Noting that the parish consisted of about seventy houses "almost all piled together in the village of Balazuc, about 200 communicants in all," the visiting priest and Louis Sauvan, curé of Balazuc, signed the account of the official visit.[39]

Of course, however much they respected the priest, sought his intervention with God, and themselves prayed to God and the saints, many, if not most, people believed in the power of various kinds of curers. Balazuc had a midwife, but no doctor, of which there were hardly any in the Vivarais. The difference between someone (*rha-billeur*) believed to be able to put muscles and joints back in place and a full-fledged healer (*guérisseur*) who had the "gift" of healing was important. In some places the power of "healing rocks" was trusted, as were remedies, depending on the illness, like eating crickets, sacrificing live poultry in the hope of better health, or placing sick infants in a pail and turning them about all. Such superstitions may have led the peripatetic Arthur Young to exclaim in October 1789 upon reaching Montélimar after traversing the Bas-Vivarais that he had finally reached a Christian land.[40]

Sorcery, a risky occupation, provided extreme measures, and the spells of its practitioners were feared. The passage under the rocks in Balazuc known as La Trouée de la Fachinière was, to repeat, that of the sorcerer. In Meyras, a village in the hills, late in the eighteenth century a sick man accused an old woman of being a sorcerer responsible for his suffering. Two of his friends hauled her to the sick man and demanded a cure. When she said that she had no means of helping him, they held her feet to a brazier and then put her into the coals, where she died.[41] It was the kind of story that quickly made its way down the mountain.

"Ungrateful" Soil

In the mid-eighteenth century, as three centuries earlier, most peasants in Balazuc still worked small, fragmented parcels of land, some of it ceded in perpetuity by seigneurs in exchange for dues, a small part of what was produced. They did so with the help of their families, friends, and neighbors in a region where traditions of mutual assistance were firmly rooted, as they had to be. Peasants looked to the sky not only in prayer but to try to predict the coming weather. They had to figure into their hopes their share of the royal tax that the *communauté* owed the king, the *dîme* owed the Church, the *cens* owed the seigneurs, as well as various other charges that weighed on them. They also had to put aside a part of the harvest to replant for the next year.[42]

Most large farms were found in the Haut-Vivarais and the Mountain (some owned by nobles), hardly any in the Bas-Vivarais, and none in Balazuc.[43] If some of the higher elevations offered relatively fertile land, the rocky, "ungrateful" soil of the small and highly detached parcels of land of the Bas-Vivarais remained notoriously unproductive. Only about a third of the land could be put to any use; in 1789 about 13 percent of the land of the Vivarais, less than half the national average, could be cultivated. Much of the land on which anything could be grown required enormous continual effort. Stones had to be cleared from land, terraces constructed and then rebuilt after violent storms had carried them away.[44] Most agricultural work in the Vivarais was still by hand. Boxwood in part compensated for the lack of animal fertilizer. Almost half the land on which grain could be grown had to be left fallow. Between 1600 and 1840 little progress in the amount of grain produced per planted seed had been made, a ratio of about five or six for one for land of medium quality (Balazuc's was generally less than that). In 1801 there was still only one plow for every six or seven households and few oxen and other beasts of labor.[45] Polyculture in the Vivarais was a strategy for survival. If all went well (and often it did not), peasants produced oats, rye, or barley, olives here and there, and, as we have seen, wine. Above about eighteen hundred feet, the chestnut tree stood as the "bread tree," at times the "tree of life."

In 1725 the États de Languedoc ordained that "no goats can be kept anywhere in the province where they could cause damage." The edict was renewed during the next two years, "[T]he grain harvest having completely failed and fearing a dearth like that of 1709, the ban was extended." Goats munch their way through almost anything they can find on any land on which they are left. Unlike cows, they eat down to the roots. However, enforcing such an edict, even if it was the work of the high and mighty in distant Montpellier, was of course impossible. The parlement's war against goats began again in 1745, when there were about twenty thousand of the sturdy creatures in the Vivarais. However, indispensable to peasants and fully adapted to rocky soil and steep slopes, the goats survived the wave of persecution. By 1789 the goat population of the Vivarais numbered at least sixty thousand, about one per family. Their milk and cheese helped people get by.[46]

Storms and Floods

Uncommonly violent storms compounded the challenges of harsh, thankless soil. The litany of disasters amazes: horrible winters in 1600, 1604, 1608, 1617–29, which, combined with the arrival of the plague in 1628, may have killed as much as 30 percent of the population, putting an end to the period of relative prosperity that had begun with the 1590s.[47] Then, following better times in the decades of mid-century, came terrible winters in the 1680s and 1692–93, devastating hail in 1696, floods the next year, then "an extremely pernicious fog" that destroyed grains and vineyards. The terrible winter of 1709–10, perhaps the worst ever, etched hunger, starving beggars, and death in the collective memory. Fate cruelly brought another bad winter the next year and then harvest failures in 1717–19. The plague followed two years later. It arrived in Balazuc from Laurac, killing all but one of the inhabitants of the hamlet of Audon. However, because troops prevented anyone from crossing the river, the rest of the population was spared.[48] Destructive hail returned in July 1727, another miserable harvest in 1728, terrible cold in 1747–51 (even freezing the Rhône River in January 1748), a ravaging hailstorm in August 1754, the "little ice age" of 1756–57 and 1765–66, droughts in 1771 and 1778–80, and then the awful winter of 1788–89, the worst since 1709–10.

A "Memoir on the Calamities that Afflict the Vivarais" speaks for many meteorological catastrophes. After freezing temperatures had killed trees and vineyards and destroyed a good part of the harvest in 1766, "the appearance of the harvest of 1767 restored the courage of this unlucky people . . . when freezing temperatures never previously seen brought back consternation and despair. . . ." A terrible storm then "crushed all hopes . . . in some places paths literally ended up at the bottom of ravines or in streams." After such calamities, there was little to trade for grain from other regions. In such times the mortality rate rose by as much as half, with the number of marriages falling. Bad times also led to land, particularly vineyards, being taken out of cultivation.[49]

Huge storms brought floods. There were at least nine in the seventeenth century (notably in 1644), and seven more in the eighteenth century, almost all in September or October, as in our day. The smaller rivers that feed into the Ardèche, principally the Drobie and the Beaume, rise rapidly, drawing from the streams that join them. The Ardèche rises up to destroy. The storms and surging rivers of September 25, 1772, destroyed "the walls of terraced hillsides, soil, leaving furrows where turbulent red, yellow and ochre-colored waters carried away in fury meadows, mulberry trees, gardens, osieries, and poplar trees, of which the leaves were counted on to feed animals during the winter."[50]

In the face of such calamities, priests led their flocks in ritual ceremonies of benediction, exorcism, and prayers, seeking protection from the scourges of nature. They frantically rang church bells to ward off storms, while their parishioners kept candles, however expensive, burning in silent prayer. The priest of one village drew complaints from parishioners who blamed him for being unable to prevent bad weather. In Aihon, near Aubenas, the faithful crowded into their church to celebrate Notre-Dame-de-la-Grêle (Our Lady of Hail), who they believed had saved them from a terrible storm.[51]

After one of the violent storms that crushed the hopes of another hard year, *communautés* petitioned the king for help. In 1727 Louis XV allocated some assistance to Balazuc following battering by hail, rain, and then flooding. Its assembly met "in the customary manner" following Mass and selected two or three men "to decide upon a just division" of the sum among ninety-seven families living in Balazuc, including the priest, who received less than 1 pound.[52] After hail had shredded vineyards in July 1732, Balazuc received another 250 pounds of the 20,000 pounds the king allocated to the Vivarais. Two years later, at the call of "the great bell," the men of Balazuc "making up the greatest and most sound part of the inhabitants" gathered in "general council . . . at the public place." The assembly chose someone to go to receive the money.[53] Royal allocations reduced the oceans of hardship following storms by several drops. The autumnal storms made the upkeep of paths leading to and from Balazuc almost impossible. Between October 8 and 12, 1754, "the surging water did so much damage to the path (leading from Lagorce leading to Balazuc) that no wagon could pass there. Two horses abreast could not take the route without risking falling . . . because of rocks all along the path on one side and the collapse of a supporting wall on the other." In 1762 and 1769, more floods seriously damaged Balazuc's paths, including that down to the boat used to cross the river. More repairs would be required to solidify support walls entirely carried away by the stream of Chaussy that in a matter of hours had become a river.[54] The storms themselves were part of the precariousness of rural life. Again, the sense of fate (*le destin*) seemed always present. Following rapid rises in the river, it was not uncommon to find bodies that had been carried down to Balazuc by the torrent.[55] The struggle against nature was constant in the life of everyone. The peasants of Balazuc began to rebuild one more time as best they could.

There was more to fear than the weather. Travelers on the roads of the Vivarais, or even on difficult paths that joined villages to one

another or to the road, feared bandits, such as those who had terrorized the region in the 1760s. In places the distances between villages
or hamlets, the latter themselves a characteristic of the lower Massif
Central, were considerable. Indeed one hamlet on the route from
Aubenas to Joyeuse, then little more than a break in the road, still
carries the bracing name Prends-toi Garde (or Watch Out!). The
rocky Vivarais and its forests, *garrigues*, brush, and caves provided
innumerable places for evildoers to hide in any number. There were
no more than a handful of rural police (the *maréchaussée*, thirty-six
men organized into brigades, with their headquarters in distant
Annonay, a good many days away under the best of circumstances).
A royal official lamented in 1766 that the people of the Vivarais "reel
under the oppression of brigandage and crimes of all nature carried
out with audacity, of which several have not been punished." A year
later a full battalion of infantry, part of the four hundred troops available in the entire Vivarais, arrived to assist local authorities, but the
brigands simply faded into the hills, woods, and rocks.[56]

Of the Vivarais, it was said during the Ancien Régime, "One kills
a man as calmly as in other provinces one kills a hare or a partridge."[57]
The peasants of the higher elevations, in particular, had a reputation
as brawlers who planted their knives in the table that separated them
from anyone with whom they were negotiating or discussing. Drink
played a role in many of the violent, occasionally murderous, inci-
dents. Beggars roamed the countryside, coming down from the
higher elevations during the worst times, of which there were many,
their sudden appearances in any village unsettling. The notorious
inefficiency of local justice may have contributed to an increase in
crimes, particularly against persons, in the last decades of the Ancien
Régime.[58]

Wolves, living in the vast rough lands that defied cultivation, also
terrorized some of the countryside, above all, on the edge of
Gévaudan to the west. There in a single year, 1767, a pack of wolves
killed eighty-three people and hurt thirty more in the region. In
Lagorce, on the other side of the hills to the southeast, attacks
occurred here and there in the region into the Restoration.[59] In
Balazuc's small church, then, there was much for which to pray.

Paths Etched in Stone

Until the early seventeenth century the only major road in the Vivarais ran along its eastern edge, the right bank of the Rhône. It met up with a passable route along the valley of the Doux that led to the Massif Central and with another, the route of the Auvergne, leading from Viviers to Alba, Aubenas, and eventually Le Puy. Routes in most of the interior of the Vivarais often were little more than rough paths on which only mules held the upper hand. The wars of religion brought more attention to maintaining roads along which troops with cannon could be transported. In 1699 the États du Vivarais decided to improve the road leading from Aubenas to the Cévennes, paralleling the Ardèche River beyond the *gras*, passing through Joyeuse. During the middle decades of the eighteenth century, the miles of roads in the Vivarais increased by about a fifth. In 1752 the intendant of Languedoc (the king's representative, or governor, in the province) authorized the payment to an entrepreneur for the annual upkeep of several "roads," mere paths, including those from Uzer to Ruoms "passing by Balazuc and La Borie" and from Balazuc to St.-Maurice.[60]

After considerable investment, by the 1770s about 280 leagues of roads were traversing the Vivarais, although many of them were difficult, indeed impassable, during the winter months, being "trails without surfaces, paving, sufficient support, ditches, aqueducts . . . narrow, steep, and tricky . . . held up only by flimsy walls made of dry stone." Two hundred and sixty-two bridges crossed valleys, rivers, and ravines. Mules carried most trade.[61] One can still see on the Balazuc's *gras* stones worn down by the metal wheels of wagons passing over them time and time again, imprinting the outline of the wheel like a prehistoric fossil in a rock. The peasants of Balazuc wanted to market some of what they produced, but the river with its rapids was of no help at all.

Reaching Balazuc from the narrow road from Aubenas to Joyeuse necessitated almost two extremely hard miles on one of two steep paths that were often impassable after storms. No road directly linked Aubenas to Vallon. The so-called royal road was in fact little more than a path leading from St.-Maurice-d'Ibie that met up with the old Roman "road" at Salles, from which another path led, with difficulty, up to Balazuc. If an ambitious traveler wanted to pay a small sum to cross the Ardèche River, he or she could then go up across the *gras* to Uzer and then to Joyeuse or Largentière. But it was an imposing, often impossible journey for any wagon. The old paths down to the water from the village had to be maintained. That meant restoring them after floods that had filled stream beds that otherwise were almost completely dry most of the time.[62]

The 1763 survey of abandoned land stressed that the access to the parish of Balazuc was so difficult that merchants did not come very often to buy its wine: "[M]ule drivers hardly ever come to this parish because it is too isolated. . . . [B]esides, it offers neither commerce nor industry, and lacks sheep because it is so poor, and has no money to buy any or even to purchase salt for them because it is too expensive. . . . [T]he land of the two parishes of Pradons and Chauzon is very well farmed, but not that of Balazuc, because it is too poor." Unconsumed wine sat until it became bitter or vinegar, not all that long. This sad fact added to "the abject poverty of this parish," where the lack of liquid wealth (besides cheap wine) made it very difficult to pay its taxes. The survey's revelation that some people "leave Balazuc to go and find a way of getting by elsewhere" anticipated the mass exodus a century later.[63]

Isolation had another important consequence. Most marriages joined couples from the village itself. This remained the case through the nineteenth century. The percentage of residents born in Balazuc remained extraordinarily high. Marriages contracted between the offspring of the seven or eight major families, several of which were subdivided over time into several branches, helped the same families keep on reproducing, a pattern that continued to our day.[64]

The Eighteenth-Century Village

A century later, at the time of a survey in 1734 of households subject to pay the *capitation*, a tax on individuals, there were no "officials of justice, gentlemen, bourgeois, lawyers, doctors, magistrates, notaries, bailiffs, sergeants, merchants, wholesale merchants, or manufacturers" in the sixty-two households of Balazuc. There were 76 people who worked land that they owned or held in some way, 3 were artisans or workers, 103 were employed as farm laborers, and 59 worked as household or farm help.[65] Families were patriarchal in organization. Until recent times generations, including brothers and non-married sisters, lived in the same house. Inheritance went in principle to the eldest son, and when that was impossible, matrilineal or parallel inheritance followed.[66]

Relationship to the land defined the social hierarchy in Balazuc.[67] At the top was the *ménager*, "who has a field and a good pair of oxen." Next came the *laboureur*, "he [who] does not have enough to live without doing something else as well," for example, working as a carpenter. In Balazuc a *laboreur* owned enough land from which to draw something of a living, at least in the best of times, a few goats, and, if he was fortunate, a pig. A *travailleur de terre*, or *domestique*, was a day laborer, often but not always landless, working for someone else.[68]

Assessments for the *taille* in 1774 merely confirm that Balazuc was a community of impoverished peasants, with precious few exceptions. One of the latter of course was the noble Julien de Vinezac, who lived in Largentière. He paid more than anyone else, above 4 pounds, but this was a drop in his large bucket. Only four other men paid more than 3 pounds, but the majority less than 2 pounds, many less than a single pound.[69] Antoine Tastevin, a day laborer, paid no *capitation* in 1789, while another Antoine Tastevin stood apart on the long list of who owed what with the unusual compliment of being referred to as *Sieur*. He paid 20 of the 973 pounds Balazuc owed in *capitation*. (To make things even more complicated, there was also a certain Antoine Tastevin Pouton, as well as the widow Antoine Tastevin.)[70]

Agricultural farm workers and domestics (the two in the Vivarais were usually the same), as well as the very poorest of the poor, were certainly members of the *communauté*, even if *néant* (nothing at all) was their part on the roll of assessed taxes. Of these, the taille, assessed by the king, remained by far the most important tax, increasing most rapidly during the Thirty Years War (1618–48), between 1675 and 1712, and again between 1773 and 1780. A collector named by the *communauté* received a small portion of the take to collect the taxes. The threat of enforcement by troops and possible seizure of the harvest was always there. In 1740, the haul Joseph Boucher collected apparently fell short by a little more than fifty-nine pounds, with interest and was to be paid within four months. In addition to direct taxes, indirect taxes, notably a tax on salt, weighed down on peasants.[71]

What resources, besides incredible energy and resigned patience, did the peasants of Balazuc have at their disposal? In 1686, Balazuc reported that the *communauté* had possessed "for all time" the desolate *gras*. For its use for marginal farming and pasturing, Balazuc owed its seigneurs twelve pounds annually.[72]

A survey in 1767 specified the rights that the inhabitants of Balazuc held on the part of the *gras* that was held communally. The *communal* lay next to Vinezac and Lanas-St.-Maurice and the path—it was nothing more than that—that led from Balazuc via Largellas to the road to Aubenas. The heads of household of Balazuc claimed the right to pasture large animals from May until the feast of St.-Thomas on December 20 and small animals (sheep and goats) from December 20 to March 25.[73] Then no one was permitted to pasture animals from that date to May 1. The assembly noted, "[N]o outsider nor nomads could come to pasture any animal large or small in any season by virtue of an agreement made in 1422." Each resident of Balazuc was limited to eight large animals (few indeed would have had to worry about this), and the seigneur to forty large animals. In addition, the number of sheep per inhabitant was limited, with the seigneurs again having the larger amount, as always. Wood could be taken as needed. Further clearing on the *gras* was not permitted. The *communauté* of Balazuc paid a guard "five *septiers* of wheat or its equivalent" to enforce this agreement.[74] The very question posed by the state reflected the complexity of and nuances between ownership and use during the Ancien Régime and the hazards of reading postrevolutionary definitions of private property back into the previous period. The *gras* later became an enormous thorn in the side of Balazuc, standing as a vestige of the complexity of Ancien Régime rights.

The *communauté* also owned the small square in front of the church. In addition, inhabitants claimed the right to fish in the river "without paying any charge" and had the right to cross the Ardèche River over and back—provided that each household paid an annual fee and someone ferried them across. Moreover, residents could use the mill and the oven, provided, of course, that they paid the seigneur or, probably, the person to whom he had leased the right to collect what was owed.[75]

Balazuc's response to the demand in 1734 by the intendant that the village list parcels of land that had been abandoned by those who owned them reflected the intensity of cultivation. There was no such land in Balazuc. The only land not under cultivation was "that which could not be cultivated by virtue of its nature, consisting of about a third of the territory of the community, made up of only rocks and badlands which can only produce a little grass for small animals."[76] An ecclesiastical survey undertaken in the early 1760s noted that Balazuc produced a little grain, a little wine, a little olive oil, and some cocoons. It was not much and often not enough. Even the best of times were not very good in Balazuc.[77]

During the Ancien Régime, Balazuc was one of 319 *communauté d'habitants* in the Vivarais. A *communauté* was not necessarily coterminous with either village or parish but most closely approximated the latter.[78] If the sacred and profane overlapped, each *communauté* had a source of local lay authority, in addition to seigneur and intendant. The *consuls*, usually two in number, one of whom was sometimes referred to as the mayor, were the principal municipal officials, men generally respected by people of the village. For their trouble, and the local prestige that went with the position, Balazuc's *consuls* received the exemption of their sons from a year's service in the militia.[79]

Balazuc had two *consuls* in 1779, Jean Leyris and Louis Boyer. They had been elected by the "principal inhabitants" or the "most sound part of the population," including local notables, artisans, and shopkeepers, thus property owners, but not the entire assembly of the *communauté*. Although the election of the *consuls* depended at least in principle on the agreement of the seigneurs, unlike Brittany and the north, the authority of the *consuls* was considerably less closely linked to the seigneur.[80]

In fact the election (usually held each year on Epiphany Sunday in

January after High Mass) of *consuls* often simply followed the wishes of one or more seigneurs, particularly in villages in which seigneurs chose to be actively involved in such local affairs. By no means were these assemblies anything like direct democracy at work. The influence of the seigneurs was considerable, even if they were nonresident and thus not actively involved in everyday life.[81] Each village had its little oligarchy; these became increasingly entrenched during the eighteenth century, with the tacit approval of the royal intendant. Balazuc had a small group of men who could read and write (and who almost certainly had spent some time in school during those years when a teacher was available). A *consul* had to be able to read and write, as did the scribe, who took minutes in French. From this small group emerged municipal officials who participated in local governance.[82]

The *consuls* called the assembly of the *communauté*, usually after High Mass on Sunday. They posted a notice on the door of the church and the bell ringer rang the bells to announce "the assembly of the principal inhabitants of the parish and the *mandement* of Balazuc" (The latter was a unit of fiscal jurisdiction, including Pradons and Chauzon). Sometimes known as the *conseil général*, the assembly included all male heads of a household who paid royal taxes (as far as we know, such assemblies remained a male domain, though female heads of household may well have made occasional appearances).

Thus, the *communauté* of Balazuc met in assembly on July 22, 1786, "at the public place in Balazuc where such deliberations take place." Hardly any villages had the luxury of a village hall, and to some extent the church fulfilled that role. In Balazuc the square in front of the church served as the public square at which assemblies were held (though one occurred at least once outside the Portail Neuf), presumably with the *consuls* sitting on the steps or perhaps even in the church. In this case, Consul Auzas informed the assembly that he had received word of the amount of royal taxes to be imposed on the *communauté* for the year.[83]

The *consuls* divided up the principal taxes (taille, *capitation*—a tax Louis XIV established in 1695, which raised by about a fourth taxes imposed on the Vivarais—and *vingtième* [twentieth], a tax on all revenue), carried the take to the tax office, assured the fulfillment of any levy for the militia ordered by the provincial governor, responded to requests for information from the intendant from Montpellier (number of households, state of the harvest, damage from floods, and so on), and insisted that the inhabitants share the tasks of the community. They also policed (in the largest sense of the term) the *communauté* and thus were rather like mayors, a title that was sometimes used for the single *consul* or for one of the two. They verified weights and measures and, in some places, tried to assure that Sunday remained a day of rest. Moreover, the *consuls* oversaw necessary repairs to church, cemetery, and presbytery, the latter being a principal preoccupation (and later source of dispute). They paid the teacher when there was one and a guard who protected the harvests.[84]

A document from October 1738 offers a rare look at the "ordinary expenses" of the *communauté de Balazuc*. Reviewing expenses since 1699, the *communauté* asked to increase the pay of the village scribe, who drew up the roll of the royal tax and copy deliberations, to 25 pounds instead of twelve and to raise the allocation for the lamp of the Holy Sacrament.[85] A similar accounting in 1778 listed Balazuc's expenses for the year at slightly more than 4,318 pounds. These included sums for the collection of taxes, the huge sum of well more than 3,000 pounds as "free gift" (*don gratuit*) to help pay off the province's debts, and more than 70 pounds to pay for the garrisoning of troops in the province. Other expenses included the salary for the teacher, small amounts for the *consuls* of the three parishes, and 20 pounds for "unforeseen expenses." The *communauté* owed 14 pounds to tax collectors (including some owed from as far back as 1610). When other expenses were counted, there was nothing left over, if not debt.[86]

In addition to taxes, royal requisitions could come at any time. In 1695, peasants transported grain provided by fifty landowners to Le Teil on the Rhône, to be transported to the Dauphiné to feed French troops. In 1722 the *communauté* was reimbursed 263 pounds "for the wood and candles supplied to troops . . . sent here at the time of the epidemic." Consuls Antoine Auzas and Guilhaume Teyssier were asked to "name several inhabitants who can sign their name to come to receive and sign for this sum." Meeting "at the Porte Neuve, the customary place to meet at the sound of the big bell," the assembly chose Auzas to travel to Viviers to receive the money.[87]

Royal decrees of 1698 and 1724 had recommended the creation of primary schools, the latter authorizing salaries of 150 pounds (Balazuc could afford but 100) for *maîtres* and 100 pounds for *maîtresses*. Inasmuch as Protestant pastors had been particularly aggressive in encouraging their faithful to attend school during the period 1680–1740, the Catholic ecclesiastical hierarchy had encouraged more village schools. In 1734 the bishop instructed teachers, hired by village authorities in collaboration with the priest to "instruct the children on the truths of religion" by reading the catechism every day. Many teachers assisted priests in their pastoral functions. In 1737, 59 percent of *communautés* of the Vivarais had schools, but many of those who attended could only read, not write. However, many *communautés* could not find or keep or did not want teachers. In the best of circumstances, teachers came and went and the schools were available only several months a year to teach the rudiments of reading (shaped almost entirely by religious texts), writing, arithmetic, and a little more about religion.[88]

Parish registers allow us to approximate literacy rates, but no more than that. After 1667, acts of marriage had to be witnessed by four men, who either signed their names or indicated that they could not sign. About 30 percent of men in the region and 14 percent of women could sign their names during the period 1686–90; by 1786–90 the percentage had risen to about 40 percent for men and dropped to 12 percent for women, rates below those of France as a whole.[89] Yet to be sure, being able to sign one's name and actually to write is not the same thing. When the families of André Auzas of Balazuc and Jeanne Girard of St.-Maurice-d'Ibie signed their contract of marriage in 1787, involving the considerable dowry of fifteen hundred pounds, most of the witnesses could not sign their names. When Jeanne Tastevin died in 1741, "age about eighteen years," both witnesses were illiterate. In 1753 the teacher Pierre Courtiol served as a witness for many births, marriages, and deaths. He and Nogier, the village priest, were often the only witnesses who could sign their names.[90]

The French language made but scattered appearances in Balazuc before the Revolution. In the mid-seventeenth century, the first priest wrote in French in the region. By the 1760s village curés could write in French, even if some spelled phonetically. The language of the Bas-Vivarais was essentially a Gallo-Roman branch of the langue d'oc (except north of the Doux River, where a Franco-Provençal dialect prevailed), or Occitan. Even within a relatively small region, dialects could vary. People at Bourg St.-Andéol spoke a patois very influenced by Provençal. In a local version of a common tale, Racine related to La Fontaine that when he reached his lodging in Valence, he asked a servant for a chamber pot. She placed a warmer under the bed, a misunderstanding that the distinguished visitor discovered in the middle of the night when he tried to use it. This was the kind of story northerners love to tell about the Midi.[91]

Seigneurialism

Even if they no longer lived there, Balazuc still had seigneurs. In 1643 the Marquis Charles de la Fare-Montclar became seigneur of the barony of Balazuc through his marriage to Jacqueline de Logères. In 1728, Charles-François, Marquis de la Fare, who had inherited the barony, sold much of his property to a wealthy Parisian banker negotiating a good price during a session of the États de Languedoc. Ten years later the banker sold "the useful domains of the barony of Balazuc" for 360,000 pounds to Comte Cérice-François de Vogüé, whose family had once been vassals of the original Balazuc family. In some ways 1738 marked the end of the barony of Balazuc. In fact, growing authority of the parlements had weakened that of the seigneurs, who were left with what was to a large extent only nominal authority.[92]

If in the seventeenth century seigneurialism had rarely been questioned, this changed in the middle decades of the eighteenth century. Although there were relatively few nobles in the Vivarais—perhaps only 150 to 200 families, ranging from struggling *hobereaux* (nobles rich only in title) to the powerful Vogüé—the weight of taxes and seigneurial exactions increased during the eighteenth century, particularly after mid-century. The seigneurs of Balazuc were rarely, if ever, to be seen in the *communauté*; their hirelings collected for them. By the late eighteenth century any sense of reciprocity or moral leadership had long since disappeared.[93]

Remaining seigneurial obligations were enforced more efficiently beginning around 1760. Payments owed in kind or cash (ever in short supply) to the seigneurs exasperated peasants by their weight and variety. The land survey for Balazuc in 1776 noted that "the seigneur of Balazuc owes a thirtieth of the royal taxes levied on the *mandement* of Balazuc," a mere pittance for a very rich man. Seigneurial rights varied considerably from place to place. Henry IV had long before promised to put a chicken in every pot, but many peasant chickens still went directly into the outsized pot of the seigneurs. In 1778 a legal specialist in feudal rights concluded that a document dating from 1544 (and confirmed in 1705) ruled that some of the peasants of Aubignas and Aps (formerly and later again Alba) owed a seigneur some oats, a lamb, a chicken, and several days of the labor of an ox each year. A lawyer proved that these rights had been bought off long before, settling this particular contest, but peasants bitterly resented remaining seigneurial obligations. One can imagine the seething hatred of peasants learning that a noble with a revenue of six thousand pounds annually had begun a complicated, expensive legal process to win the right to one more chicken each year. Certainly any peasant family would have been tempted to remit the scrawniest bird that could be found, but it did so at its own risk.[94]

Other seigneurial privileges included the right to levy fines for various transgressions—above all, including fishing and hunting in places under the direct authority of the seigneur—and the obligation to pay a fee for transfers of property. Moreover, in many places peasants had to remit to the seigneur part of what was grown or produced and, as for centuries, to bake bread only in the oven of the seigneur and pay him for doing so, as in Balazuc. If the seigneurs were not part of everyday life, peasants hated the agents who collected payments on their behalf, rights that some of the agents purchased from absentee seigneurs. Royal taxes further reduced any margin of safety when the harvest failed.[95]

As the Vivarais formed part of Languedoc, a *pays d'état*, the bad
news of taxes came from the États de Languedoc, not from the intendant representing the king even if the États had gradually given up
financial control to the centralizing monarchy. The peasants of the
Vivarais believed that their province suffered disproportionately high
taxes, a full eleventh of those imposed on the enormous province of
Languedoc, even though only about a third of its land could be cultivated at all. At the same time, taxes rose rapidly in the 1770s and
1780s, when the financial plight of the monarchy deepened.
Furthermore, the *dixième* owed the Church fell on almost everything
produced. Thus, according to an informed contemporary survey
undertaken during the period 1759–64, "Hardly two-fifths of the
revenues of the peasant remain for the cost of agriculture, to cover
unforeseen accidents, or for his subsistence."[96]

Revolt

We have seen that the seventeenth century brought religious warfare,
autumnal storms, brutal winters, devastating harvest failures, and
the plague and various other epidemics that cut a swath into its population. All this indeed combined to make life for peasants (and some
other people as well) "solitary, poor, nasty, brutish, and short," in the
memorable description of Thomas Hobbes, himself a seasoned veteran of the middle decades of that cold and in many ways unhappy
century.

Peasant revolts exploded in the valley of the Ardèche between May
and July 1670. After a bitterly cold winter, a rumor that a large new
tax was going to be imposed on the birth of every male child, every
farm worker hired, new hats, shirts, shoes, and even bread was the
final provocation. Beginning with attacks by artisans on a tax official
in Aubenas, the revolt spread through thirty parishes in the environs,
opposed by the "gentlemen" and wealthy bourgeois. Some of the latter believed the mutiny the work of the devil. In turn, some of the
insurgents may have been inspired by their conviction that "the last
shall be first" and that the "kettle might well be smitten by the
earthen pot."[97]

Unlike some peasant revolts in the seventeenth century that were directed against seigneurs or others in which disgruntled nobles participated, here the sense of popular justice did not include any inclination to overthrow the social hierarchy or to challenge the authority of the king. The rebels solicited the leadership of Antoine du Roure, a respectable gentleman farmer and former army officer married to a noble's daughter. After being called a coward by a shepherd, the incredibly naïve Roure agreed to serve as a spokesman for the five or six thousand people, a decision he later regretted. The rebels found support among some privileged landowners, as they shouted, "Down with the elect [the tax collectors]! Death to the bloodsuckers of the people!" Some wore masks or were otherwise disguised as they pillaged, coming as close to Balazuc as La Chapelle-sous-Aubenas. Royal troops at Lavilledieu defeated the insurgents, five or six hundred of whom were exiled or condemned to the galleys. Roure, foolishly believing that his king would pardon him, went to Versailles. Turned away, he fled and was captured as he sought to escape to Spain. He died on the wheel, his headless, battered body hanged on a road, a promise of dire consequences for those who would rebel against the king and his officials. Two months later a relentless force of three thousand troops imposed order by spreading terror, burning, and pillaging, searching out the poor devils hidden among the brush and rocks.

A century later the murder of Seigneur de la Mothe of Uzer and his wife in 1765 reflected another wave of popular seething resentment against impositions and against "justice" that was slow and expensive and invariably took the side of the powerful. The incredibly complicated and sometimes inefficient structure of justice left ordinary people groaning about 346 seigneurial judges and their officers, some of whom combined the functions of judge, prosecutor, lawyer, notary, and scribe. For if criminal jurisdiction had almost everywhere been taken over by royal courts, seigneurs maintained considerable civil jurisdiction, a power accentuated in a region of fragmented and often legally contested rights of property. There were still more than seventy thousand seigneurial courts in France, to whose advantage it was to encourage the multiplication of civil procedures because they profited from them.[98] The peasants of Vivarais, their fields small, scattered, and vulnerable to great storms that destroyed markers (*bornes*) establishing where one field ends and another begins, were accustomed "to chicanery, to legal proceedings." A host of magistrates abused their power and were hated for it by the peasants, many of them debt-ridden. Moreover, the seigneurs launched one legal process after another against peasants late in their payments. A *Mémoire sur le Vivarais* written in the 1760s contended that "there is hardly in the kingdom any region more badly organized or suffering in this context, lacking superior judges ready to watch over what is going on."[99]

The Vivarais formed a civil bailiwick (*bailliage*) of the *sénéchaussée* of Beaucaire-Nîmes. Chronic local complaint focused on distant Nîmes, whose judges seemed to have invaded all the jurisdictions of the Vivarais. The elevation of the secular tribunal of Villeneuve-de-Berg, along with Annonay, to the rank of *sénéchaussée* in 1780 reduced some, but not all, of the resentment against "justice." Some seigneurial judges presided over sessions in attics, dilapidated buildings, or even outside. They were popularly believed to ignore cases for which they would receive nothing, occupying themselves with those that would permit them "to pile up extravagant costs."[100] The peripatetic Englishman Arthur Young described his visit to the Vivarais: "I encountered people who are in general satisfied with their government, but never with the rendering of justice."[101]

The 1783 revolt of the Armed Masks (*Masques armés*) in the Bas-Vivarais should be understood in this context. Following another meager harvest, trouble exploded in February in villages stretching between Joyeuse and St.-Ambroix (now in the Gard). The movement started in and around Les Vans and spread rapidly, reaching two dozen parishes on the edge of the Cévennes. Bands of peasants between ten and a hundred strong, wearing masks, dressed like women, or with their faces smeared with charcoal, attacked carefully chosen magistrates, notaries, tax farmers, and merchants of means who loaned money to peasants at steep rates. Proclaiming themselves "magistrates of the poor," these peasants sacked residences and offices and burned tax registers. One explained: "We have armed ourselves against the magistrates because of their injustices; we have never wanted to do the least thing to honest folk." Masks protected the identity of the insurgents and generated fear among those who saw them. They also had a ceremonial role, serving as a "ritual of terror, selective, and not bloody," an "enraged carnival," an image reinforced by the disguises, a spectacle that also served as a rite of justice and of punishment. The Armed Masks forced innkeepers and farmers of means to feed and shelter them.[102]

Like the uprising of Roure's followers more than a century earlier, theirs was no war on noble prerogatives per se or, in any sense, on the monarchy; the rebels proclaimed their loyalty to the king (as had those led by the unfortunate Roure in 1670). They demanded a return to a standard of justice that had been betrayed by those supposed to serve the king. Twenty people were condemned to prison or the galleys for rebellion, and several were executed before a crowd of thousands in Les Vans. Yet the weight of repression seemed much less than in 1670, perhaps because the rebels were less violent and made clear the limits of their aims. Moreover, the millenarian character of popular revolt in the Vivarais had disappeared.[103] Sheer poverty remained.

Transitions

After centuries in which continuities were more imposing than changes, the middle of the eighteenth century brought significant changes and even hope to Balazuc. The population of the Vivarais rose from 213,797 in 1750 to 265,048 in 1789, the drop in the rate of mortality, beginning in about 1720, engendering a particularly sharp natural increase from 1772 to 1789. Relatively high rates of fertility and birth combined with a fall in the age of marriage (which had been at about twenty-seven years for men and twenty-five for women) built sufficient momentum to overcome the disastrous harvests of mid-century. This increase came without anything like an agricultural revolution, inasmuch as the production of grain barely increased. Chestnuts and particularly potatoes made possible the growth of the population of the Vivarais, which had stagnated or even declined between 1693 and 1734. By the mid-nineteenth century, groves of chestnut trees had doubled, making up between 25 and 40 percent of the Cévennes and 10 percent of the entire department of the Ardèche. Chestnuts and potatoes, replacements for grain, formed a major part of the peasant diet (*"Quant de tartoflas i a, Canalha s'en sauvara,"* went an old saying, tongue in cheek: "When there are potatoes, the rabble will get by"). Dry chestnuts and particularly chestnut soup, to which some peasants could add milk, formed a major part of the winter diet. Chestnuts also provided food for pigs. When, as in 1781, "the potato harvest fails in this region, the people languish in the most horrible misery." Chestnuts from the Cévennes also provided a cash crop.[104]

In Balazuc, births began to outnumber deaths more often than ever before, for example, between 1725 and 1729. In 1742, 23 deaths outnumbered 14 births. The deaths included infants of seven, ten, twelve, and fifteen days and one, seven, and thirteen months, 2 children of one and a half, and others of three, four, and five years, and young women eighteen, twenty-six, and twenty-seven years old (perhaps during childbirth). However, births achieved precedence in 1745, 1746, and 1749. Births outnumbered deaths in all years between 1781 and 1789 except 1787, when there were 9 of each.[105] Balazuc's population rose from about 400 people or a few more in 1734 to about 500 people in the 1770s and perhaps 550 in 1793.[106]

In the seventeenth century, typically less than half the children had reached five years of age. Many more did by the end of the eighteenth century. However, in the 1770s a contemporary claimed that a tenth of all infants died during their first ten days of life. Infantile cholera and smallpox still carried off infants and small children in sad numbers, at least until inoculation for the latter disease began to make headway in the first years of the nineteenth century. The presence of pock marks remained a common way of identifying people, noted, for example, on passports as well as on police descriptions of wanted people. Moreover, the peasants of the Vivarais remained undernourished.[107] Before mid-century, fevers and dysenteries seemed to arrest population growth, although these continued to return periodically during the second half of the century, as did a smallpox epidemic in 1764.

Peasants adapted their strategies to whatever might promise better times. In the eighteenth century they had begun to plant potatoes, as we have seen. Compensating in part, along with the chestnut, for the lack of grain, the potato had helped bring about population increase. Moreover, peasants planted more vineyards. The production of wine accelerated markedly in the early 1730s and then fell off. Mules hauled casks of wine up to the Velay and over to Gévaudun, exchanged for grain, and they carried oil, soap, and spices from Bas-Languedoc. Trade expanded along the valley of the Ardèche and especially the valley of the Rhône.[108]

Then, for the first time, came hope for something more. The decade of the 1730s began a marked expansion in the production of raw silk in the Vivarais, closely tied to the markets of Lyon and Nîmes. At the end of the sixteenth century, the agronomist Olivier de Serres, born in Villeneuve-de-Berg in 1539, had urged the planting of mulberry trees, the leaves of which silkworms will eat (and nothing else). The Protestant noble whom Arthur Young later called the father of French agriculture had already noted the chronic need of the peasants of the Vivarais for cash. To be sure, silk had come to France from China in the thirteenth century and had been here and there in the Vivarais the following century. In the sixteenth century royal silk manufacturers had been established in Tours and Lyon. In 1600, Serres described "the entrails of the earth and the treasure of silk that is hidden there." He convinced Henry IV to plant about twenty thousand mulberry trees (*mûriers*; *l'amourier* in Occitan) in the Tuileries Gardens. The silk industry developed slowly in the Vivarais after about 1670. A royal edit in 1692 forbade the uprooting of mulberry trees and another in the first year of the new century added a fine, half of which was to be paid to the person denouncing the act and half to the poor.[109]

Peasants in the Vivarais began to plant hundreds, thousands, hundreds of thousands of mulberry trees. The mulberry tree adapted as easily to the preexisting agrarian structure of the Bas-Vivarais as it did to its soil. Like wine, cocoons and raw silk became essential cash crops, allowing peasants to pay powerful outsiders, including the state and seigneurs.[110] In 1752 the intendant offered a bonus of twenty-five pounds for one hundred feet of mulberry trees planted and soon ordered the distribution of more than eighteen thousand young trees from a nursery in Vallon. The monarchy provided nurseries where *communautés* could get seedlings and instructions as to how to plant them. At the same time silk throwing (*moulinage*), which began in the Vivarais perhaps as early as about 1670, developed rapidly. In 1785 there were ninety-four such workshops, including those of Pont d'Aubenas, Aubenas, and Largentière. The development of silk throwing in turn encouraged peasants to produce more raw silk. This encouraged more silk spinning at home, which required little more than "a woman and some hot water." The production of raw silk gradually became part of the household economy of Vivarais peasants. Credit and debt (to be paid off after the silkworm harvest, if all went well) became an increasing part of that economy and of rural production itself. The Vivarais soon became known as "the harsh region where gold is spun."[111]

By 1770 mulberry trees stood along paths, on slopes, in front of churches, on common lands with sufficiently deep soil and even between rows of vines. At Salles below Balazuc, Antoine Tastevin, who had mulberry trees growing on two of his five properties, transformed a vast building on his property into a *magnanerie* (silkworm nursery). Antoine Auzas of Louanes, who owned fourteen properties in the hamlet, had mulberry trees planted on four of them, on another in the village itself, and on two elsewhere. Jean Thoulouze, another of the wealthier men of Balazuc, had mulberry trees on two pieces of land in Balazuc.[112]

Yet several drawbacks were not seen. Mulberry trees can thrive at the expense of nearby grain. Unlike chestnuts, they cannot help feed animals. The raw silk frenzy reorganized markets by leading many peasants toward monoculture and market saturation. Some merchants began to speculate "on the misery of most of the producers, providing them in winter with food and clothing, on the condition that they be paid in cocoons at the next harvest." They thus set what amounted to an unfair, low price, knowing that the peasants had little choice but to accept the cash in hand. Moreover, peasants had to purchase either mulberry trees or the leaves that they bore at harvesttime and, like Tastevin, construct silkworm nurseries. They also had to buy eggs, to put into incubation. To do so, many had to borrow money at 5 percent interest, a considerable amount in a time of monetary stability, or at higher rates from usurers. The production of raw silk may have made the economy of the Bas-Vivarais even more fragile.[113] Peasant indebtedness certainly contributed to the determination and contempt for those who loaned money that were manifested by the Armed Masks in the early 1780s. It also helps us understand the resolution of those who gathered outside Balazuc's church in 1789 to draw up their list of grievances in anticipation of the convocation of the Estates-General.

THREE

Through Revolution

ON SUNDAY, MARCH 22, 1789, THE MEN OF BALAZUC who were at least twenty-five years old gathered in the church. This primary assembly was to draw up the list of grievances (*cahiers de doléances*) of the *communauté* of Balazuc in anticipation of the convocation of the Estates-General in Versailles, a world away. The village scribe copied down the deliberations in the best French he could muster. Balazuc, with about 550 inhabitants, put forward its demands humbly, but with clarity and conviction.[1]

The deliberation began with the obvious: Balazuc's "extreme indigence." Those gathered enumerated some reasons for their unhappy situation. (1) They complained about taxes, particularly the royal impositions, which seemed too high given "the infertility of most of the territory" of Balazuc and the droughts, storms, and floods that devastated them. To make things worse, land owned by nobles remained exempt from most royal assessments. (2) In addition to "the *cens* imposed on each piece of their property," villagers owed seigneurs other payments that had their origins in the "heritage of feudal despotism." These included the obligation to pay the seigneur for the right to use the mill or to bake bread in the oven, the subject of many complaints in the Vivarais, and the exclusive right to hunt held by nobles. (3) They owed the *dîme* to the Church but suggested that "a fortieth" of their harvest should suffice "to procure all its help and spiritual services." (4) Balazuc was deprived "of the assistance commerce provides," having neither a market nor an annual fair and standing far from towns that had them. (5) Balazuc was the center of a barony (including the parishes of Chauzon and Pradons), but inhabitants had to travel at least six hours to Aubenas in order to find any "justice" because no court sessions were held in Balazuc. Furthermore, the village's isolation meant that crimes committed against inhabitants always remained unpunished. This left the inhabitants of Balazuc in continual fear, even as its widows and orphans "groan under the weight of oppression and wrongs."

As in the Vivarais and most of France, the strongest sentiment expressed in the cahiers was hostility to what seemed to be unwarranted privilege. The *communauté* of the inhabitants of Balazuc humbly demanded measures to alleviate some of "their deplorable misery."[2] They asked that all land owned by nobles be subject to royal taxes, that the *dîme* be collected uniformly throughout the kingdom, and at the more reasonable rate, that the administration of local justice take place in Balazuc itself, that the salt tax be ended, that a constitution establish the equal distribution of all taxes, that the fees assessed on the sale or transfer of property be eliminated or at least made more reasonable, and that Balazuc have the right to have a market every Thursday and two annual fairs (the first on July 25, the village's feast day, the other in January on the feast of St.-Antoine, patron saint of the confraternity). Finally, and perhaps most telling in a document noteworthy for its moderate yet firm tone, the cahier asked that no taxes be assessed unless they were announced in advance, made generally known, and approved by the Third Estate. At the end of the document were affixed the signatures of "those inhabitants who know how to sign." These included the two *consuls* and twenty-six other men; the families of seventeen of the men may still be found in Balazuc.[3]

The meeting in Balazuc was part of the mounting political crisis that had led King Louis XVI in August 1788 to announce the convocation of the Estates-General, which had not met since 1614. The *cahiers de doléances* were written in this context. Some sense of the political drama unfolding in France had reached Balazuc. Jean Boucher, lawyer and notary, and Antoine Tastevin, *"bourgeois,"* a prosperous property owner living at Salles along what had been the old Roman road, represented Balazuc at the preliminary assemblies in Annonay, far to the north in the Vivarais, near the Rhône, and in Villeneuve-de-Berg, much closer, in October 1788 and March–April 1789. The *communauté* of Balazuc contributed to their expenses.[4] Louis François de Balazuc, whose family had long since abandoned Balazuc and who lived near Privas, presided over the assembly of the nobles at Villeneuve-de-Berg. Because complaints about the administration of justice were common, some of the people of Balazuc would have been aware of the preoccupation in the Vivarais with the question of whether Annonay and Villeneuve-de-Berg would maintain their status as *sénéchaussées* in the face of the bigger fish of Nîmes, much farther away for those seeking justice. They also are likely to have known about the debate on whether the Vivarais would receive separate representation to the Estates-General (as it did). However, because of its isolation, most of the Vivarais "receives only by distant and faint echo news from outside."[5]

The comte d'Antraigues (Alexandre de Launay) and Boissy d'Anglas emerged as the two leading lights of the early stages of the Revolution in the Vivarais. At the end of March and in early April 1789, the question of fiscal reform preoccupied the assemblies of the *sénéchaussées*. The Third Estate demanded the absolute equality of the three orders. Whether the peasants of Balazuc and other villages in the Bas-Vivarais were aware of the machinations of d'Antraigues to maintain privileges (while maintaining his popularity by urging that the Vivarais be allowed to represent itself) or the role of Boissy d'Anglas among those demanding reforms, we simply do not know.[6]

The long drought, a poor harvest, and a nagging worry about how taxes and the *dîme* were going to be paid were far greater preoccupations in Balazuc during the early summer of 1789. News of the fall of the Bastille and some sense that unmerited privileges were at stake reached the village. The Great Fear, a general panic fueled by fears of an "aristocratic plot" against the people, swept from Aubenas on the night of July 28–29 to Joyeuse and Vallon on the twenty-ninth, then to Les Vans and Largentière, and on to Mende. Rumor had ten to fifteen thousand Piedmontese or Spanish brigands, summoned by nobles, burning harvests and pillaging the countryside. The tocsin, the rapid ringing of church bells, sounded alarm, indeed panic, from steeple after steeple, though Balazuc's isolation may have kept away even such powerful rumors. That the harvest of grain had been taken in contributed to the panic because peasants had something to burn or steal. Hastily constituted militias from Largentière and from nearby villages joined troops on patrol.[7]

In early August, villagers in Rochemaure near the Rhône began to burn tax registers. The revolt moved to the valley of the Ardèche, where châteaux were attacked. In a sign of things to come, the band of a notorious brigand took advantage of the situation to attack a nearby village before being turned back by a hastily constituted guard. On August 4, d'Antraigues, who for the moment maintained his liberal reputation, and the comte de Vogüé, who did not have one, were among those trying to convince Louis XVI to refuse to sign the measure taken late that night abolishing feudalism. In the Bas-Vivarais, many peasants had already refused to pay what they no longer believed they owed.[8] The night of August 4 in Paris finished off seigneurial rights in Balazuc. However, the law required peasants to compensate lords for their liberation from such payments as the *cens*. Outright abolition without compensation did not come until 1792–93; in practice that was already the case.

On September 21, 1789, those who possessed enough property to pay the equivalent of a day's labor in taxes met to elect "the permanent and political council of the bourg of Balazuc." The next day that body met to create a "bourgeois militia" and to name its "officers and junior officers." The 77 men listed included the noble Julien de Vinezac, who lived in Largentière but owned property in Balazuc, although he had no intention of participating. The guard then "named"—presumably elected by acclamation—Jean Teyssier as

commanding captain and Jean Leyris and Joseph Jullian as lieutenants, and a flag bearer. Leyris was a peasant of above average
means, and thus a minority, in Balazuc. He owned several small vineyards and fields. The election of a flag bearer reflected awareness of
the adoption of the tricolor, once Louis XVI had in Paris added the
red and blue of Paris to the white of the Bourbon family. The
National Guard of Balazuc existed at least on paper on the first
anniversary of the Revolution, then including the 105 "active" citizens (that is, those who paid the equivalent of three days of labor in
taxes) who had the right to bear arms.[9]

The first chaotic months of the Revolution left the village unsure
if the administrative structure that had guided and constrained them
in the past would remain the same. On November 12, 1789, the
National Assembly accorded "to each town, bourg, parish, or *communauté* of the countryside" a municipality to serve as local government.
Two decrees in December gave municipalities the right to administer common lands and village finances, although the state maintained
its control over local finances. The municipal council, mayor, and
procurer (who had represented the seigneurial court, in most places
named by the seigneur), together with several notables, would con-
stitute municipal government. The council would be elected by the
active citizens for a period of two years, half renewed each year. In this
way the old *conseil général* became the *corps municipal*, its new officials
drawn from the same group of men who had served before the
Revolution. Elected primary assemblies in turn elected the men who
would administer the Vivarais.[10]

In March 1790, the Constituent Assembly divided France into
eighty-three departments (*départements*). While seeking to rationalize
the administration of France, the revolutionaries also sought to
undercut the influence of the nobles, whose privileges and influence
were, for the most part, locally based. The Vivarais became the
department of the Ardèche (after the name Sources of the Loire had
been chosen and then quickly rejected), so named for the river over
which Balazuc stands.[11] The small, sleepy town of Privas was chosen
to be the capital of the Ardèche, by virtue of its undistinguished centrality in the Vivarais. Balazuc found itself in the canton of Vallon,

and, during much of the Revolution, in the district of Tanargue and eventually in the arrondissement of Largentière. The former *communautés* of the Vivarais were transformed into 334 communes; they included Chauzon and Pradons, each now on its own. In fact, the communes more closely approximated the parishes than had the *communautés,* corresponding to a natural grouping and mental universe organized around farmwork and religion, centered on the church, its bell tower and presbytery, and the cemetery.[12]

The creation of the department of the Ardèche passed without comment in Balazuc. The same was true of the creation of the "commune" of Balazuc, as traditions of self-government were well established in the Midi. However, although direct seigneurial domination of village affairs had not characterized Balazuc, the Revolution brought more men into the governing of villages and democratized the selection of officials.[13]

For the moment peasants had much more important things about which to worry, as always. Pounding rain and hail and subsequent floods battered mulberry trees and destroyed potatoes and grain.[14] Such catastrophes always put politics into perspective. Still, the creation of the National Guard certainly brought national events to the village, as demonstrated in 1791, when villagers planted a liberty tree, probably on the square in front of the steps leading to the church, where it uncomfortably shared space with the cross that also stood there.

Almost as if nothing had changed, in August 1790 letters from the tax commission arrived in Balazuc informing the commune that it owed 1,016 pounds, a little more than the 973 pounds the village had been assessed for the *capitation* in 1774. The mayor promised that the municipality would draw up a tax roll and name someone to assess and collect the amount owed by each household. However, the collection of any taxes in the countryside was for the moment extremely problematic, amid incendiary denunciations, threats, and even violent resistance, compounded by a series of years of bad weather and meager harvests. Moreover, bandits appeared with alarming frequency on the routes of the Vivarais.[15]

Like taxes, another overwhelming storm reminded people in

Balazuc of the limits of change. On November 7, 1790, the *conseil général de la commune de Balazuc* (the term *corps municipal* already apparently forgotten), having been elected by all active citizens, "convoked and assembled at the customary place in the customary manner, conforming to the decree of the National Assembly, by Sieur André Teyssier, mayor of the commune." Antoine Auzas, procurer (whose role was obviously no longer to represent the seigneurial court, but rather to call meetings), evoked "the misfortunes of the time, the intemperate seasons, the excessive rain and hail that ravaged this parish, and finally the terrible and repeated overflow of the Ardèche River [that] all have plunged this community into the greatest misery." The *conseil général* of Balazuc petitioned the government for assistance, estimating its losses at a hefty 31,600 pounds.[16]

The Civil Constitution of the Clergy

No single issue so divided the Vivarais and France as a whole during the Revolution as the Civil Constitution of the Clergy, adopted by the National Assembly. By creating a national church, with the state thenceforth paying clerical salaries, and proclaiming that all priests had to swear an oath of loyalty to the Revolution, the Civil Constitution brought the Revolution to the doorstep of Balazuc's Romanesque stone church. For if it was relatively easy to support a Revolution that had abolished seigneurial rights, challenging the prerogatives of the clergy was another thing. Following the designation of church lands as national property on November 2, 1789, and the suppression of the religious orders the following February, the Convention promulgated the Civil Constitution on July 12, 1790.[17] If some among the impoverished "lower" clergy of the countryside had welcomed the convocation of the Estates-General, hoping that their material condition would be improved, the Civil Constitution of the Clergy shattered their enthusiasm. It played into the hands of nobles and other determined opponents of change by challenging the authority of the clergy.[18]

On August 18, 1790, the first gathering of counterrevolutionaries, convoked by Louis Bastide de Malbosc, took place at the Plain of

Jalès near the Cévennes Mountains in the southwestern corner of the Ardèche. There the collective memory of the wars of religion remained extraordinarily strong in that part of the Ardèche, well within the orbit of news from Nîmes, France's Belfast, where Protestants had massacred Catholics on June 13–15, and from Uzès.[19] Perhaps as many as twenty thousand people from 180 parishes showed up, including many national guardsmen. The counterrevolutionary movement spread, marked by increasingly aggressive agitation by Catholics. Malbosc organized a second gathering at Jalès in February 1791, as the tocsin again rang in many parishes. There were no Protestants in Balazuc. But they were over the hills to the southeast, in Lagorce. The fear of Protestants may at least in part help explain the lack of open signs of enthusiasm for the Revolution in Balazuc.[20] Peasant indebtedness may have also played a role in popular anger toward the revolutionary authorities. Troops moved into the Vivarais to disperse what had quickly become nothing less than a counterrevolutionary movement. With the disappearance of seigneurialism, which had been welcomed, the peasant mobilization in the Bas-Vivarais ended. The next time peasants stirred would be very different.[21]

Beginning in January 1791, opposition to the Civil Constitution came into the open in many parts of France, as near to Balazuc as the villages of Laurac and Vinezac, where priests encouraged resistance to the Revolution. Most priests in the Vivarais that year refused to take the oath of loyalty. Moreover, some of the priests who took the oath announced their reservations from the pulpit or in a letter to the mayor or added phrases that qualified, modified, or contradicted their oath. In the Tanargue (the recently created district that included Balazuc), only 31 priests eventually took the oath while 138 refused.[22]

Clerical defiance helped transform some patriots into radicals in the Ardèche (found in the smattering of political clubs in small towns, including Aubenas and Largentière, that had been formed late in 1791 or the following year). At the same time, the clergy encouraged counterrevolution. Some supporters of the Revolution claimed that women under clerical influence were "tormenting their husbands, children, and servants like so many devils" in the interest of counterrevolution.[23]

Nogier, who had been curé of Balazuc for forty years, refused to take the oath to the nation. Seventy-six years old and infirm, he went home to Payzac in the Cévennes, asking that he be included among those receiving a pension. The administrators of the district of Tanargue awarded him an annual pension of five hundred pounds in his capacity as former priest of Balazuc, as well as compensation for the loss of revenue from the sale of a chapel in the parish church of Payzac, for which he had served as rector.[24]

On Sunday, August 7, 1791, Jacques Champanhet swore allegiance to the nation in Balazuc. Following the new specifications, he had been elected by the parish "in the way prescribed by the decrees by absolute majority" in June. Following the Mass said by Sieur Champanhet, he took possession of the presbytery across the stony walkway.[25]

The outbreak of war between France and Austria and Prussia in April 1792 had encouraged more resistance to the Revolution. Royalist forces were turned back on the edge of the Ardèche in July. In Les Vans a crowd killed a prominent royalist, along with nine or ten priests suspected of encouraging counterrevolutionary activity. The fall of the monarchy on August 10 and the advent of the republic hardened the determination of counterrevolutionaries, quickly showing the limits to support for the republic. Increasingly frantic attempts to raise troops through mass conscription brought stony resistance in the countryside, where service in any army had always been something to avoid at all costs. Village after village failed to provide the required contingents for service, and draft dodgers and deserters seemed to be everywhere. The Vivarais lapsed into violence, with some "patriots" attacking and burning châteaux, some fearing that the Ancien Régime would return. *Sociétés populaires* sprung up in some towns, but no club existed in the village of Balazuc.[26]

In October 1792, the municipal officials of Balazuc—Auzas, Boyer and Laroche, officers, Rieu, procurer, and Teyssier, the village scribe—gathered "at the instructions of Citizen Mayor" so that "the Citizen Champanhet" could again "take the new civil oath." The priest dutifully swore "to be faithful to the nation, to maintain liberty and equality and (if necessary) to die at my post." In January 1793, the month in which Louis XIV was guillotined in Paris, two *commissaires* of the republic came to inspect the municipal register to make sure that "Citizen Champanhet" had indeed sworn to uphold the Civil Constitution of the Clergy. They attested to the fact that he was the only priest in Balazuc and that he "lives there at the wishes of all the inhabitants." Indeed in 1793 Champanhet served as procurer of Balazuc. However, later that year he abdicated his priestly functions.[27] For a community with a long tradition of practicing its Catholic religion, not having a priest would have been a disruptive shock that affected everybody.

The beginning in March 1793 of full-scale insurrection in the west against the Revolution further radicalized the Jacobins, who established the dictatorship of Maximilien Robespierre and the Committee of Public Safety. The deputies of the Ardèche in June opposed the proscription of the Girondins, who had defended local authorities, by the Jacobins. When the Jacobin authorities on August 4, 1793, ordered municipalities to provide an accounting of grain available, only 96 of 340 communes in the Ardèche had even responded two months later. Markets were empty; hoarding was rampant. Increasingly, the "patriots" themselves increasingly split between Federalists and Jacobins. The Federalists resisted centralized revolutionary authority emanating from Paris, which the Jacobins embodied. The "Federalist revolt" was most brutally crushed in Lyon by republican troops in October. In the context of Balazuc and the Ardèche, "Federalism" remained a term of abuse directed at those who were less than enthusiastic about the Revolution.

The Jacobin victory, bringing "committees of surveillance" (though only on paper in the countryside), played into the hands of counterrevolution. In September 1793 one of the representatives of the Committee of Public Safety (*représentant en mission*) armed with special authority arrived with orders to crush opposition in the Ardèche. The Terror thus began. Two months later the Jacobin dictatorship ordered the churches closed. During the Terror, five hundred suspects were arrested, and five priests and three nuns were executed in Privas in August 1794. In many places in France, the Terror reached into villages, but it did not reach Balazuc, in part because no one wanted to denounce his or her neighbor. The revolutionary calendar begun by the Jacobins in October 1793, with the year I beginning (retroactively) on September 22, 1792, was derided and ignored. Moreover, the campaign to republicanize street names and squares was totally irrelevant in villages such as Balazuc, whose streets and passages had never had names.[28] In the meantime, amid hunger and deprivation, here and there revolutionaries were accused of knocking down crosses. Local lore, weighted against the Jacobins, has one of them suffering two broken legs when the pedestal of a cross fell on him as he sought to destroy it.

More and more priests had refused to cooperate with the increasingly aggressive, indeed desperate civil authorities as the Revolution battled foreign armies aided by émigré nobles who had fled France. In Balazuc, one dubious story has a priest by the name of Bayle remaining hidden in 1793 in the parish, not far from the church. There he is said to have heard the confession of a woman. According to this account, revolutionary forces arrived and threatened her baby. A man then jumped out with an ax and drove the soldiers away. More soldiers returned the next day to arrest the person who had saved the baby, but by then "all Balazuc had been alerted, and protested violently," so much so that the commander forgave the man who had intervened. Unfortunately, his spouse fell dead from fright.[29] Such stories, most of which were fictional, nonetheless helped turn public opinion against the Jacobin Republic.

Biens nationaux

The creation in 1790 of a national church had made the property of the Church national property. The massive sale of *biens nationaux* (national property) began at auctions in March 1791. At about the same time, the first *assignats*, hurriedly printed money backed by the value of the land to be sold, arrived in the Ardèche. While the percentage of property owned by the Church was relatively small in the Ardèche (compared, for example, to Burgundy and the Nord), about five hundred émigrés from about two hundred families, relatively few of them nobles or clergy, left the Vivarais.[30]

Balazuc contained only four small separate pieces of land "attached to the former curé de Balazuc." One parcel with mulberry trees adjoined the cemetery beyond the Portail d'Été. Jacques Mollier from the hamlet of Louanes, carrying the title of expert, assessed the value of the four parcels in January 1791 at 577 pounds.[31]

Property belonging to émigrés was added to *biens nationaux* in the years II, III, and IV, reflecting the radicalization of the Revolution.[32] Julien de Vinezac, who owned land in Balazuc, had fled the nearby town of Largentière, selling the furniture of his château to finance his hurried departure. He was shot in Lyon, where he had joined the Federalist revolt. François Melchior, the Comte de Vogüé, who had represented the nobility at the Estates-General and was the wealthiest of the émigrés in the Vivarais, left for England in October 1791. He returned a year later to fight with the Army of the Princes against the Revolution. In addition to his properties in Burgundy, his domains in the Vivarais, principally along the Ardèche River and including vineyards, mulberry trees, and mills, comprised property in Balazuc and many other villages, including Vogüé, the site of the family château, which still stands.[33]

Émigré *biens nationaux* in Balazuc consisted of the property of Julien de Vinezac and the comte de Vogüé. The auction was to begin at nine o'clock in the morning on July 11, 1792, in Joyeuse. However, no prospective purchasers showed up. The candles begun to mark the time during which bids could be taken burned out. The auction was rescheduled. On July 25 the candles burned out again without bids.[34]

However, soon purchasers came forward. The landed empire of "the émigré Vogüé" disappeared piece by piece in 1792–93 in twenty-two communes, including Balazuc. Antoine Tastevin bought some land for 14,000 pounds. Jacques Mollier purchased unimproved land with white oaks; Pierre Constant spent 7,000 pounds for "a piece of farmable land, with olive trees, called the vineyard of the boat," near the point where the small boat pulled in on the other side of the river from the village. André Teyssier purchased the mill for

25,200 pounds and the oven for 450 pounds. Louis Mollier purchased the crumbling château high in the village for 625 pounds.[35]

After consultation with the mayor, Jacques Mollier divided the property of Julien de Vinezac, valued at 33,142 pounds, into forty-six separate lots, gardens (several along the Ardèche), cultivable land, meadows, oak, walnut, and mulberry trees, vineyards, and several houses in the village itself. The description of each parcel included mention of what bordered it on each side, *bise*, *au levant*, *coucher*, and *marin* (north, east, west, and south).[36] Even as his property was on the verge of being sold, the mayor and municipal officials of the commune wrote to certify that four men who owed grain "to the émigré Louis Jullien known as Vinezac of Largentière find it impossible to pay their portion this year, given that they have absolutely no grain."[37]

At the auctions held in Jaujac and Joyeuse in February 1794, one candle after another gradually burned down until no more bids were heard. Most lots were auctioned off with little waste of wax, but some hotly contested properties took up to thirteen candles until all voices had fallen silent. For example, the second lot was a small garden near the river. The property, valued at only forty pounds, stood between "the rock" and the Ardèche. A man from Largentière bid forty-five pounds. After Joseph Montel of Balazuc bid fifty pounds, the auctioneer lit a candle. Claude Mourzial of Balazuc raised the bid to fifty-five pounds, Pierre Dubois of Largentière to sixty. When the auctioneer lit a second candle, Montel raised the bid to sixty-five pounds. As a third candle burned, Jean Roux of Balazuc went to seventy pounds, and while a fourth candle burned, Louis Boyer of Balazuc increased the bid to seventy-five pounds. A fifth candle brought Montel's bid of eighty pounds. When a sixth candle brought no more bids, Montel owned a garden.

In all, twenty-five men, all but five from Balazuc, purchased property that had belonged to Julien de Vinezac. Jean Sabatier led the way with six different acquisitions, including the four largest parcels of land; one consisted of "farmable land, some in fallow, walnut trees, and mulberry trees," and included a dovecote and a barn. After thirteen candles had burned, no one could top the 2,510 pounds he could pay. When Julien de Vinezac was shot by the Revolutionary Tribunal in Lyon, only a few of his properties remained unsold.[38]

In the district of Tanargue, ecclesiastical property (2.4 million pounds) accounted for more than that of émigrés (1.7 million pounds), though, to repeat, not in Balazuc. In all, the purchase of *biens nationaux* added to the property of peasants who were somewhat better off than their neighbors, even if the gap between them and other property owners remained relatively small and the challenges facing both were considerable. Such purchases also may have solidified the support for at least the moderate Revolution of several key figures in Balazuc. André Teyssier, who purchased some land and the mill, served as chief municipal officer of Balazuc during the Revolution. He had a vested interest in seeing that the Ancien Régime did not return. Jean Maurin was among those serving as officers in the village National Guard. Louis Duffaud and Jacques Mollier were able to purchase about twenty hectares of land along the Ardèche near Aubenas.[39] The consequences of the sale of national property were considerable. Not long after the abolition of feudalism had ended seigneurial rights, the sale of the lands of the Vogüé family and of Julien de Vinezac ended direct noble influence in Balazuc. Over the long run, the sale of émigré property mattered. While the direct influence of the seigneurs on Balazuc had largely ended well before the Revolution, the parcels of land that André Teyssier, Louis Mollier, Antoine Rieu, and other peasants purchased contributed to the shift in the family agricultural economy increasingly from the production of grain to that of raw silk and wine. They took advantage of the opportunity that the Revolution had presented them.[40]

Municipal Government during the Republic

The rapid changes that came with the radicalization of and increasing resistance to the Revolution added to the challenges confronting the municipal administration of Balazuc. Conscription, provisioning, religion, and the chaos of dealing with superior administrators who were under pressure and apt to be replaced without any notice complicated the duties of those charged with serving as intermediaries between Balazuc and the revolutionary government. Assignats plunged in value. Since liquid wealth remained extremely scarce in the Vivarais, the printing of five series of "bills of confidence" early in 1792 only added to monetary inflation. This contributed to the further fall of the assignat.[41] Balazuc was among those towns and villages that issued bills of confidence as paper currency. Two officials came to the village in December to inspect the municipal accounting and oversee the public burning of paper money that had not yet been put into circulation. Before leaving, they made Balazuc's officials personally responsible for "any problems that their negligence or inexactitude could bring about."[42]

In the meantime the expenditures of the municipality closely resembled those of the *communauté* before the Revolution. Funds had to be found to pay for the village scribe, wood and light, presumably for the building housing the municipality, and a salary of 100 pounds for the teacher, Pierre Constant, himself or his son a purchaser of *biens nationaux*, and the tax collector—a total expenditure of more than 284 pounds.[43] Life went on, but inevitably under the shadow of grand events. One sign of the turmoil may be found in the falling number of births.[44]

Little room was left moderate reformers. When on March 25, 1793, the male citizens of Balazuc met to elect new municipal officials, as part of the Jacobin purge of municipalities, the men of the village elected Antoine Teyssier to the post of national agent, replacing the procurer. This marked the passing of the effective line of authority, at least in principle, from the commune to the revolutionary Jacobin government during the Terror. Citizen Antoine Rieu *fils* became village scribe. At the time of the Revolution, Rieu had been unable to pay the grain that he owed the noble Julien de Vinezac. Now he served as an official in the municipality wrestling with the changes the Revolution had brought.[45]

Jacobin demands reached into the isolated village of Balazuc. Like the intendants of the Ancien Régime, Jacobin authorities now requisitioned grain, chestnuts, and draftees in 1793 and 1794. The *conseil général* of Balazuc elected André Teyssier, secretary of the commune, to attend a meeting in Privas in June 1793 to discuss "the delicate crisis in which the republic finds itself because of the events in Paris on May 31 and the following day" (when the Parisian sans-culottes rose up to demand a purge of the Girondins from the National Convention).[46] Some in Balazuc may have been on the verge of federalism but judiciously pulled back. In any case, to send no one would have immediately raised suspicions of counterrevolutionary sentiments in Balazuc.

The Jacobins declared the levée en masse in April 1793 in the defense of the republic. The Ardèche was ordered to provide thirty-five hundred men. Antoine Auzas was elected as one of the sergeants of the company of fifty men requisitioned from Balazuc and nearby villages at the order of the Convention to battle counterrevolution-aries in the Cévennes in April 1793. They took an oath "to maintain liberty and legality or to die defending it," whether they believed it or not.[47] Twenty-three men, most eighteen or nineteen years old, were conscripted from Balazuc to join the Army of the Alps. All but three had been born in Balazuc. With the exception of two cloth-makers, the men representing (most, certainly, unwillingly) Balazuc all either owned property in Balazuc, and were listed as *laboreurs* or *agriculteurs* (suggesting that they were property owners but owned little) or, like the three outsiders, were agricultural laborers. The three most imposing stood at five feet five inches. The smallest at four feet eight probably could have more easily hidden in an attempt to escape military service and the very real possibility of never return-ing to Balazuc.[48]

Hardly anyone desired a return to the Ancien Régime, identified with obligations to the seigneurs. But popular hostility to the exac-tions eminating from Paris, Privas, and Joyeuse meant that if rela-tively few actually joined the counterrevolutionary bands (peopled increasingly by men who had fled the draft or were deserters) becom-ing ever more common in the Bas-Vivarais, Catholics wanted their priests back. During the Terror the church had housed the munici-pality. Villages like Balazuc provided no help they could avoid to the Jacobin campaign to stamp out counterrevolutionaries.[49]

Forceful, even threatening orders arrived ever more frequently. The municipality was ordered to put an end to hoarding, rampant almost everywhere because of "the negligence of municipalities in assuring the execution of laws." Nine days later came the warning that enforcement of the laws and the arrest of deserters, "cowards who have abandoned the flags of liberty," would be the personal responsibility of municipal officials. These were serious accusations in the year II of the republic.[50]

It is of course difficult to assess the response in Balazuc to an insistent letter sent on June 1, 1793, from "the national agent of the district of Tanargue to the municipalities and the committees of surveillance." No revolutionary or surveillance committee existed in Balazuc. An earlier demand that communes send a written report every ten days detailing what measures local authorities had taken to ensure the execution of the laws had been largely ignored. This was not what was expected of "patriots." In order to "suppress malevolence, stifle discord, and protect the republic and public virtue from the passions of their enemies," Jacobin authorities wanted to hear about progress in establishing public schools, producing boots for military volunteers, and enforcing the maximum price that could be charged for grain and bread, the amount of grain produced in the village, the number of suspects and deserters arrested, counterrevolutionary agitation by émigrés and former nobles, and the activities of those who could not justify their means of existence and those "who have not constantly manifested their attachment to the Revolution."[51]

Early in January 1794 the Committee of Public Safety sent Châteauneuf-Randon to the department as *représentant en mission*. This former noble and military officer, who had crushed counterrevolutionaries in the Lozère in 1793, now waged war on the clergy who had not taken the oath to the Revolution. He also organized the requisition of grain before his transfer. His successor sent out national guardsmen from Aubenas in a search for royalist "brigands" who defied Jacobin authority.[52] The fall (the Ninth of Thermidor) and execution of Robespierre in late July 1794 brought to an end the Jacobin dictatorship. With Christmas of that year, Masses again began to be said openly where there were priests to do so.

However, orders barked by revolutionary officials, even after the fall of the Jacobins, increasingly had no effect. Authorities in Joyeuse heard new rumors that in several villages on the edge of the Cévennes above Largentière crosses had been put back up and churches had been reopened and that "what was formerly called the Angelus was being rung, and that many people promise themselves that the priests and their childish behavior would soon return." Thus Balazuc and Pradons learned that within two days twenty-five soldiers would arrive in each village, there to stay (and therefore to be lodged and fed) "until further order," terrifying news. Next, "the urgent needs of the army" necessitated the prompt transport of fodder to army camps. In the name of the law, those citizens who had wagons or hauling animals at their disposal were ordered within twenty-four hours to take them to Joyeuse, so that they could transport hay to Bourg-sur-Rhône, from which they would return with loads of grain for use by troops in Joyeuse.[53]

Counterrevolution and Brigandage

In the year III (September 1794–September 1795), the Ardèche turned against the republic in an atmosphere of tension, even violence. Many Catholics had never forgiven the Jacobins for laws against the clergy, émigrés, and deserters and bitterly resented forced loans. Compliant authorities, some of them royalists, gave returning émigrés and outlawed priests necessary papers (*certificats du civisme*). In many villages, parishioners now refused to hear Mass said by, or to receive the sacraments from, priests who had not taken the oath, and some of the latter took up other occupations. A few formally recanted their oaths in front of the faithful. In the Bas-Vivarais, particularly, political hatred now ran deep, while those denigrated by republicans as "royalists, *muscadins* [elegant royalists], *chouans* [counterrevolutionary insurgents], and brigands" attacked those republicans, particularly purchasers of *biens nationaux*, and Protestants, whom they denounced as "terrorists, anarchists, and drinkers of blood." In the meantime "patriots" in the Ardèche denounced the "returned émigrés, the refractory priests and the despots . . . ferocious animals who wish to devour the republic."[54] In some of the Bas-Vivarais, this was indeed the case.

Major revolts against the Revolution were still under way in the west and other parts of Midi. In the meantime, in 1795, the prices of grain, bread, and all food soared dramatically, bringing great hardship. The government of the Directory, which had succeeded the Jacobin dictatorship following the fall of the Committee of Public Safety on the Ninth of Thermidor, was determined to prevent hostility in the Ardèche from becoming open insurrection. At the same time, it continued to extract material resources and draftees and assure the provisioning of grain. The release of thousands of prisoners in the post-Thermidor period after the fall of the Jacobin dictatorship and the unleashing of an anti-Jacobin terror had a dramatic impact on the Ardèche.

Another official learned upon his arrival in Aubenas that trouble had occurred in Balazuc a few days earlier (April 24, 1796). Young men who were to be conscripted, their numbers swollen by suspected deserters, had cut down the liberty tree planted five years earlier, prevented other draftees from leaving the village, seized the modest *caisse* (treasury) of the municipality, and run through the village shouting, "Long live the king!" and "Down with the republic and the patriots!" The arrival of a detachment of troops scattered the group, but not before one of them fired a shot at the soldiers. He was arrested, along with twelve other men. Châteauneuf-Randon declared Balazuc under a state of siege. The village's municipal officials were to provide a list of all deserters in the village, arrest them, and take them to Aubenas to be judged by martial law. Furthermore, they were to disarm the village, leaving weapons only with two men who did not take part in the rebellion (a demand that suggests the revolt had widespread sympathy). Troops sent from the Haute-Loire hunted in the mountains for royalist "brigands," possibly including some men from Balazuc.[55] Bands of counterrevolutionaries attacked villages in several places in the Ardèche.

The government placed the Ardèche under the state of siege and sent the National Guard of Aubenas into the mountainous cantons of Burzet and Montpezat in search of "brigands." Sixty deserters, 12 priests, and a number of people who had hidden "counterrevolutionaries" were arrested. However, by this point the "brigands" clearly outnumbered national guardsmen loyal to the republic and a smattering of troops. Fearing to swell further the enemies of the republic, officials freed 150 prisoners (5 priests and 3 nuns were guillotined at Privas), as the shortage of grain became ever more pressing.[56]

Jacobin grain requisition had aided the cause of those opposed to the Revolution. Those who had purchased *biens nationaux* had reason to lie awake at night wondering if any sound they heard—say, a stone sent spiraling down a path by the mistral—might be the arrival of armed men with a score to settle. Those who had supported aggressive authorities during the brief Jacobin dictatorship had indeed much to fear.

What had begun as counterrevolutionary sentiment at the Plain of Jalès gave way to *banditisme,* bands retaining only the white cockade as a symbol of political views. Murders and holdups of merchants and wagon drivers became common. Still, bands of criminals enjoyed the tacit support of a good many villagers, particularly in the Cévennes. Troops sent to pursue the "brigands" were in tatters, poorly armed, rarely paid, and demoralized.[57]

The clergy played a major role in encouraging resistance against the Revolution and hatred of those who purchased *biens nationaux.* The confident assertation of September 30, 1796, that "the brigands have been entirely expelled from the territory of the department and twelve of these scoundrels have bitten the dust" was nothing more than bravado.[58] Bandits like Claude Duny, known as the king of Bauzon, with his headquarters in the middle of a mountain forest, enjoyed popular support, even fame and adulation.

Thereafter, when the municipality of Balazuc met, it was usually in response to the escalation of violence in the region. Despite some inevitable division of opinion, the village itself seems to have remained united in the face of all kinds of dangers. There were no denunciations.

On May 1, 1796, the commune of Balazuc met in the *maison commune* to reorganize the village National Guard and selected Antoine Rieu and Jean Thoulouze as captains of the two companies.[59] That same year the municipality named those who would participate in the "mobile column," following orders of the *commissaire du directoire exécutif*, essentially the National Guard with some new officers. A meeting called by the national agent on March 22, 1797, took place in the "former church now serving as the location of the communal assembly." The meeting "in the name of the law" ordered Citizen Jean Thoulouze, commander of the National Guard of Balazuc, "to establish a guard" and arrest all people found in the commune without passports, because of fear of "brigands." A band stormed into Montréal, visible from the *gras* of Balazuc, and burst into the house of one Blachère, who supported the Revolution. They murdered him and pillaged his house for good measure. Bold attacks took place in Joyeuse and Uzer, among many other villages near and far. Fearing for their lives, witnesses disappeared as quickly as did the bandits.[60]

Trouble on the Gras

For the moment the peasants of Balazuc again had a more immediate interest. This was a growing dispute with Chauzon and Pradons, both part of the *communauté* of Balazuc during what was already known as the Ancien Régime. The issue was the division of territory among the three communes, made more complicated by the problem that Chauzon and Balazuc had shared common land on the *gras*. An expert had been named to establish new boundaries. A decree in June 1793 had granted propertied citizens of communes the right to decide if *biens communaux*, if there were any, should be divided up. Officials of the district of Tanargue, as in many other places, warned that because "rich proprety owners seem opposed to the execution of the law on their division," they recommended closely watching the voting, in order to prevent "all of the cabals which are the fruit of injustice." A majority of two-thirds was required, as was the subsequent participation of three experts from outside the commune.

When the *conseil général* of Balazuc met to discuss the communal lands, it denounced the inhabitants of Chauzon and Pradons, who continued to claim the right to pasture their animals on, and thus do damage to, Balazuc's communal lands, particularly the woods.[61] The government soon gave the commune of Balazuc three days to respond to the claims of Pradons and Chauzon and named two different experts to draw up new boundaries among the three communes.[62]

So in 1797, even as brigands terrorized the countryside, the protection of the *gras* against people, whether from Vinezac, Lanas, or Balazuc, who were illegally pasturing animals there remained a more absorbing preoccupation in the village. Agent National Teyssier and his deputy Laroche sent six national guardsmen to the *gras* to "oversee the preservation of the rural property of the commune." On December 2 the guardsmen seized fourteen sheep on the *gras* and indeed brought them to the *maison commune*. The animals were later claimed by two men from Balazuc and by several from Lanas.[63] Nothing was resolved. Competing claims to the *gras* came back to haunt Balazuc. The struggle over contested rights to common pasture and marginal agricultural land typified peasant communities. It highlights the complexity of the meanings of property at a time when the Revolution had sanctified private ownership, a concept of ambiguous, uncertain utility within the traditions of peasant life.

Civil War

The coup d'état of 18 fructidor, year VI (September 4, 1797), annulling elections that had been favorable to royalists, brought to the Ardèche new officials, more determined to defend the republic. They replaced a good many who had been notoriously inactive in the attempt to restore order or who had resigned in fear of being compromised in the eyes of one side or the other. The hunt for refractory priests began anew; the ringing of church bells was strictly forbidden. After a surprise attack on a column of national guardsmen above Burzet, more troops poured into the region, and several leading counterrevolutionaries were arrested and shipped off to Le Puy or Lyon to be executed.

The Ardèche spun into anarchy in the years VII and VIII (September 1798–September 1800), as the revival of royalism and rampant, professionalized brigandage threatened the regime. Between September 1798 and November 1799, there were hundreds of cases of robbery, theft, pillage, arson, and the beating and even murder of noted republicans, particularly purchasers of *biens nationaux.*[64] Certainly the decision taken to double the tax on doors and windows did not help the cause of officials representing what many peasants still perceived as a godless republic. From virtually all corners of the Bas-Vivarais came frantic reports of attacks, including audacious thefts of state funds being transported or taken from local treasuries or tax offices. Well-organized bands of "brigands," in the language of officials and other supporters of the republic, operated with near impunity in Vallon and other cantons, on several occasions occupying towns.[65]

The National Guard of Balazuc was reorganized. All men between eighteen and sixty were to serve, forming one company of fifty men. Antoine Rieu was to serve as captain. Later that year Rieu called a meeting of the national guard. He announced that he was resigning as captain "because I can neither read nor write, and seeing that we are in the situation of receiving orders from a commander and in order to reply to them I must be able to write, I ask to be replaced by a citizen who would know how to reply to orders that have been given."[66]

In the meantime the Directory increasingly turned to brutal military force to restore order.[67] It created a military commission to wage war on brigandage in the Aveyron, Hérault, Gard, and Ardèche. General Nivet and his deputy commander, Monchauffé, known for his cruelty and Alsatian accent, took command of more than six hundred troops in the Ardèche. Army officers doubled as judges and immediately carried out harsh sentences against those who had attacked purchasers of the *biens nationaux* and against peasant deserters who swelled the ranks of the brigands. For twelve days Nivet's three mobile columns moved through towns and villages, arresting deserters and other suspects where they could identify and find them.

Yet the attacks continued, including in and around Balazuc in the year VII. On November 25, Vinezac's leading official learned that at about five in the morning thieves armed with rifles were stopping passersby on the road from La Chapelle to Uzer, near Balazuc, stealing their money, watches, and anything else of value. He sent two groups of national guardsmen after them, ordering them to "look further in the rocks of Lanas, Balazuc, and Uzer." The thieves had disappeared into the rugged terrain and would be back. Although there is no evidence that Balazuc itself fell into anarchy, the bands drew closer to the village, robbing a tax official in La Chapelle-sous-Aubenas and burning tax registers there and in Laurac. At least some people in Balazuc still supported the Revolution; a man described as a "patriot" was robbed near Uzer on December 2, 1798. More thefts occurred during thermidor in Laurac, Chauzon, Pradons, Ruoms, Lanas, and Balazuc.[68]

In defiance of the well-organized *battue* (not unlike that which local hunters still undertake in search of wild boar) during June and July 1799, attacks continued almost without pause. On June 22 another sizable group disarmed the guard of Chauzon, and mortally wounded a republican and purchaser of *biens nationaux*. A band that terrorized the region moved into Balazuc, where it mortally wounded Louis Pays, a member of the village National Guard. Thermidor brought more attacks, including one by fifty or sixty "brigands" on the office of the tax collector of Laurac, after which five or six men who had acquired *biens nationaux* were forced to pay up or be killed. During the night of July 7–8 they briefly blocked entrance to Pradons, forcing national guardsmen into hiding, firing shots here and there. They returned less than a week later, cut down a liberty tree and killed André Ranchin, whose father, a well-known republican, had acquired *biens nationaux* and who owned property in Balazuc.[69]

Monchauffé's men ordered raids in and around Chauzon, looking for "brigands" hiding in the vicinity who terrorized nearby villages, including Balazuc. Before a surprise operation early in the morning could be coordinated with other troops, a band showed up late at night and attacked the house of the tax collector. They fled as a detachment of the mobile column arrived.[70] Following a brazen attack near Ruoms, a third *battue* during August and September 1798 led to the arrest of thirty men. A few drowned in the Ardèche River as they tried to escape. It was a war without quarter, with Nivet's forces using "wood, straw, and sulfur" to dislodge their prey as they fled and hid where they could. Nivet's forces also arrested more than a dozen nonjuring priests, accusing them of encouraging resistance. Bold attacks continued here and there. Yet the rugged topography of the Ardèche and "the well-known character of most of the inhabitants" favored the ability of the royalist bandits to outlast the forces hunting them down. In the meantime the counterrevolutionaries gained martyrs, among them the feared Platon, known for his colossal strength and for murder, who was killed by Monchauffé's troops.[71]

On December 1, 1798, a shot shattered the right arm of Mollier of Balazuc (known to be a republican and certainly the purchaser of *biens nationaux* that had belonged to Julien of Vinezac). In January 1799, Auzas *dit* Larose, tax collector of Balazuc, was also shot and seriously wounded. When a large band drew near Ruoms at nightfall, a captain sent a detachment of fifteen troops, armed with the *mot d'ordre* "Bonaparte is here—courage," itself a sign of change from Paris. They exchanged fire as the brigands ran toward the river, leaving several guns behind. When in October 1799 a deputy from the Ardèche described the extent of counterrevolutionary banditry in Paris before the Council of Five Hundred, the second body of the legislature, he specifically cited the example of Balazuc, along with Chauzon and Laurac. Nivet's intensive military repression had been successful. But at first it won the Revolution few friends in the Bas-Vivarais. Monchauffé himself was assassinated in Aubenas on January 20, 1800.[72]

Amid anarchy and violence, hardly anyone noticed the next coup d'état in Paris, that of the 18 brumaire (November 9, 1799), which brought Napoleon Bonaparte and his friends to power. Such an event seemed a logical consequence to the militarization of the repression of royalists and brigands in the Ardèche and other regions in which virtual civil war had raged. A law in February 1800 made prefects, appointed chief administrators of the departments, cornerstones of Napoleonic centralization. The first prefect admitted that "never had the situation been as grave in the Ardèche as just before" the coup d'état.[73]

The plight of authorities representing the republic was indeed dire. They had few troops or provisions, no money, and little support. In the meantime several of the leaders of the brigands/royalists inquired discreetly if they might exchange their withdrawal from the field for an amnesty. They retained no small degree of popular toleration, even support, with many being identified with the cause of the clergy. In the Bas-Vivarais, "the dedicated brigand goes to his execution with a fanatical serenity, provided that his priest is there to help him along."[74] The senior administrative official still had not arrived in Privas, and few letters got through. Local authorities hesitated to promise what they could not yet legally offer: the amnesty that might bring peace.

Nivet's successor, General Férino, first launched a relentless repression, threatening with execution anyone caught with weapons or officials who protected "brigands" and proving that this was no idle threat. Then he offered an amnesty to those who turned in weapons. Although some attacks and even murders as well as summary executions continued, troops gradually restored order.[75] Fatigued by the anarchy and bloodshed, peasant support for rebels waned. Balazuc and the other villages in the Ardèche wanted peace above all and by this time "cared little or not at all about the form of the government that ruled them, or about the exercise of their political rights." Support for the regime increased. The Concordat between the French state and the Church, signed in 1801, removed an important pretext for systematic opposition as more priests returned and churches, in Balazuc and elsewhere, were full again.[76] The chaos had taken its toll in another way: "In half the communes one can hardly find anyone who can blindly put his signature below what a so-called secretary puts before him, ignorant even of what he believes that he knows." Some mayors admitted that "the priests alone have held on to their knowledge."[77]

"Enemies of all constraint, attached to their miserable region," as a haughty imperial prefect put it, Ardéchois continued to flee military service. During the entire revolutionary and imperial period, the number of deserters and draft dodgers remained at more than 30 percent. Those escaping military service dropped dramatically from, by one count, almost half in 1802 to just 5 percent in 1814, a "success" to which mobile columns sent out in search of the recalcitrant surely contributed. Thus conscription in 1809–12 met with relative success. Moreover although the price of bread rose in 1813, there was no trouble in the Ardèche.[78]

In some ways Balazuc, at least in appearance, had not changed at all. A new priest had long since arrived. Despite the breakdown of civil order, the sale of émigré property, and even civil war, the conservatism of the village remained intact. Peasants had struggled as they always had to survive, while the changes and dramas brought by the Revolution swirled around them, impinging in some ways on their lives. The production of raw silk, assisted by mulberry trees since planted on some of the land purchased at the auctions of *biens nationaux*, had begun to offer some peasants a glimmer of hope, as the struggle to earn a living went on. Balazuc had grown from about 550 people at the time of the Revolution (not counting soldiers on active duty) to 653 in 1804 (more than likely a good many births in devout Balazuc were not registered with the constitutional priest and then civil authorities once the registration of births, marriages, and deaths was secularized in 1792).[79] Nearly the entire population worked the land. A hundred heads of household were listed as *agriculteurs propriétaires* (with occasionally "*en petit*" added to signify particularly small holdings and thus expectations).

On the *gras* in the same stone farmhouse (*mas*) in which his family had lived for more than four centuries, Antoine Fabregoule, forty-nine years old, lived with his wife of the same age, their five children, and his brother. His wife and two of his children helped him with his land (his brother may have had his own parcel of land), and one son was a mason, a daughter a shepherd. The youngest son, Jean, nine years of age, did not attend school, probably because of the difficulty and expense of crossing the river. Nine heads of household in Balazuc owned and worked land and also were tradesmen of some kind: a hat-maker; a carder; two tailors, one destitute, the other doing well enough to have a twenty-two-year-old journeyman tailor living in the household; a blacksmith; a weaver; a woman doubling as a wool spinner; a stonecutter; and a mason, in addition to two other stone-cutters, a carpenter, a baker, two millers, a mason, another carder, and an innkeeper. Jean Daumas was one of two Balazuciens who enjoyed the status of being listed as *rentiers*. Jacques Mollier of Louanes owned and farmed land and had assessed the value of lands sold as *biens nationaux* during the Revolution. Six families had enough land and animals to employ rural domestics, but only three could afford servants. Some wives were specifically described as taking care of the household, and some of them also carded and spun. Shepherds included eighteen boys and young men and nine girls and young women.[80]

Hycinthe Baille lived in the presbytery and served as the village's priest until his death in 1831. Jean Rieu was among his poorest parishioners; at seventy-three he owned no land and worked as a day laborer. His wife, eighteen years younger, sewed and spun. With them lived their son and his wife, who begged, and their two small children. Marie Rieu was thus one of Balazuc's nineteen beggars, including several heads of household. These ranged in age from the youngest, a four-year-old girl, to a sixty-five-year-old man. Étienne Court was a tailor, a trade for which there would have been few clients in a poor village like Balazuc; his wife, Marianne, "begs for her bread." Their eldest child, a girl of eighteen, spun wool; two of their other children, ten and seven, begged, and the third at three was still too young to do even that. Louis Granier owned some land, but obviously the designation *"agriculteur propriétaire en petit"* probably underestimated his poverty. He was a widower, and his three children, twelve, eight, and four years of age, were listed as beggars. Antoine Boyer, thirty-six, was an *agriculteur propriétaire* living with his wife, Marie-Rose Cardinal. One of their children, Jean, aged eleven, went to school; his brother was three. Françoise Boyer, Antoine's sister, a beggar, also lived with them. Étienne Roury, sixty-five, also begged, as did his fifty-year-old wife and eleven-year-old daughter. Marguerite Chabriès lived nearby; at age sixty-five she begged, and her twenty-one-year-old son lived "from day to day." In an isolated village where hardly anyone had more than enough to get along, the returns from begging must have been few indeed.

The saddest among sad cases may have been a seventeen-year-old beggar, Jean Roux, the younger brother of Jeanne Roux. Jean Roux was blind. For people who had next to nothing, the sheer beauty of Balazuc must have counted for something; not to be able to see it would have been tragic. Rocky paths and steep inclines made his ventures outside perilous.

Two schools functioned in Balazuc. The 1804 census indicates which children went to school. Jean Pays, schoolteacher at the age of eighteen (the son of Jean Pays, *agriculteur propriétaire*, and the brother of the baker), taught twelve boys. Fifty-year-old Marie Roudil instructed twenty-one girls and lived in the house of her sister, the widow of a Tastevin, along with the latter's son, wife, and daughter. Only one boy, fifteen-year-old Frédéric Tastevin, the son of the late Antoine Tastevin, attended *collège* (certainly in Aubenas). That, and his family's relative wealth, earned him "M(onsieu)r" inserted before his name in the census.

In late May 1814, Jean Tastevin, who had served with the army in Spain, returned to Balazuc with many stories and a foot problem that had brought about his release from service.[81] With the (first) Restoration of the Bourbons in 1814, Antoine Auzas stayed on as mayor, and he continued through the Hundred Days of Napoleon's return. With the Second Restoration, Antoine Alexandre Tastevin, a prosperous landowner living in the family *mas* of Les Salles, thirty-two years old and deputy mayor since 1812 (his father had been mayor at the time of his death in 1801), became mayor. For a time in June and July he and his predecessor Auzas alternated signing death certificates, and both signed as mayor on October 7. Indeed Tastevin on May 15 sheepishly declared in the presence of Deputy Mayor Claude Boiron that his three children had not been properly entered on the État Civil (civil registry of births, marriages, and deaths). Tastevin stated that "by reprehensible but nonetheless excusable negligence" he had confided the task of declaring his children to his father-in-law, the mayor of nearby St.-Maurice, who had not done so. Now, accompanied by witnesses, he watched as their names were officially entered into the État Civil.[82] From then on, these crucial registers would be maintained by the mayor, not the priest, and filled out by the secretary.

The Declaration of the Rights of Man of 1793 had stated, "Education is the need of everyone," and Danton had proclaimed, "In the republic, no one is free to be ignorant."[83] However, the economic, social, and political turmoil of the revolutionary and Napoleonic periods set back considerably any kind of formal instruction. The new prefect in 1801 insisted on the importance of spreading a knowledge of French: "[W]ithout education we can hope in vain to soften the customs, which are strictly Gallic, of most of the inhabitants of the Ardèche, and to transform their fiery and savage nature, which political intrigues so well profited, during all the great events that have so agitated France."[84] The early nineteenth century was to establish the teacher as a permanent, effective presence in Balazuc. With the imprimatur of the state, the teacher emerged as a potential rival to the village priest. The school became an alternate source of instruction, solidarity, and political allegiance, increasingly a defining center of village life in a new century that brought Balazuc new challenges but also new opportunities.

FOUR

The Golden Tree

They even had cocoons in their sabots.

THE *ANNALES DU MIDI*, AN ALMANAC PUBLISHED IN 1839, did not include Balazuc among sites of interest in the Ardèche. Only very gradually did Balazuc's splendid setting and mysterious origins begin to attract a few visitors who had heard about the village. If Ovide de Valgorge, departmental inspector of historical monuments, came upon "some battered debris at the top of a rock" from the original château and visited its successor up the hill, "without pronounced architectural character," Albert du Boys, who put together an *Album du Vivarais* in 1842, had a very different reaction. Balazuc's savage beauty evoked the memory of the Saracens, who slowly assumed a larger place in the construction or vision of Balazuc's past, real and imagined. Du Boys evoked the "fearsome renown" of the Saracens in the Vivarais. "Their name resounds more than that of the Romans," even if only "popular error in the village" attributed to the "children of Muhammad the traces of antique monuments."[1]

While the mysteries of Balazuc's past compelled some reflection, the village and its region were being transformed by the production of raw silk. All hope turned toward the "golden tree," the mulberry tree, which seemed to be able to pull entire villages out of abject poverty because its leaves fed silkworms. Henri Bourdon, sent in 1836 by the minister of commerce and agriculture, reported that the mulberry tree had become "dominant . . . the product of this precious tree is the only source of income for the inhabitants. . . . The management and the height (of the tree) generally are submitted to fixed and regular principles, and the industrious touch of the peasants succeeds in drawing something from these arid hillsides."[2] On his visit, Jules Michelet noticed the visible change transforming the household economy of Balazuc and other impoverished villages in the Bas-Vivarais. His visit coincided with the silkworm harvest of 1844, a boom year. "Traveling across this rough countryside, the valleys of the Ardèche, where all is rock, or mulberry trees and chestnut trees, seem to do without soil, living from air and stone."[3] Michelet discovered the small world of "humble stone houses, rocks stuck together, where the peasants live. . . . [T]hese houses are very solemn, even sad with their small, dry gardens, poor and meager. . . . [A]t this beautiful time of the year, they produced silk, and this poor region seemed rich. In each house, under the sober arcade, could be found a young girl spinning silk, who, while pushing down on the pedal of the spooling mechanism, smiled with pretty white teeth while she spun gold."[4] It was the good old days.

In the several decades that had passed since the end of the Napoleonic adventure, the Ardèche had become what Yves Lequin calls the "kingdom of silk."[5] The production of raw silk had transformed the peasant economy of the Bas-Vivarais. Small-holding peasants proved anything but the stereotype of prisoners of tradition.[6] The Ardèche, like the Drôme, Ain, and Isère, thus remained dependent on France's second city, as well as on the international market for silk, which itself was subject to changes in fashion. Silk produced in the Ardèche won prizes at the London Exposition in 1851 and in Paris four years later.[7]

The production of raw silk seemed perfectly adapted to a region of small property owners, the vast majority of whom worked their own small plots of land with their families, perhaps also working for others in order to get by. They helped their relatives and neighbors as needed, in their tradition of mutual assistance. There were very few full-time day laborers. Balazuc's canton of Vallon had two thousand farms of less than ten acres and only thirty between ten and twenty acres, ten between twenty and forty, and only one larger than that![8] Small parcels of land changed hands frequently; many peasants owned several plots in different parts of the commune. The extreme fragmentation of property remained a characteristic of the Vivarais.[9]

The arrondissement of Largentière had thirty-four thousand parcels of land (probably many more from those owning property by secret title, to avoid being on the tax rolls). Eighty percent of the parcels were worth less than a thousand francs. The tradition of heirs trying to keep family lands together (despite the end of primogeniture by the Napoleonic Code) often led the eldest to buy out his siblings, adding more obligations to already existing debt. "Above all," said the subprefect at mid-century, "the family household and its land must be maintained: Such is the obsession of the peasant proprietor, in anticipation of the possible eventual division of his inheritance." The overriding goal was to preserve the farming family, "to preserve their identity and their position in the village community." Now the production of raw silk appeared more than ever the way to achieve that age-old goal.[10] While the production of raw silk completely absorbed all efforts from the end of April until early or mid-June, the production of raw silk could be combined with other agricultural activities.[11]

"It's better to be a mulberry tree than an almond tree," went a saying—that is, better to be wise and prudent than foolishly independent. The mulberry tree is perfectly suited to the Vivarais. It is a robust tree of modest needs that thrives in a gravelly, even granitic soil that is permeable, including the steep slopes of the hills of the Ardèche. Moreover, it can resist the lengthy droughts that afflict the region.[12]

The silkworm-breeding frenzy took hold in the Ardèche, particularly after 1820 in the Cévennes, the Bas-Vivarais, and the lower valley of the Rhône, egged on by the insatiable Lyonnais market for raw silk. Peasants planted tens of thousands of trees—an average of ten trees per hectare for the entire region by 1840—on slopes, along roads and rivers, in fields between rows of vines and olive and chestnut trees (which in the early 1850s still made up 10 percent of the entire surface of the department of the Ardèche),[13] in the courtyards of farms, and on public places. The harvest of mulberry leaves, clear and deep green, increased by eight times during the first half of the century. In 1839 more than 1.2 million mulberry trees stood in the Vivarais, producing almost fifty million kilograms of leaves. Of these, two-thirds were in the arrondissement of Largentière. In addition, another 700,000 to 800,000 other mulberry trees had been planted. The number of mulberry trees standing in the Ardèche may have risen from 2 million in 1835 to perhaps even twice that eleven years later. In Balazuc, about ninety acres were now planted in mulberry trees. One contemporary exclaimed, "[T]he mulberry tree is everywhere; one would believe it indigenous, so rapidly do they easily multiply." Another praised the benefits of the golden tree on the "half-savage peoples" of the Vivarais. The local historian Albin Mazon later remembered, "the time when the region was rich, and no one dared get in the way of the noble mulberry tree," adding that any property owner would have found a way to cancel the lease of someone who dared plant anything under the golden tree.[14]

The influential student of electoral geography André Siegfried nonetheless missed the point when, studying the results of elections in the Ardèche during the Third Republic, he emphasized the lack of innovation among the peasants of the Vivarais. He compared them unfavorably with an "agricultural entrepreneur of the American continent," or his English counterpart: "one senses two completely different humanities, two different ages of civilization."[15] In fact, what is impressive, indeed moving, about the experience of the small peasant proprietors of Balazuc and of the Bas-Vivarais is precisely their willingness to adjust their strategies for survival, as they had by resourcefully planting potatoes in the eighteenth century.[16] Struggling against the daunting obstacles presented by nature, the peasants of Balazuc were by no means prisoners of routine awaiting "modernity."

The number of silkworm eggs hatched and the kilograms of cocoons produced increased dramatically. In 1839 raw silk producers in the Ardèche hatched 38,934 ounces of silkworm eggs. These yielded 1,168,034 kilograms of cocoons, worth 4.75 francs per kilogram. In 1840 1 ounce of eggs would yield about 150 francs in revenue. Small producers put about 10 ounces of eggs annually into incubation. The next year the Ardèche produced 1,845,070 kilograms of cocoons; in 1846 1,636,000 kilograms; and in 1850, a truly exceptional year, 3.5 million kilograms. By mid-century Balazuc had produced up to 10,000 kilograms of cocoons per year. In all, the "education" of silkworms generated more than 5.5 million francs' income in the sale of cocoons or raw silk at the annual fairs of Aubenas and Joyeuse.[17]

The production of raw silk required the energetic participation of the entire family. Men and boys (and, depending on the size of the operation, hired hands who came down from the mountains to work) gathered the huge piles of mulberry leaves that would feed silkworms by sliding their hands from the bottom end of branches to the tip. (Writing in the late eighteenth century, Boissier de Sauvages commented: "The silkworms don't care at all if those who gather the leaves drink a glass of wine before going to work, and I very strongly urge that they do so.")

· The process began with the silkworm eggs (*graines*, so called because their oval and rather flat shape resembles plant seeds, particularly radish seeds). These eggs were laid (*la ponte*) on the mulberry leaves by the butterfly known as *le Bombyx du Mûrier* at the previous year's harvest. They were hatched about ten months later, the necessary period of hibernation. The producers of silkworms had to keep the eggs warm, and they used body heat, traditionally supplied by each grandmother, who wore a small cloth bag under her skirt or blouse and placed the bag under her quilt at night.

Yet even in the warm Mediterranean climate of the Bas-Vivarais, the temperature is too low at that time for the eggs to hatch by themselves. The "education" or raising of silkworms took place in spaces or structures called *magnaneries* (from the Provençal word *magnan* for someone who eats all the time—in French, *un goinfre,* thus silkworm), or silkworm nurseries. Although some stood independent of houses, most *magnaneries* were added onto existing structures above the ground floor, reached through a door from a corridor or, in some cases, from the attic. A cloth curtain covered the entrance, limiting the cold air reaching inside; oil paper–covered windows kept away direct light. Today visitors to villages in the Bas-Vivarais may think upon seeing sizable stone structures that the peasants who built them were prosperous when in fact *magnaneries* attest to the poverty of the soil on which they stood.[18]

Most silkworm nurseries were rectangular, between about fifteen and sixty feet long and about twelve feet wide, and fifteen feet or more high (I write these words in a converted silkworm nursery). Inside the silkworm nursery stood a series of structures of wood that served as sizable tables, or shelves, one on top of the other, so that they resembled bunk beds, each "shelf" covered with a straw mat and paper, on which the silkworms lived.

Many peasants believed that allowing any outsider into the silkworm nursery might compromise the silk "harvest" with an evil eye. (Olivier de Serres recommended that anyone going into a *magnanerie* drink some wine so that "in sending the smell to the silkworm, it will preserve them from stench.")[19] Just as it seems to have been common for peasants to cross themselves before feeding the silkworms, it also was traditional for priests to bless the upcoming silkworm harvest, as had been suggested long before in printed instructions in 1695 for the planting of mulberry trees and raising of silkworms. In some parts of the Bas-Vivarais, looking directly at silkworms before they had climbed onto the branches of the heath was thought to bring bad luck. In the village of Rocles, parishioners carried cocoons into the church, hoping for the best; in St.-Félicien, the priest said a special High Mass, the "most beautiful branch, that which has given the most cocoons," placed on the altar.[20] The same tradition lasted into the 1950s in Lagorce, over the hill from Balazuc. Pious families carried a selection of the most beautiful cocoons to church to thank God for having blessed the harvest.[21]

The silkworm harvest usually was about May 25, when the mulberry leaves were at their tasty peak. The eggs changed color from gray to blue forty-eight hours before they were ready to be hatched.[22] For hatching the eggs, the heat within the *magnanerie* was raised about two degrees centigrade a day from twelve to about twenty degrees. Thereafter a constant high temperature had to be maintained by a stove burning wood from white oak trees. The hotter the temperature, the more the silkworms ate, but if the silkworm nursery became too hot, the silkworms suffocated. Some minimal fresh air was required.[23]

About forty thousand silkworms, each only about eight-hundredths of an inch (two millimeters) long hatched after about fifteen days from about twenty-five kilograms of cocoons produced by one ounce (or thirty-six grams) of eggs. Once hatched, the silkworm began to eat mulberry leaves. Silkworms ate four times their weight per day, and the sound of this almost continuous chewing resembled falling rain. They had to be fed at least four times a day. As family members placed mulberry leaves on the shelves, the silkworms ate the most tender, delicious parts, while what remained from those piles of litter on which they had already dined was changed at least twelve times and fed to the pigs, which were not choosy, or used for compost. As usual, nothing was wasted. The shelves of the silkworm nursery thus had to be cleaned frequently.

From birth to maturity, a period of about thirty-five days, the weight of each silkworm increased by ten thousand times (if nascent humans ate like that, a baby weighing three kilograms at birth would end up weighing thirty tons). Thus, if six ounces of *graines* (eggs) were hatched, a sizable *magnanerie* would be quite full twenty days later. During their short (about thirty-five days) but amazingly productive lives, the silkworms had to molt four times. The period before or between two moltings (*mues*) is known as ages (thus four moltings are equal to five ages). At the end of the first age, which lasted four or five days, a single silkworm reached about twenty-eight hundredths of an inch in length. The forty thousand silkworms would have by then consumed about seventeen pounds of mulberry leaves. During the next four ages, the last two of which lasted eight or nine days each, the silkworms ate more and more mulberry leaves. Each silkworm grew to slightly more than two inches in length, and forty thousand of them required about 180 square feet of space by the end of the fifth age.

At the end of the fifth age, the silkworms stopped eating, became translucent, revealing the silk fiber within, and chose a place in which to spin. During the thirty days of their life cycle, they had now eaten several tons of mulberry leaves. They climbed up on branches of heather (*bruyères*) found in the hills of the Ardèche, placed there by the producers. For two to three days, each silkworm, rather like a spider, secreted minuscule continuous silk fiber which solidified by contact with air, and, although produced in the form of the figure eight, could stretch from twenty-four to forty-five hundred feet and even up to a mile and a half in length. They then wound themselves into the protective cocoons they had constructed (which looked something like small meringues, though without the same taste) by rotating their bodies. Thus protected, the larvae underwent a slow metamorphosis for about twenty days, transformed by powerful hormones to turn first into chrysalides, then into butterflies.

If the natural cycle was allowed to run its course, after three weeks one end of the cocoon became soft, and the mulberry bombyx or butterfly spread the fibers apart and emerged. Unable to eat or to fly, the butterflies remained hanging from or attached to the branches. The males and females (distinguishable by the shape of the cocoon) quickly mated. After the female laid about five hundred eggs, eight days later the butterflies died, their reproductive function and the natural cycle completed. Producers of raw silk then put aside some of the eggs for the following year.[24]

Several days after the silkworms had finished their work, the actual "harvest" (*déconnage*) took place. This short and extremely labor-intensive process began by the harvesters taking all the branches from the *magnanerie* and putting them outside. Family members, friends, and workers hired for the harvest took the cocoons from the branches by removing the threads that had attached them. The cocoons were placed in sturdy canvas bags (*bourras*), which were weighed and sold at fairs in Aubenas or Joyeuse to spinning mills. Producers and buyers of cocoons did not debate the price at the time of the weighing; the price was determined later according by market price.[25]

Until the middle of the nineteenth century most peasant households spun the silk themselves, after which they sold the raw silk (*soie
grège*) in Joyeuse or Aubenas. Besides the silkworm nurseries, the raising of silkworms transformed in another way the stone houses, which
became more than ever a tool of work. Families producing raw silk
added balconies or galleries on the second floor of houses, usually
reached by an exterior covered staircase. Supported by pillars or even
arcades, these covered balconies (*couradous*)[26] served as the principal
space for the actual harvest, the unraveling, and the spinning in the
late spring. The *couradou* offered the advantage of being relatively
cooler in the hot summer months, being turned to the southwest,
covered, and exposed to cooling breezes, which were used for drying
figs or cheese. During winter the *couradous* attracted some warming
sunlight, as the sun stood relatively low on the horizon.

For spinning, the cocoons were separated from the pile, and fluff
surrounding the silk likewise was removed (*déblazé*). The women put
the cocoons in very hot (eighty degrees centigrade) water. This killed
the chrysalides, which had shrunk in size, so the cocoons could not
be damaged by emerging butterflies and could be unwound. Because
the silk fibers themselves were too fine to be woven, several fibers had
to be twisted together during the unwinding, a task facilitated by the
hot water. Using a branch of heather as something of a broom, the
women prodded the cocoons in order to detach the end of a single
continuous fiber that made up each cocoon and twisted several of
them together to make more resistant raw silk. The hot water also
served to get rid of the gluelike substance that covered the thread. In
this way, the raw silk could be wound up. The size of the thread was
determined by the number of cocoons combined during the unwinding in a basin of hot water, where beating the cocoons with branches
allowed the unusable portion to be eliminated. The unwinding of raw
silk gave off awful smells (citing the "horrible smell and stench . . .
detrimental," the municipal council of Largentière in 1676 forbade
silk work for the year), another reason to place the work in fresh air.
Exposure to the air solidified the white silk thread. Then the threads
were wound onto a wheel placed near the basin. In normal times,
eight to ten kilograms of cocoons turned out about a kilogram of raw

silk. It took about forty people to harvest five hundred kilograms of cocoons (normally ten kilograms of cocoons produced one kilogram of raw silk), the labor of forty thousand silkworms.[27]

The frenetic silkworm harvest that had begun early in May then ended after six weeks in mid-June. The production of silkworms and raw silk totally preoccupied entire villages. Old people remembered the intensity of the silkworm harvest, "a difficult period with an infernal rhythm. . . . [W]e lived for nothing else, the rest was simply incidental. . . . [W]e ate only what was left from the pig, the cleaning of clothes or of the house was left for a fortnight." In some villages, large loaves of bread were baked in the elongated form of a silkworm. Another man remembered the "fervor for which no other agricultural art could replicate. . . . [W]e can say that the entire region only lives and breaths for silkworms. . . . [D]uring the period of the harvest, all other work stops, nothing is sold, nothing is bought, no agreements are made, everything is put off that can possibly be put off." All attention then focused on the fair in Joyeuse, June 20.[28]

The municipal council of Balazuc was supposed to meet on May 21, 1854, but could not because of "the ongoing silkworm harvest." Likewise, the timing of elections was determined in the region by the silkworm harvest, upon which the local economy depended. The following year the prefect suggested the first half of July for elections as the ideal time in the Ardèche because the silkworm harvest would be over and the grain harvest not yet begun.[29]

The principal tasks of the care and feeding of silkworms took place under the direction of women, who had traditionally been responsible for work inside the house, including raising the pig and looking after the chickens and other small animals of the courtyard. Male responsibility for the fields extended to gathering mulberry leaves (with the children and sometimes hired hands), hauled to the house on the backs of mules or on human shoulders, large and small (*"Cantas, cantas magnanarello Que la culido es cantarello!"* ["Sing, sing, nursery workers, because the harvest likes singing"]). Men and boys chopped and hauled the wood used to heat the silkworm nursery. Well into the late nineteenth century, children were pulled out of school to work during the hectic weeks of the silkworm harvest or, at best, "sent to the leaves" after school; sometimes they slept in the nursery. Laborers, many hired at the fair on April 1 in Les Vans, came down from the densely populated mountains to work gathering mulberry leaves.[30]

If all went well, such speculation on raw silk brought happy returns. In 1828, the prefect noted with some surprise that "the prosperity of the people of the countryside has increased measurably."[31] The Société d'agriculture de l'Ardèche claimed in 1835 that a peasant in the region of Privas could earn 150 francs per year from two acres producing grain, 300 francs for beets, and 800 francs for two acres of mulberry trees. However, even if some years in the 1840s brought unprecedented prosperity, the "kingdom of silk" remained a poor kingdom. To an upper-class observer writing in 1849, "the growing prosperity of the Ardèche has softened the way of life and sensibly modified and even improved what was too rock hard and unfortunate about the habits."[32] The silk markets of Aubenas and Joyeuse had become the second and third respectively in France. In Joyeuse, seven to eight million francs of raw silk was sold each year. Middlemen (*maisons de commissions*) made fortunes with purchases of raw silk at the markets of Joyeuse and Aubenas.[33] The value of land soared, reaching in some places as much as 6,000 francs per hectare, about twenty years' saving for most peasant proprietors. Thus the profit from a successful harvest considerably outdistanced that of vineyards. Small wonder that family after family borrowed money to buy eggs, plant mulberry trees or buy their leaves, and construct silkworm nurseries. These were calculated risks, decisions made around the huge wooden table next to the chimney in the kitchen. They were hard choices. In the Hérault and the Aude, wine became king, and the production of raw silk largely went by the wayside, while it took over the economy of the Bas-Vivarais. In about 1850, 80 percent of the families living in the canton of Les Vans depended on the production of raw silk. Half of them, however, were in debt.[34]

Cash took on an increasing role in the rural economy. A military officer noted in 1846: "Without the raising of silkworms, the people here would indeed be unfortunate and could not pay either their taxes or their farm rents."[35] After the harvest, if all had gone well, villagers had something to celebrate and could purchase the family pig. "Look at my pig," went one expression, "being shaken by the wind in the branches" of the mulberry tree.[36] The festival of St.-Jean, that annual fertility rite in late June, still celebrated with torrents of drink, came just after the silk harvest, when many Ardéchois peasant families had the most money they had ever had. Each year the raw silk produced by Ardéchois peasants brought in between eight and eleven million francs, and in 1850, it was sixteen or seventeen million. It seemed too good to last.[37]

By the middle of the nineteenth century, the most important industries of the Ardèche were offshoots of the production of raw silk in the villages of the Bas-Vivarais. Small factories for silk throwing, the spinning of the raw silk onto spools in preparation for sale to factories that produced silk cloth and clothes, dotted the banks of the Ardèche and some of the small tributaries that flowed into it. Rivers provided power for the small factories, with large basins of hot water heated by steam and mechanical spools. With 211 small factories in 1827 producing 633,000 pounds of silk, silk throwing in the Ardèche was first in France, employing nearly 8,000 workers. The handsome stone structures that served as small factories still may be seen in Pont d'Aubenas, Largentière, and other places.[38] Spinning mills began to be built along the rivers of Ardèche during the July Monarchy. Home spinning gradually disappeared in the nineteenth century; between 1850 and 1885 factory spinning took over. By 1860 there were 56 spinning workshops in the Ardèche employing 3,360 workers, almost all female, for several months a year. Industry in the Ardèche thus remained closely tied to the countryside and to the rhythms of rural life.[39]

The impact of the silk industry could be seen in domestic life and clothing. Somewhat more prosperous, many peasants now had more solid clothes, even if they were not silk. Men wore corduroy pants or sometimes short pants called *brayo*, open shirts, vests, and wide-brim felt hats and sabots that clearly distinguished them from urban dwellers, particularly from the upper classes. Boys wore tunics that were open or buttoned; girls, similar tunics that opened up in the style of skirts as well as pleated skirts. Women wore long black or brown dresses, sometimes with large pockets, made of cotton, taffetas, or sometimes silk, in brighter colors, accompanied by black hats for Mass on Sundays.⁴⁰

Yet even in the halcyon days of the July Monarchy, there remained a worrisome fragility about it all, as if fate (*destin*) lurked not far away. In 1848 the justice of the peace of Joyeuse noted that silk was the only resource in his canton. Counting those who gathered the leaves from the mulberry trees, hired themselves out to help in the silkworm nurseries in the spring, or worked as spinners or in the silk-throwing factories, he remarked that "it is difficult to find anyone whose fortune is not in some way tied to" the silk industry. Peasants borrowed money for eggs sure that they could pay the sum back after the silkworm harvest.⁴¹ In 1840 some producers of raw silk and owners of silk-throwing factories had been ruined "by the conditions of the capitalists of Lyon who advance money to be reimbursed whenever the lender wants." The role of middlemen further placed the production of raw silk even more under the control of Lyonnais capital. Despite the facts that the production of cocoons had tripled, the number of factories more than doubled, and the number of workers they employed increased by five times and that the total value of sales was up by eight times, producers lost their autonomy and were dependent on variations in the price of silk: "The fate of the production of raw silk depends on the continuing acceleration of the commerce of this product. Can this last forever?"⁴²

There was the risk of disease. The officer in 1846 had heard that "these small operations are as vulnerable as any others to the ravages of the diseases that attack silkworms."⁴³ Then along came the devastating pébrine disease (from the Provençal *pèbre*, for *poivre* [pepper]). In 1849, black pepperlike spots began to appear on silkworms: "The worms languish, their appetite diminishes, their growth becomes very uneven. They can die before they have spun the cocoon or in the cocoon, but they also can become butterflies and thus furnish the corpusculous eggs that produce only silkworms that are even more sick." The disease began to be seen in the Vaucluse in 1843 and the Drôme three years later. With cruel timing, just as the agricultural crisis of 1846–47 devastated the production of grain, potatoes, and fruit, the disease moved into the Gard. It was first seen in the Ardèche in 1849 and by 1852 had hit the arrondissement of Largentière very hard. By 1857 it had reached Italy and Spain.

Both atmospheric conditions (mild winters and rainy summers, conducive to the parasite) and the negligence of the peasants producing raw silk were in part responsible for the disease's propagation. Many producers had abandoned the habit of frequently changing or selecting eggs with care. Overwhelmed by the fever of the golden tree, they began to put too many silkworms in too small a space, piling up four or five ounces of eggs in spaces in which they had raised only one egg before. A few tried to hatch more than thirty ounces in about one-seventh of the recommended space. In the meantime each ounce of eggs now produced two or three times fewer cocoons, and they were of mediocre quality.[44]

In Largentière the subprefect Eugène Villard looked beyond the disease that most people expected would be quickly conquered to worry about the fever of speculation engulfing the mulberry tree.[45] In 1848 the price of a kilogram of cocoons was half that of the previous year, and that of a kilogram of spun silk had fallen by about a third. Overproduction, accelerated by the Ardèche's rise in population, and the lingering uncertainty generated by the commercial crisis of 1846–47 were to blame: "All at once, credit disappeared and transactions stopped; creditors and debtors in good faith recognized that they had loaned and borrowed too much."[46]

Writing in January 1852, Villard concluded that the prodigious expansion of the mulberry tree, a veritable gold rush, had brought massive debt. "Take a look at this house in the fields," he wrote. "[I]t has popped up in the middle of mulberry trees and vineyards. It took twenty years to build. From year to year, the purchase of new land has added to the domain, and a new [silkworm nursery] added to the building." The mulberry tree had pushed crops out of the fields. The production of grain and animal husbandry had suffered because of the frenzy to plant mulberry trees amid speculation on the price of raw silk. Furthermore many mulberry trees that were not at all old had begun to die for mysterious reasons. In a *pays* of small plots there was little room for error.

Villard went further, arguing that good times had led peasants toward "useless expenditures" and even "false luxury." He called for a return to "the simplicity of the life-style and habits of our fathers. . . . Let us again become a little more rustic. It does little good for the farmer to listen to the echoes of the distant world and to abandon his fields." He believed that the state should intervene to help the poor, but that collection of debts owed by those who had borrowed money to plant mulberry trees should proceed aggressively.[47]

Visitors

In 1883 Léon Védel, a writer from Lyon, came to Balazuc looking for the descendants of Pons de Balazuc. Believing that Pons had descended from the Saracens commonly thought to have founded Balazuc in the eighth century, Védel wanted to observe the descendants of his "race."[48] He believed it possible that an "Arab type" had been transmitted by a Saracen presence in the village for several centuries. The poor village perched so dramatically on and seemingly part of the limestone evoked the vision for the urban and urbane visitor of an exotic Saracen world distant in time and in space.

"It was a luminous night in July," Védel remembered. "Our small boat slid listlessly along the Ardèche River, which seemed, under the brilliant light of the moon, to be carrying precious stones in its wake. Before us, on the fantastic illuminated rock cliff, stood Balazuc and, dominating its old nucleus, the somber Tour Carrée, where Pons (de Balazuc) was born. All of nature's harmonies soothed us in the silence and splendor of that star-filled night. Seized by the strange beauty of the site, we suddenly became silent." To his traveling companion (to whom he referred only as X as if to accentuate the mystery of the site) "this strange and gripping countryside" seemed a "lost corner of the Orient, with its stunning horizons, its sky of fire."

Leaving the small boat at the river's edge, they walked up the stony path to Balazuc's sole inn, which seemed "strangely contemporary, whitewashed, with climbing vines, like an Italian villa." Védel had nothing but praise for the innkeeper's wife, a fleshy woman with fair skin, "Rubenesque," who chattered away. "A Flemish woman in Balazuc!" he exclaimed. "What a slap at the local color and harmony of the place!" (Although in the nineteenth century there were no foreigners in Balazuc, the writer's remark ironically anticipated tourists from Belgium and the Netherlands who followed Védel and his companion a century later.) Védel turned his attention to eating a trout from the river, served with eggplant from the stout woman's garden.

After lunch, Védel again rode the small boat across the river and walked to the hamlet of Servière. There he admired a cluster of poplars, alders, and willow trees across the river, mirrored by the water, with green hills of gentle slopes beyond a meadow on which a few reddish cows grazed. This seemingly prosperous scene offered a remarkable contrast with the "harsh moor, savage, and blistered by the sun!" that lay nearby. The boatman, who also served as Balazuc's weaver, spent most of his life on the river, earning his living fishing the river between Vogüé and Ruoms ("Well, you have to do something," he said). He sold what he caught to the inn and to whoever else could pay a little for a fish.

Seeing the fisherman, Lango Eldin, convinced Védel that he had found one of the missing links between Balazuc's Saracen days and the present. He seemed a veritable "historical document. . . . [H]is name, incontestably of Arab origin . . . fits together with his person . . . the most complete expression of the Saracen race, small, lean, his limbs pockmarked and nervous, dark, with a short, turned-up nose, his eyes dark like coal, short black hair set low on his forehead." Lango "resembles greatly all of his co-citizens" in Balazuc, Védel having already forgotten the Flemish-like lady who had earlier served him trout and eggplant. As for Lango, his preoccupations "only extended to the river and its inhabitants, of whom each year he carried out a census at least as exact as other more official ones!" The fisherman knew the age and habits of the residents of his domain, and "he has reserves where live and grow, under his watchful eye, the big fish that he keeps for special occasions."

Night had fallen with deafening silence, and "the village slept in a bed of blue shadow. . . . [T]he top of its Romanesque bell tower stood above the brown mass, standing alone in black on the sky-blue light. The moon skimmed over the moor . . . its light brilliantly reflecting the great smooth surfaces of the limestone." The Ardèche River, although shallow and narrow in the summer months, reflected "the clear sky and the grayish rocks. Everywhere shadow and silence, luminous shadow and murmuring silence." It's still like that.

Védel and his companion again walked up the path from the river. The village's inhabitants had themselves faded into the rock. The visitors had the impression of being engulfed by the past "ruins, the memory of people dead eight hundred years ago . . . a lugubrious sensation along these vaulted passageways, these houses dark like tombs. It seemed as though the mere noise made by our steps would wake the dead, bring life to this desert." They reached the church and then walked up toward the top of the cliff, dominating the river some three hundred feet below. Below, "the water changed colors, depending on the play of the light. As far as the eye could see, it flowed between the steep cliffs with their jagged tops laid out in the clear sky." Across the river the watchtower of Jeanne still stood guard above the cliffs.

Back in the village, Védel and his friend found themselves "in the obscure maze of vaulted passages." The difficult walk through the narrow *ruelles* took them to a remarkable, steep passageway that remains almost unchanged: "a covered path of startling appearance. . . . [N]ot a stone had been touched for six hundred years. Through these large arches that seemed to be windows opened onto a fantasy world, the countryside appeared, illuminated with a supernatural light."

They suddenly came upon a young girl, who, "framed in the small columns of a small gothic window . . . stood out like a living painting, in a light that one could not see, but which seemed to keep back the darkness all around her. Slender, with large, silky brown eyes, a mouth as red as the blooming flower of a pomegranate tree, of dull brown coloring, taking an orange tone from the light . . . her two arms graciously curving upward, she arranged her unkempt hair for the night." If the two outsiders were at first surprised and then charmed by the girl, she was frightened, crying out in terror and quickly extinguishing her lamp. Védel, his romantic imagination stirred, could now easily have believed that they had stumbled onto a princess being held captive by a renegade scoundrel knight. They had simply surprised and frightened a young girl who had no reason to expect anyone to pass by as she prepared to go to bed. But it was the early 1880s. Balazuc seemed isolated and poor, as always. Moreover, if some of its houses seemed strangely silent, it was because they were empty. Balazuc was losing population. Now Lango Eldin and the anonymous young girl struggled for survival in a very poor village already in precipitous economic and demographic decline.

Visitors to Balazuc of note (or, for that matter, visitors of any kind) were few and far between. "Dr. Francus"—Albin Mazon, the prolific local writer who published evocative accounts of his treks through the Vivarais—was another for whom Balazuc evoked the romance of imagined Saracen days. Arriving in 1884, he wanted to approach Balazuc from the river, the better to observe "the rocky valley through which flows the river." He asked a young peasant to show them a path, sending along his guide (the very term evoked a desert guide in North Africa or a scout in the American far West) to wait for them with the horses in Balazuc. The narrow path plunged them into the stifling heat of summer reflected by the burning rocks, "barely reduced by some green oak trees, a fig tree, brambles and shrubs, emerging from the cracks in the limestone."[49]

A fisherman, perhaps Lango, carried them the short distance to the edge of the river, then to "a miserable hovel, decorated by the name of 'inn,'" where they, like the Lyonnais writer before them, ate fish from the Ardèche. They also dined on an omelet and on *picodons*—goat's cheese—that they correctly found superior to that of other regions because of the aromatic plants on which local goats dined.

They then made one of those innocent humiliating mistakes of tourists, asking if it was possible to travel subsequently to Ruoms by boat. This earned them only gentle laughter and the assurance that they would have to pick themselves out of the river several times because of the rapids. Mazon then stepped into what he too was sure were the remnants of Moorish Balazuc; "If the picturesque did not exist, Balazuc would have invented it." The village strongly reflected both "feudal grouping and the Arab camp." In comments typical of the racist "ethnology" of the day, Mazon proclaimed that "the Moorish type is very pronounced in Balazuc. The men are big, sturdy, with dark coloring and eyes, and frizzy hair, and the women wear an expression that recalls something of the mischief of Gypsies." Of the villages in the Bas-Vivarais, Balazuc seemed the one "where the antique character has been best conserved." The medieval ramparts had nowhere been completely destroyed. The "prisoner tower" still stood near the old main gate; one could still see the square holes where the bars had been placed to support the wooden structures along which the village's defenders had once stood to repel sieges. Now, centuries later, the château belonged to Mollier *dit* Tartaille, a fisherman, and what once had been its most beautiful rooms served to store hay.[50]

A visit to the fortified Romanesque church carried Mazon back to medieval Balazuc. There he criticized the addition of the second nave in the sixteenth century as detracting from the architectural harmony. He visited the ruins of the Chapel of St.-Jean-Baptiste just outside the Portail d'Été, where scraggly mulberry trees grew out of "seigneurial dust." The fisherman who had rowed Mazon to the "beach" where the small boat awaited them related that several agricultural workers whose pickaxes had struck something in the ground nearby were convinced that they had come upon a treasure buried with some wealthy noble. In the end they came up only with bones. To this day a story circulates that a mysterious treasure is hidden somewhere near the deconsecrated *église romane*. His visit to Saracen Balazuc completed, Mazon departed, his horse carrying him down the road that parallels the tracks toward Ruoms.[51]

To the comte Melchior de Vogüé as well, Balazuc, where his family had lost land sold as *biens nationaux,* had "the look of a worthy African village, with its terraced houses, its vaulted paths, its meager bell tower similar to a minaret, and the donjon in ruins, a veritable picture of Barbary pirates. A look at the inhabitants completes the illusion." To legend could now be added what passed for scientific certainty. Vogüé believed that doctors had identified certain ethnic characteristics of the "Berber race . . . in particular, by the delicate nature of their joints." Balazuc fitted the part. "What light! One could say that all the treasures of the sun are found here, in the mad glow of noon, on this overwhelming moor, with the shrill cries of the cicadas . . . a melodious and perfumed heat." The *gras* could become the deserts of North Africa, the gardens along the Ardèche River compared with an Arab oasis.[52]

In 1896 a local writer, "Sylvestre" (Paul Gouy), insisting that "the Moorish type" was more evident in Balazuc than in any other village in the Bas-Vivarais "because the mixing of blood there has been without a doubt more rare," claimed that when Pons de Balazuc arrived in the Holy Land on the First Crusade, he recognized in the east his own Balazuc.[53] And so it went on. In his *Essai de géographie régionale*, Louis Bourdin reflected the advent of the "science" of race, trying to verify the presence of "an African tribe in the Vivarais" by comparing the height, hair color, forehead shape (including "a quite developed eyebrow ridge") and nose shape, skin color, length of limbs, and so on of Berbers with the inhabitants of Balazuc. Finally, in 1914, a Lyonnais paper noted that the "savage beauty" of the "extremely curious" village had begun to attract visitors.[54] However, Balazuc's brief period of relative prosperity had long since ended. As during Védel's visit more than thirty years earlier, the village confronted economic disaster and demographic decline.

Catastrophes

In *Le Tour de la France par deux enfants* (*The Tour of France by Two Children*), G. Bruno's best-selling little book, first published in 1877, which almost became required reading in French schoolhouses, two brothers fulfill a promise made to their father on his deathbed to discover the richness as well as the essential unity of France, and this was the point in the wake of defeat in the Franco-Prussian War. The boys learn about the production of raw silk in a village near the Rhône in the Drôme. Exclaiming, "What riches are due to such a simple small insect! The silkworm is to be found in and provides a livelihood of entire provinces in France," they watch as young men gather leaves from the mulberry trees and load them on their shoulders, leaving almost all the trees nearly bare. As "we follow the Rhône along Dauphiné and Provence, we see the mulberry tree almost all the time in the countryside. It appears that in these regions each house has its silkworm nursery, big or small." They are too late to see the silkworms because the season is too advanced, but they watch a young girl beat cocoons with a small broom, after having placed them in a basin of boiling water in order to separate the threads.[55]

However, the production of raw silk, though still the dominant agricultural activity of the Bas-Vivarais, had been in the state of collapse since mid-century. Fate had intervened yet again to crush the hopes of the peasants of the Ardèche. The three "pillars of rural civilization" collapsed one after another over the decades since 1850: first the production of raw silk, then the vineyards, and finally the chestnut trees.[56]

As if the silkworm disease were not enough, fate sent more disasters. The storms of the century, blows that fell in the fall of 1857, turned the Ardèche River into a torrent of destruction. The first flood on September 10 carried away three bridges, breached four dikes, ruined eight roads, and covered thirty thousand acres. The tributaries of the Ardèche rose in colossal proportions. Small rivers were spontaneously transformed into raging torrents, removing everything in their path. The grotesquely swollen Ardèche River swept away mulberry trees, leaving gardens and meadows covered with sand when the water finally receded. Another flood followed on September 24. The rampaging rivers demolished twenty-two bridges, forty-four mills, fifty-nine houses, and twelve silk-throwing and spinning factories, transforming three thousand workers in the region into the unemployed. It was not over. On October 5, amid lightning it rained for more than six hours, undoubtedly leaving some fervent Catholics wondering if the apocalypse of forty days and forty nights of rain had arrived. The rivers again rose, above the levels of the earlier storms. Fifty people perished. The prefect watched in horror as "the soil of the terraces which had just been seeded disappeared, leaving only rock; the fields, gardens, and meadows that had been spared by the first storm were destroyed or at least badly damaged. Roads and bridges that had survived the violence of the first catastrophe were not so fortunate with the second storm. It cut communications and carried away the few grain mills that had survived." The surging water poured into the small silk-throwing factories that dotted river-banks, destroying machinery and carrying away silk. The inhabitants of the Ardèche were left "in a consternation difficult to describe . . . an infinite number of poor families henceforth deprived of all means of subsistence for the winter." It seemed no exaggeration to say that the Ardèche stood half ruined. The prefect and other officials in Privas, and everybody else, gazed nervously up at "rocks suspended above the town on the point of detaching from the mountain, which if they fell would inevitably destroy houses and their inhabitants."[57] More major storms followed in 1859, 1863, 1867, 1872, 1873, 1878, and 1890, each in September or October, as if again to remind the Ardéchois of the fragility of their existence.[58]

The pébrine disease brought absolute disaster to Balazuc and the Bas-Vivarais. The production of raw silk plunged in the Ardèche from 3.5 million kilograms in 1850 to 550,000 kilograms of cocoons in 1857. Between 1850 and 1861 income from the sale of raw silk fell from sixteen million francs to four million francs. The production of the silk-throwing factories was cut in half. Not only did the quality of the silkworm eggs decline, but the yield per ounce fell from about eighteen kilograms of cocoons to ten and then eight kilograms in 1858, even as the price of good-quality raw silk soared. The disease ruined many silk producers, many of whom had taken out loans to build or improve silk nurseries or purchase cocoons. Many peasants could no longer pay their taxes.[59]

Petitions from village municipal councils rang out with desperation, but also characteristic determination and persistence. Eighty fathers of families signed that of La Chapelle-sous-Aubenas: "[W]e have bowed our heads in submission before the numerous disasters that have struck here for the last several years, considering them as the just punishment of God. We had hoped that they would come to an end. . . . Now we wait with confidence the end of these catastrophes." The peasants of the Ardèche have always been like that: "The God of goodness wanted it so."

In good times many had had to borrow money to purchase silkworm eggs. They now found that money could be found only at high and even usurious rates, "one of the wounds" of the Ardèche. By 1856 some producers of raw silk in the Bas-Vivarais had completely given up. Land lost up to 40 percent of its value between 1850 and 1870.[60]

The imperial government in 1852 provided a subsidy to begin a workshop to supply healthy eggs and proposed such untried methods as autumn harvests. In 1857 an arrondissement commission that included various officials, leading property owners, and merchants met to consider the causes of the problem. Producers tried almost anything. Some applied powders that mixed sulfur and ground coal to eggs; others tried to raise their silkworms outdoors. Attempted remedies in 1861 included various gases, sulfuric acid, vinegar, quinine sulfate, sugar, and even rum.[61] Nothing worked. Most peasant proprietors had already spent what savings and used what credit they had. Moreover, land that had been shifted from grain to planting mulberry trees now produced nothing. Monoculture now seemed to have contributed to disaster.[62]

Full-scale panic set in by the spring of 1859, after the sixth consecutive catastrophic silkworm harvest. Many poor peasants had purchased their eggs at the exorbitant price of sixteen to eighteen francs per ounce. Now, after gathering or purchasing kilos of mulberry leaves, they watched "their insects suddenly perish from an unknown disease, and [saw] all of their care over a year be wiped out in less than sixteen hours." Hard currency had again become scarce; debt was everywhere. The price of a kilogram of healthy cocoons soared to thirty-five francs because of dramatically reduced output. Expropriations reached unprecedented levels for peasants, including those in Balazuc. The value of land on which mulberry trees had been planted, some of which had been purchased by peasants who had borrowed money to do so, fell by half during this period; the value of other land fell by about a third. Many peasants were unable to sell their land or to pay the tax that weighed upon it. Others borrowed more money at even higher rates. The numbers of unemployed workers and of beggars increased, including many men from the mountains who had usually come down to what they called the good country because at least there had been jobs gathering mulberry leaves for the silkworm harvest. Those who had invested in mulberry trees could no longer sell their leaves. Even the least pessimistic of producers now wondered if their livelihood had not been "struck dead."[63]

Whereas in some places peasants planted alfalfa in the hope of stemming the tide of their losses, sudden replacements were unlikely in the "tormented soil" of the Bas-Vivarais. Peasants who could afford it now purchased eggs from other countries. In 1859, of 258 Ardéchois communes that raised silkworms, 110 used eggs imported from Tuscany, Greece, Turkey, Smyrna, or Persia. The subprefect of Largentière himself sent someone to Syria and Greece to bring back the best eggs that he could find, and the government distributed them, hoping for the best. Fifty producers formed an association to purchase eggs in Asia. Cocoons from the Levant, China, and Bengal helped silk manufacturers make up the deficit. In this way, ironically, economic hardship and depression helped insert the village into a wider, indeed global, economic network. But the strategy could not alleviate the misery of Ardéchois producers of raw silk. The 1865 harvest of silkworms was uniformly disastrous. A giant petition sent to the Senate and signed by more than thirty-five hundred mayors, municipal councilmen, and property owners in the Ardèche, Gard, Hérault, and Lozère demanded tax relief. Some peasants uprooted their mulberry trees and planted vineyards.[64]

In 1853 the commune produced thirty-six hundred kilograms of cocoons, exactly a sixth of an "ordinary" harvest, and in the canton only two villages had worse results. With winter approaching, Balazuc's municipal council set up charity workshops to assist as many people as possible by putting them to work on the village's paths. Villagers contributed three hundred francs.[65] In 1863 households in Balazuc put into incubation eggs from Romania, Macedonia, and Thessalonika. Yet again the harvest largely failed, yielding only five thousand kilograms of cocoons, less than half of an average yield. Producers and officials alike blamed "bad" eggs and extremely hot weather. The harvest two years later (for which peasant families put a third more eggs into incubation than normal) was even worse, that of the following year, only slightly better. Toward the end of the decade, producers put more eggs into incubation, using more imported from Japan. Still, yields remained disappointing, losing in 1873 about 60 percent to the pébrine. The majority of the population—at least 668 (250 families), virtually the entire village—still depended on the production of raw silk.[66]

Louis Pasteur, sent by the Ministry of Commerce and Agriculture to investigate the disease, spent harvest seasons in the Gard near Alès from 1865 to 1869. His experiments demonstrated that the silkworms were already contaminated at the time of their hatching because the butterfly was already sick, discovering the extremely contagious nature of the disease. He found that silk moths were susceptible to a tiny parasite originally found on mulberry leaves that could contaminate subsequent generations. Pasteur gradually determined how healthy eggs could be identified under a microscope, selected, and hatched. Peasant families could thus purchase healthy eggs each year instead of keeping their own eggs over the course of ten months.[67]

The corner began to be turned in 1868, when this cellular system of Pasteur was first used. By 1875, after a quarter century of crisis, the pébrine disease had been defeated. Yet the prosperity engendered by golden tree never fully returned. Competition from artificial silk, raw silk imported from Italy and Asia (the latter source dramatically accelerated by the completion of the Suez Canal in 1869), changes in fashion, and the expansion of the production of other textiles took their toll. Moreover, the long agricultural depression that began in the mid-1870s drove down prices. The number of families producing raw silk in the Ardèche fell by more than half. The quantity of eggs placed in incubation in silkworm nurseries fell by five-sixths. The price of land continued to fall. In 1879, Mazon, knowledgeable observer, sadly noted that "almost all small proprietors are threatened by expropriation and it is only their extreme misery that prevents creditors from taking things to the extreme, knowing well that even the sale of the collateral will not recoup the whole debt."[68] After 1880 increasingly more peasants turned their land over to the production of wine or to fruit.[69] When the municipality of Villeneuve-de-Berg dedicated a statue of Olivier de Serres in 1882, Pasteur was among the twenty thousand people who attended the ceremony. Yet the production of raw silk continued to decline. The good old days were long since over.[70]

To be sure, silk throwing and spinning remained important to the local economy. Almost half the silk-throwing factories in France could be found in the Ardèche, most of them in the Bas-Vivarais. Girls, beginning at age twelve, and young women walked from their villages to the small factories, where during the week they were lodged miserably and paid little more than a franc a day. They saved as much as they could for modest dowries.[71] In 1911 eleven women and young girls from Balazuc worked in the small factories in small towns or other villages.[72] But this offered little hope to local producers. Imported raw silk, principally from Piedmont but as far away as Japan, provided most of the raw material for 264 silk-throwing factories in 1889.[73]

For decades, the producers of raw silk in Balazuc (and elsewhere in the Midi) believed that the solution to their plight lay in high tariffs against imported silk (the *cahier de doléances* from Villeneuve-de-Berg in 1788 had warned against the importation of foreign silk) and state subsidies. In November 1890 the municipal council joined many other communes in the Bas-Vivarais (as well as neighboring *départements*) in demanding that a stiff duty be imposed on all imported raw silk, in proportion to that on cocoons, because it drove down prices of French cocoons and raw silk, bringing disaster to the Midi. In 1892 the state began to pay a subsidy of fifty centimes for each kilogram of cocoons, paying a subsidy to spinners as well. Five years later Balazuc's municipal council expressed eagerness that such assistance continue, pointing out that "the system of subsidies for the production of raw silk and spinning has become part of our fiscal practice."[74]

The production of raw silk remained important in Balazuc and many other villages in the Bas-Vivarais. Each year the municipal council named two members to oversee the weighing of cocoons at the Tour Carrée. Leaves from the mulberry trees owned by the commune were auctioned off. In 1909 there were still 123 households producing raw silk in Balazuc. In the canton of Vallon, only Lagorce and Ruoms, much larger communes, had more people producing raw silk than Balazuc. Even the relatively poor harvest of 1914, shortly before the outbreak of the Great War, produced in the Ardèche 1,419,800 kilograms of cocoons, for which 5.5 million francs were paid, an amount equal to the value of all grain harvested in the Ardèche.[75]

In the meantime family silk spinning on the covered balcony had declined sharply during the mid-nineteenth-century crisis and had for the most part disappeared by 1885. It had been undercut by the dramatic fall in the production of raw silk and foreign competition. Albin Mazon blamed the spinning factories, which had "killed off family spinning. . . . [N]ow one hardly ever sees these small spinning operations anymore." Families no longer brought their raw silk to the market; now many sold at increasingly disadvantageous prices to agents, specialists in speculation. Little was left of the great silk markets of Aubenas and Joyeuse.

Many families were to remember the revival of raw silk production as the good old days, "like the memory that all that is distant in the past is beautiful," in the words of a man from Lagorce. Peasants had seemed rich: "All their houses had wooden chests to store the most beautiful raw silk . . . which they sold only when the price was high. . . . [E]ach person who produced silk hurried to carry to the priest the most beautiful heather. . . . These gifts were placed in the chapel dedicated to the Virgin Mary and the product of their sale went to the upkeep of the church."[76] One man remembered that silk "was paid for in gold. . . . [A]s a little boy, I accompanied my father and remember seeing the coins stack up" in front of them. In 1926 a peasant from St.-Rémèze recalled that the profits from the sale of raw silk permitted his family the luxury of purchasing a reaper one year and a sewing machine the next. To another, "the silkworm was the appreciation of the past as if to prove that those times were better: it is still always with a smile that we speak of the worms. We add an anecdote and speak of the good fortune" of those days. In 1943 cocoons sold for less than manure.[77]

The Second Blow

Even in the halcyon days of raw silk production, the production of wine remained essential to the fragile economy of Balazuc and the

Bas-Vivarais. In the arrondissement of Largentière, the number of hectares of vineyards rose by five times from the late eighteenth century to 1864. Peasants planted vines, for the most part producing red wine of modest quality, on land reclaimed through deforestation on hillsides and on rocky terrain near the Ardèche River. The ongoing subdivision of property through inheritance increased the number of peasants producing wine. Moreover, a hectare of vineyard in the arrondissement now produced more wine: eighteen hectoliters in 1788 and twenty-four hectoliters in 1829.[78]

The expansion of vineyards presented a second hope for the smallholding peasants of the Bas-Vivarais. The new road linking Vogüé to Ruoms made it easier to market wine. Yet fate cruelly struck again. Two years after the pébrine had begun to ravage silkworms, disease hit the vineyards, beginning in the canton of Joyeuse. In June and July 1851 a grayish fungus began to appear, first on the vines, with the leaves taking on a rust color. Soon black spots began to cover vinestocks. Grapes rotted, destroying half the harvest. In 1852 the canton of Vallon, which had almost thirteen hundred hectares of vineyards, produced almost a third less wine than in a normal year. Accelerated by humidity, the oidium (fungoid blight) spread rapidly. By 1860 half the department had become affected, and over the next decade it struck all vineyards in the Bas-Vivarais. Yield, which had been twelve hectoliters per acre in a normal year, stood at two hectoliters of poor quality, though some years were less devastating than others. No one seemed sure whether washing the stumps of the vines with a sulfurous preparation or brushing vine shoots affected by oidium to keep the resulting dust from settling on the vines made any difference. The number of hectares of vineyards too had fallen by more than half. In 1862 it was impossible to estimate the value of land in the canton because vineyards "hardly can be sold since the disease arrived." Over the next years oidium resurfaced from time to time, leaving producers in a chronic state of uncertainty, even as more hectares returned to production.[79]

Yet oidium, however destructive, seemed benign compared with what came next. Phylloxera (*lou pedzoul* in patois) began attacking vineyards in the Ardèche. First noticed along the river in the Gard and

Bouches-du-Rhône in 1865, it appeared around Avignon the next year, then in 1867–68 moved into the Hérault and up into the Drôme. It crossed the Rhône and attacked the canton of Vallon in 1869.

Phylloxera, a disease brought by small plant lice that attack the leaves and roots of grapevines, ravaged the vineyards in the region. Acres of vineyards fell by 56 percent between 1872 and 1890. In Balazuc, peasants noticed the first symptoms of phylloxera in Balazuc in 1872. The disease quickly tore through ten hectares of the village's vineyards. No one knew how it spread or how to fight it. By the harvest of 1876 the phylloxera had destroyed more than a third of the vineyards in the Ardèche. Within a year the plant lice had struck every vineyard in Balazuc, overwhelming 120 acres, 200 by 1878, and 500 by 1879.[80] Worry became panic. Hurriedly constituted departmental committees had no answer. The value of an acre of vineyards dropped by 60 percent between 1874 and 1886. By 1897 almost 15,000 acres of vineyards in the arrondissement of Largentière had been wiped out. That year only about 100 acres of vineyards produced any wine in Balazuc, one-sixth of that in 1874.[81]

In order to kill the plant lice that attacked the vines, producers began to treat vines with carbonic sulfide, which had little effect in the limestone country of the Bas-Vivarais, and copper sulfate. Some producers attempted to submerge vines completely in water, in order to drown the plant lice, but this was inconceivable in Balazuc. In St.-Maurice-d'Ibie some peasants sprayed the vineyards with human or pig urine or with water in which walnut leaves had been boiled, adding a dose of prayer. In 1879 it seemed that vinestocks brought from the United States were resistant to phylloxera. Grafting and the planting of hybrid vines began to bring some good results. By 1891 most of the diseased vineyards had been replanted with American vinestocks or with grafts of the latter on indigenous ones. The vineyards gradually came to life again, but the wine they produced went for next to nothing.[82] That year Balazuc's mayor reported that the American vinestocks were bringing good results and higher prices for wine. However, more bad years followed. State subsidies afforded some assistance, although the disease made several more appearances. By the middle of the 1890s vineyards had returned to life in some of the Ardèche. Overall, the price of a hectoliter of wine had risen by almost a third, and production rose rapidly in the first decade of the new century. Thus in the long run wine producers were probably more fortunate than those who had placed their hopes on producing raw silk. Still, the crisis was obviously not over, as casks of wine, amid complaints that the old quality, such as it was, had not returned.[83]

As if to underline once more the fragility of rural life, after four days of rain, on September 22, 1890, the Ardèche River rose again, in the most violent storm ever seen, one still etched in the collective memory of Balazuc. In less than five hours the water level surged forty feet, six above the level of 1857. The secretary of the municipal council, which had met the day before, entered into the minutes that no one could remember such a flood in Balazuc. The raging water carried off the roof of the mill, leaving only damaged walls and the millstones, as well as countless trees ripped from the ground. A barn that had stood across the river was swept away in an instant; several gardens were left covered by a thick layer of gravel. In Vogüé the bridge (among twenty-eight destroyed), mill, and five houses were borne away; in Lanas, the recently constructed dike. The thirty-seven people in the arrondissement who perished included an entire family in Pont de Labeaume. The municipality estimated damage to Balazuc to be about fifty thousand francs.[84]

Then a third blow struck the fragile rural economy of the Vivarais. The disease known as encre, a tiny fungus that generates a blue-black, ink-like color of the trunk, roots, and soil and slowly kills chestnut trees, first appeared in the region of Aubenas in 1875. By 1905 it had spread throughout the Bas-Vivarais (though not directly affecting Balazuc and other villages below nine hundred feet in altitude). The bread tree joined the golden tree in the forest of disaster. Between the mid-1870s and 1929, half the acreage of chestnut trees disappeared, two-thirds by 1960.[85]

Abandoned Terraces

The middle of the nineteenth century still stands as the demographic apogee of the Ardèche. Balazuc's population, swollen by its flirtation with prosperity, peaked at 905 people in 1851. In 1861 the department reached its maximum population of 388,000 inhabitants. This growth came overwhelmingly in the countryside, where 84 percent of the people lived. The rise in population had brought agricultural saturation, the intensive cultivation of virtually all land on which something could be grown.[86]

Amazingly enough in retrospect, in 1849, the prefect of the Ardèche had tried to explain the lack of emigration from his department by noting the attachment of peasants to their land. Six years later an academic inspector's report remarked almost as an afterthought that emigration from the countryside had occurred "in weak proportions. Only artisans or people working in commerce are abandoning the countryside for towns."[87]

The inspector spoke too soon. The disastrous end to the boom years gradually led to massive emigration out of the Ardèche, part of the rural exodus that depopulated large parts of rural France. Two-thirds of the departments of France had fewer people in 1939 than in 1851. The pébrine, phylloxera, and the chestnut disease revealed the economic fragility of small property owners. The drop was moderate until 1896, then extremely rapid. Between 1861 and 1960 the Ardèche lost more than 140,000 people, almost 37 percent of its inhabitants. "The pitiful and poor arrondissement of Largentière," which had attained its maximum population of 114,428 inhabitants in 1851, had only 84,022 inhabitants in 1911 and 71,853 people in 1921.[88] The decline in the mountains was even more dramatic. Between 1906 and 1911 alone, the Ardèche lost 14,200 people, even though the birthrate remained higher than the mortality rate. The human hemorrhage began with the Cévennes, which lost half its population, as temporary migration became permanent, and then reached the limestone country.[89]

On December 22, 1857, the subprefect requested an indigent's passport, with assistance for the journey, for Marie Mollier, twenty-three years of age. From Balazuc she wanted to go all the way to Oran, Algeria, in hope of finding work. Mayor Tastevin had written a letter supporting her request. She carried almost everything she owned with her to Marseille. When Victor-Régis Chabert, a former soldier from Joannas, left for Marseille and the boat to Algeria, he carried with him well more than three hundred pounds of baggage, including the hammers and anvil of a blacksmith, as "he is hoping to go to Algeria where he can eat an honest bread."[90]

Albin Mazon's visit to Balazuc in 1884 had ended with a quick look at that most nineteenth century of buildings, the tiny railroad station, the outdoor plumbing of which was bushes: "What anachronism it was!" He recounted the story that because passengers stopping in Balazuc had been rare since the train had begun service in 1876, the stationmaster kissed everyone who stepped off the train. In fact, the train quickly became, with the decline in economic opportunity and that of population, a symbol not of arrival but of departure.[91] The advent of the railroad, although providing some temporary work for locals, made it easier to leave. As contemporaries put it, "They laid down the tracks, and then they used them to leave." Balazuc lost almost half its population, the number of inhabitants falling from 905 in 1851 to 878 in 1861 and 694 in 1881. The population rose slightly to 705 in 1891 but then began dropping again, to 680 in 1896, 605 in 1901, and 563 in 1911, a loss of 117 people in fifteen years. Balazuc's population would have fallen even more had not the cholera of 1884 spared the village.[92]

Those who remained in Balazuc continued to work their small plots of land. During the 1870s only 3 men in Balazuc had paid the tax on business: Joseph Leyris, the aged boatman; Jean Pierre, who now owned the mill; and Louis Vianès, who still had his café. According to the breakdown of professions provided by the census of 1876, 748 of the 802 inhabitants of Balazuc depended on the land for survival. Five years later all 36 leading taxpayers were farmers. In 1911 the vast majority of households worked the land. In addition, 42 agricultural workers (the occupation of "[rural] domestic" having disappeared) lived in Balazuc, in addition to 3 shepherds. Nine young women or girls worked elsewhere in silk-throwing or spinning factories. In addition to 3 grocers and a baker, there were about 10 artisans and several women who worked as seamstresses or weavers.[93]

If the families who owned property in Balazuc were less affected by the *grand départ* (although younger children joined those leaving), those without property left the Ardèche in droves. Most were young men between twenty and forty, but many women of childbearing age also moved. They left behind an aging population and thus a higher rate of death and a lower birthrate.[94] The rural exodus in some places threatened the survival of the link between families and the land they had owned for centuries. Yet in Balazuc, which has had astounding continuities over the centuries, this was less the case.

Couples married later, a fact that reflected both economic crisis and rural exodus. This in turn reduced the number of births. More villagers married from outside the village, although intermarriage between families long established in Balazuc remained common. More inhabitants of Balazuc now had been born elsewhere than ever before, although still only about 22 percent of inhabitants in 1911, and many of these came from neighboring villages and only 31 people from outside the Ardèche.[95]

In 1884 Mazon associated the overall decline in the production of raw silk with the hemorrhaging of the Ardèche's villages: "Everyone is less well off; property owners of some means have become poor and the poor have fallen into real distress."[96] Many who left were day laborers or rural domestics (although employment in the small silk-throwing and spinning factories helped slow this decline). Their departure engendered a shortage of labor; agricultural laborers, who had earned but two francs a day (only one if they were fed), thus became relatively rare, and the cost of hiring them rose. Many of those who remained could barely conceal their bitterness. Like those between the wars who constructed the myth of the "good old days," they nourished nostalgia for the "golden century" that had lasted only about thirty years.[97]

By 1911 more than 120,000 people born in the Ardèche were living elsewhere. In all, 40 percent of those born in the Ardèche had left the department for greener pastures, which then seemed to be almost anywhere else. The departures of some of them of course were motivated not only by despair but also by a readiness to look for opportunities that simply did not exist in the Ardèche. Thus, to some extent, the depopulation of Balazuc and other villages also reflects the adaptability of peasants in search of a better life.[98]

The early twentieth century expanded the attraction of Marseille and of Lyon and its region for those leaving the Bas-Vivarais. Elderly people left behind remembered "the time of the emigration of the peasantry toward the gray cities."[99] Associations of Ardéchois in Lyon, Marseille, and Avignon met every year. In 1912, *L'Ardèche parisienne* announced the twenty-first annual gathering of the Ardéchois living in Paris. A Republican Club of Ardéchois organized meetings in the capital. Although the attraction of the mines of the Gard and Loire remained considerable, increasingly those leaving the Ardèche found work as gendarmes, as railway employees, in government offices, and in the army. The grandfathers of one woman in Balazuc worked as a policeman and for the railroad, respectively, in Lyon before World War I, typical occupations for those leaving the Ardèche in search of work. At the beginning of the twentieth century one of four Ardéchois lived outside the department.[100]

Newspapers both on the right and on the left decried the mass rural exodus. *Le Républicain des Cévennes* in 1909 deplored "houses in ruin that crumble before all winds, demolished old and poor farms invaded by ivy, abandoned walls that now border only desolate fields that reflect misery and solitude. This spectacle breaks your heart." *L'Echo de Largentière* blamed collapsing morality, the weakening of the family, the falling birthrate, high taxes, and thirty years of what it considered a left-wing government: "Our region is being ruined. We have indeed built roads, railway lines, and tramways, spread education and perfected agricultural methods, but what does this serve if we are losing the most essential thing, our people?" Noting the "moral rupture" that seemed to accompany emigration, *L'Echo* suggested that a Catholic committee be set up in each canton to prepare emigrants to make their trek "in good moral conditions," so that they would not "lose themselves morally, politically, and religiously." Bishop Bonnet condemned the falling birthrate and the following year the rural exodus itself.[101]

A glance at a register of declarations for those seeking exemption from taxes during the period 1903 to 1921 gives a sense of the exodus from Balazuc. Among claims of residents that they should not have to pay a certain tax because they had lost their horses, or, in the case of Hippolyte Redon, sold his automobile (certainly the first in Balazuc), Louis Boyer (1910) declared "that he is going to leave the commune definitively at the end of the year"; Joseph Bouchet (1910) reported that "his son had left the commune for good six months ago"; Marius Mouraret (1910) asked exemption from a tax for one of his sons, who had "definitively left the commune"; Jacques Dauthueyts (1912) "no longer owns anything in the commune since his expropriation and no longer lives there"; Clément Fernand had "left Balazuc more than six months ago" and (1912) lived in Villefort (Lozère); and Louis Tastevin's brother had moved to Lyon more than six months before. Léon Mollier had left his café behind (1912); Louis Duffaud (1913) had hired himself out as a farm laborer in St.-André-de-Cruzières. Louise Vianès, presumably the aged widow of Louis, the *aubergiste* (inn keeper), had left Balazuc in 1913; a subsequent entry noted that at the end of the year she had "died as an indigent in Joyeuse, without heirs." Those leaving were often from families that did not own land in Balazuc or younger children of those that did, who left family behind.[102] When the municipality decided to sell what had been the girls' school, Giry, the boys' teacher, who assessed their value, reported that two old buildings had little value because of their location and "the great number of vacant houses in Balazuc."[103] The great hopes of the first half of the century lay in ruins. Abandoned terraces on steep slopes today offer silent witness to *le grand départ*.

FIVE

Under the Shade of the Golden Tree

JEAN-MATHIEU GIBERT, A THIRTY-SIX-YEAR-OLD BACH-elor with twelve years' teaching experience, came to Balazuc in 1833 to teach. Known for the grim Protestant from Nîmes who sponsored it, the Guizot Law, passed later the same year, specified that each commune in France should provide "an appropriate locale that can serve both as a school and a place for the teacher to live." Gibert carried with him no diploma and "little education," despite the years he had put in. He had been appointed by the district educational committee and approved by the rector of the Academy of Nîmes, probably on presentation of a certificate of morality signed by the mayor or priest of his village or a commune where he had taught.[1]

Gibert's conditions were marginal at best, barely equal to those of struggling peasants. The municipality provided lodging in the rented school near the Portail d'Été, for which the commune paid 50 francs a year. Gibert survived by collecting some of the small fees of 1 or 1.50 francs a month (less for the younger pupils) per pupil. If all the parents paid, he would have had about 300 francs to go with the 200 francs allocated by the municipal budget. How Gibert survived is difficult to imagine: In 1836 he collected only 32 centimes of what his pupils' families owed! (He may have received some small payments in kind.) He received 30 more francs for serving as the municipal secretary. The next year a small raise in the four direct taxes generated 84 extra francs, which, with a government subsidy, permitted the municipality to rent rooms for the school.[2] Six children whom the municipal council considered "indigent" were admitted free (the number rose to fourteen in 1836). The inspector had noted that one could hardly expect more from a village in such an impoverished region, which had been devastated by an epidemic that same year, "leaving Balazuc in great misery."[3]

The Guizot Law elevated the status of the village schoolmaster. It is telling that almost immediately afterward Gibert began to serve more regularly than had his predecessor (who had been from Balazuc) as an official witness to life's important events. He signed his name clearly with a confident pen, a signature for which he probably received a few centimes from those families that could afford to give him anything at all.

A man from another village takes us into the small, cramped classroom of his childhood:

> School was absolute terror for pupils. The teacher was a sort of bogeyman, whose role was to whip and punish. . . . [W]hen it was time to go to school, children cried as if they were being led to the scaffold. Most of the time the father or mother had to drag them there by force. . . . I can still see the school of my hamlet and its benches, unwieldy tables, bare walls, the teacher's desk that one approached invariably trembling, because of the ghastly cat-o'-nine-tails suspended from the chair. The blows we received are still alive in my memory, the teacher's extended hand because we had committed the terrible fault of moving or talking with our neighbor. The oldest, the "writers," alone had the right of sitting at the tables. The youngest were seated on benches without back support . . . riveted there, immobile, for whole hours, having nothing to do, because no one was paying attention to them.[4]

The children who attended school in Balazuc usually began at age six, but the average child in the Bas-Vivarais spent little more than four years there. Thirty boys attended school during the winter of 1836–37, but only fifteen in the summer.⁵ Any school fee discouraged attendance. Given the choice between having their young boys go to school or carry stones, mind goats, or help the silkworm harvest, families opted for nonattendance as the only sensible choice.

Gibert's small classroom had no blackboard and few tables or benches. In short, an inspector noted, "everything is lacking." The new teacher, who embraced the individual method of instruction (that is, calling one pupil forward, while the others just sat there), had at his disposal only a very few books of any kind from which to teach reading, writing, and basic arithmetic. They included the Bible, several catechisms (used by teachers as the basic text for learning to read), two rulers, a spelling book, several "texts about writing," a copy of *Conduite chrétienne*, a certain *Pensées d'Humbert*, and a religious manual published by the bishop of Viviers. When the school inspector came to Balazuc, he found Gibert's ability and success in imposing order and discipline in his classroom "mediocre" and his teaching "very mediocre." The inspector damned the school as "poorly run," noting the lack of progress in instruction. Nonetheless, Gibert seemed to get along well enough in the village. No one criticized his conduct or morality. However, someone, undoubtedly the mayor, noted that he got along only "passably" with municipal officials and complained about Gibert's "too extensive relations, however honorable." The teacher may have suffered hostility toward his profession, perhaps from the village priest, who could have considered him a potential rival for the allegiance of the children of Balazuc.⁶ Even in a region of relatively high religious practice, anticlericalism could be seen in the 1830s and 1840s among that generation of young teachers.⁷ Moreover, Gibert represented the state, and he and his successors were increasingly seen as such. This in itself inevitably placed him as a potential rival to the priest. His small school, however inadequate, became a focus of attention for the municipal council of Balazuc, intent on finding an appropriate local site for it, despite its chronic lack of funds.

Balazuc under the Golden Tree

Jean-Mathieu Gibert's new village was growing rapidly. The fever of the golden tree pushed Balazuc's population to its all-time peak of 905 in 1851. Yet nearly all residents still lived grouped closely together in the village itself or in one of the three hamlets, as they had for centuries. Five years earlier, at the time of a census, sixteen households lived along the *grande rue* that stretched from the Porte de la Sablière to the Portail d'Été, twelve households around the small square in front of the church. More houses, some little more than expanded stone huts (*cabanes*), had been built on the outskirts of the village: a total of 35 households and 189 people.[8] The hamlet of Servière (52 residents), Audon (88), and Louanes (50) remained important centers of population, veritable tiny villages in themselves with a total of 190 inhabitants.

A higher birthrate and a drop in the mortality also help explain the rise in population during the first half of the century.[9] The population of the Vivarais continued to grow despite the turmoil of the Revolution and Empire, from 259,504 in 1789 and 290,833 in 1806, before reaching its peak at more than 388,000 habitants in 1861. The population of the Bas-Vivarais went up even faster, the proliferation of terraces climbing steep hillside slopes a sign of this.[10]

Thus Balazuc's population soared during the first half of the nineteenth century. It rose from 653 in 1806 to 762 in 1820, to 800 in 1836, to 880 in 1846, before peaking at 905 inhabitants in 1851. Births outnumbered deaths in most years between 1801 and 1850. Yet infant mortality remained extremely high: In 1844, of thirty-three deaths, fifteen were infants of less than a year, and others included children five years or younger. The village, however, remained relatively sparsely populated, largely because of the presence of the nearly uninhabited *gras*.[11]

Most weddings, each followed by a long procession through the village led by the bride and groom and their families and witnesses, still joined men and women from Balazuc. In the other cases, one partner (with the exception of four cases it was the groom) came from a nearby or adjacent village: Lanas, Vinezac, St.-Maurice-d'Ardèche,

Pradons, Laurac. Only one bride or groom of these sixty-seven marriages had been born outside the Ardèche: thirty-six-year-old mason Joseph Exbrayat, originally from the Haute-Loire, who was married in 1835 and of whom more will later be heard.[12]

Balazuc remained a village of peasants. The fragile agricultural economy involved all members of almost all households, either working with the head of the household, in the case of women overseeing the house and the courtyard, or, in the case of older sons who were day laborers, working full- or part-time for someone else. Balazuc's increased population generated an expansion in the number of artisans, including five masons, four tailors, two blacksmiths, two barbers, a cabinetmaker, a shoemaker, and a baker, as well as two seamstresses and two *aubergistes* (innkeepers), one Louis Vianès, welcoming guests at the Porte de la Sablière, the other on the long street running from the latter entry to the Portail d'Été. However, virtually all these men with trades owned or worked land in Balazuc as well. The census also counted Cyprien Roux, the priest, Louis Fromentin and Marie Raphanel, the teachers, along with Auguste Mollier, the boatman who ferried people and animals across the river, the rural guard (*garde champêtre*), and Joseph Granier, who earned his livelihood by ringing the church bells and burying the faithful.[13]

The presence of parents and other relatives in the household added to crowded houses. For example, Louis Mollier's household included his wife, their four children, and his aunt; that of Antoine Fromentin, his wife, three children, and his parents. André Boyer lived with his wife, Anne, who was blind, and their three small children, as well as with his mother.[14]

The census reveals both changes from and continuities with the past. Six young women were *au filage,* working in the small spinning factories along the Ardèche and other rivers. Several people were indigent, "assisted by charity." These included Anne Court, the wife of a peasant proprietor, and Marguerite Granier, wife of a day laborer. The household of the aged Antoine Bouret included Rose, his thirty-eight-year-old daughter, noted as being "mentally disturbed but not dangerous," and her ten-year-old "illegitimate" (then a rarity in the Bas-Vivarais) son. Jean Roux, the blind boy whose hand we shook in chapter 3, was now fifty-six years of age and got along by making fishnets. Finally, there were ten "domestics"—male farmhands (eight of them living at the larger farms away from the village itself)—seven domestic servants, and thirteen shepherds living in households in Balazuc.

Balazuc's rising population filled the small cemetery beyond the Portail d'Été to overflowing. Even as births gradually won out over deaths, epidemics still occasionally ripped through the village. In 1833, the year after cholera had spared the arrondissement of Largentière, another decimating illness arrived in Balazuc.[15] A type of cholera known as the hot illness (*maou siaou*) killed forty-nine people in Balazuc. Of these victims, fifteen (including both children of one couple) were less than two years old and nineteen were more than sixty years. Seven men, women, or children named Mollier died. That year Balazuc had sixty-five deaths and just twenty-one births. Only one couple married in Balazuc that year, a ceremony of privilege, between Rosalie Tastevin, of the wealthiest family in the village, and Étienne Brun, of St.-Germain. In 1834 thirty-five deaths (against twenty-four births) reflected the lingering effects of the disease. However, there were forty births in 1835, against only ten deaths.[16]

These sudden deaths necessitated more space for burials. Moreover, the council believed the cause of the last epidemic to be the "miasma coming from the cemetery, which is far too close to the old ramparts . . . and with the increase in population, one cannot dig a grave without coming upon the sad spectacle of bones still not consumed by the earth." Three men agreed to sell land to the village to serve as a new cemetery, this one even closer to the church, near the river. However, the municipality at the time could not afford to pay them anything at all. The new and presumably temporary cemetery flooded easily during the frequent storms, and runoffs from graves might end up infiltrating the "fountain" below the Portail d'Été, a principal source of water throughout much of the twentieth century. It also stood too near several houses, and in 1853 two of these families tried to force the commune to move the cemetery or at least put up walls. But for the moment it had to do.[17]

Balazuc remained a village of rough paths, not roads. The one known as La Pousterle led from the shabby château to Portelas, through which those arriving via the "royal path" now passed. Another path, barely wide enough for a wagon, led around the old ramparts, outside of which stood the small place du Portail Neuf. Below that *ruelle* squatted terraced gardens, sloping down toward the cemetery. One of the paths from the church and the small *place* before it, then the center of village life, was the passage La Trouée de la Fachinière, which still cuts through and under the rock. Paths dodged stone houses, including what may have been an underground passage. Far below stood the mill; the land survey of 1825 indicates that some sort of dam directed water toward its wheels to provide enough power to turn the giant millstones. Gardens lay along the river, particularly upstream, standing vulnerable to floods.

In 1836 peasants in Balazuc had 120 acres planted in wheat, 20 acres each of rye, barley, and oats, and 10 acres each of potatoes and vegetables, in addition to the vineyards. There were few oxen, cows, or horses in the village, but rather, animals of rough terrain: thirty rams, four hundred sheep, three hundred lambs, three hundred ewes, one hundred goats, one hundred pigs, and fifty mules and two donkeys, essentially the animals of the poor. Of the hundred animals slaughtered each year, most certainly were pigs dispatched around Christmas.[18]

Municipal Preoccupations

The authority of the centralized state reached through the prefect and subprefect into the smallest village. It did so through the mayor and municipal council, as the commune gradually replaced the parish as the central focus of local identity. No one had any illusion about municipal autonomy any more under the Restoration than he or she had during the Ancien Régime. State authority and village poverty remained the two essential facts of municipal government. The municipal council of villages of the size of Balazuc during the Restoration included eight men (during subsequent regimes this rose to ten, twelve, then eleven men), two serving as mayor and deputy mayor (*adjoint*). The prefect or arrondissement subprefect had to approve each municipal budget. The state demanded that the councils vote funds to pay for the rural guard and to maintain village paths.[19] Yet these two obligations, to which was added in 1833 that of maintaining a public school for boys, saw the village to become a petitioner for assistance, regarding the state as a source of funding, sending in a constant stream of supplications. However, during the last years of Napoleon's Empire and during the Restoration, municipal council meetings were so infrequent (often only once a year during May and in 1816 not at all) that on several occasions the year was entered on the register, without month or day. Inevitably one or two members did not attend.[20]

Given impetus by the Revolution, municipal administration had become more organized during the Empire. The *greffier,* or village scribe, of the Ancien Régime became the municipal secretary. In 1806, Jacques Mollier, twenty-six years old, "landowner, knowing how to read and write," whose father had assessed the value of *biens nationaux* during the Revolution, became secretary. However, the municipality had to scramble to find even his tiny annual salary.[21] Three years later the prefect of the Ardèche, seeing that municipal council records in general were "kept in an inexact and irregular fashion," ordered Balazuc to begin keeping minutes in registers and to send them to the subprefecture for approval. The registers of minutes (*procès-verbaux*) of meetings began that year and have been kept continuously ever since.[22]

Mayors, deputy mayors, and municipal councillors were drawn from a small group of men who owned property and could read and write (as with their counterparts during the Ancien Régime) and therefore sign their names to the minutes. These farmers may have been somewhat better off than other inhabitants, but not, save one or two, by much. With the exception of 1821–23, when Jacques Mollier ("a good administrator") was mayor, Alexandre Tastevin of Salles, the wealthiest man in the village, served in that capacity. "Very devoted to the government" (though having served under the empire, his father had been among those trying to protect the interests of the Vogüé family in Balazuc during the Revolution) and secure with his modest fortune, he was appointed to the post at the end of 1815 to replace the late Antoine Auzas. Tastevin's father had served as mayor until his death in 1801. On that occasion, Balazuc and its neighbor St.-Maurice-d'Ardèche disputed the right to bury him, because Salles lies between the two. It is said that they left it up to the horse, which started off to St.-Maurice. In a village from which few people went anywhere (and in which throughout the century about 80 percent of the population had been born), Jean-Baptiste Tastevin traveled to St.-Étienne in 1846 and again the next year and two years later to Montbrison, also in the Loire. We know from his description on his passport (required in principle to travel between departments) that he stood five feet eight inches high and at sixty-three had gray hair and beard and a scar from his left cheek to his mouth.[23]

The Tastevin family was by far the wealthiest in Balazuc. In August 1806, Emmanuel Alexandre Gamond d'Antraigues, the son of a prosperous lawyer and notary and the brother of a member of the Convention during the Revolution, married Rosalie Tastavin. This was no small affair. Indeed Antoine Auzas was the only witness who could not sign his name. Jean-Baptiste Tastevin of Salles, brother of the groom, made possible a sizable dowry of thirty thousand francs, providing a large meadow in Balazuc as a guarantee. The couple agreed to the local custom for marriage contracts (*régime de l'état*), with Rosalie giving up all her possessions present and future. Upon Gamond's death, his son and bride were to inherit his house in Antraigues, furniture and household items (carefully listed: a buffet and twenty-four chairs, twelve silver services, twelve copper pots and pans, a fine clock, and four dozen napkins, totaling twelve hundred francs in value—no one else dined like that in Balazuc), small courtyard, and garden as well as his notary's practice, which his son would continue. The senior Gamond would retire, leaving his son and his new bride in fine shape. This arrangement was very much in the tradition of the Ancien Régime, when donation to an heir on the occasion of his marriage was one of the ways in which property was passed on.[24]

Antoine Alexandre Tastevin *fils* was a big eater and a hard-drinking man. Once while on horseback at the fair in Aubenas, Tastevin amused himself by cutting down the display of a pottery merchant with a sword, shouting in patois, the language of everyday life, *"T'en fazes pas, qu'oy Tastévin qué pago!"* ("Don't worry, Tastevin will pay for it!"). Tastevin's flamboyant character may well have worn on the sub-prefect, who replaced him in 1819 with Jacques Mollier. However, upon Mollier's resignation in 1823, Tastevin almost inevitably became mayor again.[25] Most councillors served until they died. Even when Claude Boiron resigned as deputy mayor after Mollier resigned in 1823, he remained on the council. Three years later Alexandre Tastevin again became mayor, with Jacques Mollier now serving as deputy mayor.[26]

The four direct taxes provided money for the municipal budget, carefully overseen by the prefect: taxes on property (*foncier* and *mobilier*), on doors and windows, and on businesses (the *patente,* paid by only a few residents). Little income generated tiny budgets: 454.60 francs in 1813 and 826.19 francs in 1844 (reflecting the vil-lage's rise in population). Expenses included a few francs for office expenses, handsomely binding the volume of the registers of births, marriages, and deaths, subscriptions to the official administrative newspaper and the inevitable *Bulletin des lois,* occasional repairs to the presbytery, obligatory contributions to pay the rent for the justice of the peace in Vallon and toward the upkeep of the cantonal jail, and allocations to pay the salary of the secretary and the tax on the com-mon lands. Finally, the upkeep of the village clock represented a modest but pressing expense.[27]

The council's deliberation establishing its budget at the paltry sum of 467 francs for 1826 added reasonably enough, "[I]t makes sense only to note items of absolute necessity, given the feeble resources of the commune." Tastevin noted in 1829 that in the five years he had never asked to be reimbursed for municipal expenses, including the salary of the secretary (to whom he still referred with the Ancien Régime term of "scribe"). That year was rare in that twenty-five francs (the equivalent of about the ten days' earnings of an urban artisan) could be allocated for "unforeseen expenses," and twenty-six francs for "public festivals."[28]

Poverty impinged on village life. The commune lacked a proper village hall. Meetings were held in the home of one of its members and even occasionally in a cabaret; the mayor kept the land survey at home. Balazuc's municipality could not remain much longer without a village hall "without compromising dignity and undermining propriety." Then a small rented space served as an extremely modest village hall. Plans to purchase and repair houses came and went.[29]

Unlike many communes, the municipality could not afford to contribute anything to the upkeep of the church. This may well have irritated Balazuc's priests. Obviously Balazuciens could hardly themselves look to the parish for much help; the church council (*fabrique*) had almost no funds.

During the first half of the nineteenth century, the salary of the rural guard jumped out as by far the largest item on the village budget. Communes had been first authorized in 1791 to hire rural guards, who had existed in many places during the Ancien Régime, and beginning in 1795, a year of great hardship, had been obligated to do so. The guard kept an eye on fields, particularly during and immediately after the harvest, and animals in order to prevent thefts both from privately owned land and on the *gras*. This was no easy task in Balazuc, a village of considerable size and notoriously difficult terrain.[30]

The rural guard had another reason to look out for outsiders. Violence remained common in Vivarais, though more in the mountains than the lower regions. In the higher elevations some men carried huge, thick sticks that they called their justices of the peace. In 1821 violent attacks and even murders included the murder of the teacher of the village of Marcols, killed by two men who mistook him for someone else. In the case of a man from Lanas set upon and murdered as he returned from the fair in Vogüé, "public outcry" accused "the named Grenier, Ladier, Malier called Cardinal and Pélé (Jean), of the commune of Balazuc."[31]

Balazuc's National Guard had disappeared with Napoleon. Following the Revolution of 1830, which chased the Bourbon monarchy from France, it revived, but again only on a register, 111 men, of whom just 4 had rifles. It thus did not matter that no one had a uniform. When in April 1831 the two officers of the National Guard of Balazuc were supposed to go to Vallon to take an oath to serve, neither showed up.[32]

This left the rural guard. However, Balazuc's meager resources in most years fell short of enough money to pay his salary of 280 francs, which in itself was not enough for anyone to live on. To come up with even that amount the council could impose additional cents on the direct taxes to pay for loans. Such a measure had to be approved by the council and by the ten inhabitants paying the most taxes and not already on the council.[33]

Balazuc's rural guard had to cover 1,890 hectares (about 3,800 acres) of rocky, difficult terrain. His principal duty remained to prevent thefts in fields, particularly during the harvest, and from trees and to watch out for illegal woodcutting. He was also to see if cafés and cabarets were closing at the proper time and to tell the mayor if that were not the case.[34] Yet rural guards, although known to villagers, did not wear uniforms (which neither they nor the communes could afford), nor did they seem to carry any special symbols of authority.

Rural guards also looked out for poachers or illegal fishermen, although some did not take charge seriously or looked the other way.[35] In 1906 two gendarmes patrolling near Le Grand Moure upriver from the village came upon about two hundred pounds of dead fish floating in the river, killed by someone whose fishing tackle consisted of dynamite and who left in haste before he could collect even part of his haul. In August 1909 two gendarmes patrolled "to put an end the damage done by the pirates of our river." The night before, two men had hurled rocks at gendarmes who expected to find them fishing. The next day the gendarmes returned to the river to find two nude men, throwing cartridges of dynamite into the river and then picking the dead fish from the surface. A long chase followed, but the two fishermen managed to escape, "helped by the thick woods and the steep slope of the rocks."[36]

With so much at stake, at least in relative terms, the rural guard could easily become an unpopular local figure. In 1812 villagers had complained that the newly appointed guard had been unable to stop the "devastation" of woods on the *gras*, the communal property, presumably by families from neighboring Lanas, Vinezac, and Uzer. Balazuc required a man "robust and energetic in order to stop this devastation and bring calm to the inhabitants." Former members of the revolutionary National Guard of Balazuc had even gone on patrol with him, a duty that "disturbs many residents." The old conflict had not been resolved. Inhabitants who depended on the sparse vegetation and wood of the common lands of the *gras* believed themselves threatened with the loss of "their means of subsistence," and they also believed that they "in the future can only live miserably, unable to pay their taxes on the little property that they have." During the 1830s and 1840s, in particular, one guard after another (often former soldiers) quit, unable to keep up with a difficult, strenuous job for which they were paid so little.[37]

Leyris, in particular, ignored his duties during the 1840s, instead earning money ferrying people and animals across the river. In the meantime *malfaiteurs* damaged property, destroyed harvests, and cut down mulberry trees, usually at night. Once on patrol, greeted by a hail of rocks, Leyris simply returned home. This earned him "no popularity" in the village. The council unanimously voted his suspension, although several of the signatures at the bottom of the deliberation were crossed out as if in protest. In May 1851 seven members refused to continue on the municipal council if Leyris maintained his functions. Yet two years later he still had his job. The following year the council refused to include his salary on that particular municipal budget.[38]

In an isolated village the presence of a rural guard sometimes did not seem to be enough. Despite the increase in settlement of parts of the left bank of the river, considerable stretches of road and fields— above all, the *gras*—stood in complete isolation. Moreover, if the pure sky offers a color of remarkably deep blue, night engulfs with utter black. There still are no lights on the road to Uzer to break its primitive beauty. This would have given any traveler some uncertainty, particularly on a moonless night, the silence broken only in the summer by the cicadas. The village today still offers steep dark inclines, paths on which anyone has to pick along with care. Even when its population was three times what it is now, a sudden, unfamiliar sound or even step—inasmuch as everyone is accustomed to how neighbors step and walk—could be unsettling. Recall the frightened, immediately suspicious reaction of the girl in the window upon whom Védel and his Lyonnais companion suddenly came in the early 1880s.

In 1893 a thief robbed and beat to death an old man living in an isolated house far from the village itself. Two years later Joseph Vacher, a twenty-seven-year-old vagrant, turned up at the village patron's saint's day festival in July.[39] This was the kind of isolated setting in which Vacher murdered children in the mid-1890s. He perpetuated a series of horrific sexual assaults and ghastly murders that began in the Ain, where someone found the disemboweled body of a sixteen-year-old boy. Two years later Vacher was arrested for assaulting a woman in the Rhône. He confessed to gruesome crimes that stretched from Burgundy to the Ardèche, including the sexual assault and murder of seven females and four males; he had probably killed four or five more than that. His victims included a fourteen-year-old boy, assaulted and killed in the Bas-Vivarais in 1895.[40] In 1910 a woman, living alone on the *gras*, heard a sound and was confronted by a man who asked for something to eat and drink, which she gave him. She then said that she had to go watch sheep and that he should leave. When she returned, he was still there, threatened her with a knife, and tied her up. He went through chests and drawers but found not a cent, because she had nothing, and he left. She freed herself and went to alert others.[41]

Most crimes consisted of thefts. One evening in 1861 someone set fire to a haystack belonging to Leyris, the former rural guard, giving him a loss of 270 francs, a considerable sum. Revenge? In 1892 villagers chased two men who, after dining copiously chez Boyer, put several bottles of wine in their pockets as they left. In 1908 an elderly man returned to find that thieves had broken into his house and found nine hundred francs that he had inadequately hidden under a barrel. There were attempted suicides (one successful case attributed to drinking), an occasional drunken outburst against gendarmes, an arrest for indecency, and a probable infanticide following the concealed birth of the baby of a twenty-three-year-old woman working in a silk factory in Aubenas. Sad events, all, but barely enough to fill a small police blotter.[42]

Three issues dominated the municipal council during the first half of the nineteenth century. First, breaking out of the isolation imposed by nature remained an obsessive priority of the municipality, intent on improving the ability of villagers to market what they produced. Second, the conflict with its neighbors over rights on the *gras* exploded. Third, the Guizot Law of 1833 stamped Balazuc's school a seal of state approval, giving Gibert and his successors enhanced prestige and an increased role in the village. Moreover, the law provided a good example of how the municipal council actively reacted to changes brought from the outside, gradually learning to manipulate them to their advantage.

The silk road of the Vivarais led from the Rhône at La Voulte to Alès via Privas, Aubenas, and Joyeuse, passing more than three long miles from Balazuc. The route from Aubenas to Barjac on the edge of the Gard led through Lagorce and Vallon, too far away to offer much to anyone from Balazuc.[43] Once a traveler to Balazuc had managed to reach the bank of the Ardèche River after having traversed the plateau of the *gras*, the river itself remained an obstacle to anyone, including the residents of Servière and Audon. The latter still attended church in Lanas and Uzer, respectively, much more easily reached, if considerably farther away than Balazuc's church. If the Ardèche River could be forded with difficulty in some places when it was low in the summer, most of the year one had to rely on the *bac*, that small boat rowed from one bank to the other, carrying people and animals for a slight fee. One can still see on the right bank of the river the place where the *bac* pulled in, and a small path led up to the larger path that led up the steep hill to the *gras* and eventually to Uzer. The right to operate the *bac* had been sold, along with the boat itself, to Jean Jullian in 1805. He paid a quarter of the lease and took possession of the boat, described as in "very bad shape" with oars and a small lock.[44]

Communal resources were insufficient to keep up the village roads or paths (*chemins vicinaux*). Not only did these paths lead to fields outside the village itself and across the river, but they led, in principle, to the outside world. So in the tradition of the corvée of the Ancien Régime, each household paying any direct taxes had annually to contribute three days of work from every able-bodied male between eighteen and sixty years of age. Property owners also had to contribute their wagons and work animals for three days. (In our day, residents of the village are asked once a year to spend a morning filling in holes in the pavement.) Technically, households could buy their way out of this obligation (as at the time with military conscription if the son of a well-off family drew a bad number in the annual lottery), but few families could consider such a luxury.[45]

When in 1837 departmental authorities first began to consider the possibility of new roads from the southern part of the Ardèche to Villeneuve-de-Berg, the municipality voiced enthusiasm for the construction of a more direct road that would lead from Ruoms to Vogüé, paralleling the river. Two years later the council members, all of whom could sign their names clearly and with newfound conviction, agreed to ask the prefect to classify (and thus to make eligible for state funds) the new road, which would intersect with the existing path.[46]

In 1846, Balazuciens complained that they were forced to accept unreasonably low prices for their goods, for example, at the two annual fairs in Ruoms, because everyone knew how difficult and thoroughly demoralizing it would be to carry unsold goods back to Balazuc. If the mulberry tree was the golden tree, the projected road linking Ruoms to Vogüé appeared like something of a yellow brick road.

The council voted to assess three additional centimes in taxes to help pay Balazuc's part for the Vogüé–Ruoms road. The pain of this sum leaps from the deliberation. The council had "carefully examined and reflected on" the proposition in view of the pressing reality that "Balazuc is so poor, having a considerable number of residents forced to work the entire day in order to assure the subsistence of their families, having no kind of commerce, and only being able to manage to transport their produce with extreme difficulty, given the pathetic situation of the commune . . . and lack of viable paths." Balazuc placed its hopes in the "great outlet" for its products that would surely result. However, when in 1847 the surveyor asked that Balazuc pay him the thirty francs it owed as its part of his fee for tracing the road from Ruoms to Vogüé, the municipality had to admit that it simply did not have thirty francs but would add it to the budget for the following year. Even this new route would not be in itself enough, unless a new path could facilitate the trek of more than a mile down to the road. In 1849, Balazuc's share of six million francs allocated by the Legislative Assembly to help rural communes extend, repair, and maintain their paths was the whopping sum of thirty-five francs. The council decided that they be employed "to improve the impractical landing place of Balazuc's boat on the opposite bank . . . given that several accidents seem to occur every day." Finally, in May 1850, the council added another five centimes to direct taxes in order to lay out a path that would lead to the new road. Four years later it voted funds toward the repair of four paths. Even the part of the village toward the river, which included the church, presbytery, girls' school, and about a third of the population of Balazuc, still had "no easy paths" leading to the more major ones, its residents destined "to live in isolation, condemned not even to be able to profit from what they can produce."[47]

Disaster on the Gras

In the meantime the long-standing dispute over rights on the *gras* transformed routine municipal poverty into catastrophe.[48] Common lands in much of France provided pasture for animals, woods that could be gleaned, bushes that could be cut, and plants, berries, and even grains that could be eaten. Most of Balazuc's common land consisted of about two hundred hectares of the rocky, limestone *gras*, that desolate, unfertile rocky Jurassic plateau above the right bank of the Ardèche, near the limits of the communes of Lanas and Vinezac.[49] We have seen that on the *gras* the difference between ownership and use had never been important, but the claims of residents of neighboring villages had raised the issue during the Revolution, which had sanctified private property.

In 1818 the municipal council decided to divide up "the communal lands known as the *gras*." They did so because "all" the inhabitants of Balazuc desired it. The hope was that what was marginal, unproductive land used for little more than pasturing and gleaning could be transformed by the intense initiative of peasant families into productive plots. The communal property would be divided into as many lots as there were households in Balazuc and sold at a modest price, paid over time. Three officially designated "experts," notaries, would assess the value of Balazuc's rugged *gras*. Balazuc's other common lands, dispersed in five different parts of the village, would eventually also be divided up. The lots seem to have been assigned by drawing straws.[50] The council decided that the *gras* would be divided into two sections: land suited for nothing more than pasture and land that offered at least some possibility of marginal agricultural production. If all worked out well, each household would receive some of both kinds of land for a small sum. At a time when the small boom in the production of raw silk seemed to offer villagers real hope, the deliberation reflected even hesitant optimism that the rocky land that now permitted little more than pasture could be converted "into vineyards, with mulberry and olive trees planted, along with the production of grain that could, with time, yield considerable revenue." Proceeds would go to maintain and improve the village paths. This was the dream.

Balazuc's decision to divide up its commons precipitated a legal war. Families from Vinezac, principally, but also from Chauzon, Pradons, Uzer, and Lanas had claimed the right to pasture their animals on what Balazuc considered its common lands for centuries. Several inhabitants of neighboring Uzer (Leyris and Auzas, almost certainly related, at least distantly, to the Leyris and Auzas families of adjacent Balazuc) joined them.[51]

In 1258 a certain Vierne de Balazuc and his son had sold the land they owned on "the land and *mandement* of Balazuc." The deed referred to the fact that the inhabitants of Vinezac had the right to pasture their cattle and cows on the "*gras de Balazuc*." Documents in 1398, 1601, and 1743 confirmed these rights.[52]

The long battle began in 1820. Some of the golden goats (*lous chabros d'or*), as the men from Balazuc were sometimes known, confiscated animals belonging to their rivals, before being forced to return them.[53] The lawsuit dragged on, but the tension surrounding its progress and potential outcome almost certainly contributed to the resignations of Mayor Jacques Mollier and his deputy in May 1823. Inhabitants of Balazuc battled their enemies from Vinezac, stoning them when they showed up on the *gras*. Shots were exchanged, and the rural guard shot and may have killed a peasant from Vinezac.[54]

In November 1824 the tribunal recognized the right of the inhabitants of Vinezac to pasture their animals on a fifth of the *gras* of Balazuc, as well as upheld the more modest claims of Chauzon, Pradons, and the two men from Uzer. It condemned poor Balazuc to pay for 90 percent of the cost of the long court battle born by Vinezac and two-thirds of those of Chauzon and Pradons and the two litigious peasants of Uzer. With understatement the mayor reported that the outcome "appears to have considerably damaged the interests of the villagers of Balazuc." The municipality launched an appeal to the court of Nîmes, which confirmed Balazuc's astronomical debt of twelve thousand francs, more than twenty-five times the annual budget. With interest tacked on, the debt had reached more than sixteen thousand francs by 1837.[55]

Clearly the village could not begin to pay its debt without selling off some of the common lands whose usage was not disputed, at least in part to avoid any chance of expropriation. In 1831 the municipality voted to ask the prefect for authorization to prepare to sell off the common lands. A royal ordinance in 1835 finally authorized their sale "to satisfy the creditors of the commune."[56] Thus, despite the hope of better times brought by the golden tree, the ruling by the court of Nîmes left Balazuc an even much poorer village.[57]

The use of the *gras*, however, still defied complete resolution. Some inhabitants of Balazuc had "usurped" willingly or "in good faith" parts of the *gras*, for which the municipality received nothing and had to pay taxes. In the early 1850s the subprefect had tried to get the mayor to begin proceedings against the "usurpers" to force them to purchase the land they had used and to pay the equivalent of rent and interest for such use. Finally, late in the century, all the land was sold.[58]

Challenges

In 1853 a financial officer of the canton of Vallon arrived in Balazuc to try to impose some order on what appeared to be a long-standing pattern of creative accounting, albeit with very small figures. He noticed more than forty mulberry trees standing along public streets, paths, and squares and in and around the old cemetery. However, it was not the commune that profited from the trees, but rather those who lived nearby. The collector estimated that their leaves should bring the municipality about twenty-seven or twenty-eight francs every year. But the municipality had not taken care of these trees and had turned over responsibility for their care to the bell ringer. Only in 1851 did the mayor sell the right to harvest these trees for fifteen francs.[59]

However, Mayor Tastevin, like his grandfather, who had failed to register the birth of three children during the Empire, had not bothered to submit a report, a mortal sin in France. He had merely noted that he had spent about twenty francs to repair the presbytery. Moreover, from 1839 to 1853, a small house owned by Jean Dours, the former mayor, served as both village hall and school. From 1839 to 1851, 720 francs had been entered as an expense for the teacher's rent. What had happened to the money? The cantonal official went along with "the most probable version": that the funds had been used to pay off the parcels of land that had been converted urgently into the temporary cemetery at the time of the epidemic of 1833. Mayor Mollier insisted that he had also used some of the money to purchase and plant four mulberry trees, bind the land survey, replace windows in the room serving as the village hall, and repair the cobblestones in front of it. There was no reason for the official to think that borrowing from Peter to pay Paul was not the case.[60]

If anything, Balazuc's problems seemed to get worse. When the subprefect visited the village on three occasions in the 1860s, he was shocked: "In Balazuc, everything remains to be done, church, presbytery, school, cemetery, etc." He dressed down the mayor, insisting that he work with the municipal council to take "effective measures to remedy this unfortunate situation." The village still lacked a sturdy path to the road that now linked Vogüé to Ruoms. In 1862, the subprefect complained, "A bad state of mind exists in this commune, marked by an unfortunate division between the village priest and the inhabitants. I took advantage of my visit to try to bring an end to all of this and called on the goodwill of everyone to calm things down." Mayor Tastevin, "a weak man without much influence," promised his help, although the subprefect could not predict what good that would do. Reflecting the alliance between Empire and Church, he suggested that the council first turn its attention to repairing the church, until a new one could be constructed. "A little goodwill from the inhabitants of Balazuc would suffice," he assured the mayor. The village after all would not require a "work of art."[61]

As Balazuc stood at a critical point, confronted by an overwhelming economic crisis, the municipal council remained obsessed with its isolation and particularly with gaining access to the railroad, creating a new cemetery, and finding at long last suitable buildings for the schools, which took on ever-greater importance in the village. As did all villages in similar situations, Balazuc asked for help from above—that is, the state, "confident in the great and benevolent solicitude of the high authorities to reduce the suffering that weighs on the countryside."[62] This, again, reflects not only the growing power and prestige of the central state but the willingness, indeed eagerness, of the municipal council to solicit assistance, as it learned the rules of the game.

France's railway network, the plans for which had been established in 1842, had slowly spread out from Paris. The state allocated routes by concessions for construction to private firms.[63] The inhabitants of Balazuc had long anticipated the arrival of the railroad as a messiah that would bring back relative prosperity. Thus parallel to economic disasters of silkworm disease and the oidium blight and then phylloxera attacking the vineyards came the village's full attention to the necessity of benefiting from modern transportation and taking what steps it could to improve its schools (as well as to find a suitable village hall).

In 1876 the first train on the seventy-five-mile line from Le Teil to Alès arrived in Balazuc. Six trains served Balazuc each day. The trip from Alès to Balazuc lasted three hours (it may now be driven in less than an hour). By the end of the century, nine lines stretched 250 miles over, alongside, under, and through imposing physical impediments in the Ardèche. Long since abandoned viaducts (including two on the territory of Balazuc) still witness the engineering feats necessary to begin service.[64]

Two decades later the municipal council of Balazuc joined other communes in placing their hope in the pipe dream of another proposed line. A deliberation in 1899 called attention to the decline of the production of raw silk and the gradual depopulation of the region. The communes asked for a line that would link the Velay (the Haute-Loire), a region that had purchased the wines from the Vivarais during the Ancien Régime, to the Bas-Vivarais, by a tortuous route of steep, dizzying turns. To bolster the case, the Balazuc council noted that the lines of the Rhône Valley could be captured with ease by invading armies from the east, leaving the proposed mountain railway inching its way to and from Le Puy to save the day.[65]

Although the expansion of the road network was arguably more important in regions like the Vivarais than was the railroad, coinciding with economic growth during the first half of the century, the railway brought a variety of new products to villages. Even amid decline, the quality of life improved modestly for the average family. Sugar gradually replaced honey, the sugar of the poor, on Ardéchois tables. Also, although potatoes remained the major part of the diet of the poor (for example, in the form of the *crique*, a potato pancake garnished with garlic and parsley), meat was no longer reserved for holidays, festivals, and periods of unusual prosperity.[66] At the same time, some lamented what appeared to be the decline in the Church's role as dictator of the values of rural life and complained that because of an overemphasis on conditions of material life, "the taste for the land is ebbing."[67]

Balazuc's cemetery was not far enough from the village to meet health requirements. Moreover, it could no longer accommodate the village's dead, to whom were added several railway workers. In 1853 and again in 1875, the municipal council discussed the possibility of moving the cemetery but each time was constrained by the lack of funds. Balazuc did not even have a regular gravedigger. Families of the defunct digging graves sometimes came upon "coffins almost intact; many people recognize the clothes of their parents, an unfortunate discovery for them."[68]

Finally, after several false starts, the municipality in 1884 purchased land that could be converted into a cemetery. They were aided by the generosity of a local entrepreneur and of Balazuciens who contributed their labor to the cemetery instead of the paths. The new cemetery was open for business in 1887. Six years later it still lacked walls on three sides and was "exposed to all sorts of profanations." It awaited more donations in money or labor from village residents, tiny annual allocations from the council's budget, and income from the purchase of "perpetual" concessions, plots six by forty feet sold for very little but of enormous importance to families.[69]

The path that led to the road that had been opened between Vogüé and Ruoms in the early 1850s offered a dangerously steep slope. Only very small wagons could risk the trek, limiting what could be taken to market in Ruoms or Vallon. By 1895 estimates for the work for a road that would lead from the river through the village to the road had reached 22,600 francs, including the purchase of land. State subsidies would be crucial.[70] In the meantime the hamlet of Audon remained isolated, awaiting funds to build a bridge over a dry stream. Audon stood less than a mile away from the village itself, but as much as five miles for anyone bringing a wagon. The purchase of land adjoining the path would be complicated, involving fifteen property owners. A loan and a state subsidy in 1902 permitted an improvement of the path to Servière, but torrential rains five years later swept away a small bridge, necessitating another loan.[71]

After all this time Balazuc still lacked a suitable village hall, which now was in a rented house near the Portail d'Été. In 1895 the council decided to turn the ground floor of the Tour Carrée into the village hall and added a door, floor tiles, and a more solid ceiling. The municipality thus rejoined the village's medieval origins. The new municipal building, inaugurated with a banquet in 1896, quickly proved woefully inadequate because the thick, prisonlike walls—several feet thick—made the room uncomfortably dark, humid, and stuffy. Rainwater routinely poured through the ceiling from the tower's upper reaches. In 1911 the municipal building moved again, this time to the large room of a building not far away that had served as the boys' school before the new school structure was built. Marriages, the annual municipal reception at the end of December, and an occasional public meeting now occupy this room, with the village hall taking up the entire building.[72]

The tradition of helping others (*entraide*) was essential in village life. "Assisted by charity" had been noted next to the names of several beggars when the census was taken in 1846. The village priest did what he could to encourage solidarity, despite the lack of resources. In 1827 the Charity Association (*Bureau de bienfaisance*) met in the presbytery. The curé, Claude Boyrou, was of course there, as was Mayor Tastevin and three other men. But it was a short gathering, because no money had come in since the last meeting, so no money had been spent. However, at the time the municipal council could help no one. Two years later the council discussed the possibility of assisting Cyprien Bayle, described as a "banned madman" who had lived in Balazuc for a decade. On principle it refused to provide any assistance to Bayle because he had not been born in Balazuc.[73] The Confraternity of St.-Antoine annually distributed meat to the poor on the occasion of its annual banquet, but as we shall see in the next chapter, its activity came to a screeching end in 1839. Assistance provided by relatives, friends, and neighbors remained necessary in a village with so little money.

Beginning with the Third Republic, municipalities could allocate extremely small sums to residents in particular need. Gradually assistance organized by the state and increasingly implemented by towns and villages developed. Communes had the responsibility of providing medical assistance for "all people recognized to be indigent or not able to procure the care of a doctor and medicine" in villages without a charity association, as well as to assist impoverished elderly people and the infirm and handicapped of any age with at least five francs a month. The municipality formed a commission of two members to consider cases of free medical assistance, which made recommendations to the municipal council.[74]

Although revenues remained minuscule, the Third Republic increased the responsibilities of the municipal council. In March 1878 the council for the first time had allocated a small sum in solidarity with someone in the commune. To thirty francs given by the prefect, in view of "the sad position in which X. finds himself," the municipal council of Balazuc added sixty francs, so that a man could be admitted to a hospital in Lyon.[75] Thereafter the municipal council was more and more under pressure to support the requests of families for assistance to relatives afflicted by debilitating physical and mental handicaps. Inevitably such decisions identified the municipal council more closely with the republic to which it answered.

However, such requests, several of which came each year, put the council in difficult situations, operating within the constraints of having precious little money. In 1885 the family of a retarded eighteen-year-old girl asked for help, apparently for hospitalization, but the commune had only one hundred francs left and could do nothing. Apparently in protest, one council member refused to sign the minutes of the meeting and stormed out. In 1893 the question arose if the council should contribute funds toward the hospitalization of a boy at Ste.-Marie, the huge asylum in Privas, "given that it is of public notoriety that X. is a victim of mental illness, and that [he] committed assault and battery on his mother and his grandfather, and that on several occasions he was found lying across the railway tracks, risking being crushed." The municipality refused to help, despite pressure from the subprefecture, ruling that the family had sufficient resources. The council noted, somewhat disingenuously, that the boy had attacked only members of his immediate family and still helped his family out in the fields. Two other families whose requests had been rejected were in even worse situations.[76]

The municipality contributed to the hospitalization in 1895 of an indigent woman who was mentally retarded and in 1906 and 1911 of men described as mentally disturbed. A year later it refused aid to a man because he had a small annual income and his wife also had some revenue. However, that year twenty people received medical help.[77] In 1907 the municipality spent more than three hundred francs for medical assistance, including hospitalization, transport, pharmacists, and doctors' fees. Unforeseen events too could strain the municipality's budget. In 1912 a doctor from Ruoms had to be summoned to Balazuc to determine the cause of death of "the indigent X., found dead at les Costes." Forty-five years old and not having "all his faculties," he had wandered away from home almost two weeks before his body had been found. The municipal council had to pay the doctor who determined the cause of his death.[78]

The availability of doctors was itself something new. Like most people in the region, Baluzuciens still relied on midwives for childbirth, on home remedies, and on healers, who advised sick people to consume such mixes as sage, thyme, and oak as well as herbs mixed with olive oil and egg yolks. In 1914, a man in Labeaume claimed to have been cured of pleurisy by cutting a live chicken in half and putting the bloody mess on his head for a very long day. Children who had difficulty walking were taken on short pilgrimages to nearby St.-Maurice-d'Ardèche.[79]

A 1905 law required municipalities to provide assistance to needy old people. Three years later the council allocated five francs per month to one man, noting that he had always lived in Balazuc; a woman who had lived in the village for forty-five years and could be cared for at home; and several other people, invariably with indications on the number of years the person had lived in the village. Sometimes the prefecture intervened in such requests, for example, in 1910 insisting that five people be removed from the list of those eligible for assistance because their children could help them.[80]

Thus the council weighed each family's situation carefully. On one occasion it deducted a franc from the ten francs to be given to a number of poor old people because they had places to live, and in one case it subtracted three francs from money provided Marie X, who was terminally ill, because she could at least count on lodging, clothes, and heat. The council deducted six francs from the monthly sum of ten francs' assistance to Madame X, who had not been born in Balazuc but had lived there for more than fifty years, because one of her children provided some financial help and another gave her a place to live. When the council failed to make such deductions, the subprefect sent back the list to be amended.[81]

Harsh winters engendered requests for help. In 1893 the municipal council distributed half the money it had left over from the sale of cemetery plots to aid "several people of poor and necessitous families" who had come during extremely cold weather in January to ask for assistance.

The council also considered requests for support from families seeking exemptions for sons from military service because of the hardship such absences would cause their families (though of course such decisions lay with military authorities). In April 1880 the council asked that Pierre X be excused from service, because he was the "unique and indispensable support of his family," of his ill father, and his sister "not possessing all her faculties." Jules X, citing "the poor harvests that the region has suffered for some time, which have left us in dire straits," asked that his son be excused. Louis D requested that his son be spared; the father had lost four fingers in the Crimean War, and his wife was sickly. The council also supported the request of a former soldier who had fought for six years in Algeria and then with the Army of the Loire in 1870. Now he could not work because he had lost use of one leg, leaving his family "in misery."[82]

In 1898, Camille Jullian, whose right hand was paralyzed, asked that his son Jean (a descendant of one of the victims of the coup d'état) be excused, as "unique and indispensable support for his family." Marius B argued that he was the sole support of a mother who was eighty but asked to be dispensed from only thirteen days of duty. In 1900 the council voted to add one more centime to direct taxes to help the families of those "under the flag." Five years later it allocated five francs to six families of reservists. Such allocations were a sign of patriotism as well as of republican solidarity, however small. In September 1913 the council supported the demand of military exemption for Joseph Fabregoule. His father was seventy-six years of age and unable to work the lands around the *mas* in which the family had lived since the Middle Ages. The property of the Fabregoule "is situated in an extremely rugged place where all farm work must be done by hand and now is almost impossible to find anyone to work."[83]

Schoolhouses

The Guizot Law of 1833 helped make Jean-Mathieu Gibert's school a preoccupation of the municipality. During the Revolution the

Convention had proclaimed that primary education in France would be free, available to all, and secular, and the Consulat had given communes the right to oversee primary education. Yet without question schooling took steps backward during the revolutionary and imperial periods.

During the Restoration, primary schooling in most of rural France remained largely shaped by the Church. An ordinance in 1816 instructed each commune to have a primary school, which indigent pupils could attend for free. In principle, each teacher was to have a minimal authorization to teach (*brevet de capacité*) from the rector of the regional school district (*académie*) and to be authorized either by the latter or by the bishop. Many village schoolteachers were "barely educated, at a level well below the important functions that have been confided to them" and taught only intermittently. Numerous villages simply ignored the directive because they could not afford a school or did not want to have one. More than a few mayors saw the arrival of a teacher as someone who could help maintain the civil registers, and some (but not all) priests (and pastors in Protestant villages) saw in a relatively educated newcomer someone who could help them.[84] Yet progress brought by the Restoration to primary education has been long underappreciated. Between 1821 and 1833 the percentage of children between five and twelve years who were in school in the Ardèche rose by almost 10 percent to 37 percent.[85]

In 1831 the Orléanist July Monarchy, which had come to power the previous year, assessed primary education in France. In the mountains of the Ardèche there were hardly any schools at all. Virtually no teachers had anything more than the lowest license (a third-class *brevet*), meaning that they could "read, write, and count" but not much more, if that. Most teachers wasted considerable time teaching pupils one at a time, the individual method. Moreover, unauthorized and even clandestine schools in operation had increased in number.[86]

In 1804, Balazuc had schools for both boys and girls. However, in 1817 the boys' school had no teacher, and the girls' school seems to have no longer existed. The next year Jacques Mollier began teaching, while still serving as municipal secretary. Thus 1818 marks the beginning of the continuous existence of Balazuc's school. Mollier taught twenty-five of the thirty-five school-age village boys, using the individual method that was rapidly falling into disrepute amid enthusiasm for the simultaneous teaching method, espoused by the Christian Brothers. A school for girls was then "projected" for twenty-five of the thirty school-age girls. Four years later, twenty-five of forty-five boys of school age attended school. Mollier taught for another six years.[87]

The July Monarchy built on the existing structure of primary schools that already existed in France.[88] Undercutting some of the influence of the Church, whose support for the recently departed Bourbon monarchy had been unwavering, the Guizot Law established committees at the arrondissement and cantonal levels that were to oversee the creation of new schools. They were to assess the performances of teachers and count the number of children to be admitted for free. A commune could opt to have a private school, run by the Church or established in Protestant areas by the pastor. Prefects retained the authority to appoint or to fire teachers independent of the wishes of the municipal council. However, the village priest invariably worked closely with the mayor, making the former, in effect, an agent of school surveillance.[89]

The Guizot Law resulted in a meeting of nearly every municipal council in France. It made communes responsible for paying male teachers at least two hundred of the minimum salary of six hundred francs. The rest was to come from fees paid by the parents of pupils who were not classified by the municipal council as "indigent." (Only in 1889 did the state begin to assume all responsibility for paying teachers.) However, this salary, in itself barely enough to survive, cannot be taken to represent the annual income of teachers, for many—and apparently in some years most—families could not or did not pay up. Many teachers earned a little more as municipal secretary, though some earned as little as ten or twenty francs per year for this work. A few teachers taught adults to read in the evening, others repaired the village clocks, and a few served as choir leaders. Some worked the summer harvest.

The minimum allocation of two hundred francs each commune

was to contribute toward a teacher's salary seemed like a very high bar to most villages. Only by virtue of a small state subsidy and by adding several centimes to each of the four direct taxes could many villages afford a school at all. The number of pupils classified as "indigent" in the Ardèche routinely reached a third and as many as half or even more. However, some municipalities placed children on the list of indigents whose parents could afford to pay. If the teacher complained to the arrondissement committee, he risked being seen as an informer, compromising his position in the village.[90]

The Guizot Law had called for the establishment of normal schools in each department in order to train lay teachers during their two years of residence. The normal school (école normale) in Privas had begun operation in 1832. The first years were difficult. A report in 1837 criticized the weakness of the course of study and the absence of adequate leadership. Inspectors complained that its students spoke French with a "very pronounced" accent. They learned arithmetic, as well as worked on their reading and writing, but neglected history and geometry. Punishment for misbehavior was indeed severe: the loss of both recess and wine. However, those who were graduated from the école normale were awarded the plum posts, which did not include Balazuc. The inspector who reported on the state of primary schools in the Ardèche in 1836 visited the schools of all the neighboring villages, but he apparently found it too difficult to reach Balazuc and skipped it completely.[91]

The assessment the inspector offered was blistering and pessimistic. Of the 330 communes in the Ardèche, 126 still had no schools. Only about half of all children attended school, and once the summer agricultural work began, half that number. The continued dominance of the individual method of instruction shocked the inspector. Pupils spent much of the time staring blankly into space while the teacher interrogated one of them after another. However, the inadequate size of most classrooms impeded the development of simultaneous instruction.[92]

To explain the poor performance of the schools, the inspector cited parental negligence. Many families sent their children to school only when it pleased them to do so, or not at all, because they did not want to spend any money, required the children's work, or believed that education carried no value. Moreover, in some places, including Balazuc, the school was far from isolated hamlets and farms. Most children turned up only five months per school year, and many came late; during the summer children forgot what they had learned in school during the winter months. Even those pupils who stayed in school until they were eleven received, in fact, only about three years of schooling or less.

Of the schools of the Ardèche, the inspector considered only seven "good" and at least two-thirds "bad." He had found "miserable straight but irregular benches, placed on stones and placed around dirty and humid walls, with large unstable tables, left in no particular order in the middle of the classroom, with the unfortunate children piled on top of one another." Small wonder teachers found it difficult to maintain discipline and teach effectively. Whether rented or owned by the commune, almost no schools in the Ardèche had been constructed for that use. In some villages the schoolroom was also used for municipal council meetings, often with the teacher serving as the secretary because he could write French. In St.-Marcel-d'Ardèche, the schoolroom was contiguous to a store from which the owner's loud voice could be constantly heard.[93]

Conditions of life for Gibert and his colleagues remained barely better than those of the old itinerant teachers. Many communes reduced the amount parents were to pay for each child per month to derisory sums, such as twenty-five, forty, or sixty centimes ("general complaint" added in the margins of the report). Some peasants were certainly jealous of "the independent position and income that we have tried to provide the teacher" and "have ingeniously worked to try to undercut the teacher and make sure he does not succeed." Well into Napoleon III's Second Empire (1852–70), municipal and departmental funds had to be used so that Balazuc's teachers could reach the minimum salary of six hundred francs and, even then, often only in principle.[94]

About a third of the teachers had no qualifications for teaching. Many were "incapable," despite the fact that most teachers were described as being "zealous" (the greatest compliment that could replace "capable"). Yet many simply quit their posts to find other kinds of work. The women who taught in the girls' schools seemed even less able than their male counterparts. Well less than half of the teachers in girls' schools, most run by religious congregations, had any kind of license. Only three or four of the boys' schools were described as "good"; the rest were in "terrible" condition. If the Guizot Law had brought more schools and progress within them, an inspector in 1849 laid out the challenges facing teachers in Balazuc and the Ardèche. Children might go to school during the winter months, but that ended "come springtime, when different herds proliferate on the hillsides, led by the village children; followed by the silkworm harvest, and then the next great preoccupation comes along, the chestnut harvest. For about seven months, the school is deserted, and fills up again only with the bad weather."[95]

Balazuc still did not yet have an adequate schoolhouse, and its rented space was far too small. Indeed the municipal council suggested that this was one reason that some children did not attend school. In the meantime the municipality hoped to be able to construct or acquire a house that could serve as both village hall and school. The plan to purchase and repair a house fell through. After Gibert's successor had left without explanation, Firmin Lafont began teaching in Balazuc in 1839. The academic inspector described his school as "well run," despite the lack of books. Two years later, thirty of the sixty-two boys of school age attended school. More than once the council and the ten leading taxpayers were summoned to impose a three additional centimes tax so that Lafont "could have enough to live."[96] When Louis Fromentin, who taught with provisional authorization, owed three years' back rent and faced eviction from his house, stopped teaching after six years in October 1849, "the furnishings of the school had been reduced to virtually nothing." For almost a year, Balazuc had no teacher. One man named to Balazuc in 1850 never showed up, despite pleas from the mayor, undoubtedly having heard that he probably would earn little more than two hundred francs.[97]

Almost miraculously, after almost two years without a teacher, a savior appeared. Benoît Vital, twenty-six years old and a former student at the normal school in Privas, had a diploma and two "certificates of morality" given by the mayors of Pradelles, his native village, and another village in which he had taught. The Falloux Law of March 1850 reaffirmed each commune's responsibility to maintain its boys' school and improve the situation of its teacher. (The law was a victory for the Church because it required religious teaching in public schools.) Vital must certainly have been disappointed, if not shocked, by the conditions he found upon arriving in Balazuc in August. Some of the promises made to him by the municipality had not been fulfilled. He taught in a single room that doubled as the mayor's office. It had one small door, through which passed the foul odors of garbage piled up "virtually in front of the door, corrupting the air." He lived in a small apartment in the same building, an arrangement that became the norm. Yet the council had used the money saved when there was no teacher to purchase school furniture, proudly noting that in the interest of "public education, the council has made all possible sacrifices." When Vital was to be transferred to another village, the municipality protested that this skilled teacher was "absolutely necessary . . . everyone is very happy with the way that he has acted and the children have made great progress since he arrived here." But in the world of French bureaucracy, even then, what was done was done.[98]

Improving Balazuc's schools, however, proved to be no easy matter, particularly against the backdrop of silk disease and three straight years of blight that had undone the vineyards. Although the district education committees now worked zealously and mayors, municipal councils, and village priests seemed to agree on the importance of educating children, Balazuc remained among thousands of French villages caught between state requirements that they provide for primary education and the harsh reality that they lacked sufficient resources to do so properly. In the early 1850s another attempt to purchase a house fell through for lack of funds. The prefect refused to help, claiming that the commune had sufficient resources and that an estimated cost of repairs had been too high. However, here again, the municipal council persisted in trying to take advantage of possible state assistance, petitioning on behalf of its school. The Ministry of Public Instruction refused Balazuc's request for supplementary funds, one of thousands of similar letters from villages pleading poverty of resources. The commune still remained in debt from the staggering cost of the legal case lost to Vinezac and Chauzon. The population was decidedly "not in the situation to make the most minimal sacrifice," while recognizing the importance of assuring its children "of civic and religious instruction for many years to come." A harsh winter and high grain prices had taken their toll as well. The council's plea was pathetic, urgent, and somewhat indignant, warning that the commune would be unable either to lodge a teacher or to provide adequate facilities for either school. Laurac and Balazuc's old rival Vinezac, "much wealthier than Balazuc" (a common, predictable refrain), had received help while it had been left "without any assistance to compensate for the misfortunes, sacrifices, and privations that have brought the village so much despair."[99]

Balazuc had had a girls' school in 1802 and probably for more years during Napoleon's Empire. Early in the Restoration, only fifteen of the forty girls of school age attended school.[100] However, the municipality at first contributed nothing to the school for girls, unlike the boys' school. In 1836, Marie Arnaud, an unmarried independent sister—thus not a full-fledged nun—received three hundred francs from parents. During those winter months, twenty-eight girls, including three indigents, attended, and eighteen girls in the summer. Arnaud taught from the Bible and a religious book, but despite her good conduct, her school was marked as "badly run." In 1841, Marie Raphanel arrived from the convent of St.-Joseph of Vesseaux to teach the girls of Balazuc. She too was an independent sister with only a "letter of obedience," meaning she had spent just several months in the convent. Marie Raphanel thus did not take the name of a sister or wear a habit to go with the simple cross around her neck.

More and more girls began to show up at the school; fifty-five (including fifteen indigents) appeared in 1843–44, and forty during the summer. Receiving nothing from the municipality, the teacher earned barely enough for her and her sister to survive.[101] Demonstrating the municipality's growing interest in schooling, the budget of 1851 finally included 80 francs' salary for Marie Raphanel. In 1850 she may have received merely 10 francs of her salary, and in

1852 her total income was only 290 francs. For months in 1853 she replaced Vital, the boys' teacher, who had fallen ill, and received a portion of his salary. She raised eyebrows, however, by putting boys and girls in the same room, violating regulations. Four years later an inspector described her as having "little ability but offering energy and devotion, earning respect and having good relations with everybody." However, the small house, "in the state of complete collapse," offered but two tiny rooms, one the inadequate classroom into which as many as sixty girls squeezed, the other the teacher's lodging. A very small window provided the only natural light, making it difficult to see in the winter.[102]

The Ministry of Public Instruction in 1854 accorded money to repair the girls' school, but this left the village four hundred francs short. In 1832 the village priest, Hyacinthe Baille, had left to the village a house that he wanted to serve as a school for poor girls, as well as lodging for the woman who would teach them. He also left a sum of money that would generate about one hundred francs each year, to pay the teacher. Unfortunately, the priest's nephew had failed to comply with his will, and the municipality had sued him in 1835. More than twenty years later, after spending sixty francs in legal fees, the council admitted that it could not afford further funds to sue the deceased priest's recalcitrant relative.[103]

The search for a suitable location for the girls' school in 1853 led to a small building behind the presbytery. Owned by the church council, it had been used by the Confraternity of St.-Antoine and then a short-lived religious confraternity (the White Penitents). In 1860, just as High Mass was being said, part of the presbytery roof collapsed, carrying with it the chimney and parts of walls. In the meantime Marie Raphanel had done her work well. Only four girls in Balazuc of school age did not attend at all. The mayor went from door to door, collecting money and promises of money or help, and the council took out another loan. Those contributing included Jean Jullian and Joseph Exbrayat, former political exiles. However, the project was abandoned because of the house's location and small size and because of problems finding a suitable space for toilets and a space for a courtyard for recess. Moreover, the church council had objected to the move, straining relations between Abbé Martin (who served in Balazuc for almost twenty years) and the municipal council. Still more seeds for future conflict.[104]

In 1857 the municipality purchased a house at the Portail d'Été that had been built into the dark stone ramparts four decades earlier. It combined "all the conveniences possible in a village as poor as Balazuc." Following needed repairs to the ramparts, the enlargement of the main door, and the addition of three outdoor toilets and the new pine floor, Balazuc had a suitable girls' school. Two years later the Convent of St.-Joseph in Vesseaux took over responsibility for the school at the request of the municipal council. The municipality agreed to furnish "a proper lodging" for the teacher, and the families of their pupils would pay a monthly fee.[105]

However, many of the children were classified as indigent. In the boys' school, in 1855, Augustin Huond, the boys' teacher, who enjoyed the respect of the village because his pupils made progress, justified the presence of twelve children whom the mayor and priest had placed on the list of indigents, by virtue of their parents' situations, including Henri Boiron ("indigence"), Louis Boyer ("evicted"), Jean Breysse ("extreme indigence"), Antoine Fromentin ("poor and with many children"), Basile Granier ("a widow, poor, with several children"), Calixte Mirabel ("absorbed by family problems"), Baptiste Maurel ("extreme indigence and family concerns"), Philippe Pays ("indigent"), Jean Thibon (a "widow whose debts leave her in need"), and Auguste Boyer ("very poor").[106]

Nevertheless, most of the indigent families contributed something; one year just three of twelve paid nothing. The family of Jean Breysse paid eleven centimes. Occasionally the mayor and priest noted that they had refused a family's request to be placed on the list, noting "abuse of the favor." Brief entries continued to tell the story: "badly off," "extreme indigence," and, cruel sign of the silk crisis, "evicted." Similar lists provide similar information on the poorest of the girls. In 1862 the sisters of St.-Joseph in Vesseaux admitted eight girls as indigents, some with brothers on the other list. In a poor village these were among the poorest of the poor.[107]

Clerical influence in education remained enormous. During the

Second Empire, many members of the conseil général, mayors, and most of the population, wanted both the boys' and girls' schools turned over to the religious orders (thus eliminating any monthly fees for those families that could afford them). In the wake of the Second Republic, the rector shared this view, considering it "the best and surest means of moralizing the masses and assuring peace and happiness." One teacher expressed the view that schools should be placed as near as possible to the presbytery, so that the village priest could more easily oversee the moral development of the pupils. He compared the "noble" and "worthy" status as a "public functionary" to "a second vocation." In 1853 the rector for the Ardèche wrote that he wanted to encourage students at the *école normale* to work on their singing, so that "each school could provide four or five young singers who will also be capable of serving Mass." After thirty-five new public schools run by teaching religious brothers opened in the Ardèche in the decade, in 1859, the religious orders, which had taught half of the children in 1847, now taught 65 percent of pupils. Although lay schools outnumbered those run by the religious orders, the latter taught more pupils, because some of their schools were in towns.[108]

Almost all the lay teachers had some sort of teaching authorization, even diplomas, although some were "of shameful ignorance." The teachers from the religious orders (*congréganistes*) lagged far behind. In fact, the Falloux Law of 1850 allowed them to teach without any diplomas at all. Many of the women had spent only three or four months in convents, leaving with the title of associated sisters and letters of obedience given by one of the religious congregations and routinely renewed each year. This gave these "sisters of the countryside" the right to open up private schools, although they were technically lay teachers.[109]

Increasingly, the lay stamp of the normal school, which had improved its reputation, came to carry weight. This irritated the clergy, some of whom were openly hostile to lay schools. Priests pressured municipal councils to ask for religious teachers. Some municipal councils, tightfisted when it came to providing funds to improve lay schools, were more generous with schools taught by teaching brothers or sisters. In any case, during the Second Empire most lay teachers still taught the catechism and escorted their pupils to Mass, following the direction of the village priest. This would change. For now most people in Balazuc welcomed the arrival of the sisters of St.-Joseph.[110]

Yet the Ardèche lagged beyond much of France. About four thousand children of school age in the Ardèche did not attend at all. Some communes with more than eight hundred people still did not have a girls' school, as required, for lack of funds or because no teacher could be found. In the mountains, many, if not most, schools were still closed three-quarters of the year. There a few clandestine schools held on, run by "nomadic" teachers who taught boys and girls in the same room, a few doubling as shepherds in the summer months, as during the Ancien Régime. No normal school for women yet existed.[111]

Even if by 1855 all communes had at least one public school, most of the schools were in bad shape, many lacking enough chairs or benches to accommodate all the pupils. A teacher in one hamlet taught in an old sheepfold, that in another village in a stable that also served as his lodging. In the public schools of the Ardèche, half the pupils were now admitted free because their families could not afford the modest monthly fee.[112]

The region still had an embarrassingly high number of conscripts who turned out to be illiterate. In 1859 one official lamented "entire villages in which not a single person with the most basic elements of primary instruction can be found. A great many of them naively say that they can read, but only the missal at Mass." In 1864 the Ardèche stood at sixty-seventh of eighty-five departments in literacy, with more than half the population still illiterate.[113]

In 1860 the Ministry of Public Instruction asked countryside schoolteachers what they required for their schools, their pupils, and themselves. Some of the responses were predictably formulaic, a few singing the praises of the emperor, his concern for his people, and so on, as if their posts depended upon it (they may have). Most tried to put themselves in the best possible light, struggling heroically against all odds to accomplish their mission. Teachers expressed considerable pride in their chosen métier, but all hinted broadly that the minimum salary of six hundred francs conferred "little of the dignity that commands respect, and the independence vis-à-vis the parents of the pupils, which we cannot do without."[114] Some parents preferred not to send their children to school rather than admit that they fell into the category of "indigents." However, the establishment of a minimum salary had the probably predictable result of discouraging other families from paying anything, hoping that officials somehow would come up with the money.[115]

The teacher in Antraigues asked how "can we inspire the children with the respect that they should have for school itself?" while teaching in "schoolhouses built for another purpose, often too small, unhealthy, and always badly lighted, ventilated, laid out, and situated. Yesterday, one danced and swore in the building; today it serves as a school." In nearby Vogüé, the school consisted of a small (little more than twelve by thirty feet), stuffy room for fifty pupils, with only three small windows, and it was so dark, in part because the château of the Vogüé family blotted out the sun, that the teacher had to light an oil lamp in the early morning and late in the afternoon. The temperature inside could reach almost a hundred degrees during the summer. Many teachers noted the lack of maps needed to "familiarize them with the region in which they live." One teacher asked how he could earn the respect of the community to which he was assigned if he lived so miserably. After all, if the most educated person in most villages lived in such conditions, the advantages of reading and writing were hardly evident for all to see.[116]

Teachers depended on the goodwill of the mayor and municipal council, as well as on the village priest. One teacher spoke for many of his colleagues, facing "often divergent expectations, even the caprices of the mayor, village priest, cantonal educational delegates, and placed under the arbitrary authority of the primary school inspector and the prefect. . . . [A]lmost everywhere [the teacher] lives in open or hidden struggle with one or another of the communal authorities, always fearing the departmental administration that can strike him down at any moment without any warning or appeal because of some calumnious invention." However, despite village intrigue, lay teachers during the Second Empire got on well enough with mayors. Many served as municipal secretaries, conscientiously copying the minutes of meetings with the kind of clear, even elegant penmanship that still is a source of pride for French primary education.[117]

In Balazuc, as elsewhere, the two schools began to make a difference. The dramatic rise in the percentage of bridegrooms who could read by the mid-1840s certainly reflects some success. But there was a long way to go. In 1857, 34 of 107 adults who signed a list promising to help improve the girls' school did so with an X (32 percent). In 1872, of the 817 inhabitants of Balazuc, almost half could neither read nor write. In 1874, 8 of 9 brides were illiterate, and when the bride could sign, the groom could not. Many of the living parents could not sign, but all the witnesses in the nine marriages could.[118] In any case, the municipal council's determination to find a better location for both schools reflected Balazuc's increased identification with, pride in, and growing recognition of the importance of its schools in providing a minimum education for village children. The school became in many ways the principal point of entry of the state and the nation into the village. The municipal council's increasing commitment to provide what slim resources it could and to petition the state for more reflected its own integration into the framework of the nation-state.

The War on the Language of Everyday Life

In *The Tour of France by Two Children*, the popular little book published in 1877, André and Julien arrive at a small farm near the Rhône where they observe part of the silk harvest. They feel isolated and alone, because they understand nothing that is spoken among the adults. When the children return from school, Julien shouts to André, "These children should know French, because they go to school. What good fortune! Now we can all talk together." When little Julien asks his brother why all the people in the region do not speak French, André replies, "It's because they don't all go to school. But in a few years, it will no longer be like this, because everyone in France will speak the language of the nation."[119] This was certainly not yet the case in Balazuc, where patois remained the language of daily life. In 1801 the departmental *Annuaire* had identified patois with resistance (implicitly that of many village curés) to "the new institutions." In its view, bringing "civilization" to a great part of the Ardèche would depend on the schoolteachers."[120]

In 1855 the priest of one village had complained that his parishioners could not understand him in church because "you have to speak to them in patois."[121] Did Jean-Mathieu Gibert and his immediate successors bring French to Balazuc? During the Revolution the Jacobins had identified French with progress. The *Annuaire* had complained, "[I]t makes us sad to see even in the largest communes children subject to the ineptitude of teachers, almost all of whom know absolutely nothing about the most rudimentary elements of the French language."[122] Priests gave sermons and judges interrogated in patois to be understood at all. The vast majority of the population still spoke patois, although they had no reason to consider themselves backward for that fact. At a minimum, teachers gradually brought bilingualism.

Even if state-sponsored primary education, in principle to be taught in the French language, increasingly represented the imposition of state strictures but also, gradually, of opportunity, French was not necessarily the language of instruction.[123] Most Ardéchois who knew French used it only when speaking with outsiders. A visitor noted that "women show even more repugnance than men to use this language." The official report on primary education in the Ardèche in 1855 stated unequivocally that in the countryside, "patois is still unfortunately the language of daily life. French is understood, to be sure, by all the population, but a great proportion remains unable to speak it, except the new generation that for the past twenty-five years has assiduously attended primary school." The parish clergy may have sometimes used missals in French but had the children recite in patois.[124] This obviously did not condemn them to eternal backwardness, despite the views of many officials. Even in Aubenas, one of the largest towns in the Ardèche and a major market, patois was still very much in use in 1849. Many peasants claimed not to understand French in order, logically enough, to dispense with further questions. Naturally, the outsider complained that he had to pay particular attention in order to understand the French spoken in the region "because they seem to have taken care to retain the pronunciation and accent of the Midi." Yet "progress" as the French state defined it came only very slowly. At mid-century the prefect estimated the percentage of men and women who could read and write French at about 40 (though barely 8 in the mountains). Almost all the teachers in the Bas-Vivarais were from the Ardèche, and most from the southern part. There is no reason to think that even as they taught the French language, they, like their predecessors, did not often speak in patois to be understood. The struggle between French and patois went on.[125]

Upper-class urban condescension already rang out in the thirteenth century toward patois, judged "an incomprehensible and vulgar language." Another, from the sixteenth century: "the way of speaking, judged inferior, of a rural locality." The word *patte* (paw) forms part of the etymology of patois, lending an animalistic resonance. Even the *Dictionnaire languedocien-français* published in 1820 began by defining patois as "a general term applied to the different crude and rustic jargons spoken by the lower people." Even today it is regarded as "an essentially oral linguistic system, utilized in a relatively small and defined area (generally rural), and perceived by even its users as inferior to the official language."[126]

Balazuc's longtime priest the abbé Chareyre was, like many priests in the region, from the mountains. He would have had to adapt to the patois of the Bas-Vivarais, based on Languedocien Occitan, in order to be really understood. But this he would have done with ease. Many clergy seemed content if pupils learned to read French while continuing to speak patois.[127]

It has been said that a language is a dialect with a powerful army. At the time of the French Revolution, perhaps almost half the population of France did not speak French in daily life. They spoke dialects of Catalan, Basque, German, Breton, Flemish, and a variety of patois descended from the langue d'oc and other spoken languages. During the French Revolution, the ex-abbé Grégoire insisted that a French citizen needed to speak French, and he submitted a report in June 1794 with thunder in its title: "On the Necessity and Means of

Annihilating Patois and Universalizing Usage of the French Language."[128] The advent of the Third Republic, which would seek to reduce clerical influence and secularize schools, would give the Church a reason not to be necessarily eager to see the faithful abandon patois for French, the language of the increasingly anticlerical state. To many among the clergy, French lay rural teachers appeared to be forceful representatives of the state, bringing nationalism through the French language. In some sense, then, the school seemed to villagers to be imposed from outside, presenting opportunities but also challenging the influence of the Church.

Yet, in fact, primary school teachers in villages like Balazuc may not have relentlessly waged war on local languages. Teachers were drawn from the regions in which they taught—true of the Ardèche—and were often obliged to speak the local dialects or patois in order to make themselves understood (and with which many were more comfortable). Moreover, they also continued to affirm the primacy of local geography and thus inevitably customs as well, in order to help their charges place village and region in the context of France.[129]

The teachers of the Ardèche who responded to the national survey (or whose reports have survived) emphasized the importance of teaching their pupils to speak French, the expected, routinized response. The teacher of Désaignes thus included among his wish list of needs "a covered courtyard where the teacher can watch the children and oblige them to speak their proper language; with time, they will learn to express their thoughts in French and to abandon their patois, which is often so crude." Those who read such reports may well have imagined that the last child who had used patois really was obliged at recess to carry a misshapen coin, passing it on to the next child who slipped into patois. Of course, a teacher could hardly have admitted that he stood by as his pupils "lapsed" into their own language or that he frequently shifted into patois with them and that many parents would have been hard pressed to speak to him in French and in any case would not have had any compelling reason to want to do so. French made progress gradually, but in many places only very slowly. A local writer noted in 1906: "We are witnessing at this moment a spectacle without analogy in human history: the gradual substitution of French for the patois of the Midi."[130] But this was to be a long process, one that lasted well into the twentieth century.

In the meantime the struggle to get children to the schools went on. Teachers were expected to count the number of pupils in their school on June 18, several weeks before the summer vacation, and on December 18 of each year—still the case today—and the number in attendance was significantly higher on the threshold of dark winter than on the edge of summer. Many families believed that their children had learned enough at the time of their first communion and viewed subsequent schooling as a waste of time. One teacher complained, "Most of the children arrive at the school without anything that they will need—books, paper, ink, or pens. And when we tell them to get them, to purchase them, they look confused, and reply, 'Papa and Mama don't have a cent to give me!'"

Farming families in Balazuc counted on the labor of even the smallest children to tend animals, haul stones, weed, and do myriad other tasks. The silkworm harvest in the spring required large and small hands, and at that time the school simply emptied out in Balazuc. The grain and grape harvests also took children away from school. Several teachers were docked two months' pay for having simply closed their schools during this period in recognition of the *fait accompli*. Moreover, the *école buissionnière*—children playing hooky, leaving the house for school but instead going off into the bushes or woods to play—continued in Balazuc, particularly for children living in Audon and Servière on the right bank of the Ardèche when heavy rains fell and the river rose. Indeed in 1853 the subprefect claimed that one of the goals of Balazuc's boys' school was to "remove children from the streets and public places."[131]

Gradually the number of school absences dropped in Balazuc's schools and those of other villages. For example, in October 1882 the list of those pupils absent more than four days included Louis Cardinal, who simply did not show up; Simon Lango, "who was absent all month—is a vagabond"; Louis Marcel, who was "held back to work" all month; and Prosper Constant, who spent October working in a factory elsewhere. Jules Fromentin missed one day because the river was too high and twelve other days because he stayed home to work. When the river could not be safely crossed, the children of Servière and Audon stayed home, seven on October 19 and five on October 27–28 (two others remained at home as well but gave work as the reason for their absences). Reports from the first years of the twentieth century reveal the same patterns. Some children stayed home frequently to watch the animals or help with the harvests (or, at the appropriate time, to prepare for their first communions).[132]

Some parents may still have remained unconvinced about the necessity of schooling, following the peasant adage "Words sow in the wind, the hoe digs the furrow."[133] However, the income of teachers in Balazuc had reached a respectable level by the early 1880s. One note added to Duchier's dossier augured trouble ahead: He was marked as being "faced with the persecutions of the curé."[134] But without question, the corner had been turned. For the first time now every child spent at least a couple of years in school, as Balazuc's lay school increasingly became part of the village's identity.

Schools for the Republic

With the advent of the Third Republic (1870–1940), republican political institutions were henceforth gradually affirmed because, as elections proved, the majority of the population wanted a republic. This was not yet the case in Balazuc and much of the Ardèche, as we shall see in the next chapter. Lay schoolteachers thereafter took on the responsibility of forming good republican citizens. For the next four decades France's schools became a battleground in the struggle between republican anticlericals and the Church, some of whose most faithful adherents struggled against lay schools because they identified them with republican godlessness. In this respect, a newly appointed inspector was quick to say that he viewed the Ardèche not as "an exile or disgrace" but rather as a challenge that could be met; his predecessors, "for the most part, had had only one preoccupation, to get out as quickly as possible."[135] Inspectors found "their work in the schools uniquely impeded by the preponderance of the religious orders." Furthermore, some lay teachers ("I won't even speak of the teachers of the congregations who are invulnerable to our authority virtually everywhere") escaped the supervision of academic inspectors. However, a new generation of qualified, certified teachers moved into the schools of the Ardèche. They included graduates of the *école normale*, whose training encompassed the history and geography of France, both republican staples. Subsidies to buy, build, or repair schools now came more frequently. Paying pupils were still absent a quarter of the time, and those attending school at no charge a third of the time. By the first years of the republic, six of every seven children of school age attended school in the Ardèche.[136]

The Ferry Laws (a series of acts passed by the Chamber of Deputies between 1879 and 1886 and named after the anticlerical politician Jules Ferry, who sponsored them) made primary education free and obligatory. The wrenching process of the laicization of public schools began, the goal being to eliminate religious teaching in them. In the meantime teachers from the religious orders still ran more than half (54 percent) of the Ardèche's schools, provided 71 percent of the teachers, and taught 62 percent of children in school. Separating the paying pupils from the indigent, some, particularly in towns, called the part of the school in which the latter sat the communal school or the school of the poor. Teaching the way they always had, they used the Bible and the lives of the saints to teach reading and writing. The religious orders tried to undermine lay schools, and petitions from some villages still asked that a lay teacher be replaced by someone from a religious order.[137]

In 1881, Balazuc borrowed money to purchase a small house not far from the Tour Carrée next to the boys' school in order to increase its size. A single mulberry tree stood in the middle of the small patch of land that came with it. The two small buildings, when combined, provided a partially covered courtyard and a cistern. The schoolroom was small, about twenty-five feet by fifteen, with a ceiling less than ten feet high. But for the first time Balazuc's school had sufficient ventilation and lighting. Jacques Ozil's own lodging, which took up the floor above the school, included four rooms and a kitchen but offered no garden. Soon Ozil won transfer to a school near his home, and Fournet, of "an unhappy and sour disposition," glared at the village children.[138]

In the meantime the girls' school at the Portail d'Été had fifty-one pupils. Again the gap between the number counted in December and that in June had narrowed. Its single room on the first floor was even smaller than that of the boys and was insufficiently ventilated and lighted. It offered no toilets, or covered courtyard, and no books other than those used directly for teaching.[139]

Two years later, amid ongoing laicizations of public schools, the girls' school of Balazuc appeared on a list to be secularized. With this in mind, "the partisans of religious education" had begun raising money to start a private school in the village. For its part, the municipal council stressed that because "religious belief is very developed in Balazuc," laicization should be put off as long as possible. To many Catholics, it seemed anathema to secularize the schools, taking down the crucifixes from the wall and replacing statues of the Virgin Mary with busts of Marianne, the female image of the republic, considered a whore by her detractors.[140]

Elvina Mathevet, who had already begun teaching Balazuc's girls, had the right to stay on as long as she could teach there if she remained "neutral" in teaching matters. Upon her death thirteen years later, in 1898, the girls' school was laicized, despite the opposition of many parents. The first lay teacher, Marie Augustine Bérard, received a national decoration at the end of the year because she faced considerable opposition to lay instruction.[141]

The girls' school had thirty-five pupils at the time of its laicization, but early in 1899 only sixteen remained. Indeed a private school taught by nuns had been started to serve the Catholic cause, and it enrolled twenty-five girls in the 1899–1900 school year. The following year its enrollment dropped to seventeen (and twelve in the summer months). With the conservative Marius Mouraret having been elected mayor in 1900, the council voted to allow the Convent of St.-Joseph of Aubenas to take over the private school, recalling services rendered by the sisters in Balazuc (perhaps teaching catechism since the secularization of the girls' school). The council insisted that families should have the freedom to provide their children with the education of their choice. However, to the subprefect, the private school represented "a permanent danger. . . . [T]he girls' school that has been laicized for two years has to struggle against a well-outfitted private school" taught by a nun.[142]

In anticipation of the laicization of the girls' school, the municipal council in 1897 had decided to build a school building that would provide substantially more classroom space and courtyards for both schools and suitable lodging for the teachers. The municipality purchased cultivable land interspersed with mulberry trees, east of the village center.[143]

In 1903, Balazuc's new school opened, although the building was not completed until two years later. Two years later thirty-three boys and twenty-five girls attended, the boys' school on one side, the girls' on the other, with separate courtyards in back. Two apartments of four rooms each for the teachers occupied the second floor. With "R[épublique] F[rançaise]" etched above the doors, the new school embodied the heyday of the prewar Third Republic.[144] The private school did not live to see the separation of church and state in 1905.

Seventy years after the Guizot Law, Balazuc finally had a proper school, constructed for that purpose. A stove, the honor of lighting of which went to the older students, provided minimal heating, with the students providing the wood. The teacher, representative of the republic, was feared but well respected. Some teachers even won affection. Few now doubted that a primary education was essential to get on in life. "Go to school, my Paul," instructed one father, "apply yourself and work hard and later you will be someone, the lazy ones never get anywhere."[145] The establishment of a certificate of primary study to be awarded to those pupils who completed their schooling and passed the test presented children and their parents with a goal.

Balazuc's teachers stood in front of their pupils, next to the blackboard and charts and drawings of various animals, the tables or desks arranged by the year of schooling. The lay teacher drilled his charges on the rules of French grammar, which then, as now, had to be learned by heart and then applied. A pupil who failed an exercise miserably might suffer the indignity of wearing a cloth dunce cap on which was inscribed "donkey." One man remembered having "to write down a dictated text under the implacable stare of the teacher who walked between the students holding a threatening wooden ruler," barking out "the seven nouns that take an 'x' in the plural form: *bijou, caillou, chou, genou, hibou, joujou, pou.*" The last—lice—was appropriate; the pupils were instructed to wear their hair short for some protection against their irritating presence (appropriately, the doctor inspecting schools in the canton of Vallon in 1880 was named Dr. Dupoux).[146]

The war against patois and local pronunciation probably continued, at least in the reports of the teachers. We can easily imagine the difficulty (indeed uselessness, except perhaps in preparation for the dreaded surprise visit of the academic inspector) of trying to teach children in Balazuc in the fin-de-siècle period not only to abandon patois but also to leave behind the powerful *g* added to the end of *vin* (wine) or *vent* (wind), two words that for obvious reasons pop up all the time, or prolonged on the number *vingt* (twenty). Children traced letters over and over, following the eternal rule of French primary schools that invariably still inculcates beautiful handwriting (sometimes valued more than what is written). Hard work and obedience became moral imperatives, along with admonitions against idleness and drunkenness (at a time when France seemed to be drinking itself to death). Stories read in class offered examples of the dire consequences that could follow the failure to obey, thus the importance of *bonne action*. These mottoes rang through handbooks provided the republic's teachers. A teacher was warned to avoid the "noisy diversions of the people of the village," to avoid compromising "his authority, his dignity, and his esteem." Attending the local market was fine, "but he must avoid behaving like a country person amused by the frivolities, or attracted by the trumpets, bells, and drums of itinerant musicians, or the bells, or duped by the crude farces of the clowns." The teacher should be a model of republican virtue, his or her apartment simple, clean, and "the teacher's wife [should] always [be] worthy of him."[147]

With the aid of maps, provided for Balazuc's boys' school in the late 1880s, children, almost all of whom had never been beyond their canton, learned the names of departments and their principal products or characteristics: the Nord, with its mines and beets, the Gironde and Côte d'or and their fine wines, the Bouches-du-Rhône and Var, with Marseille and Toulon, ports open toward North Africa, and the amputated departments of Alsace and Lorraine awaiting liberation. The children memorized the names of foreign countries and, during the heyday of the "New Imperialism" beginning in the mid-1880s, nodded in silent appreciation that an increasing number of far-off, seemingly exotic places now carried the color of France on the map of the world. With patriotic images of the republic omnipresent, as Marianne elbowed Mary out of the public schools, pupils were instructed to revere *la belle France*, memorizing the names and dates of Napoleonic victories and colonial "pacifications." Ernest Lavisse provided the history: "You should love France, because nature has made it beautiful, and because history has made her grand." Balazuc's school library had sixty-nine books, most in "good condition." Several obvious themes leap from the shelves: patriotism (*La Patrie, Our Forgotten Heroes, The War of 1870–71, The French Flag, The Revolution,* and *The Months of Joan of Arc,* which may not have lasted long on the shelves); exploring France and the world (*The Riches of France, Syria Today,* and Jules Verne's *Around the World in Eighty Days*); getting by in life (*Maintaining Hygiene, The Role of Women in Agriculture,* and *Discussions on Agriculture*); lessons for behaving properly (*The Fables of Fénelon, Practical Morality,* and *The Virtues of the People*); and appreciating France as it changes (*Social Transformation* and *Workers at Home*). Most would not be found on the shelves of a school operated by the religious orders.

The ideal curriculum in French primary schools during the last decades of the nineteenth century included instruction in optional subjects, such as linear drawing, land measuring, and elementary notions of history and geography, as well as arithmetic and some notions of physics applied to "daily life." The reality was otherwise. Like Gaul, the educational program that functioned was divided into three parts: reading, writing, and arithmetic. Girls also learned needlework. The Ardèche's teachers emphasized the importance of teaching their pupils the value of proper attention to agriculture (a lesson that they barely needed). Several cited the need for gardens where the pupils could practice what their teachers preached, perhaps an extension of the small gardens the teachers wanted for themselves so that they could grow their own vegetables. One included mutual assistance in his teaching, seeking "To inculcate successfully in their minds the concept of mutual aid that forms the basis of society." At a recent evocation of the history of primary schools in St. Lys, near Toulouse, the representative guiding principle selected to be presented on the blackboard was "If we help each other, the weight of hardship will be lighter."

Children learned to add and subtract by counting animals and vegetables—that made exquisite sense in the countryside—with more complicated calculations based on more or less real-life situations, such as the monthly expenses for fertilizer or the anticipated earnings of a farmhand: "A farm worker earns two francs a day. How many francs will he earn in a month of twenty-six days?" (Sunday was carefully subtracted as the day of rest.) They learned the importance of hygiene, perhaps taking the advice to be sure to wash their feet once a week in the summer and twice a month in the winter. During recess, they dashed around playing hide-and-seek, played games with marbles and pebbles, teased the hesitant or slow, sang songs (usually more fun than the ritual singing of such ditties as "Work Gives Joy," and whispered about or tried to guess at the facts of life). Throughout all this, the village appeared "as a vital node, a sort of heart, in more or less easy relation to other places."[148]

Balazuc's new school building, containing both the boys' and the girls' school, helped define and celebrate the republic. In Balazuc, the Ardèche, as well as many other places in France, it had not been easy. The school helped bring violent national political battles to the village, culminating in the separation of church and state in 1905.

SIX

Contentious Village Politics

WRITING IN 1879, ALBIN MAZON, PROLIFIC ARDÉCHOIS historian and raconteur, noted a new intensity of political debate in the villages of the Vivarais. He did not like it at all. Angered by having been reproached for being clerical, and at the risk "of being attacked by our modern Jupiters," he groused that "Politics has been everywhere for the last several years, especially in an infinity of places and in people where politics should not be—and no one would think that the Vivarais could have remained immune to such contagion. Today there is no longer a hamlet where one does not find its rebellious or grotesque faction, and no one who has not to some extent been touched by such contact." To his mind, the republic was not the regime "the most appropriate for our morals, traditions, and national temperament. . . . A country does not live from politics, but from bread and fertile activity. The "*Marseillaise*" is fine, but it will not feed anyone. Politics is a strong liquor that must not be abused at the risk of distaste or even death. Look at the divisions that politics has created in our towns and even to the bottom of the most humble villages." Improving agriculture seemed a better use of time than reading about politics in newspapers, "dangerous" instruments "which most often deceive political sheep and, in any case, waste considerable energy and national wealth." Coming down from the pure air and calm waters of his preferred mountains, he found the lower elevations of the Bas-Vivarais corrupted by "the pébrine, phylloxera, and politics, these three ferocious enemies of the silkworm, the vineyards, and human good sense."[1]

Quarrels with the Priest

The French Revolution had left the Church disorganized, without a sufficient number of priests, who seem to have been less able than the curés of the Ancien Régime. Many were barely educated. An entire generation of faithful had received only irregular religious instruction or none at all. During the Restoration, ecclesiastical authorities encouraged increasing the number of primary schools, which they viewed as being a means of teaching children the Bible and catechism. The number of religious congregations in the Vivarais expanded rapidly (the diocese of Viviers leading the way in France). The region underwent a particularly marked return to vigorous Catholicism during the Restoration. The new bishop arriving in Viviers in 1841 had found "faith deeply rooted in the diocese with few exceptions." With Easter observance at more than 90 percent in the countryside and 64 percent in towns, he was proud that his new diocese was one of the most faithful in France.[2]

Although the village curé interpreted God's word on earth, he was nonetheless expected to conform to some traditions of the community, or he risked becoming an outsider.[3] Tensions between village priests and the young men of the community were nothing new. The tradition that the young men of the village organize festivals had probably begun centuries earlier, like the "abbeys of young men" in early modern times (the *comité des fêtes*, primarily made up of young men and women, today carries on the tradition in the village). Balazuc's patron saint's day (*fête votive*), the feast day of Ste.-Madeleine, was celebrated on a Sunday in July. Even more, the festivity of carnival could test a priest's patience to the limit.[4]

The case of Balazuc's Abbé Salel demonstrates that the priest could quickly become an outsider, for all his influence. Balazuc had a religious confraternity, that of St.-Antoine, which may have dated from the fifteenth century. One of its religious functions in the village had been to collect about twenty sacks of wheat and ten to twelve hectoliters of wine. Eight days before the feast of St.-Antoine, the wheat was ground up, and loaves of two or three pounds were baked. Before they were distributed, the priest was to bless them. A cow was then slaughtered, and the confraternity held its annual banquet. For this reason, the confraternity had become known as the Confraternity of the Cow. The village priest, however, presided over the meal, during which the wine was consumed, and the subsequent distribution of food to the poor.[5]

In 1837 all did not go well. For some years the banquets had led "to considerable excesses." Salel, a thirty-one-year-old priest, had come to Balazuc in 1834. He decided to hold the line: "In my capacity, I had to intervene to put an end to this state of things." From the pulpit, following directions from the bishop, he had warned his parishioners as carnival season neared that if these "excesses" did not cease, he would refuse to bless the bread.[6]

Such a threat did not go over well in the village. A few parishioners reminded the priest that his predecessors had always cooperated with the confraternity. Then two members—"in the name of the others"—went to the presbytery and demanded that the priest return chandeliers that the confraternity had presented to the church. The conversation between the curé and his two late-night visitors heated up. The visitors insulted the priest. Late that night someone hurled rocks against the presbytery, and at about four or five in the morning two shots were fired at the house, leaving traces of lead. Five days later more rocks were hurled in the night against the residence of the frightened but intransigent priest. Someone tore out the gate to the presbytery's small garden behind the church and hurled it into the Ardèche River, far below. The priest beat a hasty retreat and took refuge with members of his family in another village, "following the advice of my superiors, in view of the hatred several nasty people have for me, manifested by several acts of savagery."

Judicial authorities conducted an investigation. The subprefect ordered Balazuc's mayor to forbid further gatherings of the confraternity. Père Salel later returned.[7] Believing that the threat to the priest had been exaggerated, the subprefect tactfully reduced the charges against the unknown transgressors to "the breaking of a gate" and a "nighttime disturbance." He decided that the shots had merely been directed at a window and corridor in order to scare the priest (that they did). The people of Balazuc lapsed into collective silence about the incident. The confraternity again held its annual celebration. However, the prefect dismissed Dours as mayor in 1840, and the bishop dissolved the confraternity the next year. The confraternity's house behind the presbytery became the property of the commune. It was a small, unnoticed step toward more sustained conflict over the Church in Balazuc and in France.[8]

The Republic Comes to the Village

The French Revolution helped shift the focus of territorial allegiance from the parish to the commune. This change in itself challenged the influence of the priest. Even if the Bourbon Restoration (1814–30) was based on an alliance between altar and throne, the restored monarchy maintained many of the Revolution's changes, including territorial demarcations (departments, arrondissements, cantons, communes). However, the role of the village parish priest was effaced during subsequent regimes. With the increase in the responsibilities of the mayor and the growing importance of the state-sponsored school, the Catholic Church believed itself challenged by local lay authority.

Signs of political division, or even preoccupation, were rare in Balazuc between the end of the Revolution and the Revolution of 1848. However, after the Revolution of 1830, Alexandre Tastevin, loyal to the Restoration, resigned as mayor, and the new Orléanist prefect dismissed his deputy Mollier, who had been conspicuous by his absences from recent meetings. He replaced them with two men

whose fathers had served as mayor and as officers in the National
Guard during the revolutionary period. Two other members of the
municipal council resigned, refusing to take the oath of allegiance to
the new regime.[9]

The July Monarchy (1830–48) granted the right to vote to males
paying a minimum of taxes. Municipal electors (who could select the
municipal council) in Balazuc ranged from the wealthiest men in the
village, such as Tastevin and Antoine Auzas, who paid 360 and 213
francs respectively, down to Joseph Auzas, who paid about 21 francs
in taxes. In 1840 fifty men were municipal electors in Balazuc, but
only five had the right to vote in legislative elections by virtue of paying 200 francs or more in taxes. They included Auzas and Teyssier,
whose father had purchased the mill as a *biens nationaux* during the
Revolution.[10]

In 1832 the prefect named Teyssier mayor. Here too links
between support for the Revolution and the July Monarchy may be
seen in the context of municipal political life. That all this had
begun to take a toll on the council may be suggested, but no more,
by the prefect's elimination of three from the council for having
missed three meetings in a row "without legitimate motives."[11]
Dours replaced Teyssier in 1838, but he lasted only two years, as we
have seen. The prefect then named Jean-Antoine Tastevin, son of
Alexandre, to be mayor. But Tastevin immediately resigned, citing
"grave personal reasons." Dours declined to serve. The municipal
council therefore wrote to express its confidence in Tastevin, "who
enjoys the general esteem of all of his co-citizens." Despite his
father's identification with the Bourbon Restoration, the younger
Tastevin still seemed a natural appointment. However, his resignation and that of his successor brought Teyssier back to serve again in
1844, when he was sixty-eight years old.[12] Thus mayors came and
went, leaving little trace on the historical record beyond their signatures on the municipal minutes.

The Revolution of 1848 brought the republic and mass politics to
the village of Balazuc. It began as a political revolution in Paris, but
it still must be put into the context of the "hungry forties."[13] The
potato blight and harvest failure of 1846–47 brought hardship to the

Ardèche (as did another flood in September 1846). The contraction of demand for Lyonnais silk hurt the Bas-Vivarais, in particular (as had the economic crisis in the United States in 1836–37). Many peasants who had taken out loans in the hope of capitalizing on the silk boom could not pay them back. From several cantons came demands for mortgage banks that would offer reasonable lending rates, reflecting the oppression of "the local usurer, operating as well, and, further away, the capitalist usurer, the middleman" in the silk industry. The owners of the small factories for silk throwing along the rivers of the region borrowed money from merchants in Lyon at 9 or 10 percent, loans that could be called back at any time.

Within the silk industry, unfair practices and artificially low prices were widespread. The middlemen put the squeeze on the owners of silk-throwing factories, who in turn took it out on the spinners (mechanized or family). At the bottom stood the peasant household producing raw silk, forced by circumstances to sell at what seemed to be an unfairly low price imposed by the middleman. Seizures of property increased by more than half in the arrondissement of Largentière. Hatred of those who loaned money, above all, usurers, and of the *fisc* (tax apparatus) recalled the mood that had given way to the revolt of the Armed Masks in the previous century. Early in 1848, amid an unstable market for cocoons and raw silk, "a deplorable misery" reigned in the Bas-Vivarais. The silkworm harvest was abundant, but prices for cocoons fell by half. The bishop of Viviers lamented, "[I]ndigence invades us from all sides," and called on each parish to establish a committee for charity.[14]

It was in this setting that the February Revolution of 1848 brought universal manhood suffrage and hope to the Ardèche, despite difficulties. Those men from Balazuc who wanted to vote in the legislative elections that April had to travel to Ruoms to do so, a trek of a couple of hours there and back. However, many mayors failed to respond to insistent letters asking that they submit the required list of electors. In any case, letters from many communes took ten to twelve days to come back at times, instead of three to four in normal conditions.[15]

Along with France as a whole, the Ardèche elected moderates to

the National Assembly in April 1848. The anticlerical First Republic
of the Revolution did not stand well in the collective memory of the
Vivarais. Most of the population seemed determined that the Second
would be "reassuring," guaranteeing property and religious freedom,
or it would not be at all. The year 1848 also marked the reemergence
of the Catholic Church as a political force intent on using its influence among peasants to defend its terrain.[16] The subsequent struggle
between conservative Catholicism and increasingly anticlerical
republicans shaped the politics of the Third Republic. In the meantime the Ardèche returned conservatives and moderates and only one
committed republican to the Assembly. In the presidential election
of December 1848, easily won by Louis Napoleon Bonaparte
(Napoleon's nephew), just 67 of 232 eligible voters in Balazuc bothered to vote.[17]

The first municipal council of the Second Republic was elected in
Balazuc on July 30, 1848, with a second ballot necessary the next day
in order to complete the election of twelve members.[18] Five men of
the last municipal council of the July Monarchy were elected in the
young republic. At the end of August the new municipal council
gathered to elect the mayor and deputy mayor. "Citizen" André
Teyssier was elected mayor with seven votes on a second ballot,
defeating Jean Charousset by two votes. As the Charousset family was
later known for its staunch republicanism and anticlericalism during
the Third Republic, national politics perhaps had something to do
with the outcome. Claude Mollier, whose attachment to the republic
later became clear, was elected deputy mayor, also with seven votes.
With Teyssier's death several months later, the prefect named the
young Mollier to serve as mayor.[19]

In sharp contrast with the first legislative elections of the republic, the Ardèche returned six strong republicans among eight representatives in May 1849. Certainly the role of Protestant voters
contributed to the left's success in the Ardèche. So too did rapid
Montagnard (democratic socialists of the left) political organization
and propaganda. During the past decades the expansion of the silk
industry in the countryside had integrated villages like Balazuc into
the larger economy, and despite Balazuc's relative isolation, villagers

certainly became aware of first republican and then democratic social-ist ideals.[20] The Montagnards called for the suppression of the disas-trous forty-five-centimes tax that the young republican government had foolishly imposed. Opposition to the political influence of the clergy also found resonance. Moreover, the division of the right between republican conservatives and monarchists helped the cause of the left. Yet Balazuc, Ruoms, and Pradons voted more conserva-tively than did most of the Ardèche. In addition, the attempt by the Montagnards to make primary school teachers the vanguard of lay progress at the expense of clerical influence failed with Louis Napoleon's systematic dismantling of the very institutions of the republic over which he presided.[21] The electoral law of May 31, 1850, reduced the number of voters in France by about a third, eliminating those who had not resided in the same commune for two years. The number of voters in Balazuc fell from 255 to 158 eligible in July 1850 and only 143 in January 1851.[22]

In response to the march of the repression, the summer of 1851 brought demonstrations of Montagnard solidarity in the Ardèche. At village festivals, confrontations between revelers wearing red ties and belts (illegal because the color evoked the Jacobins of the Revolution) and gendarmes occurred in several villages, notably Salavas, Laurac, Orgnac, and Grospierres. This led the prefect to believe that the Ardèche should be declared in a state of siege.[23]

That summer Balazuc seemed to be moving to the left. In the by-election of March 1850, the village gave the republican candidate a comfortable majority, although the Ardèche as a whole elected a monarchist. When in March 1851 the subprefect sought to assess the possible outcome if an election were then held in the canton of Balazuc, Lagorce, Salavas, and Vallon would offer a majority of votes to "democratic candidates." Of these four communes, all but Balazuc had strong Protestant minorities.[24]

Vigier, a police spy sent to the arrondissement (along with two others, one for each district), claimed that a radical secret society had a hundred members in Balazuc, along with seven other communes in the canton. Joseph Leyris, the rural guard, later testified that a secret society had indeed existed in Balazuc for some time, with about fifty members, a more realistic number, its meetings organized by Victor Queyroche (or Cayroche), Antoine Daumas, and Joseph Exbrayat. Rumors that there were secret signs of communication and stock-piled weapons always emanated from sources supposedly "worthy of all confidence."[25]

We can imagine issues that would radicalize at least some of the people of a poor, isolated village in the middle of the nineteenth century. Peasant ideology was very much a mix of local issues, wider political concern and commitments, and vague hope for a government that would bring social justice. Seigneurialism, obligations that had been owed to nobles during the Ancien Régime, some peasants having been subject to their "justice," still lingered in the collective memory. Michelet recalled seeing in the Vivarais "those awful black donjons that for so long collected their tribute from a poor people." In some places peasants still referred to state taxes as the taille and to money asked by the Church as the *dîme*, and some feared a return of the real ones.[26] An increase in literacy may have also played a role. Several of the Balazuc Montagnards had been pupils of Jean-Mathieu Gibert and his successors.

There were other signs of Montagnard militancy in Balazuc. In April 1851, while discussing the problems of finding a suitable location for the boys' school, the council cited "the obvious drawbacks faced by the school that is often bothered by immoral and seditious songs being sung by the people who frequent the establishment." Montagnard propaganda made much of the need to increase the opportunity for education in the countryside. Balazuc after all had no school at all in 1849 and 1850 because no teacher could be found.[27]

Fishing was another issue. The peasants of the Vivarais loved to hunt and fish.[28] Most hunters and fishermen were so poor that whatever they shot, trapped, or fished provided something consequential for dinner (much more recently a man in Balazuc, speaking of his wedding, recalled that it had been the first day of fishing season, as if he had wasted it by getting married). In October 1851 the municipal council of Balazuc unanimously expressed its view that the Ardèche River should be opened to fishing between the Pont d'Aubenas and Ruoms. It asked that a prefectoral decree, various royal ordinances, and a law from 1829 dealing with fishing be over-turned in the interest of "justice," sounding very much like the vil-lagers who had gathered together in the church to draw up the *cahiers de doléances* in 1789. Fishing rights could contribute to the "solace of the poor classes who are so numerous in this region. Without other means of subsistence, they are happy even to have a fish to give to their children, who are deprived of everything."[29]

That fall Montagnard secret societies were solidifying their links in the Bas-Vivarais, and the municipal council of Balazuc focused on an issue that made some sense to the poor of *la Belle*, whether expressed in *patois* or, more rarely, in French, the "Democratic and Social Republic." A peasant from Salavas may have said it best. He claimed that with the victory of *la Belle*, "we wouldn't have any for-est guard, any fishing guard, or a priest. We would lower taxes, we would divide the commons."[30]

Antoine Daumas, former tobacconist, had fallen under official sus-picion during the summer of 1851. Vallon's policeman, asked to pro-vide information on Daumas, admitted that it was difficult for someone not from Balazuc to come up with anything on him. Here Balazuc's relative isolation helped the Montagnards. Anyone show-ing up asking questions about someone from Balazuc would in all likelihood simply be ignored as a meddling outsider, policeman or not.[31]

Louis Napoleon Bonaparte ordered the Ardèche placed under a state of siege beginning in October. The well-organized (and widely predicted) coup d'état finally came on December 2, 1851. Great resis-tance followed, in Paris, but above all in the Midi and parts of the cen-ter, the largest national insurrection in nineteenth-century France in which more than a hundred thousand people took part. The secret societies of the Bas-Vivarais, based in perhaps as many as fifty com-munes, spearheaded the local insurrection in defense of the republic.[32]

During the night of December 6–7, a column of Montagnards formed in villages in the canton of Vallon, their numbers drawn from Vallon itself, Lagorce, Ruoms, Salavas, Labastide-de-Virac, and other villages. The band from Vallon (perhaps encouraged by rumors that a camp of five thousand insurgents at Chomérac was preparing to march on Privas and that Nîmes had fallen to Montagnards) picked up men along the way. Similar smaller groups formed around Les Vans. Probably about three in the morning, insurgents, presumably from the hamlet of Lagorce and perhaps from Pradons, arrived in Balazuc. Joseph Leyris, Balazuc's rural guard, heard noise in the streets: "[T]hey were pounding on doors everywhere. I got up and went to see what was going on, and a hail of rocks struck my house, which was surrounded by a number of men whom I could not recognize because of the night." At about five someone fired a shot, and the men disappeared. At least six men went along, carrying hunting rifles and pitchforks. They joined several thousand other people from Lagorce and other neighboring villages in an ill-fated attempt to march on the subprefecture in Largentière, eight tough miles away.[33]

Also at about five in the morning, the column of several thousand insurgents arrived at the first bridge of Largentière. The subprefect had been alerted to their arrival by shouts of "To arms!" echoing in the hills above town. Coming upon forty armed soldiers guarding the bridge, the Montagnards turned back, to be pursued by troops. The soldiers later claimed that they were fired upon as they chased the fleeing men: "[B]ullets whizzed by our ears, but not a man hesitated." The troops returned with twenty-three prisoners, two of whom had been wounded. "We chased the troublemakers for six miles, always at a rapid pace, we forty who set out with 3,000 of them in front of us!" They seized hunting rifles, picks, and pitchforks "with stains of blood."[34]

At the point where the road to Largentière meets the route to Joyeuse and beyond, a man on his way from his village to find a midwife claimed in retrospect to have come upon "a crowd, armed with rifles, pitchforks, and sticks, with sacks for pillage," singing in patois.[35] About two hundred of the insurgents ran across the *gras*. Arriving at the river, they gave Mollier and his little boat good business—it may have been his biggest day—or, more than likely, plunged into the cold December water to swim to the other side. Both Paul and Napoléon Eldin, Montagnard brothers, were seen crossing the river in Mollier's *bac*. Then the Eldins and many others headed up the path toward the village, passing through the Porte de

Balazuc: View from across the river from a postcard, c. 1910.

Portalas with the Tour Carrée, the medieval dungeon.
Note the mission cross in the foreground
and the remains of the ramparts.

The new church, about 1905, without the bell tower added in 1911.

Philippe Charousset, mayor of
Balazuc, 1892–1900, 1904–10,
and his wife.

Balazuc: General view.
Note the remains of the original château on the cliff, near the *église romane*,
the "new" château in the top left-hand corner, the remains (now gone)
of the ramparts running down to the river, and the large house
in the foreground, part of which served as an inn.

La Gare: Balazuc train station, about 1906.

The construction
of the bridge,
1884.

BALAZUC. — Pont sur l'Ardèche

Balazuc's bridge, about 1905.
During the storm of 1890
the surging river reached
the top of the bridge.

Rebuilding the bridge
after its destruction in
August 1944.

Valley of the Ardèche River, below Balazuc.

"La Maria," Maria Tastevin.
Photo by Guy Boyer.

A former silkworm nursery. Note
the mulberry tree in the front.
Photo by Carol Merriman.

A mulberry tree
still thrives.

Silkworms growing.

Vineyards distant from the village.

The romanesque church (*église romane*).

The *gras*, the Jurassic plateau.

Village passage with archways.

"Popaul" Gamel. Family photo.

Footpath down to the river.

The recently dubbed allée du
Théâtre ("walkway of the theater").

A *couradou*, a covered balcony.

Balazuc's school, about 1910.

Chez Paulette.

Jacques Imbertèche, Balazuc's teacher,
with former students Laura and Christopher Merriman,
and Mathieu Fruleux, and his father, Eric.

la Sablière. They then stopped at the auberge of Vianès, a place they almost certainly knew well. More than likely it was there that the political links between the hamlet of Leyris (and other parts of the vast commune of Lagorce) and Montagnards in Balazuc had been forged and maintained.

In the meantime troops occupied Vallon. By mid-month, mobile columns, like those of the Directory, undertook a show of force in the Bas-Vivarais, this time on the lookout for men of the left, not the right. Within a day or two after resistance ended, the mayor of Balazuc and other villages received a letter that did not mince words, demanding energetic obedience. As for the Montagnards, "threaten them on my behalf with terrible punishment if they try in any way to oppose the free expression of public opinion [*sic*]."[36] It would be like that.

With encouragement from Paris and the seemingly overwhelming mandate of that Napoleonic political tool, the plebiscite, the official account of the resistance by "3,000 barbarians" organized in a "vast network of secret societies" that had been preparing an insurrection became ever more lurid. Vallon's policeman regretted not being able to "execute all these scoundrels known to us today and who belong to the most abject strata of the canton of Vallon." He claimed that Balazuc, Salavas, Labastide-de-Virac, Orgnac, and other villages had provided about seven hundred men; the cantons of Les Vans, Largentière, and Joyeuse, "1,500 to 2,000 insurgents." On the road to Largentière, "the insurgents marched three across, literally covering the road . . . almost four miles filled with and blocked by them . . . these men organized into brigades complete with officers and junior officers. . . . [A]rms were abundant in their ranks, pitchforks, picks, swords, and the knives used to kill pigs." Arriving with drums, trumpets, and flags, they had forced the hesitant to follow them, promising that they could pillage and burn Largentière. Interestingly enough, the subprefect's account of the role of the forty soldiers credited with turning back the insurrection reflected the evolving myth of Saracen Balazuc: "These brave soldiers tell me that theirs was a veritable expedition launched against the Arabs!"[37]

Communes with large minorities of Protestants played a notable role in the resistance. For that reason, the long shadow of the wars of religion that began three centuries earlier has taken a key place in interpretations of the resistance. Communes with high rates of participation in the resistance had between 40 and 50 percent Protestants, including Vallon, Lagorce, Labastide-de-Virac, and Salavas, where the pastor stood accused of encouraging his flock to take arms. In the Ardèche, 40 percent of the men arrested came from communes with many Protestants. In 1851, Protestants accounted for about 12 percent of the population of the Ardèche (47,000 of 386,000 inhabitants).[38] However, in Balazuc, which had no Protestants, Montagnards succeeded in mobilizing ordinary Catholics with a program of practical social reform.

On January 2, 1852, the prefect dissolved the municipal council of Balazuc and replaced it with a temporary municipal commission.[39] On the eighteenth, four uniformed gendarmes from Vallon rode to Balazuc to arrest Jean Jullian and his nephew of the same name at five in the morning. They were told that the nephew, a former soldier, was visiting an aunt in another village. However, it immediately became apparent that the younger Jullian had "got away by using a rope to reach neighboring roofs." Jean Mollier *dit* Prieur, brother of the former mayor, was arrested early in the morning on January 30. Jean Vallier and Auguste Gamel were arrested on March 14. Both were found at the café at Vianès's inn.[40]

In February, the Mixed Commission of the Ardèche, consisting of the three highest administrative, judicial, and military authorities, heard the cases of hundreds of men who were accused of participation in the insurrection or whom they viewed as politically dangerous. These were very poor people, routinely described as "owning nothing." On February 18, 1852, the commission considered the cases of nine men living in Balazuc who had joined the insurrection. Seven had been born in Balazuc. Victor Queyroche stood accused of being "one of the leaders of the movement and of the secret societies of his commune, intelligent, dangerous." The thirty-year-old unmarried peasant proclaimed his innocence, insisting that he had learned of the march on Largentière from Vianès's sister-in-law when he arrived at the café at eight-thirty or nine on Sunday morning. Yet several people identified him as returning to Balazuc about ten in the morning on Sunday in the company of several men carrying rifles, with a red scarf around his neck, carrying a bottle, shouting, "Long live liberty!" He had been drinking with Claude Mollier, the mayor, when about nine in the morning seven or eight men, most armed with rifles, arrived. Eldin of Leyris, whom he had recognized by small pock marks on a cheek, but of whose first name he was not sure, was among them. Eldin asked him to drink a glass of wine with them. He had wounds on his jaw and ear and said that soldiers had fired on them and that he had fallen while fleeing. Eldin left with the others to return to Lagorce. Queyroche, who accompanied them to the *bureau de tabac* at the top of the village, improbably denied knowing any others in the small band or knowing why they had gone to Largentière. He denied belonging to the secret society or having been asked to join it. The Mixed Commission condemned him to imprisonment in Algeria.

Jean Jullian *oncle* also denied any role in the events. He had worked all day on land owned by Mollier, the boatman, in Louanes, and returned to the village at eight at night. He and his wife and child had gone to a *veillée* at the house of his brother-in-law. On Sunday morning Mollier had rowed him across the river. He had gone to Audon, where he owned a small piece of land, and he had seen some of the insurgents heading toward Balazuc but claimed not to have recognized any of them. When Mollier returned to the river, some people going over to Mass in Balazuc also rode in the *bac*. He admitted having heard of the secret society but denied either belonging to it or having been asked to join.[41] Considered "not very dangerous," he was condemned to police surveillance and was freed early in March 1852.

Antoine Fromentin faced the Mixed Commission in Privas on January 23. Married with four children, the cultivator could read, "but imperfectly." Having returned from Aubenas about midnight with his neighbor, he had only learned of the "march against Largentière" the following morning, when he saw men fleeing, carrying rifles, pitchforks, and swords. He claimed to have remained home: "I heard someone say that men from Balazuc were involved,

along with others, but I did not see or hear of anyone in particular."
(What else could he say?) He received only surveillance, having been
"led along" by the leaders and being regarded as lacking intelligence
and as "not dangerous."[42]

Claude Mollier, who had been replaced as mayor, also denied the
accusations against him. He was at the café on the morning of
December 7, just as a good many people drop by Chez Paulette in
today's Balazuc. When he headed down to the river to fish, he saw a
large group of men, some of them armed, coming from the direction
of Largentière. When he returned from the river, the café was completely full, with people coming and going. He was still there when
he heard shots being fired elsewhere in the village. The justice of the
peace ordered Claude Mollier freed.[43]

There were relatively few estrangers (those born elsewhere) in
Balazuc. Joseph Exbrayat, from the Haute-Loire, was one of a handful not born in the Ardèche. He had come to the village in 1819 and
had found work for two years as a farmhand. Then he learned the
mason's trade. When he married Marguerite Mollier in 1835, he
could not sign the marriage certificate. Now, with a wife and five
children, the eldest of whom was twelve, he worked for masters in
the trade here and there when there was work to be found, including
in Balazuc. He had been able to save enough money to buy some land
(offering to sell a piece of it to the village in 1847). He had not done
badly and now was worth about three thousand francs. Exbrayat and
Queyroche had been in prison since January 4. Fifty-two years old,
Exbrayat had gray hair and beard, "red" eyes, a dimple, was blind in
one eye, and was married with three children. He listened as he was
described as "known as a vigorous rabble-rouser but lacking brains"
who had joined the march on Largentière. The Mixed Commission
sentenced him to "probation and surveillance by the Ministry of
General Police."[44] His and all judgments imposed by the Mixed
Commission were widely publicized by large, intimidating posters.

Jean Jullian, the nephew who had temporarily escaped the gendarmes with the help of a rope, was an unmarried farm laborer
twenty-eight years of age with "some resources but not many," relatively tall, with dark brown hair, a black beard, a round, tanned face,

with a scar on the right side of his forehead. His status as a former soldier drew him a prison term followed by surveillance. Jean Mollier *dit* Prieur stood accused of having joined a secret society and the march but was freed on March 2. Auguste Gamel, thirty-two, another former soldier who was a day laborer "with no money," was the other accused from Balazuc who faced the Mixed Commission who had not been born there. He had come to Balazuc from Ucel, beyond Aubenas, and had married the daughter of Joseph Lapierre, the baker, and had a small child. He was set free that day, having "followed the insurrectionary band, neither dangerous nor intelligent."[45]

The weight of the repression fell on Antoine Daumas. Born in Balazuc in 1813, the thirty-nine-year-old cultivator, married and without children, had served for some time as the village tobacconist. Thanks to a passport that he took out to travel to Nîmes in 1845, we can see his pale, round face marked by smallpox and extended by a black beard. Fearing arrest, in April 1852, Daumas went to see Mayor Tastevin, to whom he denied that he had ever belonged to a secret society. Tastevin wrote the subprefect that he believed Daumas's "repentance" to be sincere. Before the mayor, Daumas swore obedience to the president of the republic and swore also never to "get mixed up in another insurrection." However, early in the afternoon of May 14 two uniformed gendarmes arrested him. Considered "one of the leaders of the insurrection, an active and dangerous leader of the secret societies," Daumas spent fifteen months in a Parisian prison and then was transported to Algeria, where for a year he suffered from fever at the prison of Fouka. He benefited from a pardon in February 1853 and then was placed under surveillance.[46]

Jean Jullian *neveu* and Joseph Exbrayat suffered the indignity of having to apply for and carry an "indigent's passport," providing for assistance along the route, so that they could be imprisoned in Marseille. Both were to follow an obligatory itinerary that took them to Villeneuve-de-Berg, Orange, Avignon, Aix, and then Marseille. Jullian (presumably Exbrayat as well), received sixty centimes to help him from Largentière to Aubenas, but there would be no inns for Jullian or anyone else carrying an indigent's passport.[47] After later being pardoned, the two were placed under official surveillance. This meant that they had to appear before the mayor every eight days and before the cantonal justice of the peace twice a month. As neither owned a horse, they had to walk to Vallon, a twenty-six-mile round trip.[48]

Victor Queyroche, who had picked up the nickname of Cayenne (French Guiana, the mosquito-infected northern coast of South America to which those receiving the harshest sentences were sent), appears not to have gone quietly. He was arrested in November 1852 because he had not turned up in Vallon and was briefly imprisoned there. Five years later Queyroche, described as a man who could be dangerous "in a given moment," was in jail in Épinal.[49]

Only in 1857 did authorities finally spare Exbrayat and the two Jean Jullians from the bimonthly trip to Vallon to appear before the justice of the peace. Mayor Tastevin supported their request. Moreover, a gendarme had gone to Balazuc to gather information about them. Now the mayor and other council members and villagers seemed eager to help the four men. People in Balazuc noted "their complete misery," as well as the fact that it took fifteen hours to walk to and from Vallon. All four were family fathers and had been relegated to the category of "blind instruments of several impassioned men," who now expressed regret for their actions. Auguste Gamel died at forty-six in Balazuc in 1866; Joseph Exbrayat, two years later.[50]

Official interpretations of the insurrection portrayed the Montagnard insurgents as embodying "ignorance bordering on savagery, and thus easy to lead along." Many mayors still did not understand their responsibilities. The cafés, like that of Vianès, were blamed.[51] The Second Republic had brought contentious politics to the village of Balazuc and, in doing so, challenged the authority of the Church. Napoleon III sought to identify the Empire (1852–70) with economic progress, but it also to a large extent relied on its alliance with the Catholic Church to maintain political support. In the meantime, the subprefect described "public life" in the Bas-Vivarais as "almost nonexistent."[52] More than half the men did not bother to vote in municipal elections. In very hard times economic survival remained the principal preoccupation.

Even so, the municipal elections of Balazuc in 1855 had been bitterly contested. André Mollier had been named mayor three years earlier but angrily resigned a year later, after Joseph Leyris had been allowed to take up his old job as rural guard; he had "caused and is still causing trouble in the village." Leyris had testified against some of those arrested in the wake of resistance to the coup d'état in December 1851 and given what probably was an inflated number of members of the secret society in Balazuc. Antoine Tastevin had been named mayor in 1854; he was the only choice in Balazuc, "truly so poor in every conceivable way."[53] A year later no candidate received the necessary absolute majority of votes until a second election, and the council could be filled out only by a third balloting when the prefect allowed the final two men to be elected by a simple majority. The prefect then again named Tastevin mayor. The bureau presiding over the election, however, refused to sign the record of the election. Deputy Mayor Constant complained that calumnies, "invented by several people scheming to be elected," were circulating against the previous council. When Constant posted a letter expressing his irritation, someone covered it with garbage. He suspected some of those newly elected to the council. In any case, the legacy of the coup d'état and Tastevin's role as mayor in reporting on those who had been sentenced to surveillance probably played a role in the residual bad feeling.[54]

Then it became difficult to find anyone willing to be mayor. Tastevin resigned twice, as did one of his replacements, Constant, suffering "mental illness." In two elections, only about a third of those eligible to vote did so. Besides the coming and going of mayors, another sign of hard times and perhaps indifference as well may have been the difficulty of getting members of the council and leading taxpayers (at gatherings in which additional small taxes were to be voted) to attend meetings. In 1864 the mayor cited "the bad will of the members of the municipal council as well as the leading taxpayers." The subprefect, it will be remembered, then commented bitterly that in Balazuc everything remained to be done. In 1865 a second ballot constituted the municipal council; the election of Claude Mollier, Philippe Charousset (a budding radical republican from Servière), and the innkeeper Vianès may suggest the reemergence of the left in the outcome.[55]

In the summer of 1870, France foolishly went to war against Prussia and its allies among the other German states. As it went badly (three men from Balazuc were among four hundred Ardéchois who perished),[56] new municipal elections were held in Balazuc in early August 1870. Jean Jullian, one of those arrested after resisting the coup d'état of December 1851, now forty-six years of age, was elected, as was Philippe Charousset. Both were committed republicans. However, Firmin Vincent, who was dedicated to the Empire, was elected to the council, as were some other familiar faces.

On September 4, as the war raged, France nominally became a republic when an enthusiastic crowd proclaimed it in Paris. Only very slowly in the decade following the Commune of 1871 (that uprising of ordinary Parisians against the conservative provisional government) did the republic solidify its existence. The struggle for the countryside began.[57] The members of the municipal council took their oath of loyalty to the Empire on the day on which crowds in Paris proclaimed the republic. The council did not meet again until June 1871.[58]

France entered the Republic of the Moral Order, as the nominally republican regime of the first seven years of the 1870s is known, with a conservative government that was not very republican at all. On May 16, 1877, President Marshal Patrice de MacMahon failed in his attempt to orchestrate the first stages of a restoration of the monarchy by replacing the republican prime minister with a monarchist. He then dissolved the Chamber of Deputies, which had elected him, but an election returned a republican majority. The "coup of May 16" caused great political commotion in Balazuc, because Mayor Vincent and other conservatives supported MacMahon.

In Balazuc no one regretted the end of the Second Empire more than Firmin Vincent. Safely conservative, he had been reappointed mayor by the government in 1874. Two years later he became embroiled in a battle with three members of the council over the plan to move the cemetery to a location farther from the village. When the council members accused Vincent of tricking them by underestimating the cost, the mayor expelled one of them from the room; the two others stormed out as well. The rump of the council then approved the acquisition of the necessary land. The mayor's angry opponents then immediately went to see the property owners to urge them not to sell "an iota of land." Lacking all subtlety and ignoring official reprimands, Vincent continued to use the imperial stamp, complete with its eagle outline, on official correspondence, loyally served by deputy mayor and the rural guard, Victor Boiron.[59]

During elections Vincent could no longer contain his hatred of the republic. Balazuc overwhelmingly supported the monarchist candidate for the Chamber of Deputies, giving him 222 votes and only 20 to the republican candidate, a Protestant.[60] As electors arrived at the *mairie* to vote in 1877, Vincent snarled that the republic would ruin the region. Jean Jullian *neveu* testified that Vincent had harassed one man as he voted, demanding to know if he would support the republican *canaille* (rabble). When Jullien demanded why republicans were *canaille*, the mayor replied that they had killed the archbishop of Paris during the Commune and that "the smallest eagle of the emperor is worth more than everything done by all the republicans, and that they were all rabble." The rural guard passed out ballots on which the antirepublican candidate was named and encouraged some residents to tear down posters for the republican candidate. Vincent was suspended, and then, in October 1878, a gendarme brought him the news that he had been fired, along with his right-hand man the rural guard. Jean Mollier, who had been arrested after the coup d'état of 1851, was appointed rural guard. The prefect's dismissal of Mayor Vincent was part of the purge of municipal officials who had campaigned against republican candidates.[61]

Three months later a court in Largentière condemned two well-known republicans of Balazuc, Joseph Mollier, *cultivateur*, and Charbonnier, to six days in jail each for "outrages" against Vincent when he was mayor. Yet the courts of Largentière were notoriously antirepublican, and in the subprefect's view, all this stemmed from Vincent's antirepublican vendetta. Charbonnier had asked Vincent to stop hunting in his vineyards because the mayor's dog was eating his grapes. As for Mollier, he had asked the mayor to verify a signature on a legal document, and the mayor had pushed him, "calling him a rogue." Charbonnier then ran into the former guard, and Boiron, who owed him some money. The guard insulted Charbonnier, and then wrote up a citation against him.[62] This sort of thing could have happened before, but the political connotations were now hard to miss. The year after the invalidation of the 1877 election (because of accusations of local official pressure, as in many other regions, to support the monarchists), Balazuc again voted overwhelmingly for the conservative, giving the prefect reason to consider the municipal council of Balazuc "entirely reactionary." With the stakes raised, 230 of 280 eligible voters turned up at the polls.[63]

If Firmin Vincent was a minor figure in the battle against the republic, several powerful people in high places orchestrated the electoral campaign. In 1879 Bishop Bonnet of Viviers worked to mobilize opinion against the republicans and their anticipated laicization of public schools, passing petitions in Balazuc and other villages. Bonnet, who had been appointed three years earlier at the age of forty-one, was from a family of workers in the Lozère, "young, of robust health, habituated to the ways of the mountains." Contemptuous of both Protestants and republicans, he crisscrossed his diocese, preaching against both and singing the praises of Pope Pius IX's 1864 encyclical *Syllabus of Errors*, which condemned progress and modernity. Thus inspired, some priests threatened the faithful with the fires of hell if they voted for republicans.[64]

Yet while the gradual victory of the republic brought national political issues to villages like Balazuc, family and personal rivalries continued to play an important part in municipal politics. They still do. The Tastevin, Mollier, Mouraret, Constant, Boyer, and other families had coexisted, intermarried, subdivided, allied, and fought for generations and, in some cases, centuries (to complicate things, there were several different Tastevins, Molliers, and Constants, all at least distantly related). Solidarities within and rivalries between hamlets too counted for something, even as "secular ideology provided categories for debate."[65]

For example, in 1881, Vincent, still on the municipal council but no longer mayor, accused Tastevin, then deputy mayor but later that year elected mayor by the council (a change that began in 1876), of awarding small contracts for work on the village paths to his son and one of his animals "to do absolutely nothing." Moreover, at a moment when the municipality had no secretary, anyone needing information had to go find the mayor, who was invariably working his land. Such was, and is, the world of village complaints about the mayor.[66]

The following year Cyprien Brun, a shoemaker, bitterly denounced Mayor Tastevin, claiming that he had refused to let him examine the land survey (*cadastre*) when water from a neighbor's property flooded his house. Tastevin saw the hand of Fromentin, an enemy, in the protest of Brun, who could not read and write and claimed that he, the mayor, had been denounced as a royalist. Tastevin disputed this designation and thereby illustrates for us some of the appeal of the republic: "I am not royalist for the reason that I have children and that I respect and know to appreciate very much the advantages that the Republic gives us from the point of view of education and from the military point of view." Tastevin declared that the land survey was at his house because poor weather made it difficult to read much of anything at the rented village hall as well as that Brun had been drunk. Yet the language of this minor dispute reflected the politicization of routine village affairs. André Mollier, whose property was sending water into Brun's house, was denounced as a royalist, like Tastevin; Brun signed off his letter of protest denouncing Tastevin as "a man of whim, as royalist as Mollier, while I am a citizen of the Republic."[67]

The Politics of Republican Patronage

The republic faced a daunting task in the Ardèche. Its advent pitted Marianne, its symbol, which had emerged out of the Revolution, against the Virgin Mary. In a region whose fragile economy was being devastated by the silk disease and phylloxera, religion remained "the point of anchorage in this society which closed in on itself with the series of economic crises that affected it."[68] The diocese of Viviers had proportionally more clergy than any other diocese in France. During the period 1853–62, 60 percent of newborn girls in Balazuc had first names beginning with Marie. In 1870, 70 percent of communes in the Ardèche had nuns teaching, again more than anywhere else in France. The influence of the clergy in village life remained enormous, perhaps even more than in western France. If anything, the lack of powerful nobles may have made clerical domination still greater. The religious revival in the 1870s, marked by the cult of and pilgrimages to Lourdes and other places, accentuated ecclesiastical influence. The integrative function of the Church remained strong, embedded in popular culture.[69] Attachment to patois (with nuances between the patois of the Cévennes, that of the plateau, and the limestone country "tinted with Provençal") may itself have been identified with defense of religion. French retained the reputation as the language of the upper classes, particularly of city and town; "its reference points were mostly located outside the rural community."[70]

With the vivid collective memory of the aggressive anticlericalism of the radical Jacobin republic of the Revolution and of the Montagnards of the left during the Second Republic, many Catholics viewed the very existence of a republic as opening the way to the destruction of their way of life. The legacy of the wars of religion fought against Protestants (and their role in the Second Empire) was hard to shake off for militant Catholics. The subprefect noted in 1881 that "despite the increasingly general invasion of political ideas in municipal elections, almost everywhere politics intervened it was to serve as a pretext for personal rivalries." Yet, as in the Second Republic, even in Balazuc and other places without Protestants national political debates became framed in the context of local struggles. Here "the clerical question holds the first rank." Political pamphlets and newspapers became part of village life. Even if in general the arrondissement was "not very republican," some municipal candidates had accepted "the republican label" if it did not commit them to anything specific.[71] In a region where Marxism and socialist parties had relatively little influence, the right continued to see itself as defending the Church against lay republicans. Rural democracy (however limited to universal manhood suffrage) challenged clerical authority. The Third Republic countered and undercut the influence of the Church in local political life with the patronage of the centralized state.[72]

Schools remained at the heart of the battles, even referred to as a return to the wars of religion. The Second Empire had encouraged ecclesiastical influence on education. With the republic, Church and state no longer shared the same goals, opening up villages to secular republican ideology. Taught in its public schools, it eroded the place of the church in the community.[73] Curés struggled against mayors and lay teachers in a contest for allegiance, transforming the politics of the bell tower (*la politique du clocher*). Lay schools provided an alternative source of solidarity, undercutting the age-old role of the parish and its priest in defining the values of the rural community, as well as increasingly providing opportunities for social interaction.[74] Moreover, amid the ongoing rural exodus, the schools of the republic provided modest credentials for finding jobs in cities and towns. Dreams of social promotion, however modest, no longer passed through the Church. The republican goal of eliminating the clergy from public schools became an ever more contentious focal point of conservative opposition. In the late 1880s several hundred members of religious orders teaching in both public and private schools still did not have any kinds of diploma or formal qualifications.[75]

The comte de Vogüé, whose family had lost a landed empire during the Revolution, put the new battle into context. The war now pitted the republican administration against the clergy, "the only moral authority, the only driving force of opinions in most parishes." With almost twice as many pupils in private schools at the time of the centenary of the Revolution in 1889, he estimated that half the people of the Ardèche still did not accept the republic.[76]

Villages like Balazuc split into factions. Some priests refused communion to pupils who attended lay schools and to their parents as well. Their opponents mocked religious teachers, referring to the teaching methods of the Frères d'Ignortins as "ignorantism." The lines were drawn between the future warriors of the belle époque, the clericals (*calotins*) versus the "socialists" and "anarchists." Bishop Bonnet and the Union Catholique accused anticlericals of favoring living together without marriage and of spitting on crucifixes. To the right, conservative candidates and village priests were all that could prevent the government becoming turned over to the Masonic lodges, Protestants, or both. In Coucoron the curé announced that it was a mortal sin to vote for a republican. His counterpart in Uzer threatened to refuse the last rites to anyone who voted for the electoral list that wanted to "chase Christ from our schools," while that of St.-Etienne-de-Lugdarès (in the mountains) was accused of warning, "To send your daughters to lay schools is the same as putting them in houses of prostitution." During the bitter electoral campaign of 1885, a priest accosted a man in view of the mayor and told him, "You have quite a dark mouth, you have the air of a Huguenot," before snatching an electoral ballot from his hands, an act witnessed by the mayor.[77]

Priests were accused of threatening to refuse absolution to mothers whose children attended lay school. The subprefect claimed that priests who did not engage in politics were subject to ecclesiastical disgrace, as in Lagorce. In Lavilledieu, where the municipality had requested the laicization of the school, the village priest attacked the decision from the pulpit. In Annonay, twenty-five cases of arson were believed to have been the work of opponents of laicization.[78]

In October 1890 the government suspended the salaries (paid since the creation of a national church early in the French Revolution) of thirty-seven priests because of their violent attacks on the republic, a continuation of vigorous and provocative official measures that had begun during the electoral campaign five years earlier. The government suspended the bishop's salary in 1892. In nearby Laurac, a small center of counterrevolutionary activity during the 1790s, the priest had established a clandestine school, "under the pretext of operating a day nursery." The academic inspector found thirty-four children in a house owned by the village priest. Some had catechisms or books about saints, but there were no other books or notebooks.[79] Among the priests who drew complaints was Casimir Tastevin, who had been born in Balazuc and now served as vicar in Antraigues. He was noted in 1892 as being "hostile to the republican regime."[80]

In this context, republican electoral victories came slowly. The right, which had handily won the elections of 1877, swept to victory in the bitterly contested legislative elections of 1885, capitalizing on the backlash against the Ferry Laws. The republican-dominated Chamber of Deputies invalidated the elections because of "unacceptable" clerical interference, a dubious ruling at best. The next year an electoral poster warned the peasants of the Ardèche: "Before 1789, the dovecote was a privilege, and you did not have any more the right to eat pigeons than to kill rabbits." In contrast, the memory of the "red caps" of the Second Republic lingered in the collective memory of churchmen. The left won the rematch. However, three years later a new campaign by the Church reversed republican gains in the Ardèche.[81]

During the early 1890s many churchmen in France came to accept the republic as a reality and "rallied" to it (the *ralliement*). Conservatives in the Ardèche and elsewhere tempered their antirepublicanism and identified themselves with what they considered the defense of the social order.[82] The rhetoric surrounding elections lost some of its violence during the electoral campaigns of 1893 and 1898, in part because of the *ralliement* and in part because of divisions in the left. The legislative elections of 1893 began a period of republican domination (the 1902 elections excepted) in the Ardèche. The election of Odilon Barrot as deputy signified growing support for the republic, as well as his personal popularity. Moreover, a year before the government initiated subsidies for producers of raw silk, thus increasing its popularity. Republican leaders took every opportunity to identify themselves with material progress and with the struggles of small-holding farmers.

But if the *ralliement* helped temper the bitterness of Catholic opposition, the gloves came off during the Dreyfus Affair. In a department in which only three Jews resided, the Catholic newspaper *L'Echo de Largentière* in 1895 denounced the *"traiteur Dreyfus"* with an anti-Semitic tone, reporting that on the occasion of Dreyfus's dishonorable discharge from the army at the École Militaire in Paris, shouts of "Judas!" had echoed.[83]

The advent to power in 1899 of the Radicals (socially conservative and vehemently anticlerical) restored bitterness to the question of the schools and the status of the Church. A newspaper that year warned that if the "clerical party" took power, it would return the choice of teachers to each commune. This would bring into the classroom "people perfectly incompetent and often pushed along by little village tyrants." The result would be "the return of the nation to ignorance." In reply, following the lead of the bishop, village curés denounced "the schools of the devil" from the pulpit. Many lay teachers were indeed anticlerical, and nearly all were attached to the republic they represented.[84]

As more schools were laicized, private (or free) schools were founded, 194 between 1886 and 1901. By 1897 there were 314 of them in the Ardèche, while only 163 schools had been laicized. By 1904 there were 345 free schools run by the Church and 299 lay schools. Many Catholic parents continued to take their children out of laicized schools. Several public schools had but one student. In 1898 the lay teacher in the girls' school in Ste.-Eulalie had none.[85]

Competing Symbols: Balazuc's New Bridge and New Church

If in 1881 only about half the municipalities could be considered in republican hands, this was not yet the case in Balazuc.[86] Then the patronage of the republican state demonstrated that it could make a difference in Balazuc. For generations the people of Balazuc had dreamed that a bridge would one day cross the Ardèche River. The 1882 law making primary school obligatory provided impetus for the project because the bridge would enormously facilitate the daily trek of children from the other side of the river. It would put an end to the small boat that had ferried villagers across the Ardèche for centuries, as well as to the accidents that occurred almost every year. To pay for the undertaking, the municipality had to borrow more money. Here the state would play the crucial role. Ernest Hugon, staunch republican and member of the departmental Conseil Général, who represented the canton of Vallon, came to Balazuc's assistance, using his influence to obtain a large subsidy required for the project.[87]

Balazuc's bridge across the Ardèche River was inaugurated on

September 29, 1884. The rural guard went through the village with his drum, calling on people to come welcome Hugon. The republican politician hoped that the new bridge would solidify support for the republic in the religious, conservative village. After all, the republic had come through. The subprefect congratulated Balazuc "on coming over to the republic." A plaque on the bridge commemorates the small but telling event.[88]

Almost six years later came the largest storm in Balazuc's history. On September 22, 1890, it carried the surging waters of the Ardèche above the top of the bridge. Killing thirty-seven people in the arrondissement, the flood storm did great damage in Balazuc, affecting perhaps all but ten of the hundred families. The bridge, a metaphor for the republic itself, held.

For the moment the bridge stood without a proper road providing access on either side, or even sturdy paths leading from it down to the river. In 1892, work began to remedy this situation, with the assistance of a state subsidy and another loan. The work dragged on for years. Only then could villagers more easily obtain water and sand. Dynamite blasted through rock to forge through the village a road that was inaugurated in 1897 with a procession from the bridge to the Café Roudil. Again, Hugon was there to take credit for the republic, grandly noting "the work that has put Balazuc in communication with the rest of the world."[89]

The bridge, gift of the republic, ironically led to the construction of a new church, symbol of the way things had been before. Residents of Servière and Audon could now come to church in the village, instead of going to the more easily reached neighboring villages of Lanas or Uzer, swelling the numbers attending Mass well beyond the size of the old Romanesque church. But the new church was built without any help from the republic.

The old church had been described by a priest sent by the bishop as "very small, quite irregular in size, and in a location that makes access difficult and not very agreeable." While much of France surveyed, at least from afar, the smoldering ruins of the Paris Commune in 1871, Balazuc's municipal council admitted that no major repairs could be contemplated "because we have no money and no resources."

The mayor did express to Bishop Bonnet his "regret for having been obliged to receive him in a venerable church, no doubt, by its age and memory, but not unworthy of God who resides there."[90]

In 1883, Régis Chareyre, who had just arrived to be curé of Balazuc, vowed that if Balazuc were spared from the cholera epidemic, he would build a new chapel. For the moment a new church would have to wait. The faithful raised money to build a small chapel, Notre-Dame-de-Lourdes, the name reflecting the rapid rise of religious pilgrimages in France during the early Third Republic. It is at the intersection of the two roads up to Balazuc from the road to Ruoms.[91] The faithful still needed a new church, a larger and much more visible structure that would stand tall in a changing political world.

Parishioners contributed about 2,000 workdays to construct the new church built southeast of the old ramparts. Some funds surely came from former inhabitants of Balazuc of some means. The altar was a gift. Small contributions made possible the purchase of eighteen thousand bricks. The very choice of the location of the church provided some materials, for stone extracted from the rock formation that was transformed into an esplanade could be used to build the structure. In November 1891, seventy men contributed 299 days of work. Cisterns and the river provided water; a small basin formed behind the apse to catch water from a small fault in the hillside. Mules hauled sand from the river's edge, the bells of the old church signaling when more of the sturdy animals were needed to make trips down to the water. A company on the Rhône provided the lime, carried up to the church site by a wagon, at no expense.[92]

As laicization became an ever more explosive issue, the abbé Chareyre vowed that the church would be completed before the coming "persecution" of the faithful. He might have added "before his own death," since he was terminally ill at the time of the church's construction. Chareyre drew up the plans for the church, basing them on the form of the structure in his previous parish, directed the work, and kept a "work site notebook."[93]

By late 1895 the structure of the church itself had been nearly completed, although little had been done on the inside. The sparse furnishings of the deconsecrated Romanesque church, including the altar, several paintings, several statues of the virgin, a procession cross, chandeliers, chairs, and the priest's robes, were then transferred. The large metal cross that had been in the square beneath the old church now stands on a pedestal at the base of the church. A lottery made possible the purchase of a small organ. However, the new church lacked a bell tower. Its parishioners were "worn out from days of work and money given," and the bells still hung from the crumbling bell tower of the twelfth-century church in the oldest part of the village. They remained there until fifteen years later, when the new bell tower went up, paid for by contributions.[94]

On October 17, 1895, Bishop Bonnet, eternal enemy of the republic, arrived by train at seven in the morning and was greeted at the small chapel on the road into Balazuc by "a cavalcade of young men, almost all former soldiers in fine form." He was joined by twenty priests from the region, five originally from Balazuc, and twenty-five nuns from the Convent of St.-Joseph in Aubenas. Charousset and the municipal council joined Chareyre and his parishioners for a procession to the new church, which Bishop Bonnet blessed.[95] Chareyre and two other priests then led a second procession down to the old church, from which they carried the Holy Sacrament to the new church, while parishioners sang. Solemn High Mass and benediction followed. Chareyre died on December 11 at age sixty-six. A week later his successor married the first couple to take their vows inside the new church.

Several families contributed to the stained glass windows along the nave and two small adjoining chapels of the church: Pays, Mouraret, and Tastevin (two of them priests), names that were prominent during the political battles that swirled around the role of the Catholic Church a few years later.[96] The largest of the three bells hauled from the old deconsecrated church in 1911, weighing well more than three hundred pounds, had been cast in December 1851, as if in defiance of the mobilization of the Montagnards, with then Mayor Tastevin denoted as its *parrain* (godfather).[97]

Balazuc's new church stood tall, even without its bell tower. In the meantime the village had gradually begun to celebrate the republic, even if the agricultural calendar still dominated. (The secretary of the municipal council, describing in 1885 the location of the new cemetery, still used the traditional country terms *levant* for the east and *au couchant* for the west.) In the early 1880s celebration of the republic's holiday of July 14 came not on that day but on the nearest Sunday, because of "work in the fields"; all the members of the municipal council worked the land. Balazuc now had a concrete reason to celebrate the republic, allocating a few francs to the poor on the occasion of the holiday and to illuminate the village in 1885.[98]

Mayor Tastevin had resigned early in 1884, the year that the bridge was completed and inaugurated. Referring to some difficulties that he had encountered the year before (they had brought Bishop Bonnet to Balazuc on a pastoral visit in March, an event sure to rekindle political opposition to the republic), he now claimed that he no longer enjoyed the confidence of the administration, and widely considered to have royalist sympathies despite his claims to the contrary, he was probably right.[99] The "republican list," led by Louis Pays and Philippe Charousset, was elected in its entirety. Jean Jullian *neveu*, who had been arrested and imprisoned for his part in the resistance to the coup d'état of 1851, was among those elected to the council. More than division among conservatives explains the victory of the left. One did not have to look too far to see what had given the republicans momentum and perhaps victory: It now spanned the Ardèche. Hugon, powerful member of the Conseil Général, put it with unfailing precision: "The republic did not lose the money that it consecrated to Balazuc's bridge." Funds provided by the department and the state to help repair, maintain, or improve the village paths (such as thirty thousand francs provided in 1885, a year after the republicans took over the *mairie*), embellished the republic's reputation in Balazuc.[100]

In 1885 the selection of the location for a new cemetery took on political ramifications. Mayor Pays threatened to ban further inhumations in the old, full cemetery. He proposed a new location, outside the nucleus of the village. The land belonged to his wife. Two members of the municipal council, Benjamin Boyer and Louis Constant, vociferously opposed the location of the new cemetery, but it was approved by the council. Arguing that the rocky soil (there was not much else in Balazuc) would require too much plowing, Boyer and Constant preferred other possible sites, including one near the river, a location that the majority of the council had found too distant from the village. Ninety-eight men from seventy-five families signed a petition of protest (twenty-two marked with X).

The mayor claimed that national political debates lay behind their opposition and that 90 percent of those who had signed belonged to the "reactionary party" in a year when the Church was mounting a ferocious and unrelentingly bitter campaign against laicization and the republic itself. The opening of the new cemetery in 1887 was seen by some as another small victory for the republic.[101]

In another revealing aspect of state patronage and the entrenchment of the Republic, the "insurgents of 1851" became the "victims of the coup d'état." Men who had been jailed for any length of time after the massive resistance to Louis Napoleon Bonaparte's coup now became eligible to receive indemnities from the state. In 1881 the prefect asked those survivors to elect three members of a departmental commission to review claims. The commission included three members of the departmental Conseil Général, including Hugon. The commission awarded twelve hundred francs to Antoine Daumas. The widow of Joseph Exbrayat collected four hundred francs, despite the insertion in her dossier that her political conduct now was "somewhat doubtful." Support (given "warmly") by Hugon carried the day, as it had often before.

The widow of Auguste Gamel had remarried with four children, had two more, and then been widowed a second time. The commission awarded her a small sum for the ten days in custody her husband had suffered early in 1852. Her letter (written for her because she was illiterate) recalled that her late husband had been forced to hide from the police for more than three months. It carefully noted that her grown children were republicans. Jean Jullian and his nephew of the same name were still around to collect money as well.[102]

There was again more to the government's generosity than a wish to right an old wrong. The prefect in particular called the ministry's attention to Balazuc, Vallon, Salavas, and Lagorce, "where the measure will have a double significance as absolutely justified and will produce a salutary impression in a milieu where reactionary ideas are still persistent and have not renounced the struggle."[103] Certainly Claude Mollier played his cards well. Mayor at the time of the coup d'état, he was now seventy-six years, a "widower without children and infirm . . . in Balazuc where I have always lived . . . without means of existence, and not being able to earn any money because of my age and infirmity." He added to his well-penned letter: "Returning home again in the middle of a center of monarchists, I don't believe it useful to tell you all that I had to suffer there. Not being worthy of the least consideration, the monarchists sought quarrel after quarrel with me, until they made me sell or lose the little that I owned." He received three hundred francs, not much, but at least something.[104]

In 1892, a year following his father's death, Henri Jullian, cultivator, complained to the prefect that he had tried without success to obtain the "part of the pension to which I have legal right." Now, with the beginning of "the bad season, if I have the right to the solicitude of the government of the Republic of which I have always been a convinced partisan, I would very much like to have a favorable response to my request because I really am in great need."[105]

Yet Balazuc gave the majority of its votes in legislative elections to conservative candidates in 1885, 1886, and 1888 elections. The latter election took place in the context of the phenomenal national popularity of Georges Boulanger, the nationalist general whose dashing figure posed a threat to the republic.[106] Balazuc's municipal elections in 1888 brought another conservative municipality, led by Philippe Tastevin. Yet Tastevin "would willingly march with the administration . . . it suffices to give him a sign," in the opinion of the subprefect. Here was the rallying of some conservatives to the republic, village level.[107]

During the height of the Boulanger Affair, as republicans rallied in defense of the republic, Balazuc's teacher in the boys' school was at odds with the "reactionary municipality." Moreover, he sought appointment to a commune where he could earn a little bit more by working as the secretary of the *mairie*, as was not possible with the current mayor. Here, also, Hugon, the influential *conseiller général*,

supported his demand. Within a month the teacher had been transferred to Veyras, that village's teacher moving to Balazuc. Within a
year he too was gone, Hugon's patronage again having proved decisive.[108]

The elections of 1892 marked a turning point in the Ardèche.
Amid brightly colored electoral posters Balazuc's electors returned a
fully republican municipal council, even if the subprefect considered
some of its members mere "allies." The council in turn elected
Philippe Charousset mayor. The subprefect crowed that the Balazuc
result "has been awaited for a long time. The mayor is and will be
republican." Furthermore, in the arrondissement that four years earlier had elected fifty-five municipalities that were overall hostile to
the republic and fifty-one councils considered republican, fifty-four
republican and fifty-one "reactionary" councils had now come out of
the elections.[109]

Staunch republicans and conservatives battled for control of the
municipality against the background of debates on laicization and
the role of the Church. The two sides were led by the increasingly
anticlerical Philippe Charousset and his conservative rival, Marius
Mouraret, from the hamlet of Louanes. Given momentum by significant state contributions facilitated by Odilon Barrot to the improvement of the road to Uzer, Charousset was returned to the council in
1896, again with the largest number of votes, and then was elected
mayor.[110]

One of the signs of the politicization of municipal political life was
the establishment in the late 1880s of a Republican Committee of
Balazuc, which sometimes met in the café of the small railroad station. It was a symbol of changing times. Such organizations had ties
with government officials, who were hardly neutral in their support
of the republic. In 1889, Louis Romanet, a property owner living in
Les Costes, wanted to be hired as a policeman in Lyon, a very typical
move out of the Bas-Vivarais. He was in good health and had some
education; he had earlier served in the army and then as a gendarme
for four years. Three of his uncles had had military careers, one in
Algeria. The prefect of the Ardèche, who described Romanet as a
republican, then turned to Balazuc's Republican Committee for addi-

tional information on him. The committee sent along a favorable opinion and asked the prefect of the Ardèche to pass it on to his colleague in Lyon. In this way too local politics became increasingly intertwined with state patronage.[111]

The heated political struggles of the first decades of the Third Republic brought politicians to almost every village in the Ardèche. In October 1895 Odilon Barrot came to visit the "antique village" of Balazuc. He was greeted with a reception at the Café Roudil and lunch at the Restaurant Boyer, both in the village, followed by the inevitable toasts and a short speech. At a banquet in Chauzon the subject of the possibility of having the train stop in Pradons naturally came up. When in September 1897 it came time to inaugurate the new improved road that now cut through the village, Hugon was there to take credit for the government, along with the subprefect, Deputy Barrot, and several "republican mayors."[112]

Two years after the laicization of the girls' school, national political debates shaped the election of 1900. Barrot, who that year intervened so that the Ministry of Public Instruction sent some books to the boys' school, closely followed the municipal election in the village that had supported him in the legislative election by a narrow majority. His patronage also was decisive in obtaining a large enough state subsidy in order to build the school on which work had already begun. As both sides prepared for the election, Charousset, realizing that only a few votes would separate the two lists, took a calculated risk. As rumors circulated that he had directed to political allies state payments intended to compensate villagers who had lost harvests in the freezing temperatures of the previous year, he sought the support of moderate conservatives. This move enraged some republicans and played into the hands not only of Mouraret but also of the village priest, Abbé Sablet. But there was more to it than that. For some time, there had been tension between Charousset and Benjamin Boyer, a tobacconist (which had led to the latter's resignation as deputy mayor not long before the election because of the incompatibility of that job and the functions of deputy mayor), who seems to have run an unauthorized *bureau de tabac*. Boyer would not tolerate any compromise with political adversaries of "clerical tendencies."

He blamed Charousset, who at the time still attended church, for listening too often to the clever priest, described by the prefect as "a man infinitely superior to Charousset, Boyer, and the others."[113]

In 1900 Boyer had an enthusiastic ally in Jean Mollier, son of the elderly rural guard, a former victim of the coup d'état of 1851. The younger Mollier never tired of proclaiming his anticlericalism and loudly denouncing the village priest. This made him many enemies in Balazuc. It was more than a little awkward for the rural guard that his son, albeit forty-five years of age, now vehemently criticized the mayor. Complicating matters were chronic complaints against the elder Mollier's work as rural guard, although Charousset had sung his praises in a report the previous year, citing his devotion to the republic. Mollier ignored the rowdy behavior of railwaymen who walked up the hill to Balazuc to drink late into the night almost every Sunday. Hunters and fishermen enjoyed themselves at any time with impunity. The latter included the younger Mollier, who bragged that because of his father's influence, he did not fear being arrested by the gendarmes for infractions. Most of the population seemed to want a new rural guard. Following an investigation by the gendarmerie, Mollier *père* stayed on.[114]

Boyer then formed an electoral slate with six other men, including several members of the departing council. Thus the republicans put forward two lists, dividing their support, to the irritation of Barrot and the prefect. Mouraret's single list under the umbrella "For God and for the Country!" carried the day. Behind this victory was Abbé Sablet, "who . . . will, obviously, run the new municipality. . . . [O]f a shrewd and supple character and greater intelligence than the ordinary countryside priest, he knows how to insert himself adroitly in communal affairs, acting slyly, calling himself a republican." As people in Balazuc would put it, "he sneaked around" (*il avait bien serpenté*)." The "liberals"—that is, moderate conservatives—led by Marius Mouraret (who was elected mayor by eight votes to four for Charousset), came to power. Mouraret represented Balazuc at the famous banquet for mayors (attended by almost twenty-three thousand mayors) held in Paris on the occasion of the Exposition of 1900. As if to celebrate Mouraret's victory, the Brothers of the Redemption preached a mission in Balazuc, concluding with a procession under arcs of triumph. The priest then organized a new (and apparently short-lived) confraternity, joined by about forty men.[115]

After Mouraret's victory in 1900, signs of growing political conflict jump out from the minutes of subsequent municipal council meetings. Mouraret insisted that Charousset had not provided a proper accounting from the past year, and a tax receiver had to sort things out. Charousset's accounting had been a bit loose, and he owed the commune money left over from the purchase of sacks of lime to close the cemetery wall. Forty-five francs had been maintained on the commune's budget to maintain the village clock, although the clock had not worked for six years. The money had been used to pay for modest improvements in the schools. With increasing hostility between the two sides, it became more difficult to find a quorum at municipal meetings; in 1903 two meetings had to be canceled and the third lacked a quorum.[116]

The conservatives had won in 1900 because of the double republican list. Before the legislative elections two years later, Charousset presided over a banquet in honor of Barrot; his enemy Mouraret headed the table when it was the turn of the conservative candidate Duclaux-Monteil to come to the village. Barrot won the majority of votes in Balazuc.[117] When the roof of the new school was completed late in 1902, the entrepreneur organized a banquet for the workers, who sang the *"Marseillaise"* and the *"International,"* further enraging the enemies of lay education. In 1904, the election for the Conseil Général and, later in the year, the hotly contested municipal elections brought François Vincent, anticlerical politician and Freemason, to Balazuc on two occasions, with Charousset presiding. At Vincent's second visit, the "republican electors of Balazuc" formed a Radical-Socialist Committee after his talk; sixty immediately signed up, and Vincent became the honorary president. The meeting ended with shouts of "Long live the democratic and social republic!" that, given the village's tradition and notwithstanding the Second Republic, seemed more in place in Roubaix or Limoges, large working-class cities in which Socialists dominated municipal politics, than in Balazuc.[118]

The new public school, opened in 1903, was a short walk from the new church built only seven years earlier, two competing symbols of political division as well as sources of solidarity. The behavior of the new village priest, Albert Blachère, provided ammunition for anti-clericals. In 1902 the municipality had decided to sell the presbytery, across the stone stairs and path from the deconsecrated Romanesque church. The house, still there, had a ground floor with four rooms, five more rooms above, two tapestries, a *cave*, and a terrace. The property contained a garden behind the church and a stable below the church itself and, farther up the path, an adjacent house that, once intended for the girls' school in the 1850s, now was missing a roof. However, thirty-three "property owners and republican electors of Balazuc" protested the proposed purchase, "a decision taken by a reactionary group on the municipal council" to sell a house that was of use to the village. Moreover, the municipal council would then have to find another presbytery for the village priest or else pay him an indemnity so that he could rent a house. The council voted to sell the presbytery by auction, while Charousset and his allies boycotted the meeting. Mouraret argued that repairs to make the house livable would be too expensive and that money from the sale could be used to repair a bridge on one of the paths.[119]

Then Père Blachère got into the action. He demanded that the municipality pay him an indemnity for his housing. In the meantime he resided in another house and rented out the new house that was supposed to serve as the presbytery, along with its cistern. Charousset protested to the subprefect, arguing that the sums the priest had demanded since his arrival in Balazuc in 1901 would have paid for the repairs. Ordered by the subprefect to vote an indemnity, some members of the council left the room in protest.[120]

While the abbé Blachère and the municipality were locked in combat, the 1904 municipal elections in the Ardèche reflected the national struggle between anticlericals and the Church. The state had closed the schools of St.-Joseph and St.-Régis in Aubenas and expelled a religious order from Notre-Dame-de-Bon-Secours in Lablachère the previous year. Thousands of people protested. *L'Echo de Largentière* described how "the axes of the French Army broke the locks of our convent . . . June 2, 1903, an unforgettable date in the history of the religious struggles of the Ardèche."[121]

In Balazuc, as the new school was being completed and the small private school for girls was about to close its doors for lack of pupils, the elections of 1904 took place in a charged atmosphere that one (republican) commentary described: "Since May 16 [1877], we have not seen in Balazuc a similar passion." Rumors abounded of threats and bribes, and of insults directed against Victor Giry, the boys' teacher, known for his large mustache, who preached republican unity. A "list of republican concentration" opposed what departmental authorities referred to as the "reactionary list of the mayor," Marius Mouraret. The outcome reflected the almost even split in Balazuc between staunch republicans, with seven councillors elected (six on the first ballot), and conservatives (two on the first ballot), with five councillors. Two or three votes could make the difference between victory and defeat. Mouraret led the way on the first ballot with 113 votes, followed by Charousset with one less. Moreover, the influence of national political affiliations could be seen even within the republican list, on which successful candidates (as well as others) ran under Charousset's rubric "Radical-Socialist" or simply "Radical." The subprefect simply damned the opposing list as "reactionary." The election of the mayor and deputy mayor reflected sharp political division: Charousset was elected mayor with 7 votes to 2 for Mouraret and 3 left blank. The very first issue, however small, reflected the split: The mayor argued that the previous administration had failed to vote funds to maintain a mailbox at the station. The council voted to restore the mailbox.[122] Not surprisingly, the newly constituted municipal council again rejected Blachère's demand for an indemnity. Now it was the turn of Mouraret and three other conservatives to storm out of the meeting.[123]

The separation of church and state in 1905 and, above all, the wrenching church inventories carried out by state officials the following year restored full passion to the politics of religion. Duclaux-Monteil returned to Balazuc in January 1905 for a speech and banquet in his honor. That same year a Republican Radical-Socialist Committee, over which Charousset presided, sent a letter proclaiming its devotion to the government at the time of the separation of church and state. *L'Echo de Largentière* called on Catholics to defend "religion, the country, family. . . . [T]he duty of Catholics and true French is to protest with all their forces and all the means at their disposal."[124]

That year Père Blachère stirred things up again after an elderly woman who had been known for her piety died. When her family went to see the priest, he refused—if his vociferous critics were to be believed—to prepare for the funeral until he was paid. The family had little money. Angered, they organized a civil burial, an extremely rare event in the region that immediately took on political overtones.[125] In 1906, Bishop Bonnet led the charge against Vincent. He warned his flock, "It would offend God gravely to vote badly, that is . . . to deliver the destiny of the country to men hostile to religion and dangerous to society. . . . [T]o abstain by negligence, laziness, whim, or any other cause also cannot be excused, for to abandon the struggle without good reason would make one guilty of a mortal sin," punishable, in the eyes of the Church, by eternal damnation. In contrast, Vincent and other strongly republican candidates boasted that they had something to offer peasant proprietors. Vincent ("The son of peasants, I have lived my entire life with the small and the humble!"), a member of the Conseil Général, promised to work for the renewal of subsidies for producers of raw silk (it would have been political suicide not to do so) and to "coordinate" education, carefully avoiding any mention of the wrenching separation of church and state. Duclaux-Monteil was elected to the Chamber of Deputies.[126] Balazuc and many other villages were divided right down the middle. Vincent received 105 votes, and his conservative opponent 99. The narrow margins of victory or defeat made the political contests even more heated.

In 1906 the state-directed inventories of churches led to angry and sometimes violent confrontations in the Ardèche. At Beaulieu, the ringing of the tocsin summoned the faithful in March, determined to prevent lay authorities from entering the church. In Chandolas, troops forced open the door. Locksmiths had to be called to the churches of Banne and Vinezac, among other places. Initial attempts to carry out inventories failed in Pradons, Chauzon, Lanas, St.-Maurice-d'Ibie, Vesseaux, Jaujac, and Sampzon.[127] There was trouble at Berrias, St.-Sauveur-de-Cruzières, and Laurac. Headlines in *L'Echo de Largentière* screamed: THE INVENTORY OF THE CHURCH OF LAURAC! and SIEGE OF THE CATHEDRAL OF VIVIERS! *Le Républicain des Cévennes* carried full reports providing the opposite point of view, starting, for example, that the inventory could not take place in Rosières because "the hostility of a handful of fanatics [had] prevented the tax authorities from getting to the church" or that it had been carried out in Salavas despite the fact that the village priest had barricaded the door, or that it had not occurred in Cros de Géorand because of the violent opposition of fifteen hundred "brigands," reviving a term from the counterrevolutionary years of the Directory.[128]

In Balazuc, collective memory has it that Blachère, who remained in the village for twenty-seven years, and some of his parishioners barricaded themselves inside the church. A detachment of soldiers and some gendarmes camped in the field next to the school, and "troops had to intervene in the presence of the population. A mother took along her little boy to see this so that he would always remember the act that she considered an infamy." The blows of an ax battered open the heavy wooden door, and the agents of the tax authorities went in to carry out the inventory. By common consent, the door was left unrepaired for some time as a protest against the inventory.[129]

Emboldened by the inventory, Charousset's *blocards*, as their enemies called them, adopted a more overtly anticlerical stance. If Charousset led, his lieutenants included Louis Boyer, the young secretary of the *mairie;* Chareyron, the stationmaster, who, upon his arrival to work in Balazuc, became the village's only Protestant; and Joseph-Socrate Redon, a shoemaker who, after working in Lyon for several religious communities, had returned to Balazuc "a relentless anticlerical" and took over the café at the small train station in 1907. Boyer, twenty-four, was a tiny, glib, though uneducated, man, the son of a poor farmer (this hardly made him unusual). There were others as well, such as Adrien Fromentin, descendant of a man condemned after the resistance to the coup d'état in 1851, and the Rieu brothers, both quarry workers.

The classic confrontation between lay teacher and priest intensi-
fied the bad feeling. Giry, the boys' teacher and a friend of Vincent's,
actively supported Charousset and his anticlerical list. Militants
included the mailman, who lived in Ruoms but whose daily rounds
brought him to Balazuc. His son was the Radical-Socialist candidate
for election to the Conseil d'Arrondissement. In this way, the *blocards*
of the left benefited from the support of men whose occupations took
them almost everywhere in Balazuc.[130]

In his account of political life "in primitive places like Balazuc,"
"Sylvestre," an Aubenas journalist (Paul Gouy) who followed events
in Balazuc, identified important traditions in the Bas-Vivarais, above
all, "those that impose on our peasants, as a strict duty, mutual assistance, compromise between neighbors and citizens, a moderate tone
in private or local debates, and the forms of rustic politeness even in
the case of conflict." He accused Charousset and his allies of breaking
with these traditions. Moreover, he claimed that the anticlerical
authorities in Largentière and Privas had taken advantage of "the
somewhat fearful respect of the government, the high administration, and of justice, natural to conservative populations," by supporting Charousset and his friends. In this way, he put his finger on
the ability of the centralized republican government to offer patronage to villages such as Balazuc. "Sylvestre" denounced "the new revolutionary feudalism that oppresses and exploits, under the aegis of
the centralized government unfaithful to its mission."[131]

The 1908 municipal elections threatened to be particularly ugly.
They offer a rare view of the world of village politics among close
friends and close enemies. Charousset's now-overt anticlericalism
irritated many practicing Catholics, as did the mayor's identification
with Vincent, *conseiller général* and an officer in the Masonic lodge of
Aubenas. Charousset enjoyed the support of the regional Radical-
Socialist Federation. Even as the elections began May 3, the two factions began to argue over the nomination of the members of the
bureau for the election that would oversee the balloting and declare
improperly marked ballots invalid. (Until the secret ballot was introduced in 1913, electors carried to the table ballots that were obviously for one or another candidate or for a complete list, in full view

of the various members of the electoral bureau.) By tradition, the bureau included two counters who were the oldest eligible voters and two who were the youngest. Charousset sought the exclusion of the elderly Daumas, a "liberal" (thus conservative in the French sense), because it was not clear that he could read and write, though the "liberals" claimed that he was literate. The balloting itself immediately brought accusations by the "liberals" of irregularities because they maintained that the number of votes in the urn, 197, did not match the 211 voters declared to have voted, a figure subsequently reduced to 208, and that some additional "votes" had been added to the mix. When Charousset announced that his list had been elected, each with only a margin of 1, 2, or 3 votes, the conservatives submitted a formal protest to the prefecture. In June, the administrative tribunal of Largentière invalidated Balazuc's election, noting that the oldest elector had not been allowed to serve as *assesseur*. In the meantime Charousset remained mayor, with a new election scheduled for the following year, a decision confirmed upon appeal by Charousset and his friends to the Conseil d'État in March 1909.[132]

In a region of high religious practice, two more civil burials took place in Balazuc in 1908. The first was that of "Citoyen" Bourret, a "militant democrat" and freethinker, whose funeral brought delegations from other villages. At the end of the year came the funeral of Ferdinand Pays, whose brother served on the municipal council. However, even during the height of the stormy debates over the separation, many of those who supported the latter seem to have continued to attend church. "Sylvestre" made a point of noting that Charousset had stopped going to Mass only about 1900, implying that this was at the orders of the subprefecture in Largentière, and that many "*blocards* by their votes, remain practicing Catholics by their feelings and habits."[133]

Charousset went on the attack. On August 28, 1908, he provocatively banned all "religious ceremonies . . . on the public way throughout the territory of the commune of Balazuc" with the exception of funerals.[134] Such measures were then common in cities and towns held by Socialists, but rare in villages. Certainly, for Balazuc's anticlericals, the procession under arcs of triumph at the conclusion of the religious missions (several days of fire-and-brimstone preaching and prayer) in December 1900 remained a frame of reference. In the meantime Mouraret also accused his rival of failing to account properly for the use of funds.

In January 1909 Charousset appointed as rural guard Jean Mollier, a former postman and the son of the controversial predecessor who had been arrested after the coup d'état and had resigned in 1901 during the Mouraret administration. Six men who owned land on the *gras* had filed a complaint against Gamel, the incumbent, in 1906, saying that their harvests had been almost entirely "ravaged" by sheep because of the negligence of shepherds. Antoine Mouraret claimed that the animals consumed hundreds of pounds of grapes and mulberry leaves. Gamel lost his job as rural guard.[135]

On the day of the election, June 20, 1909, on the ground floor of the small feudal donjon, the mayor set up the voting table, naming three of his allies, including the youthful secretary Boyer and an aged conservative as counters. As mayor Charousset would preside. Mouraret and his allies later claimed that the table had been set up to prevent any monitoring of the count. To be sure, two gendarmes were present, though it is unclear who first requested their presence. The conservatives may have done so, asserting that intimidation and perhaps even violence would be used against their supporters. Yet the mayor had expressed fear to the subprefect that "seditious gatherings" and even "riots are very much to fear from this band."[136] The gendarmes had been seen early that morning at Redon's small café at the railroad station, drinking with several of the mayor's friends.

Charousset penned a brief decree, referring to "an encumbrance in the room . . . that troubles that threatened to erupt at the opening of the vote." Claiming later that he had expected trouble from "a band of partisans of the Mouraret list," he forbade anyone from staying more than a quarter of an hour in the room and required everyone to stand at least five feet from the table.[137] To his opponents, such a decree in a village of 576 inhabitants with only 241 eligible voters, who would have six hours to cast their ballots, also seemed intended to prevent any effective surveillance of the process of the counting of ballots. Mouraret's allies, convinced that Charousset would stop at nothing to win, indeed sought to monitor the vote.

Enter Mollier, terribly obligated to Charousset. Mouraret claimed that the rural guard had approached the table with two ballots, thus voting twice. Another Mollier, Marius, noticed this and said to Charousset, in the patois of everyday life, *"Oqui l'y o dous bulletins"* ("He has two ballots"), to which Charousset replied, *"N'en sabé pas rien, sé pouo bé"* ("I don't know anything about it; you can appeal it"), while placing the ballot(s) in the ballot box. When Marius Mollier and Guibourdenche protested vigorously, Charousset ordered the gendarmes to evict them from the hall.

Four o'clock came. Voting was over, and inhabitants squeezed into the small, humid room. Charousset announced that 215 ballots had been cast by 218 voters, with 3 improper ballots annulled (despite opposition claims that they were valid). As the early counting ran against the *blocard* list, conservatives began to claim that Charousset, who was reading off the ballots and then putting them into the box, was counting for his list ballots that had been cast for their opponents. Boyer declared that one ballot, the writing of which he could see was that of a prominent conservative voter, had been counted for the other side. At the end of the tally, Charousset announced that of 215 ballots, 118 votes had gone to his list, and 97 to his adversaries, almost exactly the victory by 20 votes that he had predicted.

The uproar that followed took on greater political proportions in the context of the heated politics of the period. The conservatives, convinced that they had lost the election because of fraud, launched a formal protest. They asserted that in fact, of the 241 eligible men, only 197 had voted and that the other votes were imaginary. They counted eligible voters who they insisted had not cast ballots because they were dead (3 cases), absent (13 soldiers in service and 18 men away from Balazuc on election day), ill (3 confined to bed), or indifferent (6), for a total of 43. Moreover, they pointed out that the percentage of actual voters claimed by their opponents was improbably high (90 percent, particularly as only 197 votes had been cast in 1908). ELECTORAL SCANDALS IN BALAZUC! shouted the headline of *L'Echo de Largentière.* Politics had become so contentious that when

Balazuc's stationmaster was transferred in 1909, *La République des Cévennes* intoned, "Alas, Monsieur Chareyron could not please the fat clerical cockroaches of Balazuc," noting that he had obtained his post through hard work, not through the favor of "our Jesuits" and that he would leave "with the congratulations of the republican population of Balazuc."[138]

However, the next month the Conseil de Préfecture rejected the conservatives' claims because the confusion reigning in the small hall seemed to justify the mayor's actions. Furthermore, it was damaging to conservative claims that the official counter associated with the "liberal" cause, Georges, eighty-two years of age, had signed what was supposed to be the official record of the count. The appellate court in Nîmes rejected an appeal.

Balazuc remained bitterly divided politically.[139] But Charousset's star plunged, even among his political allies. The municipal council did not select him as a delegate for the senatorial elections, a sure sign of disapproval because the mayor was usually elected for this almost honorific task without debate. He resigned in August 1910, having served as mayor since 1892, a stretch broken only by the period 1900 to 1904. He left bitterly: "It is impossible for me to continue to serve as mayor [confronted with] a certain number of idiots and jealous people on the municipal council." He could no longer direct the council, whose members ignored his summons to meet. Charousset's spouse wrote of her husband: "[H]e is not mean, he is too good, and would not do harm to anyone. . . . [T]he lack of agreement with the council means that there is little that he can do." She implored the subprefect to accept his resignation, which would restore "unity to the council, peace in my family. [D]o this for me and for my children. Bad blood has done all of this to us." Then, early in 1911, the Conseil d'État turned aside the earlier decision of the Conseil de Préfecture, meaning that Balazuc's infamous elections of June 1909 were also annulled.[140]

Marius Mouraret and his entire list won back the *mairie* in March 1911. They moved it from the Tour Carrée, where it had been since 1896, to the ground floor of the boys' school not far away.[141] Soon after the elections, on May 25, the mayor reversed the ban on religious processions, which had taken place in the Catholic village "from time immemorial in the commune and have never given rise to any disorder." The council suppressed the post of rural guard. Vincent, now a senator, tried to intervene for Mollier, "without resources and worthy of the greatest consideration," his father having been persecuted after the coup d'état of 1851. Mouraret hired Damien Gamel with the new, even cheaper title of *appariteur* in May 1911.[142]

Balazuc's left republicans were in disarray. In 1912, Mouraret's entire list triumphed again. In the legislative elections two years later, Duclaux-Monteil emerged victorious.[143] Continued emigration from Balazuc may have contributed to reducing the number of voters on the left. In the meantime, sharp rhetoric and bruising accusations cascaded from both sides. In April 1914 *L'Echo de Largentière* accused "Citizen Thomas" of provocatively eating meat on Good Thursday and Holy Friday before Easter and of referring to practicing Catholics as a "bleating herd." *L'Echo Paroissial de Balazuc* (identical to that of those printed for other villages), which published such articles as "A Saint per Month," "A Force: Sanctifying Grace," "Yes, My Boy, Become a Priest!," "The France That Is Dying" [from having too few children], etc., boasted in May 1912 that there were seventy-nine lay schools with between 0 and 5 pupils and that in those same communes the same number of *écoles libres* taught 3,520 children.

Still, the existence of the republic itself was no longer really contested. Saluting the victory of Duclaux-Monteil in the elections of April 1914, *L'Echo de Largentière* distanced itself and the deputy from his political opponents on the left, but not from the republic: "A magnificent victory prepared for M. Duclaux-Monteil. . . . He demands . . . fundamental liberties, including the freedom of conscience. Long live France! Long live the republic!"[144] For many on the Catholic right, this would have been an unthinkable combination not long before. In Balazuc the bridge that stretched across the Ardèche was a daily reminder of the republic's victory.

SEVEN

Through Two Wars

ON AUGUST 3, 1914, GENDARMES FROM RUOMS BROUGHT news of war to Balazuc. Henri Duchamp, the village crier, went through the village and its hamlets beating his drum to announce the general mobilization. Men from Balazuc, sure that they would be home "before the leaves fall," soon left to fight. A telegram that evening announced the German campaign of "false news" in Alsace-Lorraine, ongoing Russian preparation for the war, news that French cavalrymen had surprised German troops at Torry-le-Sec, killing five and wounding two, with no losses, and the dubious story that the Germans had shot two fifteen-year-old boys near Longwy, while expressing confidence that reserves would be held back to help bring in an adequate harvest. A commission at the prefecture considered measures to be taken to assure the provisioning of the population. Three days later great popular enthusiasm greeted news of the entry of French troops into Alsace, the population seemingly unaware of the rapid German advance through Belgium and the threat to Paris.

In the meantime the government decree that banned absinthe certainly fell on deaf ears. *L'Echo de Largentière* carried an account of the funeral of the first French soldier killed in the war.[1]

René Viviani's proclamation on behalf of the Council of Ministers blaming Germany for the outbreak of war had made the point that fighting had begun before the harvest could be completed. This underlined the importance of completing the work that would assure food for the coming year, calling on "French women, young children, sons and daughters of the republic" to accomplish the task.

The war brought refugees from Alsace and Lorraine to the Ardèche (about a third of them speaking only their own dialects), among the more than 5,600 French refugees from the battle zones of northern France and 640 Belgians temporarily resettled. However, only one family of Belgian refugees was temporarily resettled in Balazuc during the war and then not until 1918.

By March 1915 forty-three men from Balazuc were in the army. They included three each of the Tastevins, Molliers, Fromentins, Mourarets, and Duffauds and two each of the Ranchins, Mirabels, Duffauds, Constants, and Charoussets. Antoine Charousset and Joseph Ranchin were among those who left in early August; they both were fathers of large families, and the small financial assistances due them were immediately transferred to their spouses. Marie Moulin, a widow, asked for help; her son had been mobilized, and she had only 150 francs paid by a family farming a small piece of land she owned. Philomène Ruissol, another widow, received a small monthly allocation from the state because her son, Arsène, had been called to duty. A poor village in a poor region, the municipality could do little more than raise its annual allocation of thirty francs reserved for needy families whose sons were in the military to a hundred francs to be divided among the families of the wounded. In 1915, Henri Georges Dufaud lay wounded in Hall Number 8 of the military hospital in the Grand Palais in Paris. He sent a letter asking that his mother receive what small payments he had coming. Dufaud was killed near Abbeville in 1918.[2]

War compounded the lack of labor, in part a product of the massive emigration from the countryside. Soldiers and then in some places prisoners of war were brought in to help with the harvest. But in the rough country of the Bas-Vivarais, where peasants scratched out livings with their hands and many still carried what they produced to market on their shoulders or by mule, local people were skeptical that outside labor could be used. Elderly men, women, and children brought in the harvest. Yet some land and vineyards could simply not be harvested, and their grapes were left to wither, even if the situation was better in 1916 than the previous year. Among the immediate results of the loss through mobilization (to say nothing of wounds and death) of so many men was that Balazuc's roads and paths suffered.[3] Government requisitions became commonplace. The army requisitioned mules and horses (complete with harnesses) and several vehicles and other animals and one-sixth of all wine from the harvest of 1916.[4]

When Casimir Roux went off to the Great War in the first days of August 1914 at the age of thirty-seven, he left behind Augusta Giry Roux, his twenty-eight-year-old pregnant wife, and two children, three and two years old. He soon fell wounded. On September 12, Augusta wrote the mayor of Balazuc to ask for his support in obtaining some assistance "for support of his family" from the cantonal committee that allocated small sums of assistance to families whose men were in military service. On November 4 she went to the mayor to ask for his support for help, making the case that her husband represented "my sole source of support" and that all their available resources had been used up. However, the cantonal commission unanimously rejected her appeal, agreeing with the mayor that Roux and his family "possess sufficient resources. Nothing in the dossier establishes the opposite."

Early in 1915, Roux wrote the prefect from Hall Number 21 in a military hospital of Marseille to ask that the decision be reviewed. He insisted that "my means of existence do not permit me to keep quiet about this subject, being only a simple farmer with only the labor of my wife to keep us going there, especially as at the time of my departure we were awaiting a third child."

Married to one of the few sharecroppers living in Balazuc and thus even poorer than almost everybody else, Augusta Giry Roux described her life: "I have absolutely not a cent left to obtain what is indispensable to a family of eight people." The grocer and the baker refused her any more credit. "Indeed, we own almost nothing. . . . [T]hus for us [there is] only dark misery. It was already difficult enough for us to make ends meet through the relentless work of my husband, but what is going to happen now and in our future? Do you want to force us to resort to the worst expediencies? We must live and cloth ourselves." She asked that the subprefect be "more human" than those who had provided the cantonal commission with misleading information and that he annul the decision of the justice of the peace and rule in her favor. She sent along the receipt of the taxes paid by her family in 1914, barely seven and a half francs.

Augusta Giry's letter to the president of the Appeal Commission in Largentière, written with firm hand, made a strong case as she related her life:

"My husband, Casimir Roux, had been in the trenches for already quite some time. Before the war, he was only a simple sharecropper." They had worked the small piece of land of Perbost, the former mayor, since September 1, 1913. He had paid their taxes. Thus, "[n]othing on this land belongs to us; the pair of oxen and other animals, the agricultural tools, and even the fertilizer have been purchased by the owner and not by us, for lack of money." Yet like many other extremely poor people in Balazuc, Roux owned a tiny piece of land that earned the astoundingly small sum, somehow, of sixty-seven centimes; half a piece of land earning 8.84 francs, left to him by an uncle; and a small house. "Here is our entire fortune." His mother worked a piece of land that had belonged to her husband's father, but this generated no income for them. Nothing was left: "Our small savings, so carefully put together, have been spent long ago." With no resources and no help, Augusta Roux could not farm the land that had been left fallow. "All our provisions have also been used up. We have had nothing for quite some time. My two girls and I (who will soon have a third child) survive only because of the charity of our good neighbors." (Again the long tradition of mutual assistance.) Only the "hard and cruel necessity" of begging for bread at the *mairie* remained open to her. Things could not get much worse.

The justice of the peace, confronted by many similar appeals, turned down Augusta Giry. However, a note scribbled on the margin of the letter noted that she was "almost without resources" and that most of the money that had come from the family's small harvest of cocoons had already been spent in paying off debts. Clearly, no one in the family could work the land of the wounded soldier. She would receive 2.25 francs a month, less than a good day's wages, on which she would have to feed her two and soon three children. At least it was something.⁵

No one wanted to see the man from the telegraph office at the door. Léon Charousset, who had worked his family's land, became the first soldier from Balazuc to be killed when he fell on September 22 in the Meuse. Imagine what went through the mind of Marie Granier of Balazuc, who had received a telegram bringing bad news about a certain Auguste Granier. Not knowing what to think, and hoping against hope, she sent off a return telegram indicating that her son's name was Eugène Louis Granier. A return telegram asked the mayor to inform Monsieur (but not Madame) Jean Granier that Eugène Louis Granier had died from bullet wounds at 11:15 P.M. in Temporary Hospital Number 4 at Verdun on April 17, 1915. Their son's death certificate followed in the mail.⁶

Cruelly, some death certificates were followed by bills for taxes, assessed as if those to whom they had been addressed were still alive. Léon Charousset's father wrote the tax office that his son had been killed in battle and asked that he be excused from future taxes because he was dead. Gustave Rigaud wrote to say that his nephew could not be taxed because he had been killed on October 24, 1915. Jean-Baptiste Pascal's reply noted that his son had suffered the amputation of his right arm and the loss of an eye, Madame Mirabel's that her husband had been killed by the enemy in December 1916.⁷

Twenty-four men from Balazuc were killed during the war. Of these, sixteen had lived in the village in 1914, the remainder having moved away, or had married women from Balazuc.⁸ The first two were killed in September 1914: Victorien Brun, twenty-seven years of age, who worked his family's land, and Denis Brun, both killed near Verdun. Marius Arsène Mollier lost his life shortly after his twenty-eighth birthday in the fighting at the Crête d'Ormont in September 1914. The news that Firmin Tastevin had died at age thirty-five from wounds suffered at Roclincourt, north of Arras, arrived at his mother's café in October 1915. His brother Paul had already been killed in the Meuse the previous April. One after another family received terrible news from Abbeville, Craonne in the Aisne, the Oise, the Marne, from the Somme, of course, from "sector 40," and even from Tunisia. Joseph Redon, son of the former *chef de gare*, fell in April 1916 at the fort of Souville (Meuse). Paul Mirabel fell just before his forty-fourth birthday at Hallivillers in the Somme, leaving a wife and two daughters; Frédéric Giry, son of Balazuc's teachers, was killed at Moulainville, near Verdun, in the Meuse. The news of the death of Louis Gineys at Pontavert (Aisne, a few miles from where Marius Boyer was killed the next month) in April 1917 was not communicated to his family until the following October, along with the information that he had been buried in Tomb 616 at the cemetery of Beaumarais in Pontavert. The widow of one of the two Charoussets killed during the war and Lucie Brugière, the widow of Jules Débard, henceforth received five francs a month, as did Joseph Dufaud, one of whose five children had been killed at the front.[9]

Better news, all things considered, sometimes arrived in the form of sons, brothers, and fathers returning, discharged as disabled (*mutilés de guerre*) or with lesser wounds. In Paris, several seats were reserved for them on the *métro*. Balazuc did not have one. Damien Gamel came back with a fractured leg, for which he received a pension of 300 francs for a sixth-category wound. Emile Salel, wounded by an exploding shell, could expect 100 francs less for one of the seventh category. An exploding shell at Metzeral (Haut-Rhin) in the Vosges Mountains in April 1915 paralyzed Henri Rieu's right arm (a fifth-category wound); certainly he would never return to his prewar work as a stonecutter. Marius Duffaud lost his left eye, for which he received an annual pension of 762 francs. Emile Mollier returned with the *croix de guerre*, but without his left arm. Many other soldiers from Balazuc, like soldiers from anywhere in the Great War, suffered lesser wounds (and had reason to consider themselves the lucky ones).

One such was Félix Brun, wounded in September 1914 and sent to recuperate in St.-Brieuc. Distressing but in some ways reassuring news reached seven families that close relatives had been taken prisoner and were being held in camps ranging from Münsingen in Württemberg to Hammelburg in Bavaria to the German-occupied Aisne.[10]

The home front at Balazuc held very well, however much morale itself depended on the rhythms of rural life and the degrees of privation. The role of the clergy at the military front and at home eased tensions between clericals and anticlericals. News from the war came with the return of soldiers on leave or from trips to the markets of Aubenas or Joyeuse, where newspapers were to be found.[11] At long last, after all this, news of the armistice arrived on November 11 by telegram and exuberant church bells.

With the end of the war, the municipality voted money "to erect a monument commemorating the glorious sons of the commune fallen on the field of honor during the Great War." A government subsidy of a thousand francs and a public subscription added to the funds available. The original proposed inscription, "To France's Dead," was changed to "Balazuc to Its Dead for the Country, 1914–1919."[12] A branch of vines runs up the side to a cross that surmounts the monument, on which are inscribed the names of the twenty-four men from Balazuc killed in the war.[13] The placement of the monument, just below and between the two stairs going up to the entrance of the new church, reflected the continuing close ties between the church and the community, despite the political battles of the prewar period. Although some tension between clericals and anticlericals remained, a decline in its intensity may have been one reaction to the horrors of the war. The monument was inaugurated on September 25, 1921, but not without controversy. Marius Guibourdenche, the new mayor, who served throughout the entire interwar period, was a conservative Catholic who had invited to the ceremony Xavier Vallat, the deputy of the Ardèche, a leader of the right in the Chamber of Deputies, and a vicious anti-Semite who made his mark during the Vichy years. Four municipal councillors protested by refusing to attend the ceremony, which included a Solemn High Mass.[14]

Obviously the gnawing pain of loss was virtually everywhere. The municipality advanced funds, which were to be reimbursed by the state, so that the family of Jean Pérol could have his remains transferred to Balazuc from a military cemetery near where he had been killed.[15] During the war, 12,363 ardéchois were killed, a total that fell particularly hard on the Bas-Vivarais. In St.-Jean-de-Pourcharesse, 29 of the commune's 201 inhabitants were killed. Lagorce had 57 people killed. Balazuc's dead represented 4 percent of its prewar population, slightly above the national average of 3.6 percent.[16] The percentage of males killed was of course much higher and reduced the number of prospective grooms, contributing after the war to the continued low birthrate. Rising prices (notably that of coal, for example, for heat in the schools) and unemployment added hard times to gripping sadness.[17] Demands for the small money that the municipality could provide now inevitably included mentions of sons lost in the war, such as that of one man, whose *famille nombreuse* (large family) now had one less at the table.[18]

The Great War accentuated Balazuc's decline. The armistice brought peace but did not end the exodus: From 1911 to 1921 the Ardèche lost 37,500 people, and over the next five years another 7,000 inhabitants left.[19] In all, the population of the department fell from 331,808 in 1911 first to 273,000 in 1936 and then to 249,077 in 1954.[20] Not until the 1960s did the Ardèche again gain population.[21]

Balazuc's population fell from 605 in 1911 to 456 in 1921, a loss of almost a quarter, considerably more than the decline for the canton of Vallon (16 percent) and for the Ardèche as a whole (11.3 percent). Emigrants continued to leave for the Lyon region, the valley of the Rhône, and Marseille. In addition to the men killed during the war, the 1911–20 period brought Balazuc an excess of deaths over births (131 to 57). In 1937 deaths again overtook births, reflecting the aging of the population. Some young women who had left to work in factories during the war never returned. The hemorrhaging of rural France continued, and the population aged. By 1931 Balazuc's population had fallen to 447. Five years later it had declined to 419.[22]

Even as its population continued to plunge and the silk industry declined, startling changes came to Balazuc. Radios turned up in village households. The municipality had seemed slow to act in bringing electricity to the village, whereas its neighbors St.-Maurice-d'Ardèche and Lanas had already taken steps to do so. For most of the interwar period, lamps fueled by olive oil or kerosene (with the help of old socks to keep the flame going) provided light. In September 1930 the council approved funds to complement assistance from the state in order to pay a company to start work. It lasted five years. One by one, the old oil lamps were discarded, and by the late 1930s many houses had electricity.[23] In 1928 the municipality approved the creation of a telephone office that would be linked to the nearest telegraph office. Two men were paid to run the office, and another to deliver telegrams.[24] In 1937 Balazuc joined with Chauzon and Pradons to create the Intercommunal Association to Provide Drinking Water. Bringing water to the village proved to be an enormous undertaking, at the cost of more than a 1.1 million francs and necessitating a subsidy. The village had to wait fifteen more years.[25]

Regulations in 1937 brought new standards for housing to a village with many dilapidated houses. No longer could straw be used to cover any part of a house or stable, and floors had to be at least a foot above the adjoining *ruelle* (walkway), in order to prevent flooding; mud or earth floors were forbidden. Kitchens were to be suitably aired, lighted, and ventilated and have sinks. Bedrooms and windows required minimum dimensions. Chimneys had to reach at least fifteen inches above roofs to reduce the risk of fires. Water pipes, wells, and cisterns had to be covered and placed at sufficient distances from fertilizers and cesspools. Regulations banned throwing dead animals into the river or into other sources of water.[26]

The Great War accentuated the decline of the production of raw silk. During the war itself the silkworm harvest fell by more than half to 776,000 kilograms of cocoons. The production of cocoons continued to fall. From 11 million kilograms of cocoons produced in 1875, the total in the Ardèche fell to 975,000 kilograms in 1934.[27]

Changes in the land told the story. The number of mulberry trees in the Ardèche declined with the population, from at least 2 million

in 1853 to 689,900 in 1929 to 261,030 in 1940. Shortly after World
War I, Élie Reynier, historian of the silk industry, went so far as to
suggest that it might be time "to allow to disappear from a natural
death [the silk industry], which seems preordained by the not any less
natural evolution of production and our industries." He asked point-
blank whether the power of the state should be used to sustain the
production of raw silk and spinning or the peasant component of the
industry should be allowed to disappear by itself, as would be the case
without state support.[28] Production fell to only a thousand tons of
cocoons in 1925. The extension in the late 1920s of artificial and syn-
thetic fibers hurt the industry. From nineteen thousand producers of
raw silk in 1913, the number fell to forty-five hundred in 1938, two
thousand in 1954, and one thousand in 1957. Whereas in 1900, 50
small spinning factories remained in the Ardèche, during the 1930s
only about a dozen remained, while 319 small silk-throwing mills
still were in operation.[29]

   In 1921, Balazuc had been among those communes formally
requesting that subsidies be continued as encouragement and to
prove "the solicitude of the public powers toward the population
of the most underprivileged regions of France . . . regions that can
absolutely not change their agricultural economy" and that would
continue to lose population. In 1919, the village produced only
1,000 quintals of mulberry leaves, "harvest in deficit for all products" because of drought. However, in 1929 seventy-four silkworm
nurseries could still be counted in Balazuc; that year they produced
5,538 kilograms of cocoons. In 1933 the municipality again asked
that the subsidies be maintained, to try to slow down desertion of
the countryside.[30]

   In 1938 the state still provided a subsidy of eight francs for a kilogram of cocoons that would be sold for eight francs. Some of the
shiny, rich leaves of the mulberry trees that remained now went to
feed goats.[31] Yet even then one could find posted warnings that it was
forbidden to "climb up a mulberry tree while wearing hobnailed
shoes" for fear of injuring it, which, if perhaps no longer "golden,"
still had considerable value. In 1941 a law made it illegal to cut down
a mulberry tree in twenty-four departments.[32]

Wine was now Balazuc's principal product. There were only 92 acres of vineyards in Balazuc in 1919, before vineyards began to expand again, 176 acres in 1931, and 208 acres in 1940. In 1921 the Ardèche produced 441,000 hectoliters of wine. By 1935 40,000 acres of vineyards were being cultivated in the Ardèche.[33] In addition to grapes and some barley, oats, and rye, farmers produced cherries, peaches, pears, almonds, and quinces. In 1936 a seasonal daily fruit market began operation in Vallon. Even if mules still carried goods, horses pulled wagons, and here and there a few oxen pulled plows. Mechanized farming came very slowly to Balazuc, with only five tractors and six harvesters by 1930, numbers that increased considerably during the last years of the decade. But other things had not changed. Goats and sheep easily outnumbered other large animals—and villagers as well.[34]

However, the price of wine remained low. Many peasants were furious when in 1931 the government, concerned about overproduction, banned three kinds of varietals, Jacquez, Herbemont, and Clinton (the new strictures, in any case, seemed to favor merchants). Clinton is a particularly potent grape that grows wild in some places and is still raised here and there. It is considered something of a crazy wine because of its effects on consumers. In Balazuc a story is told of one imbiber of a good many glasses of Clinton who made it up thirty or so of the stairs to his house. However, thirty-eight steps were needed to make it to the door, and he fell all the way back down again in a heap. Only producers of high-quality wines in the valley of the Rhône did more than simply survive. Here and there the first wine cooperatives started up, the first in Orgnac in 1925. Soon there were seven.[35]

Thus the entire agricultural triptych of the Ardèche—raw silk, wine, and chestnuts—had fared badly, while the price of fruit, production of which had boomed, remained too low to bring anyone much money. In the meantime the Great Depression eroded the Ardèche's few industries; many of the people who left the department between 1931 and 1936 were factory workers.[36]

Slowly what ultimately proved to be a monumental change came into view. Tourists began to arrive in Balazuc. In 1932, Mayor

Guibourdenche asked that the road from Uzer across the *gras* be reclassified so that the municipality could ask for help from the department. He underlined the fact that "these small roads are today crisscrossed by numerous automobiles, especially those of tourism." The following year the municipality contributed a small sum to help with the creation of a tourist office in the region that would encourage villages to be more welcoming to visitors. By the late 1930s, in the wake of the Popular Front's establishment of paid vacations, canoes were carrying summer visitors down the Ardèche River below Vallon–Pont d'Arc. A couple who still live in Balazuc first arrived on a tandem bike during the Popular Front. In 1937 the minister of the interior ordered that rural guards be uniformed, so that outsiders could not doubt their authority, however minimal: "For the good renown of France abroad, it matters that tourists do not return home again with the impression that in ours the maintenance of order is organized in defective conditions."[37]

Balazuc's isolation, hardly self-imposed, was over. Visitors turned up at the cafés. Those playing boules on the road through the village occasionally had to pause to let automobiles pass. Owners of automobiles in Balazuc were rare even in the late 1930s. Some passengers who got off the train at the station rode donkeys up the steep trek to Balazuc, a mode of transport that had been used for centuries. A man who had inherited an armoire carried it on his back the entire distance from Valgorge to Balazuc, twenty tough miles. Young people thought nothing of walking many miles to participate in the festivals of other villages.

French gradually won the war over patois. Many older people today recall that their parents in the 1930s spoke patois with each other and with friends their age but were apt to speak French with their children, who were immersed in the language at school. The widespread use of patois began to die out in the 1930s.

The struggle to maintain the village infrastructure went on as before. The paths to the hamlets still needed subsidies. Following "meteorological calamities" in 1928, the department provided thirty-five hundred francs to repair damaged paths. Repairs to the school were frequent.[38] The municipal council at first rejected the idea of dividing the school by class instead of by sex; "the very fact of bringing together girls and boys in the same classroom offers serious inconveniences from the point of view of morality." Then, in the early 1930s the school was divided for the first time by class, not by sex, although boys and girls still took their recesses separately.[39]

One man who grew up between the wars expresses a common sentiment that younger people do not appreciate how much they have, at least in comparison with what their parents and grandparents had in their youth. Yet though times were certainly hard, rural communities like Balazuc probably escaped the worst hardships of the Depression because of the capacity of small farmers to return to polyculture and near-subsistence farming. Still, most people in Balazuc remained extremely poor.

Balazuc had one grocery store after the war, but three by the end of the 1930s, as well as a baker in the upper village. The café run by Vianès near the Porte de la Sablière was long gone, but three cafés, including one that doubled as a grocery store, beckoned clients. Near the Tour Carrée a barber offered haircuts before Mass, though because he was known to love to drink, it was better to be shaved by his razor early in the day. There were also two shoemakers, three masons, two cabinetmakers, a butcher, a *commerçant de mode*, two seamstresses, and two roving distillers of spirits. Households had more cash and were less frugal. Balazuciens increasingly made other useful purchases not available in the village at the time of the weekly markets in Joyeuse, Aubenas, and Largentière, instead of depending on peddlers. Furthermore, as part of the Popular Front's opening up of cultural opportunities to more French families, the *bibliobus*, a traveling lending library, began to come to Balazuc and other villages once a week.

In the name of solidarity and within the constraints of its limited budget, the municipal council still allocated small sums to families and individuals who were particularly in need: mothers of newborn, elderly people, the infirm and the incurably ill, and large families (in 1913 there had been six such families in Balazuc, necessitating a small increment in taxes). For example, in 1920, the council provided assistance to four old people, six new mothers, and one large family and had to approve an additional small credit to provide free medical assistance. The following year it divided the sum of 427.50 francs, which came from part of the sale of plots in the cemetery, among ten "needy people who need to be assisted." A year later it aided a man who had been almost completely paralyzed by a stroke: "[A]s he cannot be taken care of at home, possessing no resources, his hospitalization is required for reasons of humanity." In this way, the tradition of mutual assistance continued, here administered by the council. In 1932 the minutes noted that "the municipal council met secretly" to consider a request for help. This reflected the pressures inherent in awarding some families small sums, while turning others down.[40] In 1936 the council rejected an appeal for aid from an elderly man. Although his resources were "few" by any estimate, his daughter promised to provide ten francs per month. This was barely anything, but the man also had a son with some income, and so "his existence seems assured." The village, which had so often suffered at the hands of violent storms, on several occasions voted small sums to help assist villages in France or North Africa that suffered catastrophes.[41]

The role of the Church in the defense of France during the First World War, the time elapsed since the secularization of the school system, the separation of church and state, and the inventories combined to reduce considerable political tension over education and the public place of the Church. However, the rise of the Communist party infused the right in the Ardèche with new energy. In the first elections after the Great War, four of five deputies elected represented the right. They included Gailhard-Bancel, who had lost three sons in the war; Duclaux-Monteil, the old conservative warrior now on the moderate right; and the emerging right-wing leader Xavier Vallat, who received the most votes. In the legislative elections of 1924 (in which, remarkably, all 166 eligible voters went to the polls), Balazuc gave 82 votes to Duclaux-Monteil and 76 to the list of the Cartel des Gauches, on the left, a close election, as in the prewar years. The Ardèche now had only four deputies to elect. Three came from the Cartel, and just Duclaux-Monteil from the right. However, despite Vallat, the Ardèche remained largely isolated from the influence of the parties of the far right. The royalists emerged from the war with few followers. The Catholic newspaper La Croix, aggressively hostile to the lay republic, retained considerable influence in conservative clerical circles, above all, not unexpectedly, in the mountains. In a region with few industries, Communists won small centers of support in Annonay, Aubenas, and, above all, the Rhône River town of Le Teil.

Council members identified with the right carried municipal politics in Balazuc between the wars, even if in national elections the village continued to split its votes somewhat more evenly, again suggesting the importance of personalities. In Balazuc, Catholic political energy revived in the 1920s. In March 1925 about 150 people gathered to hear two speakers defend "the eloquent words of our indefatigable apostles of religious freedom." Balazuc's priest concluded the meeting by urging Catholics to join the Committee of Catholic Union. (*L'Ancien Combattant* offered a less enthusiastic account of the meeting, referring to the speakers as "two zealots" who had summoned "reserves from neighboring communes" to come hear them evoke the memory of religious persecution and the war against the religious orders.) Balazuc's new priest, the abbé Serre, helped keep the Church a political issue. He had come with a reputation of having been influenced by progressive trends within the Church and had not followed the royalist politics of St.-Maurice-d'Ibie, where he had been posted, but in Balazuc he stood accused of refusing to bury a girl from Servière because her family had refused to agree to contribute regularly to the church. At the same time, 70 people in Balazuc belonged to the group of Radical-Socialists. In the context of municipal politics, national party labels, which had only begun to be seen after the turn of the century, remained important, even if the issues discussed at council meetings usually had nothing to do with national politics.[42]

Like his deputy mayor, Philippe Tastevin, Marius Guibourdenche had served on the list of Marius Mouraret before the war. In 1919 three candidates from the left were elected to the council. In 1925 only Hippolyte Freydier, a Radical-Socialist supporter of the Cartel des Gauches, was elected from the left and then only as the last successful candidate on the second ballot. He served with eleven conservative (URD, Union Républicaine Démocratique) republicans.[43]

After Balazuc had again supported Duclaux-Monteil, the conservative list won again in the municipal elections of 1929, with each of
its candidates elected on the first ballot, easily defeating the Radical-
Socialist opposition, and again in 1932. Thus to some extent the old
clerical and anticlerical division remained in the constitution of the
electoral lists, even if the Church itself was less of a political issue in
municipal politics.[44] Both sides had their own cafés on the road that
cuts through the village.

The rise of fascism helped mobilize the left in the Ardèche as elsewhere. On July 1, 1934, Xavier Vallat, the Ardèche's rising star of
xenophobia and anti-Semitism, gave a talk in Les Vans before three
hundred people. Two hundred people showed up to protest against
him. Following right-wing riots in Paris on February 6, 1934, an
antifascist committee organized a meeting in Vallon on the anniversary of the assassination of the great Socialist leader Jean Jaurès on
July 31, 1914. Sections of right-wing groups such as Solidarité
Française existed in the towns, protesting "the Stavisky Affair, the
shootings of February 6 and Freemasonry." For the most part, the
population of the Ardèche followed national political events with
interest but remained preoccupied with agricultural work under difficult circumstances, unemployment in the silk-throwing factories,
debates over wine production, and low prices for farm products,
while the people patiently hoped for better times.[45]

In Balazuc (where the threat of fascism seemed very distant) the
conservatives swept the 1935 municipal elections. Indeed the turnout
for municipal elections usually surpassed that for legislative elections.
Political opinion remained evenly divided, though it still favored the
right. [46] In the legislative elections of 1936, in the second election that
followed the elimination of the Communist and Radical candidates,
Thibon, former president of the Catholic Youth of the Bas-Vivarais,
had sixty-four votes, and the Socialist Blanc had sixty-three. Again,
Balazuc's vote had split right down the middle. Yet, for the moment,
the deputies from the Ardèche supported the republic, but the right-
wing local press remained conservatively Catholic, nationalist, xeno-
phobic, and antisocialist, in short, espousing much of what Vichy
would embrace once the republic had been swept aside.[47]

To be sure, personalities still played a major role in elections. Not long after the 1925 municipal elections, in which the right won all but one seat, Balazuc gave eighty-five votes to a Socialist candidate for *conseiller d'arrondissement* (and only sixty-four to his opponent); the victorious Socialist was the son of the *facteur* who brought the mail to Balazuc every day. In 1935, Balazuc split its vote in the cantonal election at sixty-three votes for each, but the right's victory in the municipal elections again suggests the role of personality in village politics.[48]

On Sunday, September 2, 1939, the church bells rang for much more than to call the faithful to Mass. The German blitzkrieg in Poland had begun, and with it World War II. Most men mobilized from Balazuc were sent to the Alps, preparing for a possible war with Italy. The *drôle de guerre*, the period of waiting that preceded the German attack on France in the spring of 1940, brought some of them back for leave. With the German invasion in the spring, bombs fell sporadically along the Rhône. Belgian refugees arrived in buses. A few, upon seeing Balazuc, asked to be taken somewhere else. About thirty or forty remained, some sleeping on the floor of abandoned houses. Gradually some of them came to love the savage beauty of the place, a world away from Brussels, Antwerp, and Liège. In early June, German troops arrived along the Rhône in the Ardèche, blowing up the bridge at Le Teil. The *drôle de guerre* no longer seemed so *drôle*. The road from Aubenas to Vogüé and then Vallon or Alès was clogged with more people from Belgium and now from the north of France and Lyon, fleeing the fighting. Refugees slept in and around Balazuc's small railroad station; a few were still carrying gas masks they had been given in Paris. Three German fighter planes circled above Balazuc. The day of the armistice, June 17, a French military unit set up camp in Lanas, where people from Balazuc had gone to buy their bread after the baker went off to war. All in all, in June 1940 some 150,000 refugees arrived in the Ardèche. In September 1940 most began the long, depressing trek back north toward an uncertain future.[49]

As almost everywhere, the people of the countryside were better

off during the war years than were residents of towns and cities. It
was a time of shortages, requisitions, and black markets. Sugar, cof-
fee, and other luxuries were hard to find, as well as meat, particularly in 1943 and 1944, but fruit, wine, and cheese (one woman
remembers exchanging goat cheese for a shirt) could be found in
abundance, along with grain. Chestnuts again helped many families
get through hard times. Even water seemed in short supply; on several occasions the train had to stop in Balazuc's station, and the
engine, leaving its cars behind, rode to Vogüé or Ruoms to get
water, then returned to pick up the rail cars. In February 1941, in
response to a ban on the sale of "stable animals," the council
announced creation of a weekly market for merchants and animal
breeders, so they could sell farm products and animals, Thursday,
eight to noon, in front of the old Portail Neuf. The municipal council met more infrequently during the war. In November 1942 it created the position of guardian of the church and named the priest to
receive a salary of 1,000 francs.⁵⁰ In 1944 the only registered business was the sale of a plot in the cemetery.

The Ardèche, as almost everywhere, had some eager collaborators.
The local Vichy press offered readers a predictable diet of views on
the war and the French state. The right-wing Légion Française des
Combattants supported Vichy with enthusiasm. Vallat, the association's general secretary, organized a parade of three thousand people
in Annonay in June 1941, two months after he had become the general commissioner for Jewish affairs.⁵¹ About 500 Ardéchois men
belonged to the *milice*. The Vichy militiamen were recognized by
their blue jackets and pants, berets that resembled that of an Alpine
soldier, khaki shirts, and black ties. In Ruoms, *miliciens* strode into
the Hôtel-Restaurant Théodore and gunned down several members
of the resistance. For years the owner left the shattered mirror on the
wall to commemorate what had happened. One hundred and thirty-
five Jews were deported from the Ardèche, many having been arrested
in Vals-les-Bains on September 30, 1943. Not one returned. In the
meantime *Le Réveil de Largentière* eagerly defended French-Nazi collaboration "against cruel and barbaric communism" and saluted
those Ardéchois who went to work in factories in Germany as "peas-

ants standing at the head of national solidarity." In 1943 the news-paper, which appears not to have had a correspondent in Balazuc (but did in Vinezac and Laurac), sang the praises of the *milice*—"it should first contribute to the maintenance of internal order and oppose the threat of communism with all its forces"— while faithfully report-ing the pronouncements and speeches of Marshal Pétain.[52] The role of the clergy was, as everywhere, mixed. Protestants from the begin-ning opposed Vichy, in part because of the Church's official embrace of the regime.

Some people in Balazuc, notably a few who had been before the war identified with the Catholic right, may have been sympathetic to Vichy. In the opinion of one man, speaking long afterward, "the peo-ple close to the church were somewhat *collabo*," following the politics of the village priest, who had been transferred to Balazuc from St.-Maurice-d'Ibie, then something of a hotbed of royalism. Yet there were no signs of outright collaboration, perhaps only complaints to the *milice*, which could be seen in the village from time to time, about a couple of families who listened to the BBC. At first, those consid-ered to have supported Vichy "were a little forgotten" in the village. The two sides "did not have too much to say to each other after the war." Gradually all was largely forgotten or at least absorbed benignly into daily life.

Under Vichy, the tone shifted to exuberant and incessant propa-ganda associated with the "peasantism" of the regime. Marshal Pétain saluted the early seventeenth-century agronomist Olivier de Serres in March 1941 and called for a return to the land. The review *Armagna du Père Menfouté*, dedicated to keeping alive patois by publishing poetry, short articles, and popular sayings, with translation into French (which had included "De Balazu en Alès" in 1938) fully sup-ported the regime, identifying it with the Church.[53] *Armagna du Père Menfouté* celebrated the values of "peasantism" embraced by Vichy. In 1941 it published "Les Paysans à la terre," homage in patois to "the wet nurses of the poor and of the rich. . . . [O]ur profession is the only one that is truly one of gold." Below was the poem: "Worthy Ardéchois, let us love the land and remain on it. If we have left it behind, let us return. The marshal has told us to do so. And the marshal is right. As always. One time yet again, the land will save France." In 1943 the review warned peasants and workers against the temptation "to revolt, to sow or harvest a bad spirit. We must put a stop to bad advice and malevolent rumors or all will be ruined." Faithful to the end, its last issue in 1944 featured a photo of Pétain.

Armagna du Père Menfouté celebrated the fortieth anniversary of the Jeunesse Catholique, which had had a presence in 1928 in 230 of 372 parishes, including Balazuc. One man remembers that early in the war, when he was about fifteen, the members of the Jeunesse Catholique met at night in the house that had once presumably formed part of the "château" on the cliff above the old church. The house had no electricity, but one of the members came from Aubenas by bike, recharging a small generator by pedaling. Religion quickly gave way to drinking wine. When the small light gave out, they picked their way down the stairs to the square below.

Gilbert Serret and France Derouret-Serret began teaching in Balazuc in the autumn of 1943. During the interwar period both had been militant *syndicalistes*. Gilbert Serret, a member of the national organization committee, represented the current of "revolutionary pacifism" within the Fédération de l'Enseignement (as opposed to what was called sentimental pacifism). Serret had joined the Communist Party in 1923, but left a year later. Thereafter Serret stood accused by the party of being a counterrevolutionary member of the group of Trotskyite-Centrists. When Trotsky was forced to flee the Soviet Union in 1934, Serret and his spouse offered him lodging in the Ardèche, after meeting him in the Isère. They shared with Trotsky a sense of the importance of mobilizing peasants for the revolution and of the role of teachers in that enterprise. In 1938, at the congress of the Confédération Général du Travail (General Confederation of Labor) in Nantes, Serret denounced the "politics of compromise" and the Popular Front, calling for "independence of syndicalism" and a return to class struggle. When the war began, the couple was teaching in the Haute-Loire. They were transferred to Balazuc (despite the opposition of Vallat, against whom Serret had led a demonstration in 1934 in Annonay), probably because Vichy authorities had placed them on a local list of those under political suspicion.

On June 28, 1943, two men in shorts, outsiders, attracted the suspicion of several people in Balazuc, including two shepherds. The next day Serret, noticeable for his limp, walked down to the river to fish. He never came back. His body was found downstream from Viel Audon, his feet tangled in a fishnet, his hand outstretched as if he had been dragged to the spot in which he was found. For decades most people held the *milice* responsible. However, although the latter organization was perfectly able and willing to murder anyone, Serret may have been the victim of his uncompromising struggle against orthodoxy within the Communist Party.[54]

On November 11, 1942, German troops occupied the "free" zone that had been controlled by Vichy. But even before, about two hundred people participated in acts of resistance in the Ardèche. The maquis (which became the name for resisters, taken from a rough scrub or brush found in the countryside in Corsica and parts of the south of France into which they could disappear) began to organize near Tournon very late in 1942. Following November 1942, the Nazi presence in the Ardèche was considerable, even if for the most part limited to the towns: concentrations of troops in Privas, Aubenas, Annonay, and small detachments along the Rhône, for a total of about four thousand men. Armored patrols drove through Balazuc occasionally during the war, but no one remembers seeing German soldiers walking through the village itself. Here Balazuc's relative isolation and strategic unimportance proved an advantage.

In the Ardèche the resistance consisted of a fusion of Communist and non-Communist groups joined to become the Armée Secrète (AS, Secret Army) of the Unified Movements of Resistance, an organization particularly based in the Cévennes, the members of which were divided on whether or not attacks should be launched before the awaited national uprising against the Nazis and the Vichy collaborators. Problems of communication were considerable, and isolated farmhouses were essential to the enterprise. In all, there were about fifteen different groups of resisters. The Francs-Tireurs et Partisans Français (FTPF, the military wing of the Communist-dominated Front National) concentrated their efforts on acts of sabotage (139 of which occurred from the beginning of 1943 until D-Day), particularly near the Rhône. These attacks led German commanders to place French civilians armed with hunting rifles on the front of trains. The AS, more cautious, at first remained in the hills and mountains. By late 1943 the two groups were working more closely together, more so after D-Day in June 1944. Allied planes occasionally dropped arms to them, such as those that landed near Lanas (at least twenty-one Allied aviators perished in the Ardèche).[55] A few maquis hid in Audon from time to time during 1943 and early 1944. Resisters included some Spanish refugees exiled during or after the Civil War across the Pyrenees. Others in Balazuc served as "occasional resisters," such as several who were asked to go down to the tracks and count the number of German trains that went by. One woman remembers that a particular group invariably took large kegs of wine with them and by the end of their duty were unable to identify just who exactly had been on how many trains.

The repression organized by the Gestapo and the French collaborators within the *milice* swelled the ranks of resisters. German soldiers surprised *maquisards* of the FTPF, killing many, including a ninety-year-old man, in the mountain hamlet of Thines on August 4, 1943. German troops also massacred residents of a hamlet in Labastide-de-Virac and executed 10 people from Le Teil at Sanilhac. Another 150 people were deported from the Ardèche for acts of resistance.

The number of maquis, as elsewhere, grew with the German imposition of the Service du Travail Obligatoire in February 1943, which required the supply of French workers for factories in Germany. The resistance helped *réfractaires* hide. The woods, caverns, and brush of the *pays calcaire* offered shelter, as they had in prehistoric times and during the Revolution and Directory as well. Of the 6,650 men recruited, 2,200 were excluded for medical reasons, and about 2,330 disappeared "into nature," aided by the fact that some police simply looked the other way. This number included 2 men from Balazuc, while several men, including one from Balazuc, went to Germany. In 1942 only 242 men who were called to work in Germany actually left, and during the war 2,100 (32 percent) left.[56]

Continued attacks by resisters, carried out at great risk and with increasing confidence in 1943 and early 1944, raised the costs of collaboration. From 1942 to June 6, 1944, maquis undertook more than 250 acts of sabotage in the Ardèche, most carried out by the FTPF. Attacks on known collaborators took place here and there. These included the execution of a woman providing information to the Gestapo about the resistance in the twin Rhône towns of Tournon and Tain–l'Hermitage in May 1944.[57] In November 1943 a *maquisard* shot a policeman dead in Tournon. Acts of sabotage on the railway in the valley of the Rhône became more common. An arms depot was discovered hidden in an abandoned cement factory in Le Teil. Soon thereafter a bomb exploded outside the door of a notary, a known collaborator, in Le Pouzin. In February 1944 a *milicien* fell to bullets in La Voulte, and an explosion blew up a bridge over the Doux River. The next month Vichy *milice* and German troops fought the first pitched battle with maquis at the *mas de Levret*, in which German troops were killed. Reprisals came quickly. Nazi troops executed men, women, and children in a field. German troops, gendarmes, and Gestapo searched the area near the Pont d'Arc near Vallon for resisters, sending a car bearing the Lorraine cross ahead of them in the hope of enticing the maquis into the light of day. Another bomb exploded outside the house of the brother of the president of the Légion des Anciens Combattants in Tournon. Next, a bomb placed along the tracks blew up a train, killing twenty-five Germans north of that town. *Maquisards* opened fire on *miliciens* in Labeaume early in April, gravely wounding their commander. In late July 1943 someone warned German troops that maquis were awaiting arms to be parachuted in near Thines in the Cévennes. At dawn on August 4, an entire company of German infantry moved in to encircle and massacre them.[58] In Privas a peasant shouted in patois at a column of German soldiers, who understood only the courageous gesture: *"Podètz ben bramar, souvatgé, vos arras-taretz ben un jorn!"* ("You can shout all you want, savages, but you will stop yourselves one day").[59]

By the time of the Allied invasion of Normandy on June 6, 1944, perhaps as many as 4,000 men had joined the resistance, which increasingly controlled the countryside, at least by night, and was supplied largely by women. Numbers rose to as many as 7,000 by August. During the summer, successful sabotage repeatedly cut the main rail lines. Resistance attacks increased in confidence and scope, despite reprisals by Nazi troops, leading to several small pitched battles, including one near Annonay and another near Banne at the end of July. Allied air attacks destroyed several bridges across the Rhône, but misdirected bombs fell on Bourg-St.-Andéol on August 15, 1944, killing 146 people.

As the Allied army advanced from the south, thousands of German troops then fled toward the Rhône. They crossed the Ardèche in two large columns. One reached the Rhône via Bourg-St.-Andéol; the second headed via Vallon, Lagorce, Vogüé-Gare, and Lavilledieu, where they executed fourteen civilians. About seven thousand German troops surrendered in the Ardèche, many along the mountainous road between Aubenas and Privas when attacked by the French forces of the Interior (FFI). In the meantime, when a German convoy left Privas, moving toward Chomérac, on August 12, troops of the FFI arrived in Privas and set up a Comité Départemental de Libération. Privas thus became the first prefecture freed by the resistance.

More than 1,000 German troops were killed in the Ardèche, and 7,400 taken prisoner. In all, about 600 people were killed by the Nazis or by the *milice*. Thus it is not difficult to understand that much score settling accompanied the liberation, although some, who knows how many, may have had little or nothing to do with the questions of collaboration and resistance. During the *épuration* that followed the liberation, 570 people in the Ardèche faced charges for some degree of collaboration.[60]

In Balazuc, Allied planes increasingly broke the silence of night. As Allied troops moved up the Rhône Valley and the Germans departed, maquis blew up Balazuc's bridge on Sunday, August 6.[61] Following the explosion, which could be heard for miles, some people burst into tears, seeing the central arch of the bridge destroyed. The bridges of Chauzon and Lanas too were blown up, along with a small bridge traversing the Claduègne near Villeneuve-de-Berg, the goal being to make it more difficult for German troops to escape Allied pursuit, however unlikely crossing the Ardèche River at Balazuc would seem.

By August 20, when news of the insurrection in Paris arrived, in Balazuc a Communal Committee of Liberation of four men had sprung into existence; it included Marcel Evesque, who had replaced Gilbert Serret in the boys' school.[62] A woman who was a young girl at the time has vivid memories of seeing Canadian soldiers camped near the *gare* of Balazuc. In the meantime, a number of *faux maquis* terrorized the *pays*, though none was from Balazuc, threatening and requisitioning.

In Balazuc, on August 24, the Committee of Liberation met "to take possession of municipal powers replacing Marius Guibourdenche, mayor, and the municipal council, declared having resigned." Guibourdenche had served as mayor throughout Vichy. Criticized by some as somewhat sympathetic to Vichy, he had hidden his brother-in-law, who was sought by the *milice*, for some time during the war. There would be no reprisals in Balazuc, though there were tensions for some years.[63] In the meantime, the Committee of Liberation added seven members, "to fill the functions of mayor and the officers of the civil state, under the responsibility of four members of the executive committee." The group, self-consciously functioning as the municipal council, unanimously elected Hippolyte Freydier, identified with the moderate left, as its president.[64]

On October 10 the new prefect, Robert Pissère, confirmed the role of this committee, calling it a Municipal Delegation. It included Freydier, who had been asked to join the Committee of Liberation with the role of smoothing over differences of opinion; Evesque, who belonged to the Communist party and had joined the FFI; Noël Boyer, who had served as a municipal councillor since 1924; and eight others. None had served on the municipal council during the Vichy period. Twelve days later this group established a commission to revise electoral lists and passed a preliminary budget for the following year. It also undertook the routine tasks of the *mairie*, such as establishing a commission to revise the electoral lists and the salaries of the secretary and the rural guard. Reconstructing the bridge held first priority. Until the central arch could be solidly repaired, a wooden passage, which on the first three attempts to link the two sides fell into the river, served as passage for men, women, children, goats, and even oxen. Before its erection, ladders had allowed one to climb up from the original *passerelle* to the remaining spans of the bridge on either side of the missing central arch. The bridge was reopened on August 31, 1945, "under the aegis of the Committee of Liberation."

The first municipal elections of the postwar era took place in May 1945, with only one list put forward, "placed under the sign of patriotic unity."[65] It mixed moderates, practicing Catholics, Socialists, and Communists, and it included four members of the Committee of Liberation. All were elected with between 105 and 146 votes. The council elected Freydier mayor and Gabriel Boyer deputy mayor, and it soon named committees for education and public assistance. That same month, with the help of government funds, a municipal "celebration of victory," was held including a *goûter* (snack) for the children of the village, to welcome back a few returning prisoners of war. One man remembers that at the school Evesque told the pupils to take out their notebooks and write by hand the name Franklin D. Roosevelt, who had died on April 12, 1945.[66]

The discrediting of some of the right by the experience of Vichy helped the left revive following the war. In the fall of 1945 the Communists, carrying the prestige of their role in the resistance, won seventy votes, more than any other party in Balazuc, to sixty for "independents and peasants," twenty-nine for the Socialists, and twenty-seven for the moderately conservative Catholic MRP. In the crucial legislative elections, the first of the Fourth Republic, in November 1946, the list of "independents and peasants" edged out the Communists by eighty votes to seventy-one, with Socialists receiving twenty-four and the MRP only eighteen. The 1947 elections brought another single list, headed by Freydier and elected in its entirety.[67] The Ardèche itself during the Fourth Republic moved slowly toward the right, where it remained until the legislative elections of 1997.

Balazuc stood in considerable disrepair, if not near ruin. Many houses were abandoned, without roofs. Yet the real damage to Balazuc came not from *faits de guerre* but from decades of continued decline.

EIGHT

The New Golden Tree

NOT LONG AFTER THE END OF WORLD WAR II, THE COM-
munist newspaper *Combat* undertook a campaign "in favor of villages
in perdition." It focused attention on several villages in the Bas-
Vivarais. The journalist who visited Balazuc asked his readers to
imagine an old village built on rocks that plunge vertically toward
the Ardèche River, "running among the pebbles and the fine sand.
Rocks lock in the beautiful river with their almost animal muscula-
tures and the paddlers who descend with the current are enchanted
by such ramparts which were, according to one theory, made by
solemn monsters." In the company of M. Boyer, deputy mayor, he
found his tour of the village "extremely moving." They walked from
the river up through the Porte de la Sablière, passing a house that had
been constructed in the sixteenth century. "We go up a rough path
bordering uninhabited houses, some of which still are used to keep
animals or fodder." The "sad visit" continues. The path rises, falls,
goes up again, and then suddenly bifurcates. Deserted porches stand

"above closed doors and innumerable rocks which move under our steps frighten only a stray chicken." Children do not come to play here, "so crushing is the solitude there." They go into a house, almost certainly the original "château"—"one could still save" it—with a fine view of the river far below and a Renaissance chimney that "ennobles this little structure sitting among debris, its scraped walls revealing some Louis-Philippe wallpaper." From the *place* beneath the Romanesque church, "of poignant beauty . . . bordered by deserted doorways," the journalist and his guide walked up toward the bell tower, "of which only one part remains." A goat preceded them, nibbling at the grass that grew between the remaining tiles of the roof: "It makes me sad to think of the fate of the vaulted ceiling below. . . . Should one wait until some disaster arrives to protect this roof?"

Who could save such a magnificent village? The journalist wanted "to draw the attention to Balazuc of those heroes who desire to save something of what we still have of the old houses, who can search in vain in the most beautiful and touching ruins." No hotel would greet any prospective savior interested in restoration, only, at best, "a table in an inn where one can eat lunch, indeed *chez* Monsieur Balazuc!" On the other hand, anyone interested in visiting or helping save Balazuc would find a mayor eager to help and "the nicest of guides," the deputy mayor. He closed by adding that Balazuc was served by rail, locating it for readers as only twenty-four miles from Viviers, improbably described as "one of the most beautiful towns in France."[1]

In the late 1940s, André Lhôte, the cubist painter and professor at the École des Beaux-Arts in Paris, urged his students to visit villages of great beauty that risked falling into complete ruin and to consider buying houses in them. Balazuc, offering "uninhabited houses with cracked walls and collapsed roofs," fitted the bill. One student answered the call, followed by a painter, an art critic, a Parisian doctor, and a singer from Montmartre. Over the next two decades they were joined by a smattering of Marseillais and Lyonnais. Humans began to outnumber the sheep drinking at the water's edge.

However, signs of the depopulation of rural France were everywhere. An account in 1947 was pessimistic: In the limestone country of the Bas-Vivarais, peasants, "fatigued by an incessant struggle against nature, abandon the fields fathers have left behind . . . a human uprooting" compounded by France's low birthrate. Large families, once common in the Bas-Vivarais, were now extremely rare. Every year young men and women moved away in search of work. In 1946 more than 18 percent of the population of the Ardèche was more than sixty years old, almost 16 percent in France as a whole. In Balazuc after the war more than a quarter of the people were at least sixty. The village's population continued to drop with each census, relentlessly, from 347 in 1946 to 301 in 1954, 248 in 1962, 218 in 1968, bottoming out at 211 in 1975.[2]

The sense of decline was hard to miss. In 1952 the village protested the elimination of the tribunal that had been in Largentière since the first year of the French Revolution. Two years later Balazuc's municipality enthusiastically contributed some money to help maintain the small airport that had been created in nearby Lanas, on the spot where British airplanes had dropped supplies to the maquis during World War II. There has never been any passenger service. In 1959, 68 communes out of 338 in the Ardèche had no schools at all; a handful of mountain villages still did not have electricity. In 1975 the population density of the Ardèche had fallen to half the national average.[3]

After the war two trains a day still served Balazuc, carrying workers to a small factory in Ruoms or to a *moulinage* remaining in Lavilledieu.[4] In 1951 the SNCF (national railway company) closed Balazuc's small station although the train still stopped to pick up or drop off passengers. The municipality protested angrily that the closing would prevent residents from sending or receiving packages at the station or from sending their baggage in advance; moreover, travelers would be exposed to the elements as they waited for the train. Furthermore, inasmuch as the village had been classified as a "picturesque site," the absence of a functioning railroad station seemed incongruous. Still, as the region's population declined, so did the trains. In 1955 the SNCF ended winter service between Alès and Aubenas. After struggling so long to break out of its imposing isolation, Balazuc was again losing ground. Passenger service ended completely in 1969.[5]

With the exception of the freight line running along the Rhône River, the last branch of the railway, which had been used to haul fruit, closed down in the late 1980s. Now the Ardèche is the only one of France's ninety-five departments with no passenger service. Even the adjoining Lozère, by far France's least populous department, has a train to and from Mende. The Ardèche has freight tracks passing along the right bank of the Rhône. Balazuc's abandoned station stands as an eerie monument to distant times. Appropriately enough, the only two "trains" that accommodate passengers carry tourists in the summer season: an old steam train that slowly climbs up the hills from Tournon on the Rhône to the small town of Lamastre and a short battered red and yellow train that operates only on Sundays, the "route Picasso" (for whatever reason), which carries visitors a few miles from Vogüé. Once in a while work on the tracks on the left bank of the Rhône or demonstrations against the extension of the TGV from Valence to Marseille, force TGV and Corail trains to "borrow" the Ardèche side of the Rhône. A century earlier it was possible to board a train at the Gare de Lyon and get off in Balazuc.

Permanent departures from the village left behind many adandoned houses. Others stood with no roofs or with gaping holes, some of their owners hesitating to repair them for fear of incurring more taxes.[6] Thus some were sold for almost nothing. A man who lived in Lyon with a house to sell in Balazuc finally found a purchaser. The day that the contract was to be signed he took a day off from work and traveled to Balazuc. It was said that he earned less from the sale of the house than he lost by missing a single day of work!

Only walls without roofs stood along the path leading from the *place* in front of the Romanesque church down to the river. One house near the old church was in such bad shape that it seemed on the verge of literally collapsing and thus posed a danger to anyone walking by. In 1950 the council voted funds to repair the house (having been ordered to do so by the prefect), in anticipation of being reimbursed by the two brothers who owned the property, against whom the commune had begun legal action.

The postwar period brought Balazuc, with an even smaller tax base, no relief from financial problems. The commune had to pay back loans that had brought it electricity, as well as keep up the village paths. When the municipality announced the new price for cemetery plots in 1948, the prefect annulled its deliberation because final resting places in Balazuc cost below the minimum established by the department. In 1951 the municipality agreed to repair the church's roof and gutters. But an even larger bill soon arrived for the repair of the stained glass windows. When the municipal council voted by a majority to pay it anyway, Freydier resigned. Needed repairs to the church came in 1952. The walls of the cemetery were collapsing. Its roof half fallen in, the former presbytery was in terrible shape, and understandably, the commune had been unable to rent it out for the past fifteen years. Expensive repairs would be required before its sale could even be contemplated. Some parts of the village remained in total darkness at night, as they had when Léon Védel picked his way up the stony paths in 1883. Only in 1952 were lamps installed at the *place* beneath the old church and the Portail d'Été. Seven years later the municipality admitted the need for more electrical current in the village "because of electric kitchen appliances" and, joining another intercommunal association for electrification with neighbors Chauzon and Pradons, took out loans in the early 1960s to make the change possible. Gradually electricity reached outlying houses, including one only in the late 1990s.[7]

Deficit spending was unthinkable. In the 1940s and 1950s regular expenses included salaries for the secretary of the *mairie* and the rural guard, and small sums allocated to the woman who swept out the school, the manager of the communal phone, the man who monitored the condition of the village paths and looked after the cemetery, and the municipal tax receiver named to oversee the municipality's accounting of its budget, as well as small indemnities to compensate the mayor and deputy mayor.[8]

The municipality still rented out the old cemetery as a garden for the derisory annual sum of 130 francs (then worth 26 cents!) and, when the number of pupils in the school fell below the number necessary for two classes, one of the two apartments that had been built for teachers. The Tour Carrée was rented out as a garage to one of the schoolteachers for a small amount and later as a storage area. The village was hard pressed to meet even essential expenses, including keeping the clock on the bell tower of the church running more or less on time. In 1975 the commune could not afford to join an inter-communal organization seeking to facilitate the disposal of garbage. Until a contract was finally signed with a company, the municipality paid someone from the village to assure the weekly pickup of garbage. A second collection was added in July and August.[9]

Early in the Third Republic the municipal council had assumed the role of allocating small sums to families and individuals in great need. In this way the council took over for the church by adminis-tering minimal assistance. Aid to the particularly poor (such as four helped in 1954 with a few francs), the incapacitated, the very old and sick, or young mothers continued when possible. Often, however, the sums required for hospitalization were clearly beyond the capacity of the village's resources. Some requests for assistance have always had to be turned down. Whenever it could, the municipality aided peo-ple who could be cared for at home. The council reviewed possible sources of help from family members; in the case of a widow who asked for help in 1963, the council decided that she was indeed infirm, that her sources of income were "insignificant," and that her son, who lived elsewhere, was not in a position to provide any help. Such assistance could be renewed, as in the case of a woman in 1964 recognized as being "an invalid, 100%." These could be unpopular decisions, however secret they were—at least in principle. Moreover, the council was sometimes still asked to support (and usually did) the request of someone to avoid military service because his absence would cause great hardship at home.[10]

The struggle to maintain Balazuc's roads and paths still necessi-tated loans and subsidies. The condition of the paths leading to the village itself from Audon, Servière, and Louanes were absolutely essential to their residents, whose children took them to school. In 1953 the age-old tradition of the obligation of three days' work for each adult on the paths of the commune ended with its conversion into a new tax.[11] The next year the council again asked for help from the state to maintain and, it hoped, widen the essential road that led to the two main routes. In September 1960, after another terrible storm, the mayor invoked "the deplorable state of our paths damaged and even carried away by the water of the last storm. . . . [T]he surface of our paths has only loose stones instead of a proper surface." Patching here and there fell far short of assuring a "rational and durable upkeep." Large loans and state subsidies in the early 1960s brought considerable improvement in the narrow road that, passing through the village, joins the two main roads. Requests for subsidies for village roads invariably noted that they were "frequented by many tourists."[12]

The years since the war have dramatically changed the land. At mid-century, there were still oxen and horses. Almost all houses still had one or more goats to provide milk and cheese. One can still see the ground floor *caves* in which the goats resided. The path once grandly called the *chemin royal* was completely brown, goats having chewed up anything that grew. Goats seemed to be everywhere, masses of them going down to the river to drink, then returning home on their own, or going up on their own to graze above the imposing cliffs across the river and then returning when it was time to head home. Those who remember the first years after the war recall the absence of greenery, the goats dining on virtually everything that grew. Photos from mid-century make Balazuc seem barren, the cliffs across the river completely devoid of greenery. In the *vieux village* (old village), goats climbed up the stairs to the roof of the *église romane* to eat the weeds that grew between the tiles. Goats remained omnipresent until the early 1960s. The paths were clear because the animals ate everything along them. The color of Balazuc has now changed from brown to green. On the *gras*, nature has fully "taken back its rights." Except for a few cows grazing here and there, it has returned to its dramatic fully natural state.

Pigs, once lords of the animal roost, also disappeared. The annual slaughter around Christmastime and accompanying festivity is but a memory. "Père Balazuc," one of the last men who butchered pigs for families in Balazuc in exchange for some wine and a small part of each pig, died almost twenty years ago.

The 1950s brought lasting changes that transformed the village. The war had interrupted the project first considered in 1937 to bring fresh drinking water to Balazuc. In the years immediately after the war, most women still washed the family clothes in the river, and a few still drew drinking water from it during the summer months. Ten women each morning went down from the upper village to La Fontaine, a prime source, to get water. Runoff from roofs into cisterns provided much water. Baths and showers remained a luxury, and washing machines were a curiosity. In 1950, Balazuc formed an association with Chauzon and Pradons to bring drinking water to these villages, and three years later they took out a loan. Dynamite blasted the way for pipes. In 1956 faucets began to appear here and there, almost twenty years after the municipal council had first approved the project. Finally, by the end of the decade, water reached all houses of the village itself, and toilets soon followed.[13]

The telephone became more common. In 1946 a phone was put in the mayor's house because he lived too far away from the public phone. In 1978 the village had its first telephone booth, replacing the person who looked after the phone and carried messages to and from residents who did not have phones.[14] Then came television sets, which sometimes preceded running water. The first set in Balazuc stood in a house in the upper village in about 1958. It was standing room only. The crowd of those gathering to watch evening serials (*feuilletons*) sometimes stretched onto the patio. But without a nearby tower, those with sets in Balazuc could receive only very poor images, or none at all, until in 1960 a television tower was built in the Ardèche. The municipal council's request for a nearer tower rang with (certainly misplaced) enthusiasm for the new world of television, "[C]onsidering that the television, a magnificent instrument of culture and distraction, can usefully help cause our countryside populations to remain at home and halt the rural exodus!"[15] In the sixties, televisions became more common, although for the moment one station had to do. At a minimum, broken antennas ultimately became near-perfect devices for measuring the distance between the boules and the *cochenet* (cork target). Most people agree that television put to an end the *veillée*, that traditional institution of evening sociability between Toussaint (All Saints' Day) and carnival around the kitchen fireplace, at which friends and relatives told stories, ate roasted chestnuts, and played cards. While some older people lament the replacement of the *veillée* by television, one has given the noisy box its due by pointing out that programs provide companionship for a good many people living alone (though some wag in Paris may have got it right when he claimed after de Gaulle's death that the general may well have died of boredom from watching French TV). About ten years ago a group of about six or seven began to gather on Friday nights to play the recorder, alternating houses and desserts. It lasted off and on for about two years, but then the deaths of two of the group helped bring about the end of what had been the equivalent of a *veillée*.

Another enduring feature of village life went by the wayside when the municipal council ended the position of rural guard with the retirement of the last one in 1959 after thirty-six years of carrying news to each part of the village and every hamlet, beating his drum as a reminder of a meeting, standing at the Portail d'Été or in front of the *église romane*. The municipal secretary and the village employee now carry out some of the tasks of the old rural guard.[16]

Between the wars, adult villagers still spoke patois. But it has virtually disappeared from daily life, except for some very old residents who speak it among themselves. There are fewer and fewer of them around.[17] La Maria, as she was known to everyone, spoke patois. A keenly perceptive woman who spent her childhood and much of her adult life taking care of goats, in her last years she reigned over the small square—really just seven parking places—in front of her daughter's small grocery store (*libre-service*). Over the past twenty years the supermarkets—*grandes surfaces* or *hypermarchés*—have transformed the way families shop.[18] One by one rural stores have closed down. People in Balazuc appreciate the store, and many who use the less expensive supermarkets purchase some goods at the grocery store as well. A few also shop at the market in Joyeuse on Wednesday or Aubenas on Saturday. Balazuc's store provides a real service by selling canisters of gas, used by almost everyone, as well as vegetables, canned goods, matches, small toys, postcards, and cookies and candy. It is also one of two places where one can catch up on the news, of which there is not much in winter. The other place is Chez Paulette, the café operated by Paulette Balazuc, who came to the village decades ago.

In the decade preceding her death, La Maria's stocky frame could be seen in one of the two aisles of the small store, observing who was purchasing what, claiming that once she had caught a child shoplifting during the vacation season. During the afternoon, even in the winter, La Maria assumed the same pose, dressed in black, as elderly women almost always did, leaning against the stone wall behind the few parking places across from the store. Knitting, she missed absolutely nothing that happened anywhere near, while also carrying on conversations. She was known affectionately as Radio Balazuc because she knew everything about Balazuc and everybody who lived there.

One of the things in which she was most interested in knowing was of course to what extent villagers were availing themselves of the *hypermarché* rather than her store. When once a week we passed the store with our car trunk stuffed with straw bags filled with fresh vegetables and fruits and cheeses from the markets at Joyeuse, Aubenas, or Les Vans or with Leclerc bags holding milk and juice purchased in bulk, we always were careful to note if La Maria was standing guard, because in order to unload our cargo, we would be in her sight, at least for a second or two. Her elderly neighbor beyond the store would ask that his son hand such bags quickly over the fence, rather than risk attracting her attention by opening the gate. "Just think," La Maria once told me in a loud whisper, "some villagers would rather save a few centimes on certain foods by driving to the supermarket than purchase them at our grocery store! Don't they realize that our little store might have to close, and then what will happen to the village?" She had a point. But we and others continued to buy enough there every day to demonstrate our loyalty and avoid a trip.

La Maria could be relied on for good advice, of course, for example, informing us that the choicest and most tasty truffles are those upon which a pig has recently peed. The Ardèche is not known for truffles, but she knew where to find them. She recalled the omelet made with truffles served at her wedding a half century earlier. Like many people of her generation, she had different ideas about distance from those of subsequent generations. Once La Maria asked us if we had come from America by airplane or train. Upon seeing us prepare to leave Balazuc in our car, she asked where we were going. "Les Vans," we replied, twenty-five minutes away, and on Saturday morning there is a market there. She warned us about going to Les Vans. One of her elderly friends had gone there and never come back. She seemed genuinely surprised when we nonetheless got into the car and drove away. *"Au revoir!"* she called dramatically after us, as if we were leaving for Finland or as if she truly believed that we might never see her again. Still, she always seemed very happy to see us, particularly the children. Once, knitting against the stone wall in the small parking area across from the store to take advantage of some wintry sun, she told our son, Christopher, then age three, to be careful not to step on her knitting as he scampered up a wall. He stepped right on her wool, and when chided, he replied with what he had recently heard someone say at the playground: *"Ta guele!"* ("Shut up!" or even "Shove it!") She loved his response, and soon everybody in Balazuc knew about Christopher's encounter with La Maria. News got around like that. La Maria is now gone.

Working the Land

After World War II the rural economy of the Bas-Vivarais underwent considerable changes. The continued rural exodus and the sale and rental of land reduced the percentage of small property owners. However, *remembrement*, the government-orchestrated regrouping of parcels of land in order to reduce fragmentation in the interest of efficiency and productivity, did not take place in Balazuc.[19]

World War II provided the coup de grace to the silk industry of the Ardèche. The region had produced only 90,831 kilograms of cocoons in 1950, and eleven years later, it was even less, 16,000 kilograms. Nineteen thousand producers of raw silk in 1913 were reduced to forty-five hundred in 1938, two thousand in 1954, and only a thousand in 1957. Today just six producers of raw silk remain in the Vivarais. From producing more than 10,000 kilograms of cocoons in 1909, Balazuc produced less than a tenth of that in 1951. Cocoons were weighed for the last time from the scale hanging above the door of the Tour Carrée in the early 1950s.[20] State assistance, which had helped prolong the life of the industry, ended in 1968. The *royaume de la soie*, which by then had been reduced to a small principality, is no more.

After World War II transportation by train and the decline of the production of raw silk had accelerated the production in the Ardèche of fruits, especially peaches, but also apples, cherries, and prunes. Vivacoop, an enormous fruit cooperative begun in 1949, encouraged production and new fruits in the region, above all, the kiwi. In 1987 cooperatives accounted for half of the fruits grown. Producers, logically enough, have adjusted their strategies to state subsidies.

Yet, in 1950, although about three-quarters of the population still worked the land, less than a quarter of the surface of Balazuc was under cultivation, even less than in the nineteenth century. Those who worked the land still struggled to make ends meet. One man recalls that in the late 1950s it took two people a half day of work to extract enough potatoes from the hard soil to fill a medium-size sack. The rural guard looked the other way as young men and boys sneaked down to the river to place nets across the river to snare fish. A friend recounts that when he was about fourteen, in about 1941, his father would wake him at midnight. He went down to the river and checked the nets, then rode his bicycle all the way to Vals-les-Bains and sold the trout to the hotels. It was a tough way to make a living. The *gras* still makes up about half the territory of Balazuc. However, tractors and other farm machinery became increasingly common, though the lay of the land limited their use. A photo that hung for years in the *salle polyvalente* (all-purpose room) shows Père Balazuc in the early 1960s in a wagon being pulled by two oxen.

Vineyards became an ever more important source of income, particularly on the slopes to the east across the Vogüé–Ruoms road. Polyculture has practically disappeared, and the production of grains and potatoes is almost a thing of the past. By 1950 vineyards made up about a quarter of land under cultivation in Balazuc producing wine, although the number of producers had declined. Intercommunal

cooperatives multiplied throughout the wine-producing parts of the
Ardèche, particularly after World War II. This permitted the introduction of more modern production techniques, aiding small producers (and these were almost all of them) without the resources to benefit
from improved technology. In the 1960s producers realized that they
would have to improve the quality of wine from the Ardèche if they
were to survive. Cooperatives helped convince them to select the best
possible vines. In 1987 cooperatives in the Ardèche produced
750,000 hectoliters of the nectar of the gods, 85 percent of the
departmental total, the highest percentage in France. Gone forever
are the days when one could see laborers hired for the harvest having
a drink at Chez Paulette at noon. Virtually all vineyards are now harvested mechanically.

The quality of wines has improved dramatically, with the success
of such "noble vine stocks" as Chardonnay, Merlot, and Gamay. The
arrival of Louis Latour in the Bas-Vivarais itself signaled the global-
ization of sales. In the mid-1990s, photos of Balazuc and Vogüé and
then of the cave paintings from the Grotte Chauvet began to adorn
cases of Ardéchois Chardonnay, which can be purchased in
Connecticut, among other places. In Lagorce winegrowers began in
the 1980s to plant Viognier grapes and to produce an excellent white
wine at a fraction of the price of the upper Rhône Condrieu.
Ardéchois Viognier has found a market in the United States. From
the subsistence economy of struggling polyculture, the Bas-Vivarais
has moved closer to monoculture. Yet the shortage of labor, the division of property, and low prices remain problems. There are only fifteen farming families left in Balazuc. Above all, they produce wine
on two hundred acres of vineyards.[21]

Besides the herd of a couple that produces (excellent) goat cheese
and that of the restored hamlet-farm at Viel Audon across the river,
there are few goats left in Balazuc, whose inhabitants at one time they
easily outnumbered, and all are on farms far from the village itself.
The transhumance still takes place, but those taking goats by foot up
into the mountains must avoid the police to do so, because local
authorities believe that it poses a threat to the circulation of traffic.
Cars, not mules and donkeys, now carry provisions. Those going

along sleep under the stars for several nights, and the outing has something of the ambiance of a picnic.

Church

Without question, the role of the church in Balazuc has declined dramatically since World War II. As a local observer put it, "The bell tower no longer exercises its powerful social and psychological pull." Or as the priest who has retired to Balazuc puts it, "society has changed." In a region that is still considered relatively faithful in terms of religious practice, the bitter battles over the laicization of schools, the separation of church and state in 1905, and the inventories of churches in 1906 have long since been forgotten.[22] Thus village priests have considerably less influence in municipal political life.

Several times since the war, the new church was gradually restored, with the help of parishioners, the commune, the departmental Conseil Général, or the state, and included a heating system and later, gas heating, then the electrified bells.[23] The municipal council sometimes refused to pay for repairs to the church, remembering when the village priest tried to get it to pay for the restitution of the stained glass windows. Thanks to the declaration of the church as a historical monument, state funds facilitated painting, some varnish, and the introduction of a new heating system in 1994.

However, as the population of the village dropped, the Church's crisis in France could be felt even in the traditionally religious Bas-Vivarais and in Balazuc, with its many stone crosses or their remnants, standing here and there. Fewer people heard Balazuc's priests say Mass. (Well after World War II, men and women continued to sit on opposite sides of the church, a tradition that began to erode with the arrival during the summer months of Parisians and other visitors who were unaware of such a division.) Certainly, as one woman put it, the *brassage* of the population of Balazuc, the arrival by marriage or for other reasons of *estrangers* from other regions after World War II, eroded allegiance to the Church. Moreover, several priests did not help the Church's cause by regularly angering parishioners. One curé, who served in Balazuc for seventeen years, including the Vichy years, when he was known for supporting the collaborationist regime of Marshal Pétain, earned a reputation for a temper that he showed by loudly denouncing almost every leisure activity from the pulpit. He also caused a stir even among the faithful by refusing to bury an unmarried woman who had lived with a man. A second priest drank heavily, shouted at people from the pulpit and in the confessional, and was suspected of other vices. A third was known as a ladies' man, and the rumored discovery after his departure of what appeared to be a secret passage that led from his bedroom through a closet into a maid's room did not help. Some parishioners started to go to Mass elsewhere. Yet one priest seemed attached to the notion of Christian democracy (in contrast with the bishop of Viviers, invariably conservative), calming political divisions that had often centered on religion. Another is recalled as having announced from the pulpit candidates for whom parishioners should vote in departmental and national elections, but he knew enough to let the municipal elections alone.

In 1970 Père Veyre dynamited rock formations near the church to facilitate additional parking. The explosion damaged the church's ceiling, so that some of the faithful who came to Mass gazed toward the heavens not in quiet prayer but in worry that the roof might collapse. The municipality refused to contribute to the work the priest had ordered and told the construction company that had carried out the work that it should send any bills to the curé. When the priest went to the village hall with the bill, the mayor, who had angered some residents by having some cypress trees cut down in the cemetery, told the curé that he, as mayor, may have irritated the dead, but that the priest had enraged the living. The faithful contributed funds to pay the bill, but that priest left a debt of five thousand francs.[24]

Balazuc's church survived its most explosive curé, but beginning in the mid-1980s the village no longer had a full-time priest. (The number of priests in France has fallen by about 30 percent since 1978.) Since the eighties Mass has been said in the village about once a month, with the schedule for Masses in other churches in the region posted on the door of the church. This is now a common arrangement in rural France. Attendance is sparse in Balazuc, and as in most places, it is a decidedly older crowd. (When Laura was nine or ten, she went into the back of church during a Mass and noted in a loud voice, *"Même les femmes sont chauve!"* [Even the women are bald!]) Yet, when a violent storm so shook the church that the statue of the Virgin Mary crashed to the floor into many pieces, small boxes left at the store and at Chez Paulette asking for contributions were quickly filled, and a new statue was purchased. Many (but no longer all) weddings (and recently a combined marriage-baptism) still take place in the church, then, and only then, filled to capacity, with the inevitable firecrackers hurled as the bride and groom walk out under a small shower of rice. Gone forever are the days when the priest's role was *Monsieur-le-curé-homme-orchestre.* A very pleasant, socially committed retired priest lives in Balazuc's presbytery. He participates in village events and gets on extremely well with everyone. He has found assistance for people in particular need. In his view, the Church should be "organized around things that need to be done" in society.[25] The church functions in Balazuc as only one organization among others. Without question, its role as a political lightning rod has long disappeared.

Politics

Historians have sometimes debated when "modern" politics came to the French countryside. Eugen Weber insists that "peasants" could become "Frenchmen" only when agencies of modernization, which he identifies as mass education and conscription and the railroad, have broken provincial autarky and brought about the integration of rural France into the nation.[26] In this view, "national" politics gradually replaced the "face-to-face" confrontations defined by family rivalries and traditional resentments between, for example, villages or hamlets and villages. However, municipal politics in Balazuc now has almost nothing to do with political parties, but a good deal with personalities, with longtime family rivalries often playing an important part.

The presentation of two rival electoral lists for municipal elections, as in the bitterly disputatious pre–World War I period, has always been a sign of political division, even if personalities and longtime family and personal disputes have often shaped such fissures. In 1953 Balazuc returned to the prewar pattern of preparing two lists for the municipal election. Six years later, Berre, originally from Marseille, was elected with a moderate list without competition, and voters returned essentially the same list six years later.[27] In 1971 Berre presented another single list, one that marked something of a drift to the left (one wonders if the priest's dynamiting of the area near the church had anything to do with this). In national politics, Balazuc continued to lean to the right.[28]

The municipality commemorates Armistice Day, November 11, with a small ceremony. In 1989 it planted a tree in honor of the French Revolution (a number of us chose to celebrate the night of August 4, the abolition of feudalism, rather than July 14, with a barbecue and face painting of the children in red, white, and blue).

Municipal minutes very rarely mention national political events. In April 1961 the municipality did, in view of the "grave events" in Algeria, renew "all its confidence in and sympathy for General de Gaule [*sic*], president of the republic."[29] But the mandate of the council is limited—to oversee local affairs, to represent the village to higher authorities, and vise versa—and the risk of censure by the subprefect or prefect was always there. Indeed the prefect or subprefect has always had the power to annul any deliberation that did not seem in proper order to the higher authorities. The stamp of the subprefecture affixed to the top left-hand corner of each page as a sign of approval makes the relation between the higher authorities and the village council perfectly clear.

It therefore seemed logical for the municipality to express its unanimous support in 1963 for the declaration of a congress of mayors that opposed any "attack against local liberties, notably by the reduction or suppression of the powers of municipalities . . . essential bases of democracy." The petition complained about financial obligations that seemed to increase each year, augmenting local taxes. That same year the council expressed its anger at a sizable increase in direct taxes that would hit marginal (third category) land especially hard. Many property owners in Balazuc owned such marginal land, much of it not cultivated or else planted in vineyards. The municipality asked for the establishment of a fourth category that would be assessed at a lower rate.[30]

The debates over France's joining Europe counted for very little, and the referendum generated only mild interest in Balazuc at best, despite an overwhelming vote in favor. European subsidies have assisted some of the remaining agricultural producers to switch crops, for example, from fruit to vines or from wine to kiwis. But farmers do not know or particularly care whether the subsidies they receive come from "Europe" or from France. In either case, they arrive via the French Ministry of Agriculture. Few people analyze the consequences of the increasing reach of the European Union, the support of which could be crucial in finally bringing about the completion of a proper sewage system. Virtually no one knows that a small subsidy from Brussels paid for much of the fancy sign describing Balazuc's attractions. People in Balazuc showed little interest in the campaign of José Bové, a leader of agricultural protest most known for a symbolic trashing of a McDonald's in Millau, a town about three hours west in the Aveyron. The few remaining farmers in general remain conservative (though for most, the church plays no role in this continuity), viewing Bové as a *soixante-huitard* (a student activist in the late 1960s). European "norms" have left producers of goat's cheese, along with cheese merchants in towns and at the markets, something to worry about. Yet occasionally Europe reveals itself. A couple that grows fruit suddenly sent out handwritten invitations to their wedding. They had been together for more than fifteen years and have three children but had never married. Why were they marrying after all these years? Was it a coincidence that a notice advised fruit growers that in order to conform to the norms of production established by the European Community, a course being offered would be free for the wives of farmers?

In the postwar period, the members of Balazuc's municipal council were invariably farmers, almost always drawn from families of property owners who had lived in the village for decades and more often for centuries. The election of Jean-Baptiste Redon, who ran the railroad station, in 1953 was exceptional in the decades immediately following the war. The council elected in 1965 included only farmers, most drawn from families with roots in Balazuc extending well into the Ancien Régime, some of whose ancestors had gathered in the old church in March 1789 to draw up the list of grievances in 1789.[31] In 1977 the first woman was elected to the municipal council.[32] The intrusion of new family names began only in the 1970s, and in most cases, the person elected had married into one of the old families of Balazuc. Prior to this new century, only two mayors had not been born in the village, but both had married women from Balazuc and lived in the village long enough that they almost counted. Municipal council members not originally from Balazuc have sometimes been picked out for special criticism, despite their being from the Bas-Vivarais. But because of the infusion of new blood and the reduction in size or even the disappearance of some of the old families, the number of people born and raised in Balazuc and eager to be a member of the municipal council has dropped demonstrably.

The gap between those originally from Balazuc and those who are not remains important and is frequently noted, particularly in the context of municipal elections. To be sure, the days are long gone when babies were actually born in the houses of their parents. The public hospital and the private clinic of Aubenas are no longer that far away. Those who are not from Balazuc are sometimes referred to as *estrangers*, as one would have said in patois, but not with hostility (although some from the village have been slow to give business to those living in the village but not born there). Someone who asked where someone who lived in Balazuc was from heard the response "the flat country" and thought, logically enough, that despite the lack of a telling accent, the answer meant Belgium or the north of France. The *plat pays* turned out to be the village of St.-Germain, less than ten miles away. A friend in jest asked a woman who had married a man from the village fifty years ago but was from an adjacent village, how she liked Balazuc after half a century. She replied with great seriousness, "Sometimes I get homesick." But since World War II the number of couples from Balazuc has declined considerably.

One longtime resident insists that since World War II, "there has been no political cleavage in Balazuc," despite the fact that especially in the immediate postwar period, party differences did count for at least something.[33] The last two municipal elections, 1995 and 2001, again demonstrated that municipal politics in Balazuc, and thousands of other villages, has very little to do with national politics. (To be sure, in villages with particularly high percentages of unemployment or where the presence of ethnic minorities has played into the hands of the extreme right, this is sometimes not the case.) This certainly does not mean that municipal politics cannot be divisive, as the elections of 1995 revealed. The mayor and the other council members indicated that they would not seek another term and thus not oppose a list of candidates being prepared. In fact a second list, carrying other names, apparently began to circulate, though not openly, after negotiations broke down between the two emerging sides—the outgoing council and the new list. Thus the supposedly "single" list presented to voters (who could vote for the entire list or cross out any number of names and add others) encountered opposition. On the day of the first election, seven from the "single" list were elected, necessitating a second balloting a week later, when the remainder were easily elected. Charges and countercharges flew. Some people stopped speaking to others, and at the Feux St. Jean, the two sides kept their distances, the winners more often seen near the bar, the defeated preferring the chairs near the store. Very few people went to greet both sides.

The residual bad feeling gradually ebbed. In retrospect, even those extremely involved in the elections are hard pressed to come up with specific issues that lay behind what turned out to be a bitter contest in 1995. It was about personalities. Guy Boyer's list included candidates whose national party sympathies stretched from the left to the far right. Issues in Balazuc—financial strictures, maintaining the school, the role of tourism, the designation of where houses can be built—basically have little or nothing to do with national political issues or party affiliations. If in Ardéchois villages any group is remarkably well organized, it is the hunters (who blast away at migratory birds from the Col d'Escrinet and recently purchased an old hotel-restaurant there to serve as their headquarters); signs reading HUNTERS, TO THE URNS! popped up along the road before the 2001 elections.

The job of being mayor remains challenging, to say the least. Georges Clemenceau may have been correct when he said, "If you are not ready to eat a bowl of toads every morning, then it's not worth getting into politics."[34] The mayor has, to be sure, three deputy mayors who carry out some of the work. Deputy mayors sometimes get blamed for unpopular decisions, but much blame and credit inevitably fall on the mayor. In many ways it is a no-win situation. A village mayor is particularly vulnerable to malicious gossip (by *les mauvaises langues*), that staple of village life, spreading rumors, exaggerating, or occasionally misrepresenting what has occurred or been said. You cannot please everybody. When an elderly lady left money to the village and to someone in the village, rumors spread about the origins of her goodwill toward a place where she had lived for about ninety years. How far should the mayor go to try to force an entrepreneur to remove building materials abandoned on communally owned land? The mayor must be ready to answer telephoned complaints from people about almost anything (light bulbs burned out, lights on too late, cars blocking garages, and so on) and hear that it was not like this under the last administration. Inevitably mayors stand accused of favoring old families and so on.

During the summer of 2000 several angry boules players marched to the mayor's house about midnight to complain that the lights in the old cemetery had gone out and they could not play until three in the morning, to the relief of those living nearby, who themselves call to complain about the constant clack, clack and boisterous conversation. The small group of angry nocturnal protesters asked the mayor to explain his boules policy, and he replied that he did not have one. He then asked them if they would go to Lyon and make such a demand of Raymond Barre, its mayor at the time.

In the opinion of one resident, Balazuc's mayors have perhaps been too willing to answer complaints by telephone. Another noted that the municipality had forgotten to hold events in each café and restaurant (when in fact there is precious little money available for such events). Yet another critic complained that the municipality had done little more than plant flowers to please tourists and should have been more aggressive in requesting departmental subsidies, for example, to improve the lighting in the old church. The criticism is part of the job, all for thirty-eight hundred francs a year in compensation (now a little more than six hundred dollars). Thus mayors must have occupations that permit them to carry out their duties and be available (obviously a mayor has to reside in the commune, though one deputy mayor lived in Lyon and returned to Balazuc each weekend). They must also love their village and have an endless reservoir of patience.

More than this, the modest resources of villages like Balazuc are continually earmarked for intercommunal associations (at the most basic, joining with other villages to pay for firefighters based in Ruoms or to pay for water or to clean up the Ardèche River). As little as 20 percent of the budget is left to the municipality, and the future may bring more intercommunal associations, further reducing options.

The question of where anything can be built, and what, remains crucial and inevitably controversial in any village. During the term of the last mayor, an expert from outside worked with the municipal council to come up with a plan that classifies all the land in the commune. He or she makes the final decision, but the influence of council members is considerable. Some land is classified as *non constructible*—for example, because building would interfere with natural beauty or because bringing electricity would be too expensive. In several cases people from inside or outside the village have purchased land in the hope of building a house, only to have the land declared out of bounds for construction. Accusations have occasionally circulated that members of the council influence such decisions because of their own family interests. One family living in another village owns land in the commune, but as much as it would like to build a house and move to Balazuc (and as much as the municipality would love to be able to count on its children in the school), the plan designated the property as *non constructible*. With reference to the problem of where houses could be constructed, one critic offered a harsh description of village politics: "the village, it's only chicanery" (*"le village, ce n'est que de la magouille"*).

Then there is the question of what can be built. Several large concrete storage structures have popped up, eyesores on the horizon;

although farming families have the right to build on their property if the structures are related to agricultural work, some such structures do not conform to legally established standards. Proponents and opponents of such construction pressure the mayor, who, again, cannot please everyone.

In November 2000, Guy Boyer invited the people of Balazuc to a meeting at the *mairie*. After discussing the financial situation of the municipality, answering questions, and hearing impassioned complaints about the problems of being blocked by tourist cars in the summer months, he announced that he would not seek a second term in the elections of March 2001. In turn, all the members of the council who were present, save one, said that they too would not run for reelection. The mayor then proposed a second meeting just before Christmas to discuss related issues. He also expressed the hope that a single list might be formed and in a letter to each household described his decision as "definitive, irrevocable, and confirmed."[35]

Amid no small degree of discussion and even acrimony, a single list gradually took shape. It was headed by a woman originally from the north of France who had recently moved to Balazuc. She seemed both competent and retired from business and would have time to serve in that capacity. The electoral list called Live Well in Balazuc consisted of eleven candidates "men and women offering different perspectives," eager "to serve better the interests of the commune," and offering "experiences and abilities with faith, enthusiasm, and realism." Their program included "communication (listening, solidarity, and conviviality)"; "preservation," including "the maintenance of commerce, the school, artisanal activity, associational life, and attempts to attract young farmers"; "security," including the improvement of spaces for children and for sports, bus stops for students, parking and road maintenance; "tourism" ("improved and more beneficial integration in local life"); "the development through active research of funding for priority projects," and, with a sense of urgency, *assainissement*, the creation of a purification station for village waste. Urging electors to return the entire list (despite the fact that several candidates were unknown to many people), it ended with the hope "that Balazuc will remain one of the most beautiful and most lively villages of France!"

Efforts to bring one of the outgoing deputy mayors onto the new list failed because of disagreements and clashes of personality. That deputy mayor called a meeting to present his program, which highlighted the urgency of finally completing a proper sewage system that would end the system of "all into the sewer" that for some houses in the lower part of the village means "all into the river." But after also stressing the importance of maintaining and attracting small businesses like the store and Chez Paulette ("A village without commerce will soon become a village without life") and of constructing apartments to attract families, he announced that he would not run for election.[36] Thus no one on the new list had been on the former council (with the exception of one woman who had been elected to the council in 1995 but had soon resigned). The Senior Citizens Club seemed to split into factions. Some people arriving at school to pick up their children no longer said hello to each other. Complaints were voiced that there would be no one on the council to represent farmers (though, in fact, one of the elected members raises goats and another is the wife of a farmer). Rumors began to circulate on why so-and-so had agreed to join the list or had been accepted (or refused). Despite no shortage of criticism of the list and the fact that only one person on the list (not the proposed mayor) had been born in Balazuc, no second list appeared. About two weeks before the election, someone mailed an anonymous letter to some people in the village. It denounced "A leftist, speculating, and very self-serving clan" that "practices the exclusion and the rejection of some valuable and respectable people." The letter called on voters to "Think of the forgotten: people, businessmen, peasants, the hamlets, the village" by crossing off four names on the ballot and replacing them with four others. Beyond the letter's fundamental incoherence, its anonymity and the fact that in principle none of the people suggested had been consulted by the person who wrote it drew harsh criticism.

Until the day of the election one did not know if shorter lists of several or of individual candidates would appear. It took much more than two hours to determine the outcome (80 percent of the eligible voters had cast their ballots) because of so many "partial" ballots that had one or more names crossed out, along with votes for people not on the list.[37] In all, more than sixty people (including the great Marseillais soccer player Zidane) received at least one vote; the former mayor and several members of the former municipal council received more than twenty.[38] As the counting process went on and on, with people squeezed into the room and gathered outside near the door, occasional signs of displeasure or even hoots were sounded when a name that did not meet someone's fancy was called out. A woman who received about ten votes greeted each one with a whoop, though she fell ninety-eight votes short of election. This provided some ambiance. The entire list, again representing a wide range of political views in terms of national politics, was elected, and Balazuc had its first female mayor. However, the *mairesse* knows few people in the village, a fact that some people believe will give her neutrality but that has disadvantages. Her candidacy, as an outsider who at the time of her election knew very little about Balazuc, unthinkable even a decade ago, and the election in itself show how much Balazuc has changed.

The new municipality faces several daunting challenges, none more important than cleaning the river. In 1980, Operation Ardèche Claire started up, with the goal, via huge investments, of increasing the flow of water during the summer season through the use of dams at higher elevations and improving the quality of water and of treating waste with the natural filtration process of alluvial terraces and by constructing purification stations. Thirty-five "Ardéchois communes in solidarity" signed on to reach the minimum norms established by the European Community for the quality of water in which one can swim. In 1989, Balazuc joined other communes along the Ardèche with the goal of protecting "the natural and tourist patrimony shared by member communes, and the preservation of the environment." Subsequently a local initiative began, the Syndicat des Eaux de la Basse-Ardèche (SEBA).[39] After twenty years of planning and projects, starts and stops, Balazuc remains the only village of the middle Ardèche River valley without fully proper treatment for sewage. As a result, some sewage empties into the river. Year after year (most recently because of the inopportune resignation of the president of the organization charged with undertaking the expensive work), the construction of a proper purification station has been put off into the future. The project is now projected for completion in 2005. Balazuc must contribute 1.6 million francs of the total cost of about 10 million francs.[40] With this in mind, young people in the summer wisely choose to swim above the village at a point known as the Grand Moure, where they jump into the river from rocks high above. The commune is obliged to post the results of tests carried out on the water; these results usually tactfully report that on the basis of the fecal content, the quality of the water is "mediocre" or even "good." In years of drought, in particular, the water can get quite low in depth and "sandy" or "muddy," suspect in quality.

The School

Balazuc's falling population had worrisome consequences for the school. In 1946 the municipality had to argue against the closing of one of the two classes in Balazuc and against the creation of a one-room schoolhouse (*classe unique*). Yet at that moment, with forty children at the school, there was some reason for optimism.[41]

The primary school has always remained a centerpiece of the village's collective endeavors and thus of the preoccupations of the municipality. Over the years, council meetings allocated funds to repair the aging school (constructed at the beginning of the twentieth century), as well as make more serviceable its small walled *cour de récréation*. Minuscule departmental subsidies for the school went toward painting, redoing woodwork, repairing the ceiling, doors, and outdoor toilets, whitewashing, and purchasing new tables, chairs, maps, a blackboard, and, increasingly, books. The municipality provided money for school supplies for indigent children.[42] Little by little, the apartments of the teachers, and then the single apartment, were made more livable. The kitchens were improved, and in 1958 a was toilet added. Yet in 1961, when it came time to repair and improve both the girls' and boys' toilets, not enough money was available.[43] In 1979 the roof required immediate attention, and as Balazuc (or at least some people in the village) celebrated the bicentennial of the French Revolution, the ceiling of the school again seemed on the verge of collapsing. Another sixty thousand francs would have to be found.[44]

More serious challenges lurked. In 1961 the academic inspector asked the departmental school authorities to transform Balazuc's two classes—that is, one for boys and one for girls—into a one-room schoolhouse for boys and girls. At the time, the number of children in both classes had fallen to thirty-two; the following year it stood at twenty-five. More threatening, only four children who had yet to attain the minimum school age lived in the village. There was little the municipal council could do once the inspector had made a decision.[45] In 1970, Balazuc's *classe unique* had only eight children, with no sign that the number would increase in the near future. For the first time the very survival of Balazuc's school seemed uncertain, before the number of students rose somewhat again.[46] In 1990–91 there were only nine pupils in the school, eight girls and one boy. The next year, when our daughter, Laura, began CP (first grade), the school did not then have a kindergarten for our son, Christopher. In 1996, Mayor Boyer called the communal school a "worrying subject."

As the "participation" of the state through funding some school activities declined, efforts to raise money became even more important. In December the school sponsors a Sunday afternoon Lotto, essentially a bingo game, for which prizes (some are better not to win) are donated. There is also a drawing (*tombola*) for more prizes. One can purchase tasty pieces of cake and *tarte*, as well as wine, pastis, and soft drinks. The event draws a good number of people from the village, especially parents of children in the school, and two sisters, with an uncanny knack for winning prizes, who make the rounds from village to village. In addition, on another day during the winter, the restaurateur comes to make crêpes and waffles, which, along with drinks, are sold to benefit the school.

Everyone agrees about the importance of the school as a focal point of community life and identity. It still is a frequent frame of reference for inhabitants of all ages. Since his arrival in 1988, our teacher, Jacques Imbertèche, has become a highly respected member of the community, essential to its life.[47] In a village without a *place* to provide a natural center to meet, parents picking up children at four-thirty catch up on what is going on. Even families and individuals who have disagreed about much in the past agree on the school.

Primary school teachers in the region (as in others) use activities and excursions to teach children about their regions. The children in Balazuc have thus gone on hunts for fossils in the village, visited *grottes* (several months before the discovery of the Grotte Chauvet, they had been near Vallon not far from the place of discovery), and learned to canoe or kayak. Jacques's predecessor brought cocoons to school, showing the children what once had been the principal source of the livelihood of the Bas-Vivarais.

The schools in St.-Maurice-d'Ardèche, Lanas, and Vogüé were "regrouped" to form a single school, with each village's formerly independent school now housing two of the six years of elementary school. Balazuc kept its one-room schoolhouse, its *classe unique*, even as others shut down completely or were "regrouped" in the Bas-Vivarais and throughout France. A 1996 study concluded that pupils who had been in a *classe unique*, from CP to CM2 (first through fifth grade with one teacher, or several levels in the same class) had slightly better results than those schools with a "normal" organization of one teacher for each grade. Yet thousands of one-room schoolhouses were forced to close their doors in the 1970s and 1980s in villages throughout France. St.-Maurice-d'Ibie provides a good example. In 1856 its population stood at 771. In 1911 it was 387, in 1931 290, and now it is less than 100. In the late 1990s, the school shut down. At the time of its closing, the teacher had just 5 pupils, 3 of whom were his children. Likewise, Labeaume, where there were three schools in the early 1950s (two public and one private), has no school. Advocates of one-room schoolhouses argue that shutting them does not really save money because of the cost of transporting children, paid by the communes, to schools in other villages.[48] Moreover, when villages lose their primary schools, their own survival is at risk.

For a village to do more than barely exist, it requires a church, a school, a café, and a grocery store, as well as some associational life. In the nineteenth century the school, in Balazuc and in thousands of other villages, represented in some ways both the intrusion of the state in local life (the use of French versus patois, dialects, or languages, or Marianne versus Mary, as we have seen) and the opportunities presented by the state (minimum education that could lead to positions, often administrative, in a town in or out of the region). Of course, as we have seen, the church bitterly resisted the lay school, some of its followers having opposed the lay republic itself. Certainly over the long run of the nineteenth century, state-sponsored schooling helped erode traditional rural France.

Now it seems that in some ways this relationship has been reversed. Balazuc's attempt to maintain its school to some extent represents the village's trying to protect itself against state decisions that can undercut its very existence. The one-room schoolhouse helped the village retain its identity as a country place. If television helped erode the sense of community that always existed, to some extent it might have been already disappearing. Thus the school takes on even greater significance. The *classe unique* is very special, not only because Balazuc has been fortunate over the last thirteen years (and even before) in having a wonderful teacher but also because the involvement of the parents in a one-room schoolhouse has been considerable. The older children help teach the younger children. Dogs and an occasional cat show up, participating in their own ways. The school stands as something of an extended family. One proof is that the pupils have always taken the *tu* form when talking to the teacher, indeed often calling him by his first name, instead of *maître*. (This is certainly preferable; in Paris I have met people so formal that they address their cats as *vous*.) This familiarity has never prevented Jacques from disciplining his charges. To those who remember the teachers of old, this was quite a change and, to us, a good one. Moreover, Jacques has always served as an informal counselor to families in the village, continuing a tradition dating back generations. With the decline in the influence of the Church—indeed the departure of the last full-time priest in the mid-1980s—this role became even more important.[49]

The meetings of parents with the teacher invariably ended with the appearance of a bottle of Armagnac. We originally got to know our closest friends in the village through the school, its meetings and planning, and participating in the Lotto and other school activities. Late in June or early in July most families involved in the school go on a picnic together, lots of pastis, wine, Fanta, food, and boules. We used to have enough people, counting some former students and their parents, to rent a bus. Of late, those going on this very enjoyable afternoon excursion have become fewer in number and take cars to a site usually much less ambitious than that of the old days. Every year, fewer and fewer people show up, and *les anciens* (we whose children were in the school awhile ago) complain that the parents now are less involved than before.

The survival of the school, in the long run, would depend on the number of children enrolled each year. In order to add to that number, the first step was to establish a kindergarten (previously a few special requests to admit a child of kindergarten age had been granted). In order to accommodate four- and five-year-olds, an assistant had to be hired to be with the smallest children in the other room; any teacher in a *classe unique* is stretched very thin by the necessity of teaching students at every grade and preparing, in particular, the fourth and fifth graders to move on to *collège*. Accepting children of kindergarten age added a few more pupils. In 1997–98 the number was up to eighteen children. It reached twenty-three the following year, then fell to twelve in 1999–2000 and eleven the next year.[50]

The *cantine scolaire* (lunchroom) had in the early 1990s long since disappeared. Because of this, a few mothers who worked in Aubenas or Joyeuse received permission to put their children in primary school there, thus reducing the number of children in Balazuc's school. Then Jacques, the teacher, announced that the mayor would be attending the parents' meeting one evening. His presence lent a different tone to the early stages of the meeting. The teacher introduced "*Monsieur le maire*," M. Mouraret. He did so with unusual formality. The topic was ways of starting a *cantine*. The mayor immediately broke the tension by stating, only half in jest, that we had gathered to see how best to cheat the state! The relationship among the state, school, and village had arguably been reversed. The school no longer represented the state, but rather the way in which the village attempted to maintain one of the centerpieces of country life by establishing a *cantine* in any possible way, getting around, at least temporarily, the usual strictures of administrative rules and regulations. With that in mind, parents began considering ways of providing lunch for pupils in Balazuc. For some time five mothers alternated preparing meals and serving them either in the school or in their houses to pupils who did not go home to lunch. Finally, conforming to official norms, the municipality helped pay for the transformation of a room in the basement of the school into a *cantine* and engaged a caterer in Ruoms to bring daily lunch, which inevitably includes mashed potatoes. The lunchroom was inaugurated late in 1996. The next year the municipality hired a young woman to oversee a care center, so that children whose parents work could stay and play after school.[51]

In the fall of 1996 our teacher became ill. A substitute teacher from another village came to Balazuc. Without question, she got off to a rough start. She might have been amazed to find in the classroom a large dead bird (*grand duc*) that had been electrocuted after landing on an electrical line. The bird was to be the subject of discussion that day. She angered parents who turned up at a meeting with her very early in her stay when she said that in coming to our school, she had the impression of entering the nineteenth century. Things got much better (they had to; some of the children at first referred to her behind her back as *Madame Con*!) and she ended up liking Balazuc.

In 1998, almost inevitably, the decision was taken to "regroup" Balazuc's school with that of Uzer, on the other side of the *gras*. Parents were invited to "discuss" the matter with a school inspector. A representative from Uzer was present as well. He explained Uzer's situation rather pathetically, saying that his village did not want to remain only a "corridor" on the road between Aubenas and Joyeuse. In 1912 the prefect had dissolved the municipal council of Uzer because it was so bitterly divided into two factions that virtually no business could be done. Now the situation was more or less the same. The year before, only a single pupil, the son of the mayor, had been in the public school. At the meeting the inspector explained the rationale for such a merger, which would benefit everyone, of course. He was about to move on to another job but explained all this with no signs of irritation. There were a few questions, but not many. Carol Merriman asked the person sitting next to her if we were going to vote, a question that drew a look of absolute amazement. This was France, of course, and the decision had already been made. The deed was done.

The merger with Uzer's school, which sent our *petits* to their school and their *grands* to Balazuc, has been a mixed success. The first year, five of Balazuc's kindergarten-age children rode a small bus over the *gras* to Uzer. Both schools have terrific teachers, and the addition of several older children increased the number of pupils in Balazuc's school. But several of the newcomers offered particular challenges. Our teacher, with more than twenty years' experience teaching in challenging neighborhoods in Paris (he remembered mornings when pupils arrived hurriedly being chased by shopkeepers from whom they had lifted something), called the first year of the merger the most difficult year of his career. The November 2000 bulletin for parents in Uzer did not help things by referring to Balazuc's school as "gray and sad" in appearance. Some parents from Uzer began to enroll their children in private schools, as they had before the merger. But the mayor put it very well: "[The most important thing is to maintain the school." Toward the end of every school year, the mayor, teacher, and just about everyone else begin to count the number of pupils thought to be returning, or entering, Balazuc's school the next year, with the numbers anticipated coming from Uzer now figuring into the equation. The official report is, naturally, that "the pedagogical merging [of the two schools] has perfectly responded to the wishes of the Ministry of National Education and to the wishes of the parents," tellingly placing the "wishes of the ministry" first. Balazuc still has its school. However, the merging seems to have undercut the energy of parents on its behalf, perhaps because it is less closely identified with the village. Jacques Imbertèche retired at the end of the 2000–01 school year. Despite the merging with the school of Uzer and the appointment of a new teacher, the future of the school remains uncertain.

Just before his retirement, the parents of his students and the municipality organized several official events for Jacques. The last of these took place at the school, several days before his retirement on July 2, 2001. The pupils prepared songs and poems in his honor. They were to take place in the *salle polyvalente*. As luck would have it, the recently elected municipality had ordered about two hundred new plastic garbage cans, complete with wheels, for those who wanted them. Because the tiny all-purpose room was the only place to stack them, the children had to work around the garbage cans. As the parents (and former parents) of pupils squeezed into the room, some standing behind the bar to have room to see, the children pretended that the stacks of gray garbage cans were a forest. The children waved their hands from behind the trees and darted out when it was time for them to say something. It went well. A cocktail hour followed in Jacques's honor. Balazuc, as always, had done the best that it could with what was available.

The New Golden Tree

Before the 1950s tourists came to Balazuc only in very small numbers, despite the legislation of the Popular Front that gave people the right to take a month's vacation. A woman who purchased a house in Balazuc in 1949 remembers that anyone who swam in the river "would be taken for a crazy person." The German invasion brought a Belgian refugee to Balazuc, a village she immediately came to love. She later purchased several small houses standing along the path up from the Porte de la Sablière and rented them to compatriots. To furnish the lodgings, she convinced some residents to exchange wooden armoires and tables for Formica kitchens, which had come into vogue. Mayor Freydier encouraged the rebuilding and protecting of village houses and selling them to people who would properly maintain them. In the postwar years, cars began to arrive in greater numbers, but café tables could still be left in the roadway. Likewise, *boulistes* only occasionally had to move aside so that a car could pass. In 1947 the municipal council noted that the village center offered no place for automobiles to park or, for that matter, to turn around, causing "serious difficulties for tourists who have been arriving in ever greater numbers to visit our old village." Three years later the mayor had to establish rules for the parking of automobiles in the village, forbidding parking in public places or along streets, and limiting speed to twelve miles an hour.[52]

In 1955 the municipality finally voted funds to repair the *église romane*, "witness to the past." Its half-crumbling bell tower has become the symbol of Balazuc. Two years later two Parisians contributed money to restore further the old church.[53] The 1960s brought many more tourists to Balazuc, which the *Guide Michelin* had awarded a star. In 1978, the Collection Sélection du Reader's Digest selected Balazuc as one of the hundred "most beautiful villages of France." Amazingly enough, it characterized the village as being divided between Protestants and Catholics, each religious faction with its own café, grocery store, and so on! "[G]iven the needs during the tourist season," the construction of public toilets followed in 1979.[54] In 1982 the Association Les Plus Beaux Villages de France was founded with 138 member villages ("the harmony of their silhouettes, the colors of the facades of their houses and roofs, and of the surrounding countryside generates a special emotion").[55] In the Ardèche, Vogüé, Alba (which became Alba-la-Romane), and St.-Montant near the Rhône were asked to join the association.

In 1984, Mayor Mouraret, whose grandfather had led conservatives in the contentious politics before World War I and served as mayor for two terms, finished a short speech on the occasion of celebrating the centenary of the bridge by assuring visitors that they would always be welcome in Balazuc, where they would find "calm, the human calm of its inhabitants and vestiges of a past always present." More and more people have accepted his invitation. The number of tourists perhaps doubled in the late 1980s and 1990s. A constant theme cited by people who write in the notebooks left in the "new" church (besides occasional references like "A church is only a church. A statue is only a statue. The air inside is simply cooler than it is outside") is the relative calm of Balazuc. One note left stressed the village's "human scale"; another wrote it was "a charming village, a good place to live"; yet others (one a Belgian family), "Your village makes us dream . . . an unforgettable encounter" and "There exists a paradise on earth, the Ardèche is joyously it."⁵⁶

Tourism, replacing the mulberry tree as the new golden tree, in some ways has saved the Ardèche. If over the centuries nature often seemed to get the best of the inhabitants of Balazuc, villagers now turned the special gifts of nature of the Bas-Vivarais into an attraction to attract visitors and money. The valley of the Ardèche became a favored site. Renting out canoes became a lucrative business, particularly between Vallon–Pont-d'Arc to St.-Marcel d'Ardèche, the Gorges of the Ardèche themselves. Now, in July and August, thousands of visitors step into canoes near Vallon to begin the "descent" down the Ardèche, and gendarmes are sent to direct traffic on the river. Hotels, restaurants, cafés, rural *gîtes* (lodgings), and, above all, campsites have proliferated.⁵⁷ Dutch and Belgians come in droves, leaving behind their *plat pays* to spend a couple of weeks or even a month camping in the rugged terrain of the Ardèche.⁵⁸ Most Belgians have been appreciated in the Ardèche as considerate and somewhat free-spending tourists (one Belgian complained: "There are lots of Belgians here, but precious few from Liège!"). Dutch visitors have shed their reputation for being relatively tightfisted. Local lore (perhaps unfairly) had their camping cars packed full of virtually every item (especially Dutch beer and cheese) to be consumed during the vacation, so that only lettuce, bread, and little more were purchased locally. During the late 1970s, Dutch families bought up houses in the Cévennes; one can still see occasional cruel graffiti telling them to go home, but those days were brief and are over. Appropriately enough, even the old station of Balazuc has been fixed up to house summer visitors, who would have to be quite deaf, with all the cars whizzing nearby. Germans too come to Balazuc, above all, during Easter, but in considerably smaller numbers.

There were 7 *gîtes ruraux* in the Ardèche in 1956, 586 in 1965, and 900 in 1976 (three-quarters owned by peasants or by rural communes). Nicely affirming the transition from the old tree of gold to the new one, some silkworm nurseries were transformed into *gîtes*.⁵⁹ In Balazuc in the late 1970s a group of young people began to rebuild Viel Audon, the small group of houses on the right bank of the river that had been abandoned for more than a century since their occupants headed for the safer ground of Audon above the massive cliff. They formed an association called Le Mat (or "crazy" in old French) and *fou*, and they raise goats and produce cheese, while creating a center for young people in the summer. Viel Audon now enjoys a nice reputation, also welcoming schoolchildren during the year. Moreover, it annually does well over a million francs in business.

At the same time, the number of secondary residences doubled between 1962 and 1975 in the Ardèche. They continue to increase and now account for about 16 percent of houses in the department. However, in particularly attractive villages, the percentage is much higher, and it is well over half in Balazuc today. To be sure, some of the owners were originally from the village. But an increasing number are from other countries, particularly Belgium, the Netherlands, and Switzerland. Several other Belgian families purchased houses, and the very small *quartier* just above the Portail d'Été is sometimes jokingly referred to as the *quartier belge*.[60]

If the landscape is now more heavily wooded than for many centuries, it is also more cluttered with buildings than ever before. Michel Carlat, an expert on the rural Vivarais and its architecture, deplores "the invasion of secondary residences." He laments that new constructions lack the originality of village houses and isolated farmhouses, some of which have stood for centuries. From a "tool of work," the stone house of the Bas-Vivarais has been transformed into an "object of pleasure." In this way, the *couradou*, that covered balcony so essential to the convergence of house and work, has been either eliminated or covered up, for example, by large bay windows that have transformed it into something very different. Carlat links rural architecture to the very survival of the peasantry: "These houses stand as witnesses to our past as much as abbeys or châteaux." He insists that the slope of hills should be preserved as much as possible, with houses adapting to the lay of the land, not the other way around. One inappropriate house sticking out like a sore thumb can destroy "the charm and value of a site or of a hamlet." He calls for a sobriety in harmony with the traditions of the Bas-Vivarais. One of his colleagues asks: "Does there exist a purgatory for those who destroy the past, those who wreck the countryside?" Carlat calls out for a defense of the *patrimoine*: "The land is sick. Sick from tourism, sick from speculation, sick from the rural exodus, and it is dying from them. And when a region is incapable of understanding the problem and of remedying it, it will die as well."[61] Indeed the final chapter of a recent book of recollections about another village in the region is entitled "A Village without Peasants."[62]

Preservationists have already lost the battle against electricity and television."[63] But where possible, electric lines have been placed underground—for example, the road across the *gras* and the stunning drive down to the river. However, white satellite dishes for television (*parabols*) appear like peppermint life savers protruding from red tile roofs, including ours. When the Association Les Plus Beaux Villages recently sent officials to Balazuc to evaluate the welcome accorded to tourists, they renewed Balazuc's membership but expressed reservations about the number of *parabols* visible from almost anywhere.

The old village of Balazuc is protected as a historical site (although the state does not pick up the tab) so that changes in the village itself have to be approved at the departmental level. But even if some houses have been left more or less intact even after being purchased by outsiders, some newcomers have constructed horrendous secondary residences out of totally inappropriate materials and with complete disregard for the way the village has evolved. Thankfully, most of these (including a house built in the German rustic style!) lie in merited isolation away from the village.

As mayor, Guy Boyer (who served from 1995 to 2001), a man of inexhaustible goodwill, has been a forceful advocate of tourism in Balazuc and its region. He encouraged articles about Balazuc that appeared in the local paper, *Le Dauphiné*, Lyon's mass-circulation *Le Progrès*, *La Marseillaise*, *La Tribune de Genève*, and papers in Belgium and Luxembourg. On the occasion of his presentation of the good wishes of the municipality at the end of one December, he noted that the mayor of a small town in Luxembourg had sent the good wishes of his town as well as some chairs to Balazuc. A picture of Balazuc graced the cover of the departmental phone book in 1997. The new council worked to "Favor the welcome offered to tourists and vacationers!"[64]

One of the priorities of the newly elected council was to "accustom and encourage the population to develop *gîtes*, guest rooms, and farm camping."[65] The *mairie* prepared a list of twenty-seven available rentals in the village ("Balazuc . . . sun, water, nature, sport, leisure activities, discover natural feelings in a preserved environment"), with prices in "high," "middle," and "low season" depending on the number of people who could be accommodated. Rentals ranged from the relatively modest sum of eighteen hundred francs to fifty-four hundred francs per week, with the scary "Ask about it" for the largest available house, invariably rented to German tourists. The municipal secretary responded to many telephone calls requesting information on rentals.

An *extra-municipal* commission (that is, including some people from outside the council) met to consider ways to "develop new structures of welcome" for tourists, as well as to make the village cleaner; the ominous "carcasses of automobiles" and the "random dumping of garbage on the *gras*" were items for discussion. Other steps included creating information boards at the four local campsites and planning for additional parking, the "flowering of the village" program to encourage residents to put flowers in their windows (with the motto "One window, one flower"), cleaning up the ruins of the Chapel of St.-Jean-Baptiste near the Portail d'Été and the small garden behind the *église romane*, enforcing the ban on *camping sauvage* (camping outside the "official" campsites) that was enacted in 1988. The light dangling from the corner of our house over the *ruelle* had only an old plastic Évian bottle to protect it until the municipality added a handsome case for it.[66]

The new council voted the imposition of a tourist tax (*taxe de séjour*) to be paid by those renting to visitors (two francs per adult per day and one franc for each child above ten, fifty centimes below that age, excusing children under four, vacation colonies, and disabled former soldiers). Three years later this tax added thirty-five thousand francs to the severely stretched municipal budget, twice the amount raised from the tax on businesses in the village.

In Balazuc, among other villages, entrepreneurs have built summer rental houses. (Inevitably some things escape all control: A construction permit is authorized to build a small garage, which miraculously is transformed into a tiny *gîte rural*.) In Balazuc this has probably helped make lodgings scarce for families wanting to live there all the year round, because owners insist on collecting the full summer rent. The cost of houses and particularly of rents has risen rapidly in Balazuc. Many of the houses that go up for sale in Balazuc are too expensive for local people to afford. In spring 2000 a prefabricated house went on the market for a million francs. Such houses are increasingly snapped up by foreigners, for most of whom the connection to the village will be only several weeks a year. When a Parisian decided that she wanted to sell her house, she telephoned me to see if I knew any wealthy Parisians or Americans and then priced the house at an astronomical sum (it later came down and was sold to friends). Furthermore, attempts by the municipality to attract permanent residents, particularly families with children of school age, have sometimes failed because of the lack of suitable all-year rentals. The commune owns two HLM apartments (modest-income housing), both in a wonderful old building, but they are relatively small. The municipality owns land a good distance away from the village on which an HLM could be built, yet the cost of bringing water to such structure would be enormous, perhaps prohibitive. Moreover, despite the attraction of rural life, the shortage of work nearby is another impediment to attracting young families with children.[67] The municipality has hoped to attract one or two more families interested in raising sheep by convincing those who own land on the *gras* to allow newcomers to pasture animals there.

Yet largely because of the large number of retired persons living in the village, the population of Balazuc jumped from 282 in 1995 to 339 in 1999. Balazuc has become in part a *village dortoir* (bedroom village). Some people go to work in Aubenas, other small towns, or a regional institution for the handicapped. This has helped the population reverse more than a century of continual decline.[68] Moreover, with the waning and then disappearance of the small industries linked to the silk industry, the structure of work remains increasingly tied to the service sector, specifically tourism.[69]

Summer tourism swells the population of the village to about a thousand people, severely straining the modest resources of the commune. People driving into Balazuc see signs telling them that they are entering one of the most beautiful villages of France. The Association Les Plus Beaux Villages publishes a guide to these villages. Balazuc has been classified a village of character (*village de caractère*), along with Vogüé and Alba.

Villages de caractère are supposed to have street names so that tourists can find their way around with maps. This seems odd, in that through its long history, references to the location of houses were simply given by, roughly, *quartier* (section) of the village: Chazotte, Le vieux village, Frigoulet, and so on. To be sure, the long stretch between the Porte de la Sablière and the Portail d'Été appeared on the 1846 census as the *rue principale* because it was the longest and led into the village. Inhabitants have always referred to "the *ruelle* where there once was a forge" or "the path where X lives." The nineteenth- and twentieth-century censuses do not note names of streets, even when the population stood at a few more than nine hundred. Our mail arrives to "Merriman, Balazuc 07120." Sometimes *quartiers* are helpfully added to names in the phone book, again "Le Village," or "Le Vieux Village," or "Portail d'Été," but nothing more. The postman knows everyone and manages even the summer months with great aplomb. (One forgetful colleague, sending me a note from Strasbourg, had begun to write on the envelope when obviously something distracted his attention. The letter reached me in one day addressed simply to "John, Balazuc.")

The insistence of the association of *villages de caractère* that its sites have street names again witnesses the extent to which the preservation of beautiful rural places reflects the construction of what the French would call the urban imaginary, or urban preconceptions of rural life. Cities after all have streets with names, and as the rural population of France continues to shrink, most tourists come from cities and towns. One of the goals of naming *ruelles* and passages that have served their function for centuries is to make it easier for tourists to follow recommended itineraries on maps when visiting the village.

The municipality created street names that never existed, names evoking noble families disappeared centuries ago or representing a physical characteristic, a hill, a slope, proximity to the old church. However, instead of the urban white on blue, Balazuc's are light brown, with the names etched in green, colors apparently chosen by a Parisian artist. And so tourists purchase maps on which are inscribed the names of streets that mean absolutely nothing. The streets of the various Disneylands also have names. In both cases, tourism arguably has helped create a false cultural heritage (*patrimoine*).

Thus, Balazuc finds itself with, among others, a "rue du Château," "rue de la Tour Carrée," "rue Guillaume Le Troubadour," an "allée des Remparts," "rue de la Plage" (a nod to tourism), "Passage des Grottes," a "Passage du Sarcophage," and a "rue du Bac." Some lifelong residents of Balazuc, hearing tourists refer to some of these names, themselves ask where these places are to be found. Some in the village who groused about the palpable increase in summer tourism were not happy to see the plaques go up, giving streets names they had never before had. They cited their cost and the fact that better use could be found for the money and that they would just be stolen. After all, the municipal employee could drill only so deep into the rock, and at worst, they resemble decals. Said one, the owner of the company that makes the plaques must be rubbing his or her hands in glee, at three to five hundred francs each. Moreover, even (or indeed especially) older people born in Balazuc seemed confused by them. The main road has been dubbed the Grande rue Pons de Balazuc, after the seigneur killed in the First Crusade nine hundred years ago. A local woman who cannot see very well logically enough thought it said Grande rue du Pont de Balazuc, or the bridge of Balazuc. The allée du Théâtre leads down to the old cemetery (and thus the Children's Garden or the pitch for boules, depending on your view). I took a picture of the plaque in September 2000, and when I returned the next month, the plaque had been stolen.

Everyone who lives in Balazuc is justly proud of the extraordinary beauty of the village, and most are happy that visitors enjoy seeing it. Yet complaints about the number of summer tourists are now heard more often than a few years ago. One resident blamed the publicity in newspapers and on television ("too much publicity—*trop de* pub"). For the most part Balazuc attracts a family tourism, with strollers and dogs on leash omnipresent. However, *commerçants* agree that the August crowd is somewhat different. "Look what happened last summer when kids destroyed the public toilets in the middle of one August night!" said one man. "It's different in August." He insisted that the days were gone when one knew the summer folks; "it was more of a cultivated tourism." He was now thinking of selling his house and moving to a village in another department where it is quiet all year long. A woman born in the village also complains about the "avalanche" of tourism and the fact that she no longer gets to know the people who come to Balazuc in July and August, whereas she has good memories of "good moments" spent with regular summer tourists.[70] Yet another woman notes philosophically "one has to live in one's time" ("*Il faut vivre de son temps*").

In response to the dramatic increase in tourism, several more cafés and restaurants opened up for the months when visitors could be expected. None are now open outside the peak tourist season. In 1994, Balazuc had twenty-three businesses of some sort. In the early 1990s, a pizzeria/crêperie opened up just off the main road. It was joined by a restaurant visible from the main road, L'Amourier. An *amourier*, it will be remembered, is the patois name for *mûrier*, the mulberry tree. The name thus joins the old golden tree to the new one, tourism. Its neon sign can be seen from the road below, next to the large yellow and black sign advertising Mini-Golf. Next to the village store, Lou Cigalou offers snacks, light meals, and karaoke. Various small stores selling "regional" items started up. One on the road has nice colorful place mats and herbs of Provence. A couple from Paris opened a Maison des Artisans, selling, among other things, pottery that they produce. A couple from the Nord, who had sold porcelain and then small stones and jewels at several markets in the region, opened a store in a cavern next to their home at the Portail d'Été. They called their store Espace Minéral and attracted some tourists. For two or three years they organized an "artisanal fair" in May, drawing some artisans, painters, and those offering "products from the land of the region," as most widely defined. Musicians played; the inevitable *buvette* sold drinks and sausages. Children from

Balazuc organized a garage sale (*vide grenier*). However, after one successful undertaking, rainy weather virtually wiped out the next two annual events, and the artisanal fair disappeared.

Espace Minéral had not been open very long when it encountered what one person called nasty competition (*concurrence méchante*). A woman who has a store in Ruoms removed her car from her garage on the street, and soon there began Espace Naturel. Then posters for each store began to disappear in turn. Two gendarmes, with decidedly better things to do, appeared, asking for information, exhibiting slight smiles and annoyance. There, and elsewhere, one can buy inexpensive stones and jewelry, products that for the most part have very little or even nothing to do with the Bas-Vivarais and can be found in similar stores from Biarritz to Charleville-Mezières. Some products sold in the village are made in Indonesia.

Local merchants and other entrepreneurs have of course not always seen eye to eye. Furthermore, the new golden tree has not helped all those who invested in tourism. Some local people have noted that with a couple of notable exceptions, most of those with shops in Balazuc do not participate in village life. However, as more stores and restaurants open up, the pie of tourist spending has inevitably been cut into smaller pieces. Balazuc fell victim to the hard reality that tourists began to take shorter vacations and spend less. They spend time sunning themselves or swimming (and about one a year drowns in doing so), but many, if not most, buy little or nothing, except perhaps a postcard or two, a beer, and an ice-cream bar. A second couple producing pottery gave up after one disappointing summer in Balazuc. A small store, Expression Textile à Balazuc, has just opened up.

Tourism augments the income of some families in Balazuc, but hardly all. It rewards those with houses to rent, as well as commerce. It also brings with it some fundamental problems. With the exception of buses of older visitors in the spring and late summer, almost all tourists arrive by car. Hundreds of automobiles pour into the village each day of the summer season, clogging the principal road, which in some places is too narrow for two cars at the same time. Balazuc has thus gone from impoverished isolation to having too many people, but only during the summer months. Despite signs that warn buses not to try to negotiate the steep, winding road down to the bridge, every summer at least one gets stuck, backing up traffic through the village, across the bridge, and up the hill on the other side of the river. Cars park almost anywhere possible along the roads down to the river, making it even more difficult for others to get by. The construction of a parking lot near the river, which entailed ripping up a small vineyard, only temporarily alleviated the problem. Two more lots have been added. Moreover, since only one car can cross the bridge at a time, standoffs between two cars whose drivers refuse to back up are frequent. On one occasion, two Belgian cars (as luck would have it) confronted each other at mid-bridge, both drivers (perhaps one Walloon and one Fleming, but who knows?) refusing to give in. Twenty minutes later cars were backed up as far as one could see. The crisis was resolved only when pedestrians began hurling insults at both drivers, and one backed up, as a Belgian woman shouted to the nearest driver that he was a "disgrace to Belgium." Trailers used to transport canoes for the "descent" down the Ardèche pose another threat, careening through the village, their trailers following like a Chinese dragon, seeming to bounce from side to side, irrespective of the presence of the old, young, or those in between. Signs on the main roads telling travelers that Balazuc offers a "nautical base" give the impression that the ports of Marseille or Toulon lie ahead. The old stone farmhouse at Les Salles, near which Roman legions marched centuries ago, offers a campsite and rents out canoes.

Balazuc still does not have a proper central square. The new church and, increasingly, the construction of more houses outside the village have further minimized the role of the small *place* in front of the old church. The road forged through the village in 1897 following the construction of the bridge passes by the small grocery store. A loan after World War II permitted its widening to form what amounts to an inadequate small *place*, space for the annual festivities of the *Feux St.-Jean* in late June, when children and young adults (and some older leapers as well) jump over a bonfire—the traditional fertility rite, as well as one that was to guarantee a year in which fleas would leave you alone—while adults stand at the *buvette* or sit in chairs around the edge of what serves as a small square. For the last couple of years a disk jockey has provided music and banter. In 1989 the purchase of land between the new church and the *mairie* facilitated the laying out of a somewhat dusty public place where cars can park. This *place* is used for one or two dances (*bals*) in the summer and for the drinks offered at the time of the inauguration of the recently elected municipal council.[71] Servière, which once had its own celebration of the Fires of St.-John, hosted a bread festival several years ago, using the hamlet's old oven. But unlike most villages, Balazuc still lacks a place where people can chat, although the grocery and main café provide something of that function, as long as they survive. This lack of any kind of rustic forum continues to fragment village life, compounded by the tourist onslaught.

Tourism has brought other problems. Tourists, particularly young tourists, make noise. Young people climb up to the bell tower of the *église romane* and talk at night. Chez Paulette is the only café open throughout the year. From Easter through September, the outside terrace draws considerable numbers of visitors. For half the year, one small room serves as the café, a small bar with several stools and a number of tables. Cases of vandalism, though happily rare, became more frequent with the increase in tourism. These ranged from tearing down signs identifying the locations of various artisans and stores, taking the chairs from Chez Paulette in the middle of the night and placing them in the street, and destroying with iron bars the public toilet facilities in the middle of the night. The common tendency is to blame "the young" or, to some, "gangs from Largentière." The mayor's annual summer bulletin in 1998 put it delicately: "For the tourist season to go well, with harmony between the permanent and tourist populations, necessitates attention, understanding, indeed discipline."[72]

Moreover, Balazuc remains weighed down by an extremely limited budget, with one million francs' expenses per year and loans to pay back (most recently to purchase land next to the school for additional parking, with the hope against hope that one day it might be used to expand the school). After all these centuries Balazuc remains one of the poorest villages in a region, at least in terms of its budget.[73]

Balazuc pays taxes on communally owned land that earns nothing.[74] The municipality is still responsible for the upkeep on Balazuc's small roads and paths and is hoping, like its predecessors in the nineteenth century, that the road to Uzer will be reclassified as a departmental road so that some funds will be forthcoming. In the meantime, the *salle polyvalente*, the all-purpose room that once served as one-half the school until the number of pupils declined, is far too small for even a village of Balazuc's size, paling in comparison with that of tiny Pradons. The small soccer field remains rocky, subject to flooding, and of little use. The village bells sometimes do not work because of an electrical problem. The clock sometimes gets stuck at about 3:00 P.M.

Despite appearances, tourism does not significantly augment Balazuc's resources. Only those who rent out houses to tourists or operate campsites pay the tourism tax. It takes considerable resources to welcome tourists and keep up the village and Balazuc. Beginning in 1989, the municipality began to pay for what became a full-time employee who devotes much of his attention to the roads and paths. With relatively small campsites and no hotels, Balazuc simply does not have the financial resources to provide more than the bare minimum of "welcome" for tourists.[75] The four small campsites are often full and beyond (thus the vacation tax is not necessarily forthcoming for those lodged above official capacity). Although the plan designating areas on which one can and cannot build takes precedence, Balazuc could accommodate three more campsites, which would increase revenue. At the moment a "four-star" campsite is in the early stages of planning for the *gras*. In 1999 the mayor protested to the prefecture and at the annual congress of the mayors of the Ardèche about the pathetically small sum of seven thousand francs (now about a thousand dollars) contributed by the state for the development of tourism in Balazuc, an amount that was set in 1993 and subsequently frozen. Other nearby communes received up to twenty times that amount.[76] At a meeting in December 2000, as the mayor was explaining why the tourist onslaught did not pour money into Balazuc's coffers, one man yelled out, "We need some way of making them pay!" (*"Il faut trouver un truc pour les faire payer!"*)

Tourism and garbage go hand in hand in Balazuc, as everywhere.

Most of the year the garbage truck sweeps through the village only once a week, very late Sunday night or early Monday morning, and during "the season" of July and August, a second pickup is added. But tourists coming for an hour, four hours, or a day must dispose of ice-cream wrappers or beer cans; those staying for a week, a fortnight, or a month accumulate large ugly black plastic garbage sacks that must go somewhere. In a silent protest against the high cost of garbage sacks in France, I began to put rolls of very inexpensive Stop & Shop garbage bags into my suitcase when coming over from the United States. I have never been checked at any customs desk, so I have never had to explain why I bring garbage sacks in huge rolls to France, and in any case, I doubt that the French government will respond to the recent doubling of the entry tax on foie gras and shallots from Brittany by imposing a daunting tax on garbage bags.

In 1995 the municipality still had several large containers, or bins, for garbage here and there, with signs clearly stating that they were "reserved for Tourists passing through"—note the capitalization—and recognizing that "the cleanliness of the village is one of the essential criteria of the quality of the welcome" afforded to visitors. Some residents began to sneak down at night or early in the morning to place their sacks in the containers, which were within a matter of hours full, overfilled, and attracting bees, flies, and, inevitably, cats and dogs, despite the frequent efforts of the *mairie* ("Our appeals have not been heard!") to remind owners not to allow their dogs to *se sauver*—to escape into the village.

The last thing I wanted was to be seen violating a municipal ordinance. More than once early in the morning I drove several large black sacks resembling body bags down to the green container near the bridge, fearful that someone would recognize our red Renault 19 that had committed the transgression. But as I was hardly alone in occasional sin, and as the number of tourists continued to increase, the municipality had the containers hauled away. This has left only a couple of very small garbage containers placed discreetly in key places, their openings too small to accommodate much more than plastic Orangina bottles and ice-cream bar wrappers. This sometimes leaves one with garbage sacks in the car and the hope of coming upon

a garbage container in a nearby commune before the smells over-
whelm driver and family or before some contents begin to ooze
toward the suitcases. (Once, after discovering a container, I caught
myself shouting to no one in particular, "St.-Maurice has garbage
containers!!" It was a not inconsiderable discovery.)

The municipality has continued its efforts to enhance tourism. A
shining new telephone booth has been put up near the river. A stone
shelter, in harmony with the rural architecture of the Bas-Vivarais,
greets those driving into Balazuc from the Vogüé–Ruoms road. It
looks nice but serves no purpose at all. The old donjon, which in the
nineteenth century served for some decades as the town hall, now provides several panels of information on the history of Balazuc. In the
summer, one or two young people work at "Point I," where a brief
exposition, "A Thousand Years of History in Balazuc," has been set
up in the Tour Carrée, which still leaks. They provide the maps of the
village, now complete with street names. Twice a week a woman,
known as La Conteuse (the storyteller), takes visitors on a tour of the
village, narrating tall tales about medieval village life to applause. In
1997 two not terribly successful cocktail hours (apéros) were held outside the mairie for "the summer tourists," but the idea was abandoned
after few tourists or residents turned up. In 1999 the municipality
celebrated the completion of a copy, placed outside the village hall,
of the fifth-century sarcophagus discovered near the old Roman road
in the seventeenth century and now in the Gallo-Roman museum in
Lyon. In August 2001 the mayor made a special point of thanking
tourists who participated in the Festival of Bread and Wine.

The Association de la Roche Haute provides some cultural anima-
tion of the summer season. Most of the activity centers on the église
romane. The view from the top of the old church is superb, and the
dilapidated but charming bell tower, symbol of Balazuc, beckons any
visitor to scale the slippery stone staircase to reach the top. Beginning
about mid-July, the association makes possible the opening of the old
Romanesque church to thousands of visitors (the "new" church draws
many visitors, a good many of whom leave thinking they have seen
the église romane). In order to give visitors something to look at in the
quite barren church, the Association de la Roche Haute (principally

one or two members) organizes an exposition in the two naves. It begins in mid-July with a short introduction of the artists in the church, followed by drinks in the *place* below. Generally, there are two parts of the exposition, one for each nave. The first usually presents the paintings or sculptures by an artist, usually from Paris and brought to Balazuc by one of the members of the association who lives in the capital. The paintings, drawings, or sculptures are for sale, but few, if any, are sold. In the past, the second nave sometimes presented a theme, such as "World War I in the Ardèche," "The Silk Industry in the Ardèche," "From the Table of Yesterday to the Gastronomic Palace of Today" (my favorite), "Hats and Umbrellas from the Beginning of the Century to Our Day," "*Les Objets de Toilette d'Autrefois*" (items used in the past for washing up or grooming, provided by villagers), and so on. Because the association receives a modest subsidy from the departmental Conseil Général (as well as from the municipal council), each day a member of the association (which had sixty members in 2001) sits and counts the number of people who come in to see the exposition. Those counted include those who come in only briefly, to get out of the sun (my own rule is that they must have two feet inside the door to be counted; dogs are supposed to be excluded, but many come in, though they are rarely counted). In 1996 the exposition on eating in the Ardèche attracted almost ten thousand visitors. Thus the exposition generally succeeds in providing something cultural for visitors to do, if only for a few minutes. In addition, the church provides a nice setting for concerts, usually with a classical theme, despite the occasional entry of a bird zooming close to the heads of the audience. The association each year also organizes a "cultural visit" to a site of interest, such as the old Roman town of Vienne, Lyon, or Marseille. Unfortunately, most full-time residents of Balazuc show little, if any, interest in the annual expositions, and few belong to the association.

In the early 1990s a teaching couple from Normandy began the Association Balazuc Cavernes (ABC), with the goal of enhancing the appreciation of Balazuc's prehistoric past and its remnants and thus advancing cultural tourism. They discovered and charted the location of prehistoric sites and printed a periodic bulletin. They also laid out a series of possible walks or hikes of varying lengths to parts of Balazuc, principally on the *gras*, where there are prehistoric *grottes* and dolmens, including a "tomb of a giant." The "grand circuit of the Megoliths" takes one on a six-mile trek; the "botanical circuit around Balazuc," indicated by green markers, lasts a mile and a half and exposes one to at least twenty-eight kinds of plants, including wild asparagus, hellebore, and thyme. However, some of the small signs providing information along the paths have fallen victim to vandalism.

The organizers of ABC have orchestrated summer activities for children, and adults as well, including afternoons of spelunking (*stages spéléo*) and an occasional talk by a local expert on the prehistory of the region. The sale of *marquisette* (a white sangria, made with fruit, rum, soda water, and sparkling wine), beer, and Cokes, at the association's annual *bal* in July raises money for printing hiking routes and equipment for spelunking. However, in the summer of 2000, ABC's dance did not take place. Its organizers complained that there could not be an association of only two persons, who did almost all the work. Without the commitment of more than a few full-time residents of the village, the association seemed on the verge of disappearing, a blow to cultivated tourism in Balazuc. Yet, hoping that a new municipality would be more encouraging, in 2001 the association sponsored its annual *bal*, its faithful bartenders selling many gallons of *marquisette*.

Balazuc will always be there, privileged by its fantastic settings. However, the new golden tree does not necessarily guarantee the future. Again, Michel Carlat: "The most important thing is that the land remain farmed, that people can live from it. . . . Never will the arrival of tourists during the summer compensate for the absence of people during the rest of the year." Even if encouraging people to purchase country houses is the only way of saving the "rural architectural patrimony," the tradeoff may be that "our region falls in a tomb, the price of returning to a desert."[77]

Another risk, simply put, is that as the rural patrimony is threatened, a new, false patrimony is being created. The *Guide Michelin* of course lends considerable credibility to the sites of the French patrimony. Balazuc retains its star (and deserves two). Yet, to be sure, the

GM also awards stars to Euro-Disney, which could not have less in common with any aspect of the patrimony of the French hexagon and may well merit having been damned by a government minister awhile back as a "cultural Chernobyl."

Furthermore, the quest for profit from tourism can damage the most beautiful sites of the patrimony. In Provence, across the Rhône and to the south, the magnificent site of Les Baux en Provence, which became a center of a Provençal revival in the late nineteenth and early twentieth centuries, has been transformed into the equivalent of Provençal-land. Avignon in some ways is just awful. Recently, someone had the idea of creating not far from the Grotte Chauvet (which will be closed to all but a few specialists) a "Grotto-land" (the idea perhaps coming from a store in Ruoms called Cadeauland or Giftland), complete with rides and copies of the cave drawings.

The hustle and bustle of summer tourism give a completely misleading impression of the village, just as seeing handsome stone *magnaneries* could lead a visitor to assume that Balazuc and its neighboring villages are wealthy. Most of the year the village seems deserted. Indeed Carlat uses Balazuc as an example of the discontinuity between the summer season and the rest of the year: "There is no one in the village. It's a desert. Go to Balazuc from October to April."[78]

Balazuc's demographic profile is not encouraging. More than a third (115) of the residents belong to the Club du Troisième Age (Senior Citizens Club). It meets one or two times a month in the *salle polyvalente*. One spring a small group of its members went on a trip to Catalonia. Relatively few young people remain in Balazuc. Not that long ago very few children went beyond primary school, leaving with—or without—the Certificate of Primary Studies (*certificat d'études primaires*) at age thirteen. Now attendance at the *lycée* in Aubenas or some sort of professional school is routine. More young people take and succeed in the *baccalauréat*. A handful of young people go on to the university, increasing the chances that they will then leave Balazuc to work somewhere else. There is nothing for most of them in Balazuc. At one point, Mathieu, who later spent a school year living with us in Connecticut, was the only boy in the village between ages eleven and eighteen. He could not understand my fascination with Balazuc (though now, at eighteen, he has changed his mind and appreciates it very much). "There is nothing to do in Balazuc!" he once said. "There are two hundred eighty people: two hundred old ladies, fifty old men, and about thirty people more or less young!" The number of adolescents increased in the 1990s, but there is nowhere for them to hang out. In 1999 almost 40 percent of residents were at least sixty years old. All too frequently the church bell rings slowly to alert Balazuc to the fact that another resident has died.[79]

Outside the tourist season, the grocery store is open only in the morning. Since the baker closed in the 1970s, the bakery in Vogüé delivers bread early in the morning to the store. The store stays open in the winter as something of a public service, since some older people have no means of leaving Balazuc to shop. A butcher brings his wagon to the village once or twice a week, stopping in two or three places and honking to make his presence known. Several times a year a truck loaded with haberdashery and sewing materials shows up. The *bibliobus*, the small library bus that began service during the Popular Front offering a modest selection of books that may be borrowed, still comes to the village for about an hour several times a month. None of the restaurants is now open outside the tourist season.

During most of the year, Chez Paulette opens in the morning for the same people who come every day at about the same time and an occasional deliveryman, but it closes from about lunchtime to five o'clock. Then the regulars of a small card game of *bélote* turn up to play until seven o'clock or seven-thirty, perhaps a little later on Friday or Saturday evening. (Now one regular asks if soon there will be even four left to play.) Stories are told of those who sat around the table in the past. One was known as the prefect because he had worked in the prefecture of Marseille but had been sent packing for illegally selling permits for this and that. During the early years of the presidency of François Mitterrand, he occasionally announced that he could not play cards that night because a plane was coming to take him to dinner with the president. But well into the evening he was still seated at the table.

Sunday about noon a few people come to have a drink. One could not imagine a friendlier place, but all seems like marking time until the first cars of tourists arrive. Over the last few years, the number of people showing up in the evening has declined. Photos of several faithful clients, Paulette's friends who have died, now adorn the walls. During the summer of 2001, a man who had come to Balazuc a few years after World War II died. He had left money so that following his burial his friends would drink a pastis or two Chez Paulette. Now Paulette is also about to retire. Who will keep the keys to many of the houses? The grocery store closed at the end of September 2001. No successor is in sight at the moment. A public meeting to discuss the problem reflected village concern. That the store that offers local products, above all, wine, and is open all year long, decided for the moment to sell bread from a nearby bakery (thus arguably combining two of life's essential, bread and wine) only partially alleviates the problem.

The calendar does provide occasions for people in the village to get together, but here too some of these are in the summer. The *fête votive*, the feast day of the patron saint of the church and thus the village, occurs in the third week of July. A *bal* takes place, but the majority of people who attend are tourists. There are strobe lights, music played by a disk jockey or cassettes, and a bar (*buvette*), animated by children hopping up and down. A "country meal" (*repas campagnard*) is held late in the spring, sometimes with an entertainer and songs sung by several people from the village, a few in patois. It is a much smaller occasion now than in years past, with fewer young in attendance. In November, a light meal around roasted chestnuts is served, and the soccer club (which does not have a team but sponsors a series of brief matches at the rocky field in August) and an association for those who like boules, most of whose members no longer play—organize a dinner in a restaurant in a nearby town. Sparse decorations remind one that Christmas is coming, but the village, if anything, becomes even more deserted, as a good many families not natives of Balazuc return home to their original homes in the north of France.

Most permanent residents now live in parts of the village that had no or very few houses until late in the nineteenth or the twentieth century. Some residents have built comfortable, spacious modern houses away from the village itself during the last several decades. The old village seems almost deserted during the winter months, when only two houses are occupied in part of the village near the old church, proximate to the old *place* that was once the village center.

In the summer of 2001 a resident, one of those whose ancestors had resisted the coup d'état of 1851, who himself had first come to Balazuc at the age of six months and moved back after years of working in Lyon, sold his house to a Swiss family. The winters had become too lonely (*"Je me trouve tout seul"*). The departure in the summer of 2001 of Popaul Gamel, one of Balazuc's most beloved figures, who, with his long hair and flowing beard, was a reassuring fixture at the café, winter and summer, has greatly saddened the village. His moving out, when many people said he would never really leave, led to voiced concern, indeed some pessimism, about Balazuc's future. If in the nineteenth and the first half of the twentieth centuries, the silk industry, the production of wine, and chestnuts represented (arguably with the church a fourth) the triptych of rural life in the Bas-Vivarais, on a smaller but very human scale Balazuc's triptych has over the past two decades been the school, the café, and the store. The existence of none seems assured for the future. Thinking of Popaul's leaving, one resident put it strongly, *"C'est un coup d'arrêt* [This is the final blow]," while Paulette despaired, *"Balazuc, c'est fini,"* at least the Balazuc she and many others still remember. Sadly, these are epitaphs for much of rural France.

One longtime resident recently complained that now it's *"tout le monde dans son coin"* ("everybody keeping to himself"). One frequently hears that village life is far less intense than in the past, perhaps today because most of the population lives away from the village center. Here again television and the telephone are frequently mentioned as culprits. The absence of a true village square may also contribute to bringing people together less frequently than before. "Nothing goes on anymore," lamented one woman, insisting that the difference can be felt even since a good number of us celebrated the bicentennial in 1989.

However, among the continuities worth treasuring is the persistence of being able to rely on neighbors and friends as well as family. In its long past, mutual assistance has always counted for much. Those with cars sometimes do shopping for those without them or drive the elderly to their doctors' appointments. The term *entraide* (mutual assistantce) is still used because it still means something. Just like the role of the school, such solidarity has helped people overcome their differences. In 1998 a friend of many fell desperately ill. One day someone made it known at the café that it was time to prune his vines. The next day several people put together food for lunch, in the hope that a few people would show up to help. Fifty people were there the next morning, and they included a few who had not spoken to one another for some time. Not long after noon, the entire job was completed. Also, recently, when a man fell while hunting, a sign went up outside the café asking for people to come help with the vines that he could not look after.[80] Balazuc remains a great place.

Another tradition, perhaps surprisingly, lingers, almost reassuringly, as French villages struggle for survival. The Vivarais is one of those regions in which healers were always esteemed. Some people in Balazuc still believe in their powers. An esteemed healer lived until his death in the old village. The woman recently elected first deputy mayor has an excellent reputation as a healer of burns. Several years back a friend who had cut himself wide open with a power tool refused to see a doctor. He went instead to a healer up in the mountains, an elderly man who passed his hand over, without touching, the wound, which healed. More recently Mathieu, who had developed several warts while spending a school year in the United States, found no success there with various tubes of medications. However, after returning to France, the warts went away. I asked him what he had done, asking, half in jest, if he had gone to see a healer. No, he had not gone to see a healer. He had called him on his cell phone. Balazuc changes.

NOTES

Preface

1. Laurence Wylie, *Village in the Vaucluse* (Cambridge, Mass., 1974 [first published in 1954]). Among others: Susan Carol Rogers, *Shaping Modern Times in Rural France: The Transformation and Reproduction of an Averyronais Community Village* (Princeton, 1991); Pierre-Jakes Hélias, *The Horse of Pride: Life in a Breton Village* (New Haven, 1978); Roger Thibault, *Mon village* (Paris, 1982); Thomas F. Sheppard, *Loumarin in the Eighteenth Century* (Baltimore, 1971); Harriet G. Rosenberg, *A Negotiated World: Three Centuries of Change in a French Alpine Community* (Toronto, 1988); Gérard Bouchard, *Le Village immobile* (Paris, 1972); Patrice Higonnet, *Pont-de-Montvert: Social Structure and Politics in a French Village, 1700–1914* (Cambridge, Mass., 1971); Liana Vardi, *The Land and the Loom: Peasants and Profit in Northern France, 1680–1800* (Durham, N.C., 1993); Gillian Tindall, *Celestine: Voices from a French Village* (New York, 1996); Deborah Reed-Danahay, *Education and Identity in Rural France: The Politics of Schooling* (Cambridge, England, 1996).

2. See Christopher H. Johnson, *The Life and Death of Industrial Languedoc 1700–1920* (New York, 1995).

3. Peter Jones, "Towards a Village History of the French Revolution: Some Problems of Method," *French History,* 14, 1 (March 2000), p. 80.

Chapter One

1. Quote from *Notre France* by Michel Carlat, *L'Ardèche traditionnelle* (Poët-Laval, 1982), p. 135. Stone from the quarry in nearby Ruoms forms the base of the Statue of Liberty in New York Harbor.
2. Michel Carlat, *L'Ardèche: Les Chemins du coeur* (Voreppe, 1990).
3. Vicomte E.-M. de Vogüé, *Notes sur le Bas-Vivarais* (Paris, 1893).
4. See Jean Cottes, Jean-Marie Chauvet, et al., "Les Peintres paléolithiques de la Grotte Chavuet, à Vallon-Pont-d'Arc (Ardèche, France): Datations directes et indirectes par la méthode du radiocarbone," *C.R. Académie de sciences de Paris,* t. 30, series II (1995), pp. 1133–40; Jean-Louis Roudil, *Préhistoire de l'Ardèche* (Soubès, 1995), p. 32.
5. Pierre Bozon, *La Vie rurale en Vivarais* (Valence, 1961), p. 254.
6. Maurice Allignol, *Balazuc et le Bas Vivarais* (n.p., 1992), pp. 16–19. The area near the Tower of "Queen Jeanne" and the Combes, dominating the *gras,* seem to have been principal sites of habitation, as well as Frigoulet, on the left bank of the river.
7. Bozon, *La Vie rurale,* pp. 56–70.
8. Evoked in Paul Perrève, *La Burle* (Montferrat, 1994).
9. Elie Reynier, *Le Pays du Vivarais* (Vals-les-Bains, 1923), pp. 47–51.
10. About 30 percent of the Ardèche's population lives there, on only a tenth of its territory. At the northernmost part of the department are Annonay, the largest town in the Ardèche, and Tournon to the south on the Rhône.
11. Paul Joanne, *Géographie du départment de l'Ardèche* (Paris, 1911), p. 20.
12. Carlat, *L'Ardèche: Les Chemins du Coeur,* p. 89.
13. Bozon, *La Vie rurale,* pp. 48–49; Pierre Bozon, *L'Ardèche: La Terre et les hommes du Vivarais* (Poët-Laval, 1985), p. 43; Reynier, *Le Pays du Vivarais,* pp. 90–91, 103–04.
14. Charles Forot and Michel Carlat, *Le Feu sous la cendre: Le paysan vivarois et sa maison* (St.-Félicien, 1979), p. 44.
15. Bozon, *L'Ardèche,* (Poët-Laval, 1985), p. 7.
16. Jean Volane, *L'Ardèche pittoresque* (St.-Etienne, 1989; first published, 1899), p. 5.

17. André Siegfried, *Géographie électorale de l'Ardèche sous la IIIe République* (Paris, 1949), pp. 19–20; Carlat, *L'Ardèche traditionnelle*, p. 71.

18. Vogüe, *Notes*, p. 49.

19. Bozon, *L'Ardèche*, p. 49; BN, Collection Languedoc-Bénédictins, XIV–XVI (24), noted that the region's forests were now viewed as "an illusory resource, nonetheless the Vivarais is alarmed by the lack of wood. . . . The forests are becoming precious and are disappearing."

20. Carlat, *Architecture rurale en Vivarais*, pp. 60, 173; Alain Molinier, *Stagnations et croissance: Le Vivarais aux XVIIe–XVIIIe siècles* (Paris, 1985), p. 34, notes that during the July Monarchy, the Ardèche stood eighty-first, thus almost last, among departments in the numbers of doors and windows, with only sixty-eight per hundred inhabitants.

21. Michel Carlat, *Architecture populaire de l'Ardèche* (Poët-Laval, 1984), p. 66.

22. Michel Carlat, *Architecture rurale en Vivarais* (Paris, 1982), pp. 204–06; Reynier, *Le Pays de Vivarais*, p. 30. In 1876, thirty-one inches of rain fell on Joyeuse in twenty-one hours.

23. See Bozon, *La Vie rurale*, pp. 183–86. However, Vogüé certainly exaggerates when he dubbed it "an example of rural democracy, a little French Switzerland" (*Notes*, p. 145, n. 1). See Wylie, *Village in the Vaucluse* for his analysis on the role of the family in "Peyrane" (Roussillon).

24. Carlat, *Architecture rurale*, pp. 82, 129, quoting H. Gaudin: The house "submits itself to the natural lines of the countryside to which it adapts with remarkable suppleness. . . . Adjusted, shaped, it marries the lay of the land [and] becomes part of the countryside, integrated into it, by establishing a compromise with the milieu."

25. The construction of vaulted rooms of stone (often built stone upon stone, without mortar) itself reflects the fact that peasants of the Bas-Vivarais had relatively little access to solid wood for use in houses (Carlat, *Architecture rurale en Vivarais*, p. 184).

26. Bozon, *La vie rurale*, pp. 230–33.

27. Forot and Carlat, *Le Feu sous le cendre*, p. 40; Carlat, *Architecture populaire de l'Ardèche*, p. 74.

28. Régis Sahuc, *Le Fils du pauvre: Mémoires et portraits* (Le Puy, 1994), pp. 23–24, 74; Carlot, *L'Ardèche: Les chemins du coeur.*

29. Carlat, *L'Ardèche traditionnelle*, pp. 75–76.

30. Carlat, *Architecture populaire de l'Ardèche*, pp. 71–72, 116; Carlat, *Architecture rurale en Vivarais*, pp. 69, 76–81.

31. Forot and Carlat, *Le Feu sous le cendre*, p. 32.

32. Sahuc, *Le fils du pauvre,* p. 219.

33. Louis Bourdin, *Le Vivarais: Essai de géographie régionale* (Paris, 1898), p. 102.

34. Carlat, *Architecture rurale en Vivarais,* pp. 160–68.

35. Reynier, *Le Pays de Vivarais,* pp. 90–95. This description owes much to that of Bozon, *L'Ardèche,* pp. 222–32. Bozon traces the origin of the term *gras* to the root of *Kar=la pierre* (p. 223).

36. Fonds Mazon.

37. Michel Rouvière, *Paysages de pierre, paysages de vie* (Chirols, 1991), pp. 4, 77.

38. Michel Rouvière, "Le Gras de Balazuc, Vinezac, Lanas," unpublished paper, 1998, pp. 5–6.

39. BN, Collection Languedoc-Bénédictins, XIV–VI (24), (written after 1766).

40. Pierre Cornu, *Une Économie rurale dans la débacle: Cévenne vivaraise, 1852–1892* (Paris, 1993), pp. 5–8, 35–36. See Jean-François Blanc, *Paysages et paysans des terrasses de l'Ardèche* (Annonay, 1984), 288–91; MR 1248, (Military survey), 1846; Bozon, *La Vie rurale,* p. 38; Ovide de Valgorge, *Souvenirs de l'Ardèche* (Paris, 1846), p. 300.

41. Volane, *L'Ardèche pittoresque,* quoting from Bourdin, *Le Vivarais,* p. 191.

42. Carlat, *L'Ardèche traditionnelle,* p. 5.

43. Volane, *L'Ardèche pittoresque,* p. 8, quoting Boiron, *Lettres Ardéchoises.*

44. Carlat, *Architecture rurale en Vivarais,* p. 33.

45. Forot and Carlat, *Le Feu sous la cendre,* pp. 39-40.

46. Charles Ambroise Caffarelli, *Observations sur l'agriculture du département de l'Ardèche* (Paris, [Year IX]), p. 92. See Marie-Noël Bourguet, *Déchiffrer la France: La Statistique départementale à l'époque napoléonienne* (Paris, 1989).

Chapter Two

1. It now stands in Lyon's Gallo-Roman museum.

2. Volane, *L'Ardèche pittoresque,* pp. 157–61; Jean Boyer, "Historique de Balazuc," unpublished paper, available to visitors to Balazuc, attributes the founding of Balazuc to *des gens d'Emir Yousouf.* An offshoot of this story has Charles Martel choosing Balazuc as capital of a vast seigneury, with which he rewarded, along with Largentière and its mines, Wilhelm d'Hastafracta, first seigneur de Balazuc; Allignol,

Balazuc et le Bas Vivarais, p. 157, has d'Hastafracta restoring a primitive chapel that had been vandalized by the Saracens, adding the altar made of limestone. He also claims without evidence that the first Christians of Balazuc worshiped in the fourth or early fifth century.

3. The trefoil shape of a window or two sometimes been described as reflecting Saracen influence. The windows most likely represent an imitation of Renaissance style in the sixteenth or seventeenth century.

4. See Gérard Cholvy, ed., *Histoire du Vivarais* (Toulouse, 1988), pp. 10–58.

5. Jean-Pierre Gutton, *La Sociabilité villageoise dans la France d'ancien régime* (Paris, 1979), p. 23; Cholvy, ed., pp. 59–60, 66-67; Michel Noir, *1789, Des faubourgs de Paris aux montagnes d'Ardèche* (Paris, 1988), pp. 15–17; Monique Bourin-Derruau, *Villages médiévaux en Bas-Languedoc: Genèse d'une sociabilité (xe–xive siècle)*, 2 vols. (Paris, 1987), vol. 2, pp. 333–36.

6. That *zuc* sounds like *souk,* which can mean "market" in Arabic, provides some comfort for those seeking Saracen origins for Balazuc. Baladunum could be written *Balazunu* (*Balasu* in Languedocien).

7. Bozon, *La Vie rurale,* p. 88.

8. Volane, *L'Ardèche pittoresque,* p. 157, dates the arrival of the first seigneurs about A.D. 1000. Pons de Balazuc left with his friend Raymond d'Aguylen (or d'Agiles), chaplain of St.-Gilles, count of Toulouse. Together they began to write an account of the conquest of Jerusalem, *L'Histoire des français qui prirent Jérusalem.* Gérard and Pons are sometimes credited with ordering the construction of the walls of Balazuc.

9. Boyer, "Historique de Balazuc."

10. Chauzon and Pradons were separated from Balazuc in the seventeenth century, although remaining part of what became the *mandement de Balazuc.*

11. Allignol, *Balazuc et les Bas Vivarais,* pp. 147, 269; Boyer, "Historique de Balazuc." In 1367 Jean de Cacello, curé de Balazuc, was invested before Pierre de Balazuc, chevalier (Vicomte L. de Montravel, "Balazuc" [1902], n. 9, p. 440). The Balazucs were suzerains of Vogüé, Vinezac, St.-Maurice, Rochecolombe, and St.-Montant.

12. J. H. M. Salmon, "Peasant Revolt in Vivarais, 1575–1580," *French Historical Studies,* p. 5.

13. Noir, *Des faubourgs de Paris,* pp. 18–19. Salmon, "Peasant Revolt in Vivarais," notes (p. 3): "Most of the Bas-Vivarais had been under the

temporal administration of the bishop of Viviers, whose overlordship had been steadily eroded by the southern barons since his acknowledgement of the royal suzerainty of Philippe-le-Bel." In 1320–22, the Vivarais became a *bailliage*, with two courts of justice dependent on the senechal of Beaucaire.

14. Cholvy, ed., *Histoire du Vivarais,* p. 82.

15. Ibid., p. 89. The États included the seigneurs of baronies, such as Balazuc, and representatives of thirteen towns (in later centuries, a number of royal officials were added and the bishop was subtracted). The king chose the *bailli* (chief judicial official), from among nobles.

16. Noir, *Des faubourgs de Paris,* pp. 21–22. The *estimes* corresponded to the *terrier* in the north, an inventory of property rights, etc. See Montravel, "Balazuc,"pp. 435–42. This account draws on Maurice Allignol in *Balazuc et le Bas Vivarais,* pp. 507–51. The *estimes* included forty-three declarations made by fifty families. Jean Régné, *La Vie économique et sociale et les classes sociales en Vivarais au lendemoin de la guere de cent ans* (Aubenas, 1925), pp. 8–9, gives sixty-two as the number of taxpaying families. The *estimes* mentions a chapel along the old Roman road, perhaps the site of the quartier Estrade, and another at "*le territoire de Cham-Sant-Geli,*" or Champ Gely. The sale or leasing to other nobles of these obligations may in the long run have put peasants under harsher seigneurial domination, because the purchasers could claim seigneurial judicial authority.

17. There were (at least) 30 oxen, 16 cows, 33 cattle, 53 pigs, 13 mules (the brothers Yccard were *maîtres muletiers*), and 26 donkeys in Balazuc, along with 1,290 goats producing milk, cheese, and butter.

18. Carlat, *L'Ardèche traditionnelle,* pp. 61–62. In some cases, the shepherd took goats or sheep every day and returned them at night.

19. Allignol, *Balazuc et le Bas Vivarais,* pp. 540–41.

20. See Régné, *La Vie économique et sociale,* p. 20.

21. In 1345 Albert de Balazuc had added Montréal to the family name by marrying Pelette de Montréal, although by then the barony of Balazuc included only the parishes of Balazuc, Chauzon, Pradons, and St.-Maurice-d'Ibie.

22. A point Peter Jones, *Politics and Rural Society: The Southern Massif Central, 1750–1880* (Cambridge, England, 1985), makes for the lower Massif Central in particular.

23. Cholvy, ed., *Histoire du Vivarais,* p. 77.

24. See Michel Joly, *L'Architecture des églises romanes du Vivarais* (Paris,

1966), pp. 24, 51–55. Allignol claims *(Balazuc et les Bas Vivarais,* p. 45, note 8) that the church of Balazuc "is in all likelihood the only church in France to have as its foundation a megalithic construction."

25. Allignol, *Balazuc et les Bas Vivarais,* pp. 418–20.

26. C 1141 (2 Mi 547). Henceforth (unless noted otherwise) all archival documents cited are from the Archives Départementales de l'Ardèche in Privas. Jean de Balazuc became known as *brave Montréal* for his efforts.

27. Salmon, "Peasant Revolt in Vivarais,": "When the peasants rose against the garrisons and the seigneurs they associated with them, they were acting out a kind of spontaneous judicial process against those whom they saw as murderers, robbers, and infractors of royal peace edicts" (p. 27).

28. BN, Collection Languedoc-Bénédictins, I (103); Cholvy, ed., *Histoire du Vivarais,* p. 127. By contrast, *"une foule de petits seigneurs"* led the Protestants. Neighboring Uzer was on a list of villages with Protestant churches in 1562.

29. C 1051, letters of May 30 and July 9, 1628, and "Comptes avec pièces justificatives des dépenses et avances faites par les communautés d'Antraigues, etc." Joanne, *Géographie du département de l'Ardèche;* Cholvy, ed., *Histoire du Vivarais,* etc. Guillaume de Balazuc served as one of the royal lieutenants during this military campaign.

30. At the beginning of the twentieth century, only the Gard had more Protestants than the Ardèche.

31. Cholvy, ed., *Histoire du Vivarais,* p. 111.

32. Molinier, *Stagnations et croissance,* p. 281.

33. Gutton, *La Sociabilité villageoise,* pp. 19, 112, 245; Molinier, *Stagnations et croissance,* p. 85.

34. See Carlat's discussion, *Architecture rurale en Vivarais,* pp. 147–48. A newly completed house was feted by a meal (as elaborate as material conditions permitted) known as the *reboule.*

35. Molinier, *Stagnations et croissance,* p. 81. Cholvy notes *(Histoire du Vivarais,* p. 138) that 55 percent of the *communautés* in the Vivarais had two *consuls.* A *communauté* was an artificial administrative unit that most often corresponded to a village, if not always to a parish.

36. A sol (or sou) was equal to a twentieth of a pound, and a denier was worth one two-hundred-fortieth of a pound.

37. Institutions, such as hospices and religious orders, that organized assistance for or even welcomed the poor were far from Balazuc. See

"Ardèche charitable . . . Ardèche solidaire," *Mémoire d'Ardèche et Temps présent,* 70 (April 2001). The poor person was seen by some as a *misérable honteux,* by others as the living image of Christ.

38. François Thomas and Marthe Thomas, *Le Vivarais* (Paris, 1947), pp. 83–84.

39. Montravel, "Balazuc," pp. 435, 441–42. Curés identified in various documents formally witnessing ceremonies or taking oaths include Philippe Faget, 1460; Tristan Bechard, 1493; Pierre Pastelli, 1529; Thomas Bigoge, 1610; François Salel, 1647; Claude Roussel, 1651; Jacques Volo, 1687; and François Champalbert, 1693. In 1651 the noble Jean de Montand was canon and prior of Chapelle sous Aubenas, and archdeacon of Balazuc, Uzer, and Chauzon. Sauvan, originally from the parish of Lablachère, signed his will on December 13, 1739, asking to be buried in Balazuc and making his nephew his heir.

40. Molinier, *Stagnations et croissance,* pp. 317–18; Carlat, *L'Ardèche: Les Chemins du coeur,* p. 23.

41. Carlat, *L'Ardèche traditionnelle,* p. 128.

42. Gutton, *La Sociabilité villageoise,* p. 256. However, the *communauté* of Balazuc included the villages of Chauzon and Pradons. Between 1644 and 1801 only about 8 percent of the population of the Vivarais lived in towns (Cholvy, ed., *Histoire du Vivarais,* p. 141).

43. Molinier, *Stagnations et croissance,* pp. 158–63. In the Vivarais as a whole, 60.8% percent of the farms were worked by the peasants who owned them, compared with 51 percent for France as a whole. Molinier has studied thirty-five parishes in the Bas-Vivarais (primarily the lower or edge of the Cévennes) during the early modern period. There the average parcel of land was 1.89 hectares: 33.2 percent were less than a single hectare.

44. Molinier, *Stagnations et croissance,* p. 115. Volane (pp. 120–21), however, says that about 23 percent of the land of the department was cultivated (10 percent formed meadows, 8 percent orchards, 3 percent vineyards, 18 percent in forest, and 37 percent in moors). Cholvy, (*Histoire du Vivarais,* p. 121) notes that the average farm in the Bas-Vivarais was about ten ares in size (only about three thousand square feet) and describes the revival of agriculture in the 1590s following the first wave of the wars of religion.

45. Cholvy, ed., *Histoire du Vivarais,* p. 146.

46. Molinier, *Stagnations et croissance,* pp. 58–59; Reynier, *Le Pays de Vivarais,* p. 210.

47. Molinier, *Stagnations et croissance,* p. 245. Beginning in 1648, the États du Vivarais began to consider periodically how much money could be allocated in assistance to *communautés* hit hard by calamities. These amounts, to be sure, were negligible, rarely compensating for more than 2 or 3 percent of losses (Molinier, *Stagnations et croissance,* p. 12). A third of the 460 people in the parish of Jaujac died of cold and hunger during the winter of 1709–10.

48. See Pierre Goubert, *Louis XIV and Twenty Million Frenchmen* (London, 1970) and Goubert, *Les Paysans français au XVIIIe siècle* (Paris, 1998); Molinier, *Stagnations et croissance,* pp. 11–27.

49. C 1511; Molinier, *Stagnations et croissance,* pp. 40–41, 172–74; Jolivet, *La Révolution en Ardèche* p. 41.

50. Molinier, *Stagnations et croissance,* pp. 22–25, 303; Reynier, *Le Pays de Vivarais,* pp. 22, 52.

51. Molinier, *Stagnations et croissance,* pp. 31–33.

52. C 1242. The procès-verbal was signed by "Gaunan *curé*; Auzas *consul,* Teissier *consul* and Constan [certainly the clerk or *greffier*] . . . en presence de nous soussigné Jean Maurin collecteur de la comm.(té) de Balazuc," December 14, 1728.

53. C 1254, letter to *consuls,* January 20, 1734, signed by Tastevin, mayor; Teissier and Auzas, *consuls;* Pays, *greffier;* Vallier, Teissier and Auzas, Brun, Boyron, Barthélemey Mollier, Roudil, François Roux, Antoine Rieu, Antoine Boyer, Claude Leyris, Claude Boucher, Pierre Daumas, and Jean Constant.

54. C 843, December 17–18, 1754, September 18, 1756, and October 17, 1762, accounting of extraordinary repairs, September 1, 1763.

55. After a swift rise in the river in 1824, three men noticed a body in the water near the mill. The dead man, certainly drowned by a sudden surge of the river, was about sixty years of age, of normal height (that is, about five feet one inch tall), with a round face and prominent nose, black hair, and a gray beard. On his last day, the man, "known to be a beggar, wore a dark jacket and short pants, and had with him a sack for his belongings" (October 26, 1824, report inserted into municipal council register).

56. Molinier, *Stagnations et croissance,* pp. 55–56; Noir, *Des faubourgs de Paris,* p. 72.

57. Emannuel Le Roy Ladurie, *The Peasants of Languedoc* (Urbana, Ill., 1976), pp. 265–69; Cholvy, ed., *Histoire du Vivarais,* pp. 135–36 and 154–55; Gérard Sabatier, "De la révolte du Roure (1670) aux Masques

armés (1783): "La mutation du phenomène contestataire en Vivarais," in Jean Nicolas, ed., *Mouvements populaires et conscience sociale, XVIe–XIXe siècles* (Paris, 1985), pp. 121–47 (quote, p. 128); Mémoire, BN, Collection Languedoc-Bénédictins XIV–XVI (24).

58. Salmon, "Peasant Revolt in Vivarais," p. 6, and Molinier, *Stagnations et croissance*, pp. 389, 141–42.

59. Cholvy, ed., *Histoire du Vivarais*, pp. 143–55.

60. Albin Mazon, *Notice sur Vinezac* (Privas, 1897; reprinted Villeneuve-de-Berg, 1987); AD Hérault, C 4019, June 29, 1752, noting that the repairs had been successful. Molinier, *Stagnations et croissance*, p. 168.

61. BN, Collection Languedoc-Bénédictins, XIV–XVI (24), *Mémoire sur le Vivarais*; Reynier, *Le Pays de Vivarais*, p. 138.

62. C 1361, October 27, 1787. Thus, in 1787 Teyssier of Balazuc received sixty pounds "for the price of the crowning of the wall of support for the port of Balazuc." A route went from Ruoms through Lagorce, near its distant *hameau* of Leyris, and then, near Vogüé, went off toward Villeneuve-de-Berg.

63. C 18, July 27, 1763. The report noted that the land survey was "in pretty good shape, dating from 1615 and rebound not long ago."

64. André Chambon, *Paysans de Vivarais* (Vals-les-Bains, 1985), p. 143, shows the extraordinarily narrow geographic range of marriages of the peasants of a village in the Bas-Vivarais during the Ancien Régime, only three occurring beyond the range of twelve miles, the two most distant in Viviers.

65. C 81, list of inhabitants of the Vivarais paying the *capitation* (1734). Balazuc, Pradons, and Chauzon paid a total of 551 pounds. The survey counted "about four persons" per family (counting widows and those unmarried), 166 households for the three villages. Balazuc had a notary, but he did not necessarily live there. The position of notary was extremely important in Languedoc, a *pays* of Roman and thus written law, and all transactions had to be signed publicly before a notary to be binding. Allignol (*Balazuc et la Bas Vivarais*, p. 550) refers to another survey, the *estimes*, of the early seventeenth century, which counted 138 households and at least 820 people, but this surely counts all three villages, as does Alain Molinier's figure of 150 households in 1644. Molinier, *Paroisses et communes de France: Dictionnaire d'histoire adminstrative et démographique, Ardèche* (Paris, 1976), puts the number of households in Balazuc in 1687 at 72.

66. Marie-Hélène Balazuc, *Mémoires de soie* (Robiac-Rochessadoule, 1992),

p. 132; Molinier, *Stagnations et croissance,* pp. 346, 352; Jones, *Politics and Rural Society,* pp. 95, 100, notes that until the Revolution, within the context of Roman law, the transmission of property could be arranged "by immediate and irrevocable donation during the lifetime of the donor; by testament; and by donation to a nominated heir upon his marriage," the most common arrangement. Roman law did not impose primogeniture. Jones remarks that patriarchical and stem families were essentially the same in the region.

67. The land survey known as the *compoix* became essential for the assessment of taxes and for the historian. The *mairie* of Balazuc possesses two *compoix:* a register of 939 pages, subsequently noted to be a *compoix, "sans préambule ni répertoire,"* sometime before 1677 and probably from at least 1617; and a *compoix terrien,* 1776, with subsequent notes adjusting the amounts (reflecting sales of land, inheritance, assessments now *"à la décharge de,"* ["the responsibility of,"] and so on) each head of household owed, until year IV of the republic.

68. Molinier, *Stagnations et croissance,* pp. 144–45.

69. Mairie de Balazuc, register of the taille. Heads of household who were relatively well off included Antoine Tastevin, Jean Boucher, and André Auzas, each of whom was assessed more than three pounds. In May 1789 the syndic of the Vivarais levied twenty-six pounds and nine deniers on all *"négocians, marchands en gros et en détail, fabricans de toute espèce, hôtes, cabaretiers, etc.* [wholesalers and retail merchants, manufacturers of all kinds, innkeepers, cabaretiers, etc.]," indicating that there were at least such people in Balazuc.

70. 1Z 532, *"Capitation* list for 1789." I have here not separated from Balazuc seventeen people listed as paying the *capitation* in Chauzon (and presumably Pradons), including the village priest. In 1776, eleven Tastevins who were heads of household, eight Auzas, and six Molliers could be found in Balazuc.

71. C 42, ordinance of June 27, 1740. In 1780 the taille represented 76.8 percent of direct taxes and 31.7 percent of the deniers *royaux, provinçiaux et diocésains.* In order to pay it, many villages went into debt, some having to sell communal land. Cholvy, ed., (*Histoire du Vivarais,* p. 151) notes that in 1750 such indirect taxes represented 58 percent of the take in the diocese of Viviers.

72. Allignol, *Balazuc et le Bas Vivarais,* p. 543. In 1636 a notarial act granted Georges Tastevin the right to sell meat, establishing limits on the prices he could charge. He could pasture animals on the common

land. No one else could slaughter animals in his house or sell meat. If anyone did so, he could be hauled before the senechal court at Nîmes.

73. Jones, *Politics and Rural Society,* p. 45. See also Jones, "Common Rights and Agrarian Individualism in the Southern Massif Central 1750–1880," in Gwynn Lewis and Colin Lucas, eds., *Beyond the Terror* (Cambridge, England, 1983), pp. 121–51, in which he notes (p. 123) that in the south, where Roman law had been the rule, collective agricultural practices could be found in the region. Jones argues that "demographic pressure within a closed economy did more to focus attention upon the commons and collective practices than any number of legislative pronouncements" (p. 127). Albert Soboul long ago emphasized the solidarity of the *communauté* of the Ancien Régime, suggesting that collective practices, particularly those relating to common lands, accentuated the capacity for resistance to seigneur, church, and monarchy. Among his implications was that the Revolution, by sanctifying private property, undercut the solidarity of the village, accentuating social divisions (Gutton, *La Sociabilité villageoise,* p. 115, and Jones, "Common Rights," pp. 121–22).

74. 2 O 187 and C 991, October 23, 1768. Some signed the document; "the others [were] illiterate." Yet a deliberation of the principal inhabitants, dated April 25, 1779, stated "with unanimous voice" that Balazuc owned no common land (C 991 and 2O 187, deliberations of April 25, 1779), Boyer and Leyris, *consuls.* The contradiction probably comes from the fact that the *communauté* paid the seigneur an annual fee for use of the *gras* and wanted to avoid paying any taxes on the land.

75. A. D. Hérault, C 3014. In 1644 villagers paid four seigneurs for the right to fish in the river (8J 26/10 [Fonds Reynier]). Some seigneurs were more lax than others, but the leasing out of rights sometimes led to harsher conditions because those who purchased the leases wanted to make money.

76. C 17, procès-verbal, November 16, 1734.

77. Régné, *La Vie économique et les classes sociales en Vivarais,* p. 17; Molinier, *Stagnations et croissance,* pp. 155–56, notes that the annual revenue for each inhabitant in France at the end of the Ancien Régime was 126.95 francs, while it was 104.45 in the Vivarais. Probably about half the land that could be cultivated in Balazuc at the time consisted of vineyards.

78. On problems of defining a village, see Jones, "Towards a Village History of the French Revolution," *French History,* 14, 1 (March 2000), pp.

67–82. He defines (pp. 68–69) villages as "small, nucleated settlements containing individuals who worked a fixed agricultural territory. Place, physical space, and community were thus superimposed; indeed bounded together by the common disciplines of crop rotation and collective vigilance against the incursions of marauding seigneurs," a definition more closely corresponding to the cases in northern France.

79. Gutton, *La Sociabilité villageoise,* pp. 86–90; Régné, *Histoire du Vivarais,* vol. 3, pp. 72–73, drawing upon BN, Languedoc-Bénédictins, XIV–XVI (25). The goal of the decree of June 1787 was to increase the responsibility of *communautés* for following directives from the state. It mandated the election of municipal assemblies. In most parts of France, it was barely applied. These municipalities gave way to those established by the Constitutional Assembly in 1790. In some places seigneurs or even the departing *consuls* named them.

80. Gutton, *La Sociabilité villageoise,* pp. 69, 77; Cholvy, ed., *Histoire du Vivarais,* pp. 138–39. Jones, "Towards a Village History of the Revolution," p. 77, makes the point that *la plus saine* part of the population should not give the idea that a majority necessarily participated in decision making but rather represented relatively "well-to-do heads of household and property-owners."

81. See Robert Schwartz, "Tocqueville and Rural Politics in Eighteenth-Century France," unpublished paper, quoting Turgot's mean and probably wrong description of French villages as "a congery of huts and country folk as inert as their huts" (p. 2).

82. Gutton, *La Sociabilité villageoise,* pp. 81–82; Jolivet, *La Révolution en Ardèche,* p. 45. Schwartz portrays peasants in the village he has studied in Burgundy as differing "from the hapless, down-trodden victims portrayed in Tocqueville's account of rural society" (p. 21).

83. Mairie de Balazuc, deliberation of July 22, 1786, and July 13, 1788. Similarly, on July 13, 1788, "after Mass," another such meeting agreed to pay the collector Antoine Chabasset more than eleven pounds. AD Hérault, B 1214 and B 1217, contain documents (kindly noted by Peter McPhee) detailing a bitter dispute between Pierre Lapierre, *exacteur des tailles de la paroisse de Balazuc* in 1688, and Claude Daumas, *consul,* who apparently failed to collect the taille. The dame of the barony of Balazuc, widow of the *maréchal de camp,* who lived in Balazuc, in 1702 gave the figure of the taille paid in the *mandement* of Balazuc at eighty-three hundred pounds.

84. Molinier, *Stagnations et croissance,* pp. 83–84; Gutton, *La Sociabilité villageoise,* pp. 86–87, 95–99ff.

85. C 43, État des dépenses ordinaires de la communauté de Balazuc, 19-10-1738. The *montant des impositions* is given as 3,079 pounds, 3 deniers and 6 sols.

86. C 54, 1778, "preamble of the tax roll levied on the communities of B.P. and C., diocese of Viviers . . . deliberation of the ordinary council of the community, July 12."

87. C 1063, "State of grain transported to Le Teil by the inhabitants of Balazuc, 1695–97," signed, Tastevin, *maire,* January 8, 1695. Presumably those from whom the grain was requisitioned were reimbursed. C 1239, letters, of February 20 and 26, 1722.

88. Gutton, *La Sociabilité villageoise,* pp. 102–06, notes that in the diocese of Reims in 1774, only 10 percent of *communautés* had a school; Molinier, *Stagnations et croissance,* pp. 393–405; Cholvy, ed., *Histoire du Vivarais,* pp. 155–57. In 1737, 59 percent of the *communautés* in the diocese of Viviers had schools. Molinier, "Les Difficultés de la scolarisation et de l'alphabétisation sous la Restauration: L'Exemple ardéchois," *Annales du Midi* (1985), p. 129. Balazuc may have had a school for girls, but we simply do not know.

89. Molinier, *Stagnations et croissance,* p. 405; "Les Difficultés de la scolarisation," pp. 129–30, remarks that the Bas-Vivarais, particularly the edge of the Cévennes Mountains and the edge of the Rhône River did a little better. Compared with rates in France of about 27 percent for brides and 47 percent for grooms at the time of the Revolution (Isser Woloch, *The New Regime: Transformations of the French Civic Order, 1789-1820s* [New York, 1994], p. 174). On March 2, 1698, Suzanne Dalmas was baptized, before her godmother, godfather, and parents. Only the priest, Champalbert, signed.

90. B 138 (1787), 6MI 188, contract of September 18, 1787; 5Mi 19. When the body of Jean Vernet of Mercuer washed up in the river on August 6, 1752, Courtiol, Nogier, and Louis Tastevin signed their names, and Louis Pinchon could not. In 1750, Nogier, the priest, was the only one of nine witnesses who could sign his name attesting to the five deaths that year.

91. Jones, *Politics and Rural Society,* pp. 73, 123; Carlat, *L'Ardèche traditionnelle,* p. 136; Noir, *Des faubourgs de Paris,* p. 37. The spoken language of the Mountain, in contrast, reflected proximity to Auvergne.

92. Allignol, *Balazuc et le Bas Vivarais,* pp. 451–52, 622. The banker was Bonnier de La Mosson.

93. Molinier, *Stagnations et croissance,* p. 141; Noir, *Des faubourgs de Paris,* pp. 77–87; Jones, *Politics and Rural Society,* pp. 75, 162–64. Despite the resurgence of aggressive seigneurialism, the authority of the seigneur over the peasantry was less in Languedoc and Provence than in much of northern France. Two adages nicely draw the difference: If in northern France it was said, *"Nulle terre sans seigneur,"* much of the Midi had it *"Nul seigneur sans titre"* (Gutton, *La Sociabilité villageoise,* p. 155).

94. Jolivet, *La Révolution en Ardèche,* pp. 16–17; Schwartz, "Tocqueville and Rural Politics," p. 3; Mairie de Balazuc; Noir, *Des faubourgs de Paris,* pp. 91–93.

95. Noir, *Des faubourgs de Paris,* pp. 77–87; Gutton, *La Sociabilité villageoise,* p. 171.

96. BN, Collection Languedoc-Bénédictins, XIV–XVI (24); Jolivet, *La Révolution en Ardèche,* pp. 18–19; Jones, *Politics and Rural Society,* pp. 155, 158. The taille was assessed according to calculations of revenue and population density that had been determined in about 1530.

97. Quoted by Sabatier, *"De la révolte de Roure,"* p. 122. See Cholvy, ed., *Histoire du Vivarais,* pp. 135–36. This prophetic aspect was found in earlier revolts in Romans in the Dauphiné in 1580 and in the Rouergue in 1627.

98. Michael Sonenscher, "Royalists and Patriots: Nîmes and Its Hinterland in the Late Eighteenth Century," doctoral dissertation, University of Warwick, 1977, p. 387; Gutton, *La Sociabilité villageoise,* pp. 18, 173–76; Cholvy, ed., *Histoire du Vivarais,* cites the murder of sieur de Pierreplane in 1757.

99. BN, Collection Languedoc-Bénédictins XIV–XVI (24). That the Vivarais was under written law may have made the peasants more litigious.

100. Jolivet, *La Révolution en Ardèche,* pp. 21–22; Noir, *1789, Des faubourgs de Paris,* p. 7. See also BN, Collection Languedoc-Bénédictins, XIV–XVI (24).

101. Noir, *Des faubourgs de Paris,* p. 126.

102. Sabatier, "De la révolte de Roure, 1789, p. 134, adding with reference to 1670, "It seems impossible that the traumatic nature of past revolts not be inscribed in popular collective memory" (p. 138). See Sonen-

scher, "Royalists and Patriots," pp. 422 and 995 ff. Sonenscher places
the revolt in the context of the evolution of the seigneurial system's
being transformed "into a parasitic relationship with commercial cap-
italism," contributing to "the monetarisation of social relations," a
revolt undertaken by those victimized by the network of rural credit.
Rebels sought a "re-affirmation of local control over an area which had
fallen outside of the traditional means of enforcing sanctions." See
John Merriman, "The 'Demoiselles' of the Ariège, 1829–1831," in
Merriman, ed., *1830 in France* (New York, 1975).

103. Cholvy, ed., *Histoire du Vivarais,* p. 116–17, 152–54, and Maurice
Boulle, *Révoltes et espoirs en Vivarais 1780–1789* (Privas, 1988), p. 12;
Sabatier, "De la révolte de Roure," pp. 121–47. Sabatier notes (pp.
124, 128) that the *masques armés* were more moderate than the "followers" of Roure in 1670, who had pillaged several churches, killed a
priest, and "profaned" several cadavers. He concludes that by the time
of the *masques,* "the societies of order had succeeded the society of
order." Riots had become part of the rules of the game, and a millenarian content was no more (p. 144).

104. Molinier, *Stagnations et croissance,* pp. 202–05, 207–09, 233–40; Jones,
Politics and Rural Society, pp. 12–13, 54; *La Vie rurale,* pp. 82–87; Cholvy,
ed., *Histoire du Vivarais,* p. 147, notes the production of grain rose only
from 350,000 quintaux in 1690 to about 385,000 in 1789. The growth
in population was less than that during the period 1644–93, a time that
drew to a close with harvest failure and probably also the departure of
Protestants. The birthrate stood between 36.7 per 1,000 and 40.1 per
1,000 toward the end of the Ancien Régime, mortality falling to about
32 per 1,000 (Cholvy, ed. pp. 141, 144). Earlier age of marriage and
sturdier clothes may also have contributed. A "confraternity of the chestnut" exists in the Ardèche today. The difference between recipes for "the
crique [potato pancake] of the poor" and "the *crique* of the rich" is today
the addition of *crème fraîche* in the latter. Chestnuts were sold as marrons
de Lyon, particularly to France's second city.

105. 5Mi 19.

106. Molinier, *Paroisses et communes de France.* In the early 1760s a survey of
Languedoc gave Balazuc 203 households and a population of 903, but
these totals certainly would have included Pradons and Chauzon and
seem far too high: BN, Collection de Languedoc-Bénédictins,
XIV–XVI (24), "État de lieux qui forment le bas pays de Vivarais [Sur-
vey of the Bas-Vivarais]."

107. Molinier, *Stagnations et croissance,* pp. 271, 320. In 1789 the average person consumed 137 kilograms of bread, 47 kilograms of potatoes, 32 kilograms of chestnuts (considerably less in Balazuc), 20 kilograms of fruit, 2.8 kilograms of dry vegetables, and 1 kilogram of sugar. Vaccinations had knocked out smallpox in France by 1809.

108. Molinier, *Stagnations et croissance,* pp. 212–17, 228; Jolivet, *La Révolution en Ardèche* p. 4. In the late eighteenth century the Vivarais produced the equivalent of about 200,000 hectoliters of wine. In 1730, an ordinary year, it exported 65,000 hectolitres of wine, and in 1780 it produced two-fifth more than could be consumed locally. In 1768 the diocese of Viviers imported about 4.5 million pounds of goods and exported a little more than 1 million pounds.

109. 12M 81; Bozon, *La Vie rurale,* pp. 131–33. Olivier de Serres quoted by Élie Reynier, *La Soie en Vivarais* (Largentière, 1921), pp. 14, 12–21; Hervé Ozil, *Magnaneries et vers à soie: La Sériciculture en pays vivarois et Cévenol* (Lavilledieu, 1986), p. 41. A document from 1361 relates the purchase by a merchant from Anduze of slightly less than two quintaux of cocoons from Privas.

110. Chambon, *Paysans de Vivarais,* p. 140; Bozon, *La Vie rurale,* p. 130; Molinier, *Stagnations et croissance,* p. 175.

111. Sonenscher, "Royalists and Patriots," pp. 260–61, 315; Noir, *Des faubourgs de Paris,* p. 32.

112. Mairie de Balazuc, "États de section, 1791."

113. Molinier, *Stagnations et croissance,* p. 210;. Reynier, pp. 44–57. Ozil, *Magnaneries et vers à soie,* pp. 41–42; Jacques Schnetzler, "Une économie fragile," *Mémoire d'Ardèche et Temps présent,* 24 (November 1989), pp. 7–14.

Chapter Three

1. L 1637, District de Tanargue, population of communes, n.d. (1793?); B 142 (2MI 76). See Jolivet, *La Révolution en Ardèche,* pp. 80–90. There was, to be sure, a formulaic aspect to the cahiers, models of which had circulated.

2. In nearby Largentière 116 men signed a petition in 1787 asserting that "the people complain bitterly that those who pay more than half of the taxes" were represented by only one person on the Conseil politique de la Ville, while the nobility had three representatives and the "bourgeoisie" two. Whether this lively debate had any influence on Balazuc,

we do not know (see Jolivet, *La Révolution en Ardèche,* pp. 46–48).

3. Brun, *consul;* Thoulouze, *consul;* and Pays, Rieu, Tastevin, Lauriol, Auzas, Rieu, Mollier, Charousset, Fromentin, Boulle, Boyer, Teyssier, Fabregoulle, Constant, Auzas, Mollier, Courtiol, Mollier, Pays, Marcel, Tastevin, Guérin, Boyer, Laroche, Tarterrey, and Boucher.

4. B 141, *Mémoire touchant les états généraux de France,* 1788, Vivarais. Jean Boyer suggests that Tastevin and Boucher may well have written much of the *cahier de doléance.* The spouse of Antoine Tastevin was Thérèse Dubois-Maurin, sister of a deputy of the Bas-Vivarais to the Estates-General. Only the Tastevins of Salles had the right to have a *pigeonnier* (dovecote).

5. Jolivet, p. 2.

6. Noir, *1789, Des faubourgs de Paris,* p. 134, quoting d'Antraigues: "The Third Estate is the people and the people form the base of the state. They are the state itself."

7. Jolivet, *La Révolution en Ardèche,* p. 133.

8. Pierre Ladet, ed., *Entre Coiron et Tanargue: Aubenas sous le vent de l'histoire* (Privas, 1991), pp. 127, 205; Cholvy, ed., *Histoire du Vivarais,* p. 165; Jolivet, *La Révolution en Ardèche,* p. 142.

9. Mairie de Balazuc, "Liste des citoyens actifs de la communauté de Balazuc"; L 901, "Listes des citoyens actifs et éligibles, 1790–91"; L 968, "Liste civique de la garde nationale de Balazuc du 15 juillet 1790"; document also found in Balazuc.

10. Jolivet, *La Révolution en Ardèche,* pp. 157–58.

11. Several villages that had been within the Vivarais were attached to the Haute-Loire, and several that might have become part of the Gard to the south joined the Ardèche.

12. Molinier, *Stagnations et croissance,* p. 82. The Vivarais had included 320 *communautés* and 350 parishes. See Peter Jones, "Towards a Village History of the French Revolution."

13. Woloch, *The New Regime,* p. 35.

14. Chambon, *Paysans de Vivarais,* p. 164.

15. Mairie de Balazuc, August 15, 1790; L 968, mayor, August 15, 1790; Jolivet, *La Révolution en Ardèche,* pp. 200–08.

16. L 897, list of declaration of losses, 1790. That of Balazuc was signed by *"Teiyssier maire, Brun officier, Toulouze officier, Marcel notable, Scabaiter aussi notable Constant notable Boyé notable, Auzas notable, Auzas procurer de la commune, Tastevin, greffier-commis."*

17. See Jolivet, *La Révolution en Ardèche,* pp. 209–311, and Cholvy, ed.,

Histoire du Vivarais, p. 168. The law of November 27, 1790, required priests to swear obedience to the Civil Constitution.

18. See Timothy Tackett's definitive study *Religion, Revolution, and Regional Culture in Eighteenth-Century France: The Ecclesiastical Oath of 1791* (Princeton, 1986).

19. See Sonenscher, "Royalists and Patriots," who sees the events at Jalès as a "product of a specific perception of a relationship to Nîmes" based on the commercial network that stretched into its hinterland (p. 254). The Catholics of Nîmes paid the Protestants back in 1815.

20. Sonenscher, "Royalists and Patriots," places emerging differences between "royalists" and "patriots" in the context of "the different places occupied by 'royalists' and 'patriots' within a developing structure of commodity exchange" (pp. 532–33).

21. Jones, *Politics and Rural Society,* pp. 75, 172–73 ("when some of them next took to the field, it was to defend the old order"); Chambon, *Paysans de Vivarais,* p. 169.

22. Jolivet, *La Révolution en Ardèche,* pp. 236, 269–78; Thierry Chailan, "Les Réactions à la Constitution civile du clergé dans le district du Tanargue," pp. 187–200, in *Églises, pouvoirs et société en Ardèche (milieu xviiième siècle-milieu XIXème siècle)* (Ucel, 1993), p. 191. Of the twelve parishes that made up Balazuc's canton of Vallon, none of the curés took the oath in 1791; 6 did in 1792, and 11 in 1793. In the Ardèche overall, 279 priests took the oath (some albeit with reservations), and 246 refused outright (Cholvy, ed., *Histoire du Vivarais,* p. 168, gives a figure of 158 out of 195 taking the oath in the diocese of Viviers late in 1790 or early in 1791). Allignol's views on the whole history of the Revolution and, for that matter, the subsequent history of the Church may perhaps unfortunately be summed up by his account of the war of the radical Jacobin republic against the clergy: "Here the horror of the Nazi concentration camps was surpassed" (*Balazuc and le Bas Vivarais,* p. 633)!

23. Jolivet, *La Révolution en Ardèche,* p. 261n.

24. L 560, "Nogier ancien curé de Balasuc [*sic*]," January 27, 1792, and deliberation of May 9, 1792, April 18, 1792. A list of priests in 1792 (L 974) still lists Nogier as the curé of Balazuc. L 1566 (1793) indicates that Nogier had paid his taxes.

25. L 559, Champanhet's petition of September 30 and deliberation of December 16, 1791, in the "Registre des délibérations du directoire du département de l'Ardèche, livre 1" lists his salary at one thousand pounds.

26. Mazon, *Notice sur Vinezac,* pp. 120–43; Cholvy, ed., *Histoire du Vivarais,* pp. 166–67.

27. L 967; procès-verbal of August 7, 1791, signed by Champanhet, curé; Teyssier, mayor; Leyris, officer; and Auzas, procurer; L 267; "extrait des régistres des délibérations de la commune de Balazuc," June 27, 1793, year II, signed Jean Leyris, mayor, and Joseph Charousset, François Laroche, muncipal officials, as well as Jean-Louis Boyer, Jean Maurin, Louis Mollier, Jean Pays, *notables*; Jacques Christophe Champanhet, procurer, and André Teyssier, secretary/scribe, *"assemblé en conseil général dans la maison commune"*; L 544, list of priests who "abdicated" their functions following the decree of 2 frimaire. By the revolutionary calendar, his resignation came on 14 germinal, year II.

28. See Jolivet, *La Révolution en Ardèche,* chapters 10, 11, and 12, statistics from pp. 472, 478, and 496.

29. Allignol, *Balazuc et le Bas Vivarais,* p. 636. This is a nice story, but Allignol provides no sources.

30. Cholvy, ed., *Histoire du Vivarais,* p. 169. The auctions ended in the year IV and, by placing responsibility in the hands of *commissaires départementaux* following an assessment of the value of property, made sales more difficult. Jolivet (*La Révolution en Ardèche,* p. 487) gives a lower estimate of the number of émigrés, 200 to 210.

31. Q 195, Jacques Mollier, January 31, 1791. A somewhat disjointed letter written by Deputy Pamplone on May 6, 1790, sent to Balazuc concerned the administration of *biens ecclesiastiques,* "counting on your friendship for me" to see that "divine services" not suffer. The letter suggests that the proceeds of the small amount of ecclesiastical property went to Pamplone.

32. Michel Riou, "La Vente des biens nationaux dans le département de l'Ardèche," in *Communautés d'Oc et Révolution française* (Largentière: Imprimerie Humbert et fils, 1987), vol. 2, pp. 77–89. The decree of June 3, 1793, authorized the sale of property belonging to émigrés.

33. Riou, "La Vente de beins nationaux," pp. 81–82. The comte de Vogüé returned to France in 1801 and died in 1812 at the age of eighty, with nothing left of his lands in the Ardèche; his family received forty-five hundred francs in 1828 from the *milliard des émigrés.* John Markoff, *The Abolition of Feudalism: Peasants, Lords, and Legislators in the French Revolution* (University Park, 1996) cites a report from the Ardèche in March 1792: "There is a decree which orders the demolition of all the

towers of the châteaux because they are no longer regarded as anything but houses" (p. 223, n. 33).

34. Q 195; Q 248, suggests that two previous dates, December 30, 1791, and January 16, 1792, had also brought no bidders; Q 270, sale of July 25, 1792; Q 282, Bournet, procurer syndic, July 11, 1792 ("the year four" [*sic*]); Q 486, registered 26 thermidor, year IV.

35. Q 316; Riou, "La Vente des biens nationaux," p. 84. This huge sum suggests that more than one purchaser was involved, which was actually illegal but fairly common.

36. Q 47, Q 283 (procès-verbal), Q 486. Purchasers were to pay a tenth of the price within a month and a tenth with accumulated interest each subsequent year until all was paid. Jacques Mollier himself purchased land at Salerne for 205 francs, which was to be paid for over twelve payments, and property in Grospierres that had been owned by the priory there.

37. L 1212, 25 nivôse, year III, signed in the *maison commune* (probably already the church) by Leyris, *maire;* Laroche, *officier;* Maurin, *notaire;* Teyssier, *agent national;* Pays; Boyer, *notable,* Mollier, *notable.*

38. Q 486, Q 270, and Q 316 (on 15 and 16 pluviôse and 18 germinal, year II). Two of those who purchased land—François Tendil of Lagorce and Claude Laurent of Largentière—never did pay for the property, which was subsequently sold off. F20 161, decree of 30 frimaire, year XIII. Sabatier's purchases were made on his behalf by Louis Auzas and Jean Pays.

39. Mairie de Balazuc, "États de section," 1791, with subsequent notation; Ladet, *Entre Coiron et Tanargue,* p. 205.

40. Riou, "La Vente des biens nationaux," p. 89: "[I]t would be these enriched peasants who, at the beginning of the nineteenth century, would develop the great speculative adventures, vineyards and raw silk." A Tastevin purchased 150,000 pounds of property in the middle valley of the Ardèche (p. 88).

41. Ladet, *Entre coiron et Tanargue,* pp. 381–83.

42. L 1212. Of three thousand pounds in bills, only six hundred had not been issued.

43. L 1637, District of Tanargue, "State of local taxes, the year II, established on 18 messidor," slightly more than 284 pounds.

44. État Civil. Birthrates fell from twenty in the years II and III, to thirteen in the years IV and V, and eleven in the year VI, rose to fifteen in the year VII, and fell back to a mere four in the year VIII, before the

birthrate rose to thirty in the years IX and X. Apparently only two marriages took place in the year VIII.

45. L 1212, extract of procès-verbal of the registry of the commune of Balazuc, 5 germinal, year II. Signed by Leyris, mayor; Teyssier, national agent; Charousset, officer; François Laroche and Mollier, notables, as well as Boyer, Pays, and Jacques Mollier, serving as secretary.

46. L 267. Teyssier was reimbursed for his journey.

47. L 1607, procès-verbal of organization, April 17, 1793, "l'an 2 de la République."

48. L 1212, "État des hommes, armée des Alpes . . . commune de Balazuc." A list of national volunteers (L 939) from the district of Tanargue in 1793 included one from Pradons and seven from Lagorce, but none from Balazuc, as "currently in service of the nation," May 5, 1793.

49. Jolivet, *La Révolution en Ardèche,* p. 564, notes (p. 558) that the sale of Church property encountered little active resistance.

50. L 877, letters of 16 and 23 prairial and 5 ventôse, year II.

51. L 877, including 2 nivôse, year II, letter to the municipality and agent municipal of Laurac; Jolivet, *La Révolution en Ardèche,* p. 279.

52. Cholvy, ed., *Histoire du Vivarais,* pp. 174–75.

53. L 1167; L 877, letters of 16 prairial and 16 and 17 messidor, 5 ventôse, 14 ventôse, 2 nivôse, 28 nivôse, 18 frimaire, year II; Mairie de Balazuc, letter of departmental administration, 17 frimaire, year III.

54. Claude Jolivet, *L'Agitation contre-révolutionnaire dans l'Ardèche sous le Directoire* (Lyon, 1930), pp. 10–14, 17; Donald Sutherland, *France 1789–1815* (New York, 1986), pp. 310–11.

55. L 1212, including letter of 7 floréal, year IV; L 252, 13 thermidor, year IV. A general added that "several of those arrested were not armed . . . and was assured that they did come to Balazuc without bad intent. They have all been sent before the justice of the peace."

56. Cholvy, ed., *Histoire du Vivarais,* pp. 173–75.

57. Ibid., pp. 178–79.

58. AD, Paul Delichères, "Notes de Delichères sur l'histoire d'Aubenas pendant la Révolution"; F1cIII Ardèche 10.

59. Mairie de Balazuc, procès-verbal, thermidor, year VII. The reorganization may have reflected a conservative drift in Balazuc.

60. F7 3652(2); Jolivet, "La Revolution en Ardèche," pp. 60–75. The Montréal attack came on 4 fructidor, year V. The law of 10 vendémiaire, year IV, made communes responsible for damages in demonstrable cases of negligence.

61. L 877, Directory of Tanargue, 3 messidor, year II letter of 28 nivôse, year II, and procès-verbal of *conseil général* of Balazuc, 8 thermidor, year II. This issue had long antecedents. In 1780 "*les officiers ordinaires de la baronnie de Balazuc*" heard six witnesses in a dispute over the right to pasture animals on the *gras* (L 931). A decree of August 14, 1792, authorized the division of common land "but offered no guidance as to how this was to be accomplished." The decree of June 10, 1793, authorized a municipality to hold a general assembly of all inhabitants to debate and vote (with a third of those eligible to vote required) on the selling off of non-wooded common land into equal parcels (Jones, "Common Rights," p. 131). In 1813, Napoleon, short of revenue, simply seized the *biens communaux* (see Woloch, *The New Regime,* pp. 151–53).

62. L 877, 16 messidor, year II; L 931, 8 thermidor, year II, signed by Laroche, *officier municipal,* Teyssier, *agent national,* Leyris, *maire,* Boyer, Mollier, and the secretary clerk (name illegible).

63. Mairie de Balazuc.

64. L 1561; see also Howard G. Brown's excellent article "From Organic Society to Security State: The War on Brigandage in France, 1797–1802," *Journal of Modern History,* 69 (1997), pp. 661–95. The law of January 18, 1798, aided the repression by defining highway robbery and breaking and entering by more than two people as capital crimes.

65. F1cIII Ardèche 10, commissaire of executive authority, 9 fructidor, year VII; municipal administration of the canton of Aubenas, 15 fructidor year VII; commissaire of the executive authority, 27 fructidor, year VII; minister of interior, 7 thermidor, year VII; F7 3652(2); Jolivet, *La Révolution en Ardèche,* pp. 82–84.

66. Mairie de Balazuc, thermidor year VII. The Guard then named Antoine Vital, first lieutenant, to replace him and Jean Leyris, a former *consul* who had been elected to be an officer in September 1789, to serve as lieutenant. In the years V and VI, André Teyssier served as mayor and Antoine Brun as his deputy, with a note indicating that "the same should remain in place." In the year VIII, Tastevin de Salles became mayor, and Rieu *fils aîné* his deputy (3M 44).

67. Brown, "From Organic Society to Security State," argues that this strategy, however brutal and in contradiction to what was still a nominally republican regime, gave the "new administrative and judicial structure of France an opportunity to take hold in rural communes" such as Balazuc (p. 662), a process that continued until 1802.

68. L 1561, procès-verbaux, 12 ventôse, year VII.

69. L 1561, Tribunal civil et criminel, "État des assassinats et vols commis depuis le 15 prairial de l'an VII"; Nivet, report on 20, 21, 22, and 23 messidor, year VII.

70. L 1561, petition from twenty-five men from Chauzon complaining about Monchauffé's methods; report of Sihol, 2 ventôse, year VII. .

71. F1cIII Ardèche 10, L'Administration centrale du département de l'Ardèche, 12 nivôse, year VII; Nivet, report 16 messidor, year VII, to 16 nivôse, year VIII; F7 3652(2).

72. F1cIII Ardèche 10, L'Administration centrale du département de l'Ardèche, 16 nivôse, year VIII; Bulletin de la police générale, 25 vendémiaire to 1 brumaire, year VIII; Jolivet, *La Révolution en Ardèche,* pp. 85–92; Howard G. Brown, "Bonaparte's 'Booted Justice' in Bas-Languedoc," *Proceedings of the Annual Meeting of the Western Society for French History,* 24 (1998), quote from page 4 of the original unpublished version. In the year VI the electors of the canton of Vallon included André Teyssier, Jean Toulouse, Antoine Fabregoule, Antoine Brun, and Antoine Auzas (L 269, Assemblée primaire du canton de Vallon, 1 and 2 germinal, year VI).

73. F1cIII Ardèche 10, report of prefect, 28 prairial, year VIII.

74. F1cIII Ardèche 10, L'Administration centrale du département de l'Ardèche, 24 ventôse, year VIII and prefect (Charles Caffarelli), 1 nivôse and 2 brumaire, year IX.

75. Cholvy, ed., *Histoire du Vivarais,* pp. 180–84; AN, F20 161 prefect, 15 floréal, year XIII. See Brown, "From Organic Society to Security State," pp. 661–95. Tristan Blanc, a well-known bandit from Uzer, was executed in 1802, and the band of Claude Duny, the "king of Bauzon," lasted until 1805.

76. Cholvy, ed., *Histoire du Vivarais,* pp. 179–81; F7 3652(2), commissaire du gouvernement, 1 pluviôse, year VIII.

77. F1cIII Ardèche 10, prefect, 27 prairial, year IX.

78. F1CIII Ardèche 10, prefect, January 12, March 12, and October 6, 1813; F20 161, prefect, May 9, 1811; Alan Forrest, *Déserteurs et insoumis sous la Révolution et l'empire* (Paris, 1988). Molinier, *Stagnations et croissance,* p. 391: 1802, 46.7; 1805, 16.6; 1806, 29.1; 1807, 17.1; 1813, 15.7; 1814, 4.9 percent. F20 161 gives different figures, but the same trend, for a total of 2,039 *réfractaires* during the period of 4,922 draftees: 38 percent in 1801–02, 18 percent in 1805, 13 percent in 1809. Most were rejected for insufficient height, followed in order of importance by various infirmities.

79. There were 653 inhabitants in 127 households (about 5 persons per household).

80. Census of the year XII (Mairie de Balazuc). Balazuc also then had a *propriétaire-officier de santé*, Joseph Salel. Those with servants included Jacques Mollier, who also had a rural domestic and a shepherd living in the household, and the family of the late Antoine Tastevin, who employed three domestics and two servants.

81. Mairie de Balazuc, May 23, 1814.

82. F1bII Ardèche 2 and État Civil. Tastevin was born in 1782, Boiron in 1777. With a personal fortune estimated at twelve thousand francs, Tastevin was by far the wealthiest man in Balazuc; in the region, among mayors only that of Charbonnas, a marquis, had a greater fortune (by almost four times).

83. Woloch, *The New Regime*, pp. 178, 180–83. The ambitious Lakanal Law of 27 brumaire, year III (November 17, 1794) proposed the first national system of primary education.

84. *Annuaire du département de l'Ardèche*, year IX, pp. 60–63.

Chapter 4

1. Ovide de Valgorge, *Souvenirs de l'Ardèche*, p. 57; Albert du Boys, *Album du Vivarais* (Grenoble, 1842), pp. 11, 223.

2. Élie Reynier, *La Soie en Vivarais,* p. 86.

3. Quoted by Charles Blain (Albin Mazon), *Quelques scènes et récits de l'Ardèche* (Aubenas, 1981), p. 65.

4. Quoted by Carlat, *Architecture rurale en Vivarais,* p. 105. In Michelet's account, a passerby says to one of the girls spinning, "What a shame, innocent fairies, that the gold you spin is not for you!"

5. Yves Lequin, *Les Ouvriers de la région lyonnaise* (Lyon, 1977), vol. I, p. 34.

6. For an elegantly presented but often attacked view on modernization, see Eugen Weber, *Peasants into Frenchmen: The Modernization of France, 1880–1914* (Stanford, 1978).

7. Philip E. Ogden, "Industry, Mobility and the Evolution of Rural Society in the Ardèche in the Later Nineteenth and Early Twentieth Centuries," in Philip E. Ogden and Paul E. White, *Migrants in Modern France: Population Mobility in the Later Nineteenth and Twentieth Centuries* (London,1989), emphasizes the control of the industry by Lyon capital (p. 124).

8. 12M 181, agriculture survey of 1852. See also AN F11 2697, 1862.

In the canton of Vallon in 1852, only 39 property owners lived outside the canton, 100 who lived in the canton did not cultivate their own land, while 1,250 cultivated their own land and another 650 worked their own land and that of someone else.

9. Bozon, *La Vie rurale,* pp. 175–76. In Vinezac in 1850, 80 percent of the peasants had less than five hectares, including moor and there were only 21 *ouvriers agricoles* for 196 families of *cultivateurs.* In the year XIII, Louis Duffaud, *cultivateur* living in Audon, sold to Antoine Boyer, *maréchal à forge* living in the village, a parcel of land forty-four ares (*ou mille et douze toises anciennes)* for 150 francs (2E ML 631).

SIZE OF FARMS IN THE ARDÈCHE, MID-NINETEENTH CENTURY
(Reynier, *Le Pays de Vivarais,* p. 121.)

77,000 EXPLOITATIONS RURALES

More than 40 hectares	1,400
10–40 hectares	10,000
1–10 hectares	35,500
Less than 1 hectares	28,000

10. Eugène Villard, De *la situation des intérêts agricoles dans l'arrondissement de Largentière* (Nîmes, 1852), pp. 11–14, 18–19, 22–25; Jean-Luc Mayaud, *La Petite Exploitation rurale triomphante* (Paris, 1999), pp. 186–87.

11. Cholvy, ed., *Histoire du Vivarais,* p. 199.

12. *La Belle Lurette,* 8 (Summer 1997), pp. 8–12; Cholvy, ed., *Histoire du Vivarais,* p. 199. See particularly Reynier, *La Soie en Vivarais,* pp. 3–8.

13. Cholvy, ed., *Histoire du Vivarais,* p. 197.

14. 12M 76, prefect, January 18, 1840; 12M 179; Bozon, *La Vie rurale,* pp. 130–34; Ozil, *Magnaneries,* pp. 45–49. Leaves sold for about twelve francs per quintal. The smaller black mulberry trees are valued for their oil, for their fruit, and as a natural medicine.

15. Siegfried, *Géographie électorale de l'Ardèche,* p. 30.

16. Mayaud, *La Petite Exploitation,* p. 115; Cholvy, ed., *Histoire du Vivarais,* p. 196.

17. 12M 76; 12M 179. Each kilogram thus yielded about thirty kilograms of cocoons per ounce of eggs.

18. Hervé Ozil, "La Sericiculture en Ardèche: Survivance d'une production?," doctoral dissertation, Université de Lyon II, 1983, vol. III, p. 173.

19. Carlat, *Architecture rurale en Vivarais,* pp. 88–92, 145.

20. Forot and Carlat, *Le Feu sous la cendre*, vol. 1, pp. 233–34, 484.

21. Ozil, *Magnaneries,* pp. 75–98, 154–63; Bozon, *La Vie rurale*, p. 136.

22. This account draws on information provided by "Visite de ma magnanerie," by M. Monhomme, Les Mazes, Vallon–Pont d'Arc.

23. Balazuc, *Mémoires de soie*, p. 96. During stormy weather, some *éducateurs* burned thyme to freshen the air.

24. However, the producers had to make very sure that the butterflies did not leave the cocoon because if they did, they would cut the silk thread.

25. In 1847, the spinning factory of Mazellier in St.-Privat, beyond Aubenas, drew about 5 percent of its raw silk from Balazuc, Lanas, Rochecolombe, and St.-Maurice (Yves Morel, "Les Maîtres du fil: Une industrie textile en milieu rural: Le moulinage ardéchois au XIXe siècle," doctoral dissertation, Université Lumière—Lyon II, 1999, p. 195).

26. In witness to the nuances and bewildering variety of patois, a *couradou* in Balazuc and Vallon was known as a *couderc* in Rochecolombe, five miles from Balazuc, a *placet* in Grospierres, a *barda* in St.-Andéol-de-Berg and St.-Paul-le-Jeune, and in some places an *onto* (Carlat, *Architecture rurale en Vivarais*, p. 76).

27. Ibid., p. 158; Reynier, *La Soie en Vivarais*, p. 88. The fluff was sometimes carded, spun, and given to weavers to make *bourrette*, a tough fabric.

28. Balazuc, *Mémoires de soie*, p. 90. Peasants placed the spinning wheel in the shelter of the covered balcony.

29. F1bII Ardèche 4, prefect, May 25, 1855.

30. Ozil, *Magnaneries*, pp. 33, 131–57.

31. Bozon, *La Vie rurale*, p. 260.

32. Annet Reboul, *Moeurs de l'Ardèche au XIXe siècle* (Valence, 1849), p. 183.

33. Reynier, *La Soie en Vivarais*, pp. 100–08.

34. Bozon, *La Vie rurale,* p. 269; Cholvy, ed., *Histoire du Vivarais*, p. 199.

35. MR 1248, 1846.

36. Bozon, *La Vie rurale*, p. 137.

37. Reynier, *La Soie en Vivarais,* pp. 90–91; 15M 1, prefect, February 28, 1849; Ozil, *Magnaneries*, pp. 49, 131–46; Morel, "Les Maîtres du fil," p. 161.

38. Reynier, *La Soie en Vivarais,* pp. 95–96; Morel, *"Les Maîtres du fil,"* pp. 455, 457, notes, "to send one's daughter to a silk-throwing factory was in some way to admit inferior social status."

39. Bozon, *La Vie rurale,* p. 137; Cholvy, ed., *Histoire du Vivarais,* p. 201.
    In 1846 the department produced 282,272 kilograms in *soies ouvrées,*
    sold for about twenty-two million francs. By 1848 ten to twelve thou-
    sand workers, mostly women, were employed in silk throwing or spin-
    ning workshops.

40. Forot and Carlat, *Le Feu sous la centre,* vol. II, p. 685; Albin Mazon, *Voy-
    age le long de la rivière Ardèche* (Aubenas, 1885); Reboul, *Moeurs de
    l'Ardèche,* pp. 184–87.

41. Ozil, *Magnaneries,* p. 45. See Reynier, *La Soie en Vivarais,* p. 9. In 1846,
    the canton of Vallon alone produced between 200,000 and 250,000
    kilograms of raw silk, and the canton of Joyeuse more than 300,000
    kilograms.

42. Cornu, *Une économie rurale,* pp. 44–45.

43. MR 1248. The harvest in 1845 had been mediocre because a long win-
    ter had been followed by drought in the spring, retarding the growth
    of leaves and forcing *éducateurs* to throw out part of the *graines* already
    hatched.

44. Ozil, *Magnaneries,* pp. 72–75; Cholvy, ed., *Histoire du Vivarais,* pp.
    205–06.

45. Villard, *De la situation des intérêts agricoles,* p. 21ff.

46. 12M 76; Villard, *De la situation des intérêts agricoles,* pp. 30–31.

47. Villard, *De la situation des intérêts agricoles,* pp. 13, 30–34. He noted that
    many transactions were hidden to avoid the payment of money to the state.
    Reflecting the official mood of the post–coup d'état of December 2, 1851,
    he added that any help from the state should resist subverting the princi-
    ple of private property, "this indispensable basis of human societies."

48. Léon Védel, *À travers le Vivarais: Balazuc et Pons de Balazuc* (Lyon,
    1884), pp. 7–13.

49. Mazon, *Voyage le long de la rivière Ardèche,* pp. 61–62.

50. Ibid., pp. 36, 63–68.

51. Ibid., p. 69. In 1884 Mazon met some children on the bridge of
    Ruoms and again believed he had stumbled onto descendants of the
    Saracens (Balazuc, *Mémoires de soie,* p. 9).

52. Vogüé, *Notes sur le Bas-Vivarais,* pp. 49–52; Balazuc, *Mémoires de soie,*
    p. 66.

53. *Le Courrier d'Aubenas,* February 29, 1896, written by "Sylvestre" (Paul
    Gouy). A sonnet made the connection for his readers: "When Pons de
    Balazuc, having left for the Crusade/ Rode under the hot Oriental sun,/
    In a harsh valley near Tibériade/ he believed that he was again seeing

his fief and his native manor./ He recognized the Saracen tower, across the way/ On the crest of the rocks, the door, and its arcade,/The rustic dwellings around the esplanade,/The meager olive trees on the burned flanks of the valley."

54. Bourdin, *Le Vivarais,* pp. 131–32; *L'Exprès de Lyon*, January 8, 1914. Those who wanted to erect a monument to Pons de Balazuc desired a festival of appreciation that would also elaborate "the cult of the past and respect for religious and patriotic traditions." No one from Balazuc was involved, but the association reflected the influence of the Touring Club and the Automobile-Club de France (*Le Républicain des Cévennes*, February 27, 1909).

55. G. Bruno, *Le Tour de France par deux enfants* (Paris, 1877), pp. 162–66.

56. See 15M 1, survey of 1848.

57. FicIII Ardèche 11, P07, prefect, June 6 and August 2, 1856, September 12 and October 1, 8, and 10, 1857, April 10 and July 7, 1858. An undated note indicated that in January 1858 more than eight thousand workers had been let go during the past three months and that there were thousands of beggars, with only about 40 percent of workers employed and more factories closing every day.

58. 12M 76, Mayor Tastevin, June 23, 1857, petition, and mayor of Lagorce, June 16, 1857, prefect, October 1, 1857; Bourdin, *Le Vivarais,* p. 105. In the canton only Ruoms and Vagnas produced more kilograms of cocoons than Balazuc.

59. Ozil, *Magnaneries,* p. 51; Cholvy, ed., *Histoire du Vivarais,* p. 205; Balazuc, *Mémoires de soie,* pp. 32, notes (p. 48) high rates of suicide and problems with alcholism among peasants, at least in Labeaume. She remarks that within households, growing financial problems may well have strained relations, for example, between mothers-in-law and daughers-in-law. In France production fell from 24 million kilograms during the period 1846–52 to 5.5 million kilograms in 1865 and less than 2.4 million kilograms in 1876, barely 10 percent of the total twenty-four years earlier.

60. 12M 182, cantonal statistics; 12M 76, Mayor Tastevin, June 23, 1857; petition, and Mayor Dumas of Lagorce, June 16, 1857. Yet only Ruoms and Vagnas produced more kilograms of cocoons than Balazuc.The petition of La Chapelle-sous-Aubenas attacked "abuses invented one by one by the greed of certain purchasers of cocoons and of silk," including price-fixing and a mysterious *retenue* of 1 percent called "by the ridiculous name of the gift," and, more recently, another *retenue* of another per-

cent, unfairly assessed in anticipation that some of what they purchased would be flawed. The worst examples were in the vicinity of Aubenas, where the Tribunal de Commerce was "composed almost entirely by judges themselves involved in the commerce of cocoons or of silk." See Cholvy, ed., *Histoire du Vivarais,* pp. 205–06.

61. Pierre Bozon, *La Vie rurale,* pp. 372–73.

62. Subprefect, October 20, 1856, January 15, April 23, and July 4, 1857. Jones, *Politics and Rural Society,* "[T]he dangers inherent in a rural economy geared increasingly to monoculture became painfully evident" (p. 58).

63. Flc III Ardèche 11, prefect, July 26, 1856, April 26 and July 27, 1859. In 1855, the Société ardéchoise d'encouragement à l'agriculture was founded and published a review, but had little impact.

64. Reynier, *La Soie en Vivarais,* pp. 114–35; Cholvy, ed., *Histoire du Vivarais,* pp. 205–07; Reynier, *La Vie rurale,* pp. 372–73; Ozil, *Magnaneries,* pp. 52 ff; 12M 76, prefect, March 25 and April 26, 1859. The pébrine then moved east into the Italian states beginning in 1853 and reached Illyria in 1857, Macedonia in 1861, Bucharest in 1864, and the Caucusus in 1865. It eventually spared only Japan. No one from Balazuc apparently produced eggs in 1868, but a year later 160 inhabitants were listed as doing so. In 1871 the figures were 281 producing cocoons and 132 producing *graines.*

65. Mairie de Balazuc, nonclassified, prefect's decree of September 14, 1893.

66. 12M 81. Subprefect, July 4, 1857. Harvest in 1865: 4,000 kilograms; in 1866, 6,000. The 1869 survey reported that there were 160 producers in Balazuc. Figures from the 1873 harvest indicate sales of 14, 900 kilograms of cocoons totaling about 96,400 francs (at 7 francs per kilo for cocoons from French eggs and 6 francs for imported *graines*), which if we take 186 as the number of households involved in the production of raw silk, gives an average return of 518 francs per family. One hundred sixty families were *petits éducateurs,* and 26 were more than that.

67. Ozil, *Magnaneries,* pp. 60–61. Pasteur saw that silkworms were infected with the disease from birth. They could not be saved, but if they became infected later, they could still "spin a good cocoon, but the chrysalis and the butterfly are carriers of a germ that becomes active in the eggs."

68. Quoted by Cornu, *Une économie rurale,* pp. 142–43. Land values fell by 40 percent in the canton of Joyeuse from 1852 to 1882.

69. Bozon, *La Vie rurale,* p. 374; Cornu, *Une économie rurale,* pp. 129–30. The number of families producing silk fell from 40,300 in 1872 to 17,510 in 1914. The quantity of eggs placed in incubation in the Ardèche fell from 178,000 in 1882 to 47,219 in 1902 to 29,470 in 1914. However, those who persisted enjoyed better yields than before because of improved hygiene and better spacing in the *magnaneries.* In Labeaume, there were about 200 producers in 1900, 150 in 1918, 108 in 1930, 66 in 1940, 50 in 1950, and none at all in 1966 (Balazuc, *Mémoires de soie,* p. 88).

70. Cholvy, ed., *Histoire du Vivarais,* p. 206. The price of indigenous cocoons continued to fall steadily, from 7.60 francs per kilogram in 1857 to 4.74 francs from 1876 to 1880, 3.71 francs from 1886 to 1890, and reached only 2.87 francs during 1896 through 1900. The Ardèche retained its place in the production of French raw silk, producing with the Gard half of France's total of 8.5 million kilograms of cocoons, 2.4 and 2 million kilograms, respectively, in 1909, while neighboring Drôme produced 1.5 million.

71. 15M 1, survey of 1873. In 1905, when the Balazuc municipal council asked the railway company to build a shelter near the now-empty railway station, it complained that thirty or so women workers were "exposed to the cold of winter and the burning sun during the summer" as they waited for the train that would take them to the workshops of Lavilledieu.

72. Municipal council minutes, November 19, 1905 (henceforth a footnoted date without other indication refers to a municipal council meeting); census of 1911.

73. Reynier, *La Soie en Vivarais,* pp. 131–55; Morel, *Les Maîtres du fil;* in 1913, 23.5 percent of spun silk in France came from the Ardèche, 40 percent from the Gard, and 9.7 percent from the Drôme. There were 381 *moulinages* remaining in the Ardèche in 1912.

74. November 30, 1890, and November 28, 1897; Cholvy, ed., *Histoire du Vivarais,* p. 206. Beginning in 1892, two representatives of the municipal council were chosen as observers for the weighing of the cocoons from the scale attached to the old donjon tower.

75. 2 O 187; Reynier, *La Soie en Vivarais,* pp. 2, 147. In 1909 peasants in Balazuc put 320 ounces into incubation, producing 13,852 kilograms of cocoons, a yield of 43 kilograms per ounce.

76. Blain (Mazon), *Quelques scènes et récits du Vivarais,* pp. 63–66.

77. Ozil, *Magnaneries,* vol. III, p. 176.

78. Michel Rouvière, *Paysages de pierre*, p. 4; Cholvy, ed., *Histoire du Vivarais,* pp. 194–97; 12M 53, 12M 55, 12M 181. In an average year, wine brought about fifteen francs per hectoliter.

79. 12M 55, Int., August 9, 1852, prefect, n.d., and notice of July 7, 1854, January 22 and October 24, 1857, and April 22, 1861; 12M 181, 1852 statistics; F11 2697.

80. 12 M 53. The number of hectares of vineyards in the Ardèche fell from more than thirty thousand in 1872 to seventeen thousand in 1890; the number of hectoliters of wine produced dropped from 375,000 in 1862 to 7,500 in 1884!

81. 12M 54, survey, Cholvy, ed., *Histoire du Vivarais,* p. 206. A hectare of vineyards was worth twenty-five hundred francs in 1874 and one thousand in 1886. In Balazuc, some peasants planted grain in what had been vineyards. In 1940, 36,000 *viticulteurs* worked 20,700 hectares (Reynier, p. 197), and only 15 had more than 20 hectares; 15 had between 10 and 20 hectares; 224 between 4 and 10 hectares; 3,000 between 2 and 4; 3,300 between 1 and 2 hectares, and 26,000 less than 1 hectare!

THE PHYLLOXERA IN BALAZUC

YEAR	HECTARES OF VINEYARDS	HECTARES DESTROYED	HECTARES "INVADED"	HECTARES REPLANTED
1874	300	60	260	
1878	200	100	180	
1885	250	75	225	2
1891	130	20	300	110
1893	235	20	58	80
1894	160	60	110	100
1896	240	239	1	15
1897	50	195	1	49

Source: AD Ardèche, 12M 56 and 12M59

82. 1Z 233, prefect, September 8, 1891, March 26, 1894, and October 29, 1906.

83. 12M 58, Tastevin, September 4, 1891, and Charousset, September 22, 1892, and August 27, 1894; prefect. September 8, 1891; 5M 45, sub-prefect, October 10, 1894; 12M 186; 12M 192; Cholvy, ed., *Histoire du Vivarais,* pp. 206. In 1900, Balazuc had 54 of 60 hectares of vineyards in cultivation, 60 in 1902, and 68 hectares in 1908.

84. September 23, 1890.

85. Pierre Bozon, *La Vie rurale,* pp. 381–82; Cholvy, ed., *Histoire du*

Vivarais, p. 207: "The convergence of these crises is not accidential. It reflects the fact that the equilibrium of the old agricultural economy had been broken by overpopulation. Above all, this prevented both individual enrichment and the evolution of methods of production and exchange." To be sure, it may have been providential in that improved standards of living brought considerably less dependence on chestnuts for food.

86. Bozon, *L'Ardèche*, pp. 57–58.

87. 15M 1, prefect, February 28, 1849; F17 9322; Ozil, *Magnaneries*, pp. 52–63. Ogden, "Industry, Mobility and the Evolution of Rural Society," pp. 121–22. Pierre Gourinard, "La Part de l'Ardèche à la mise en valeur de l'Algérie," *Revue du Vivarais*, 73 (April–June, 1969), pp. 91–93. The density of population per square kilometer fell from 59.4 in 1851 to 37.3 in 1921.

88. The canton of Vallon fell from its peak of 10,910 people in 1856 to 5,721 in 1946, losing 41.9 percent of its population. See Reynier, *Le Pays de Vivarais*, pp. 85–86.

89. Cholvy, ed., *Histoire du Vivarais*, pp. 209–10.

90. Gourinard, "La Part de l'Ardèche," pp. 92–93.

91. Mazon, *Voyage dans le Midi de l'Ardèche* (Aubenas, 1884), p. 69.

92. Fonds Mazon; Chareyre to Mazon, August 27 and September 27, 1884. Mazon believed the village's perched location brought fresh air. Of Balazuc's two major sources of fresh water, one, "reputed to be very good," was below the river; the other, the "fountain" six hundred feet farther away, near the river, was supposed to have water that was "heavy" (others used the cistern of the presbytery, believed to offer the best water). Mazon believed that the cisterns were a potential source of infection. One person stopped drinking the water when he noticed "little insects going here and there," using it only for cooking. However, a relatively dry winter, leaving empty cisterns, seemed to explain in part why Balazuc escaped the epidemic, which killed fifty-three in Vogüé and forty-four in Ruoms.

93. Censuses of 1876 and 1911; *Annuaire*, 1870 and 1888; *Almanach*, 1905. The exception in 1875 was Jean Cartoux, *maréchal*. In 1888 there were two *cafetiers* (one of whom had a *tabac*), two *épiciers*, a *marchand de graines de vers à soie*, a *courtier en savons et huiles*, a mason, two millers, a shoemaker, and a blacksmith. In 1905, there were seven cafés or restaurants. In 1911, of 152 households in Balazuc, 105 were headed by proprietors-cultivators, 10 by property owners, 3 by *rentiers*, and

4 by tenant farmers. In addition, of 10 heads of household without listed occupations, almost all had a son living there who worked the family land.

94. 10M 91, census of 1911: Bozon, *L'Ardèche,* p. 65; Cornu, *Une économie
rurale,* p. 125; 6E 23/1, État Civil. Deaths outnumbered births in Balazuc during the period 1863–72 (130 to 117), equaled each other during the following ten years (119 each in 1873–82), and, after an excess
of 30 births in 1883–92, took precedence again by 109 to 75 in the
1893–1902 period. Those married in 1823–25 had an average age of
twenty-five years; in 1843–54, it was thirty, and in 1883–85, grooms
averaged thirty-four years of age, their spouses twenty-eight years.
One sign of the exodus was that the average size of household in Balazuc fell to 3.70 in 1911.

95. Census of 1911: 123 of 563 (21.8 percent), including Chauzon (9),
Vinezac (8), Pradons (6), Lanas (6), and Montréal, Ruoms, Laurac,
Uzer, and Lagorce, 2 each. Six had been born in Marseille, 2 in Lyon,
and 1 in Paris. The Gard led the way among other departments.

96. Cited by Cornu, *Une économie rurale,* p. 127.

97. 12M 181; Cornu, *Une économie rurale,* p. 151. A *valet de ferme* earned
between one and three hundred francs per year; a servant between fifty
and one hundred francs, including lodging and food.

98. Reynier, *Le Vivarais,* p. 154. By contrast, only 31,500 residents had not
been born in the Ardèche, with the Drôme, Rhône, and Gard leading
the way. In 1911, 24,000 Ardéchois lived in the Drôme, 22,000 in the
Rhône, 16,400 in the Gard, 9,000 to 10,000 people each in the industrial Loire, Marseille and the Bouches-du-Rhône, and the Seine, 5,500
in the Isère, 5,400 in the Haute-Loire, and 4,000 in the Vaucluse.

99. Sahuc, *Le Fils du pauvre,* p. 255.

100. Bozon, *La Vie rurale,* pp. 282–303; Bozon, *L'Ardèche,* pp. 65–66;1Z
344. During the last half of the nineteenth century, the Bas-Vivarais
had a lower birthrate than other parts of the Ardèche (in part because
of Protestants). Only about 10 percent of those living in the Ardèche
in 1914 had been born elsewhere, and by 1939 the percentage had
risen only to 15 percent, the majority from neighboring departments.
Of those born in Balazuc in 1875 for whom we have places of death,
two died in Marseille and one in St.-Ambroix in the Gard. Of those
born ten years later, deaths occurred in Sète, Marseille, Paris, and the
Isère.

101. *Le Républicain des Cévennes,* December 18, 1909 and *L'Echo de Largen-*

tière, March 5 and July 16, 1910; Cholvy, ed., *Histoire du Vivarais*, p. 254.

102. Mairie de Balazuc, "Registre d'inscription des déclarations."
103. Mairie de Balazuc, October 30, 1905.

Chapter 5

1. F17*83 and T 499, "État de l'instruction primaire, 1833."
2. T 211 and T 499; 2 O 184, mc, May 10, 1836. In Bessas, the fee was 75 centimes per pupil; in Lagorce, 1.50. The average pupil spent three years in school in Labastide and four in Lagorce, which was largely Protestant, and only one in Bessas.
3. 2 O 184, May 10, 1836. The municipality paid fifty francs to rent the house that served both as the school and the teacher's lodging (T 43).
4. Jean Peyrard and Jules Joly, *En Ardèche, notre école au bon vieux temps* (Lyon, 1993), p. 32.
5. T 211; Alain Molinier, "Les Difficultés de la scolarisation et de l'alphabetisation sous la restauration: l'exemple ardéchois," *Annales du Midi,* 97, 170 (April–June 1985), p. 148.
6. F17 *83. Sharif Gemie has emphasized the isolation of the teachers he studied in the Rhône (Sharif Gemie, "'A Danger to Society'? Teachers and Authority in France, 1833–1850," *French History*, 2, 3 [September 1988], pp. 264–87).
7. Molinier, "Les difficultés de la scolarisation," p. 146, n. 33. Cardinal Bourret, an Ardéchois, affirmed that "few dioceses were as religious as that of Viviers. The taking of the sacraments there was universal."
8. The land survey (*cadastre*) was drawn up under the supervision of an inspector for direct taxes, with the assistance of three inhabitants of Balazuc and two "experts" in the value of land (July 25, 1826). It divided land into land that could be cultivated, vineyards, meadows, woods, moors (*landes),* pastureland, willows, gardens, and houses, and within each category, it established the quality and the approximate value of the property. Land on which mulberry trees were planted was considered agricultural land; olive trees were counted as vineyards. Twenty-five houses stood outside the village itself and its hamlets, including one at Coste la Beaume, two at Savel, two at Retourtier, one at Mourre Frais, two at Chaussy, two at Les Plagnes, one at Les Costes, two at Couzamas, two at Montagussonon, three at La Gardette, and seven at Croix-du-Bois.

9. Birthrate: 32 per 1,000. Death rate: 24.8 per 1,000.

10. Bozon, *La Vie rurale,* p. 259. The population of the Bas-Vivarais rose from 29,561 in 1801 to 51,521 in 1861; Rouvière, *Paysages de pierre, paysages de vie,* p. 14; État Civil. In 1823–32, births 151 and deaths 122; in 1833–42, births 168 and deaths 154 (this included the disastrous year of 1833); in 1843–54, births 188, deaths 146 (6E 23/1). Thus the average age of death (twenty-six in 1823 and thirty-four in 1824; twenty-nine in 1843 and twenty in 1844) misleads because of the large percentage of children who did not survive their first year.

11. 5M 51; Bozon, *La Vie rurale,* pp. 260–68. Other figures: 596 in the year IX, 611 in the year X, 629 in the year XI, 783 in 1826, 787 in 1831, falling briefly to 780 in 1841 (a result of the epidemic of 1833).

12. Of sixty-seven couples marrying in 1813–15, 1823–25, and 1833–35, thirty-seven marriages brought together a bride and groom from the village (État Civil).

13. Census of 1846 (Mairie de Balazuc). At the time of the 1846 census, 133 of 174 heads of household were *cultivateurs,* and 2 were laborers (some of those counted as cultivators were also day laborers, who probably did not own the land they worked). Also, 3 widows and 3 other single women headed families. Three men were comfortable enough to be listed as *rentiers,* and another simply as a property owner. *Rentiers:* André Teyssier at the Marché aux oeufs; Jean Antoine Tastevin at Salles; and his son, Jean Antoine Tastevin, at Portelas. A list of electors from July 1850 in the Mairie de Balazuc included 75 *propriétaires,* 64 *cultivateurs,* 1 *rentier* (Jean Tastevin), 3 masons, 2 blacksmiths, 2 innkeepers, and a handful of other trades.

14. Census of 1846 (Mairie de Balazuc): 156 households and 880 people. The average household included 5.64 people.

15. Jean Cheyron, *Epidémies du choléra en Ardèche* (Largentière, 1985), p. 3.

16. État Civil.

17. September 4, 1839, February 20, 1842, n.d. [May 16, 1847], August 1, 1852, May 28, 1853; Jean Boyer; letter, March 7, 1853, Caveny, attorney in Largentière, to Mayor Mollier, December 19, 1853. In 1852 the three owners of the cemetery land apparently had still not been paid for the land in which some of their neighbors now lay.

18. 12M 179; Bozon, *La Vie rurale,* p. 131. Villagers consumed nine thousand kilograms of meat per year. This meant that the average person consumed about twenty-eight pounds of meat annually. This in itself reflects increased prosperity, contributing to a decline in mortality and

population growth. Balazuc's mulberry trees produced about forty-five thousand kilograms of leaves each year.

19. See Woloch, *The New Regime,* p. 428.

20. For example, a note, n.d. (July 1831) says that "Jean Vallier, Henri Constant; François Gineys; and Jean were in great indigence" and would not be included on the tax roll.

21. July 20, 1806. Woloch writes (*The New Regime,* p. 155): "Thus was the old-regime legacy of governmental 'tutelage' over the communes renewed by the Directory, carried to an extreme by Napoleon, and perpetuated under the Restoration."

22. Prefect, June 20, 1809, following the law of 28 pluviôse, year VIII.

23. Mairie de Balazuc. Tastevin's fortune was estimated as between six and twelve thousand francs.

24. 2E ML 631; Jones, *Politics and Rural Society,* p. 100.

25. Jean Boyer; May 18, 1823.

26. July 22, 1823, and June 7, 1826.

27. May 10, 1812; May 5, May 14, 1813; May 22, 1817; May 8, 1822; May 12, 1824; May 15, 1828; May 9, 1830; and June 6, 1835. The cantonal municipal receiver oversaw the municipal budget. Thus a circular of the minister of the interior in 1821: "You must never forget that the communes are merely usufructuaries of the wealth and property in their possession. . . . Guardianship essentially belongs to the [national] government" (Woloch, *The New Regime,* p. 151). The secretary's salary was thirty francs in 1825 and forty francs in 1844. Maintenance of the clock cost twenty-two francs early in the Restoration, forty francs per year in the first years of the July Monarchy.

28. May 12, 1825; May 15, 1828; May 10, 1829. In 2000 the mayor of Balazuc refused to accept the thirty-eight-hundred-franc annual payment (about five hundred dollars) awarded to a village mayor. In 1834 the municipal council had to add a few more centimes even to pay back thirty-two francs still owed for the collection of taxes in the village over the past four years (July 13, 1834).

29. February 6, 1842, noting that it was "indispensable" to find a suitable place for the council to meet, suggesting the purchase of a building for eight hundred francs; May 16, 1847; June 29, 1848. However, the meeting of May 9, 1845, referred to gathering in the *maison commune* instead of "the ordinary room for its sessions."

30. Woloch, *The New Regime,* pp. 156–58. Supplementary communal

levies were authorized in 1805. Balazuc also had some sort of night guard, refered to as the *piéton*.

31. F7 9632, minister of the interior, January 31, 1821; reports of August 15, 1823; February 15, May 15, and October 4, 1826.

32. Mairie de Balazuc; F7 437, prefect, March 19 and June 4, report of September 6, 1831, and July 2, 1831.

33. For example, July 12 and November 22, 1818; May 9, 1830; and May 9, 1832. On July 13, 1834, the commune had to undertake a loan for a mere 224 francs to pay the rural guard. After 1814 the ten leading taxpayers were to approve the mayor's budget (Woloch, *The New Regime,* pp. 153–54), confirmed by the law of May 15, 1818.

34. 1MP 34, Int., October 30, 1865. 1M 34, article 36 of the law of April 19, 1829, noted in a circular from the minister of the interior, January 10, 1865; Article 5 of the law of February 28, 1872; Law of April 5, 1884, and minister of the interior circular of April 25, 1889. Rural guards were technically judicial officials; after 1830 they took oaths, before justices of the peace.

35. 5M 32, police for the canton of Vallon, July 15, and gendarmerie report, July 27, 1861.

36. *L'Echo de Largentière,* August 7, 1909.

37. May 10, 1812; May 15, 1814; December 3, 1815; April 15, 1832; August 1, 1834; April 14, 1837, May 16, 1846; and mayor's decree of May 9, 1845, naming Vianès, the innkeeper, as rural guard.

38. May 28, 1851; November 6, 1853; June 6, 1854.

39. Jean Boyer places Vacher in Balazuc.

40. Angus McLaren, *Trials of Masculinity: Policing Sexual Boundaries 1870–1930* (Chicago, 1997), pp. 159–64. The story is told in the film *Le Juge et l'assassin* (1979), which considers the relationship between the judge and the killer. Vacher was born in the Isère in 1869, one of eleven children in a very poor family. He claimed to have been bitten by a rabid animal and tried to strangle a brother at age twelve, before an abbreviated, disastrous stint in a monastery. Following brief employment as a papermaker, he went into the army, where he suffered "the sexual conflicts he experienced in dealing with males." Dismissed on convalescent leave, in Besançon he shot and wounded a woman who had had the good sense to turn down his request that she marry him. Medical experts declared him sane, and he was guillotined on a public place in Bourg-en-Bresse on the last day of 1898.

41. *L'Echo de Largentière,* August 13, 1910. Jean Boyer's account of this is

somewhat different. He has the woman claiming to have been raped but an investigation decided that both were "joyously" drunk.

42. 1Z 311, based on records 1897–1925, July 22, 1905; *Le Républicain des Cévennes,* April 23 and December 17, 1892; January 6, 1912; March 19 and April 23, 1892; *L'Echo de Largentière,* August 26, 1906, August 7, 1909, and December 24, 1910. In 1856 thieves stole from the mayor himself, as well as two other *agriculteurs* (1Z 245, Tastevin, August 4, 1856).

43. F20 161, "Situation du département de l'Ardèche pendant l'an 13."

44. Mairie de Balazuc, dated 1 brumaire, year XIII. In 1853, Claude Mollier *dit* Prieur, asked permission to operate a boat for his own use, including attending the land he owned on the right bank of the river (subprefect, March 5, 1853).

45. October 12, 1836, July 7, 1844, and May 9, 1845. October 12, 1836, July 7, 1844, and May 9, 1845. Such labor obligations were authorized by virtue of a 1797 law, an 1802 decree, and the law of July 28, 1824, as described by Woloch, *The New Regime,* pp. 166–70.

46. August 12, 1839. The council also rejected the idea of contributing to the financing of either of two other roads being considered along the Chassezac River, neither of which had anything to offer Balazuciens.

47. November 15, 1846, n.d. (May 16, 1847); September 17 and October 12, 1848; July 1, 1849; and May 5, 1850; December 19, 1853; 2 O 184, subprefect, August 26, 1854. Not until 1843 did a coach link Aubenas and Alès via Joyeuse. To be sure, few councils were able to resist the temptation to exaggerate village misery in the ill-placed hope of avoiding taxes. Residents of Audon and Servière were criticized for not contributing to the construction of a suitable path from Balazuc down to the new road, which after all was on the other side of the river.

48. Jones, *Politics and Rural Society,* p. 42. The Vivarais "remained subject to a variety of collective practices which the Revolution challenged but failed to destroy." The law of 1837 allowed "the sub-division of commonland into small leasehold plots (p. 144)."

49. 2 O 187, "biens de la commune de Balazuc," n.d. (about 1820), noting 137 hectares, whereas other documents refer to 200 hectares. This land was estimated to be worth two hundred francs per hectare. In addition, less than half a hectare of vineyards could be found there (worth, in principle, a thousand francs per hectare, but cultivation had been abandoned "for a very long time") and on a tiny patch of cul-

tivable land. The marquis de la Fare and then the comte de Vogüé had owned some of the *gras* during the eighteenth century, some of which had been sold as *biens nationaux.*

50. November 29, 1818, September 20, 1819, and August 18, 1822. Common land could be found in Croix-du-Bois, Chazotte, les Costes, and the Serre Barbaud, Serre Rimbaud, and Serre Lauriol. In 1822 one of the Constants participated in the drawing and "accepted a parcel" of land on the Serre Chastagnon, even as the municipality awaited official authorization to go ahead.

51. On February 16, 1820, the council asked the mayor to take "all necessary actions . . . to bring to an end any trouble that could be brought by this commune (Vinezac) against that of Balazuc, whose possession of the place in question should be free and exempt from any limitations of usage." Mayaud (*La Petite Exploitation,* p. 115) writes, "The community of a village is equally an agricultural community, at the same time the agent organizing work, the organ regulating collective uses, and the instrument managing collective property."

52. Rouvière, "Le Gras," pp. 2–3. Another act in 1599 by the Senechal of Nîmes maintained these rights. The animals of Balazuc could drink from the *fontaine de Loda* and the pasture near it. Vinezac brought forward documents from 1422, 1398, 1599, and 1624 giving its villagers the right to pasture their animals on the land Balazuc intended to divide and sell (February 16, 1820). Bozon, *La Vie rurale,* pp. 98–100, discusses the dispute, noting that in 1485 the men of Uzer gave those of Balazuc the right to lead their animals to drink from the fountain of Beaumegiraud, while another in 1548 allowed them to take their animals to drink from a stream but not to cross into Uzer.

53. On November 9, 1820, the council rejected the claims of Antoine Rieu and Philippe Constant. Two inhabitants of Balazuc claimed that the experts had overlooked the fact that they had possessed "from time immemorial" land on the Serre Chastagnon on the *gras*, which was to be included in the sale.

54. 2 O 187, subprefect, May 22, 1820; Mazon, *Notice sur Vinezac,* p. 153, relates the alleged shooting; May 18, 1823, the resignation of Jacques Mollier, mayor, replaced by Jean-Baptiste Alexandre Tastevin.

55. May 12, 1825. The council also undertook a lawsuit against Jean Constant for "usurping" rights held by the commune on the *gras*, as cited by the rural guard in 1822, noting that the village had held rights on

the *gras* "from time immemorial." Lanas had dropped out of the contest. Michel Rouvière refers to a second decision rendered by the tribunal of Largentière on August 14, 1825.

56. May 15, 1828, February 17, 1829, and May 16, 1831; September 20, 1835; May 15, 1837. On July 28, 1828, an expert submitted a report on the advantages of the sale to the commune. In 1836 the prefect estimated that the sale should produce 15,580 francs, which would be payable by the purchasers with interest within four years (1Z 535, February 25). Royal authorization came on February 2, 1835, for the sale of slightly more than 201 hectares to 133 households.

57. Purchasers in principle were to pay within four years, at 5 percent interest. After the sale, Balazuc still held parcels of land in Croix-du-Bois, Chazotte, les Clos, Charousset, Louanes, and les Plagnes. The tax inspector on November 27, 1853, counted seven *usurpateurs*, including Jean-Baptiste Tastevin, André Auzas, Jean Pays, Jean-Baptiste Thibon, Jean Ranchin, and Joseph Lapierre, the baker.

58. 1Z 535, subprefect, December 27, 1843, report of tax official, November 27, 1853, and expert, December 13, 1853, and May 21 and August 1 and 6, 1854; Mairie de Balazuc, subprefect, January 10, 1854, and July 7, 1858. During that decade and the 1860s, accusations of usurpation of the communal by residents of neighboring communes flew about. In 1882 the municipality hired an "expert" to try to make some sense of the whole mess, amid complaints and legal contests. The sale of some of the remaining common land led to enormous confusion; the municipality continued to pay taxes on land that had been purchased by its residents. Five years later the adminstration annulled all prior arrangements. Finally, in 1898, an authorized surveyor took charge, and the municipality forced those purchasers of communal land to pay back taxes the commune had been paying on the land (December 26, 1886, October 23, 1887, and June 5 and August 24, 1898; Jean Boyer).

59. 1Z 535, Fleuvaux, tax collector, of Vallon, September 27, 1853.

60. Mairie de Balazuc, April 10, 1853, and n.d. The meeting of June 2, 1854, voted that 390 francs be allocated to reimburse Dours. The sum of 913.86 francs for the cemetery was owed to Pays, Tastevin, Perbost, Constant, Auzas, and Dours. Mathieu Valladier of Vallon was finally paid off in principal and interest in 1850.

61. 1Z 233, subprefect of Largentière, July 26, 1862, January 29, 1863, December 9, 1865, and March 21, 1866. In 1840 even the most basic

repairs to the church had been estimated at two thousand francs, but the church council had only four hundred francs (1Z 801, Mayor Teyssier, March 6, 1846).

62. 1Z 570, November 4, 1860.

63. Gordon Wright summarizes in *France in Modern Times* (New York, 1995), p. 150: "The state first took on more than half the construction cost by providing the land, the roadbed, and the bridges and later shifted to a kind of cost-plus arrangement by which it guaranteed to the private firms a fixed return on their investment."

64. November 18, 1894. Telegraph service began from the small station in 1894.

65. December 10, 1899. The Freycinet Plan of 1879 created a plan for state-subsidized construction of secondary lines, some of them of marginal utility, however, viewed by those competing for them as essential to their region and town. On winners and losers, see Christopher Johnson, *The Life and Death of Industrial Languedoc 1700–1920,* especially chapters 6 and 7.

66. A sad account of a meal in 1897 near Issarlès: "[T]he children are seated near the chimney, where potatoes are cooking in water. The latter are emptied into a strainer to drain, then put on the table. The father crushes them with a blow of his fist, grinds salt with the aid of a bottle, and each person takes a salted potato from the table. A little milk for everyone and dinner is over" (Carlat and Forot, *Le Feu sous la cendre,* pp. 37–39).

67. Roger Ferlet, *Le Vivarais d'antan,* 2 vols. (Valence, 1981–82), p. 65; Bozon, *La Vie rurale,* pp. 278–79.

68. August 15, 1875, providing a list of the leading taxpayers of Balazuc.

69. August 15 and September 28, 1884; 2 o 184, subprefect, August 25, 1854; August 15 and November 9 and 23, 1884; May 3, 1885; May 16, 1886; December 7, 1892, and November 18, 1894. Louis Constant and Benjamin Boyer refused to go along with the proposal, claiming that the terrain was inappropriate. In 1890 Marie Boissin still had not been paid for the land she had sold. The municipality took out more loans for the cemetery (T 322, subprefect, September 14, 1994, and 2 O 185), for example, those cemetary plots sold to Henri Cartoux, December 8, 1890 (42 francs), Philippe Ranchin, January 31, 1914 (105 francs), etc.

70. August 20, 1895. In 1869 the municipality borrowed forty-five hundred francs from the *caisse vicinale* (a fund for village roads and paths) in

order to improve the path down to the Vogüé–Ruoms road, but apparently the money was not actually paid to Balazuc. *Propriétaires* who had sold adjoining land to the commune still had not been paid by 1871.

71. May 5, 1895, November 23, 1902, February 16, 1902 (the 6,232.40 francs would be financed 15.45 percent by the commune, 24.25 percent by the department, and 60.20 percent by the state); October 20, November 24, 1907, March 15, 1908, and January 26, 1913.

72. 2 O 186 (dossier titled "Tour prisonnière"); architect's report, February 22, 1895, and estimate; subprefect, April 1, 1895; March 3, 1895, January 31, 1897, and May 7, 1911. On September 2, 1898, the municipality sold the building in the *quartier* of the Portail d'Été that had housed the municipal council for 150 francs.

73. V 53; May 4, 1827; May 10, 1829.

74. By virtue of laws in 1879 on medical assistance to the poor and another law in 1893; September 10, 1893; January 30, 1895, and November 19, 1905 and circular of Ministry of the Interior, July 29, 1905. This included small indemnities for travel to see the nearest doctor available, five miles away in Ruoms.

75. March 3, 1878.

76. August 23, 1885; June 9, July 23, and August n.d., 1893. In the end, following a survey undertaken by the gendarmerie, the father agreed to pay half of the cost, with the department chipping in as well.

77. June 23, 1895; September 23, 1906; February 19, 1911; February 25, 1912; July 21, 1912.

78. February 10, 1901, and February 9, 1908, October 15, 1912, and *Le Républicain des Cévennes,* October 5,1912.

79. Balazuc, *Mémoires de soie,* p. 147.

80. October 23 and November 15, 1908; August 7 and November 13, 1910.

81. December 3, 1911, March 17, 1912, and February 9, 1913. Of course, political considerations may have come inevitably into play (particularly during the first decade of the twentieth century, when the Charousset and Mouraret factions were at war), but we have no evidence of this.

82. April 13 and 30, 1880; May 3, 1885; May 16, 1886; February 19, 1893, February 25 and March 17, 1894; February 18, 1896; and August 8, 1897.

83. November 13, 1898, July 14 and August 19, 1900, and April 12, 1903; June 13, 1900; October 6, 1901; November 18, 1906; and September 17, 1913.

84. F17 10374, report of the Commission de l'Instruction Publique, 1817; a report in V 51 notes that Balazuc had one boys' school with twenty-five pupils. Balazuc was part of the academy of Nîmes until mid-century, that of Grenoble thereafter.

85. Raymond Grew and Patrick J. Harrigan, *School, State, and Society: The Growth of Elementary Schooling in Nineteenth-Century France—A Quantitative Analysis* (Ann Arbor, 1991), p. 31. F20 741; Cholvy, ed., *Histoire du Vivarais,* p. 218. In 1821, the percentage of children twelve years of age who could be considered at the primary level stood at 29.9 percent in the canton of Vallon, 22.5 percent in the Ardèche. An ordinance of 1824 gave ecclesiastics considerable leeway in overseeing primary schools. Cantonal committees established by the Ordinance of February 29, 1816, had little impact.

86. T 498 SP Largentière, April 21, 1831; 10T 8, report of October 25, 1831; T 576.

87. État Civil (4E 23/4). Mollier was succeeded by Jean Besson in 1826 and Joseph Avias two years later. The literacy rate (of those able to sign their names) for conscripts in 1827–29 stood at only 32.9 percent in the Ardèche, 37.2 percent for the canton of Vallon (Molinier, *Paroisses et communes de France,* p. 49).

88. Stephen Harp writes, "Intervention by the French state . . . took over a patchwork of local and religious institutions and transformed them into a primary school system" (*Learning to be Loyal: Primary Schooling as Nation Building in Alsace and Lorraine, 1850–1940* (De Kalb, Ill., 1998), p. 7. See F17 10260.

89. Ibid., pp. 33–35; F17 11345, inspector, August 28, 1834; Molinier, "Les Difficultés de la scolarisation," p. 135. The 1816 ordinance established a cantonal committee, then presided over by a priest, to watch over primary schools and encourage the establishment of schools in communes that did not have them. Molinier also notes that the number of communes without any school had fallen from 164 communes in 1821 to 82 by 1833.

90. AD Gard, 10T 8 (1831–33), report of August 6, 1833; F17 10260, J. Bouvret, February 16, 1841.

91. T 495, November 9, 1833; F17 9632, report of 1837, notes "especially stuttering and what is known as *le sésérément* ('s' for 'ch' et 'z' for 'g') as the two vices that most need to be fought, but in theory more than in practice." By the late 1830s the number of schools had jumped to 532, with 23,850 pupils, of whom more than 8,000 were admitted free (F17 10260).

92. F17 9370, inspector's report, Airolle Condujorgues, August 1836. During the winter, 8,742 boys between six and sixteen but only 482 girls were in public schools. However, if children in schools run by the church were added, 11,524 boys and 9,085 girls were receiving some education (6,160, a third, were carried on the list of indigents). Yet with 42,591 school-age children in the Ardèche, this meant that more than half (21,982) did not attend at all. Moreover, only about half of these (5,459 boys and 4,658 girls) attended during the summer months. Of 212 schools, 117 still used the individual method.

93. Molinier, "Les Difficultés de la scolarisation," p. 141, drawing on F17 83; T 211.

94. T 211. August 12, 1841, indicates that in Balazuc 143 families "would be able to pay for their children's schooling"; October 24, 1852. The inspector calculated that the average teacher in the Ardèche earned 495 francs per year, barely enough to survive—if parents provided 295 francs in fees (1Z 765, May 9, 1845, May 18, 1846, February 1, 1846; October 6, 1848; T 3290, authorization of February 3, 1849).

95. F17 9313, "Rapport général sur la situation de l'instruction primaire dans le département de l'Ardèche en 1849"; Molinier, "Les Difficultés de la scolarisation," pp. 142–44; Jacqueline Roux, "L'Enseignement primaire dans l'Ardèche sous la monarchie de juillet: La contribution des congrégations religieuses à l'enseignement elémentaire," in *Eglises, pouvoirs et société en Ardèche (milieu xviiième siècle–milieu XIXème siècle)* (Ucel, 1993), pp. 125–26. Actes du Colloque de Charmes-sur-Rhône, April 4 and 5, 1993. By 1847 the Ardèche could boast 502 primary schools in 330 communes, 226 public and 276 private. Only 25 communes still had no schools.

96. August 12, 1841; May 16, 1847; and May [n.d.], 1838, and December 12, 1839, set the monthly sum parents were to pay at 1, 1.50, and 2 francs. F17 11369 and F17 11373. The combination of the 200 municipal francs, departmental allocations, and whatever parents managed to pay (180 francs his first year) raised Lafont's income to somewhere near the minimum of 600 francs.

97. July 14, 1832; February 10 and August 28, 1834; December 12, 1839; February 3, 1850; 1Z 535, prefect, August 21, 1834. The house belonged to Joseph Leyris; February 6, 1842, indicates that no purchase had been made and identifies another possible acquisition.

98. August 4 and November 4, 1850, and April 20, 1851; 1Z 773, Mayor

Tastevin, January 2, 1851.Vital taught fifty-six boys, but only twenty in the summer. The familes of thirty paid, and twenty-six were admitted free, as "indigents."

99. Mairie de Balazuc, plan signed by the architect Frey, August 6, 1853; *agent-voyer,* February 4, 1852; subprefect, February 7, 1852; January 12, February 12, 1852, September 20 and 25, 1853, November 6, 1853, January 19, August 20, February 20, and September 24, 1854; SPL, April 9, 1852; 2 O 184, sale, May 14, 1855, minister of public instruction, July 31, 1854; T 209. When the mayor proposed the 1855 budget, which included funds to acquire the house belonging to Charousset (of Largellas), the council members and leading taxpayers turned it down by a vote of ten to eight.

100. F17 10382, "État de l'instruction primaire," December 8, 1821.

101. T 499; T 212. The Pelet Law of June 23, 1836, authorized the title of *institutrice communale* if the municipal council allocated a salary. Twenty-eight female orders were established or returned to the Vivarais between 1796 and 1839, including fifteen communities of St.-Joseph, among them those of Aubenas and Vesseaux (p. 220). The school inspector in 1850 considered Marie Raphanel's "letter of obedience" of "no value."

102. T 209 and 211, "État de situation des écoles primaires," 1836–37, 1839–40, 1841–42, 1843–44; T 175, 1851; 1Z 773, prefect, February 1, 1854, and Deputy Mayor Constant, November 1853; n.d. (May 16, 1847), February [?], May 19, 1852, September 25, and November 6, 1853; T 74, subprefect, December 6, 1853.

103. November 11, 1832; 2 O 188, members of the Charity Association, June 6, 1835, voted unanimously to begin a lawsuit; January 19, 1836, and subprefect, January 9, 1836; August 20, September 10 and 24, 1854, and February 22, 1857, and November 7, 1858. Père Baille had left the village his house at the Portail d'Été. A suit began the following year (November 7, 1858), with 193 francs paid to the lawyer who handled the commune's suit.

104. 1Z 520, letter of Tastevin, Mollier, Cartoux, Auzas, and the village priest, November 14, 1860; January 19, 1854. T 175 and T 209. In all, 105 people contributed 321 francs in cash or work, themselves and their mules. Mairie de Balazuc, plan approved by the subprefect, May 10, 1856; 2 o 184, agreement September 20, 1856, mayor, January 4, 1856, subprefect, March 23, 1854, and April 10, 1857; prefect, June 21, 1854, architect, June 24, 1854, and council, September 25, 1854; list of subscribers; mayor, October 13, 1858; notarial doc-

ument, July 28, 1860; March 25, 1862; 1Z 520, mayor, November 4, 1862.

105. 2 O 184, procès-verbal of hearing before the justice of the peace of Vallon, March 15, 1857; subprefect authorization, April 10, 1857, and act of sale, registered July 15, 1857; T 216; August 26, 1859. The house then had two floors, a *cave*, a stable, and an attic. [It was purchased from Antoine Tastevin *dit* Julien. The latter had debts, owing money to Louis Vianès, innkeeper and grocer; two men in Vallon; a wholesale merchant in Lagorge; and Auguste Perbost of Balazuc, by virtue of an old marriage contract (November 20, 1856)]; T 27, mayor, September 5, 1858. Parents were to pay 1 or 1.50 francs, depending on the age of the pupil. In 1866 the girls' school had twenty-three paying pupils and eight indigents.

106. February 18, 1855. In contrast, an inspector in 1857 described Huond as "routine-minded, sick, can no longer teach in this school."

107. Mairie de Balazuc. Huond, who was in his sixties, "ingenious and honorable," fell ill with an incurable illness and left his post in 1857. A colleague in Vallon wrote to ask the prefect to facilitate the payment of his last salary, because Mayor Tastevin had not taken any action (1Z 773, subprefect, November 18, 1857; letter of Cherité, October 22, 1857).

108. F17 9374; F17 9279, report of rector, June 1854; F17 9374. T 209, 1853–54); Cholvy, ed., *Histoire du Vivarais,* p. 244. In 1879, the percentage of boys in their schools had risen to 46.6 (compared with 20.2 in France as a whole) and of girls to 77 (compared with 54.1 in France).

109. T 212, inspector, January 27, 1850; F17 9314 (1853); F17 9319 (1855); F17 9317, February 8, 1855. Of those 45 in public schools, 18 were lay teachers, and 27 nuns; of the 78 teaching in private schools, 50 were lay Catholic teachers, 24 were nuns, and 4 Protestants. Presumably a good many of the lay teachers had letters of obedience from convents. During the 1853–54 school year, of 123 women teaching in primary schools for girls (public or private), only 19 had *brevets*, 49 had letters of obedience, and 55 had only provisional authorizations given by departmental authorities or none at all.

110. F17 9322, inspection, 1855. See Robert Gildea's excellent *Education in Provincial France, 1800–1914: A Study of Three Departments* (New York, 1983).

111. F17 9322, 1859, despite the fact that in many places the school fee had been lowered.

112. F17 9336, 1858 and F17 9322 (1855, 1859, 1865); F17 9374, "Rapport au Conseil académique." Of 216 *instituteurs* armed with *brevets* in 1859, 76 had received them from the *école normale* de Privas. In 1877, only 16 candidates, all from the Ardèche, entered each year (Cholvy, ed., *Histoire du Vivarais*, p. 241). The raw silk disaster may have helped convince municipalities to be more generous and increased the interest in schools.

113. 10M 28, 1872, subprefect, March 31, 1859.

114. F17 10779. The minimum salary was raised to seven hundred francs in 1862 after five years of service and in 1875 to nine hundred francs.

115. F17 9319, *inspection académique*, arrondissement of Largentière, 1855; BB30 382, *procureur général* of Nîmes, July 9, 1867.

116. F17 10779. See Jean-François Chanet, *L'École républicaine et les petites patries* (Paris, 1996).

117. In 1912, 158 teachers served as secretaries out of 346 communes in the Ardèche (T 246, *inspecteur d'académie*, October 23, 1912).

118. According to a document in the Mairie of Balazuc, 382 people could neither read nor write (47 percent), 141 could read but not write (17 percent), and only 295 could both read and write (36 percent). These statistics are very approximative and a little misleading because they include children below school age. A decade later, in 1884, in five marriages, only 1 bride and 3 grooms could sign, but all the witnesses save 2 could do so.

BRIDES AND GROOMS WHO COULD
SIGN THEIR MARRIAGE CERTIFICATES IN BALAZUC

YEARS	GROOMS (percentages)	BRIDES (percentages)
1813–15	50	36
1823–25	21	14
1833–35	45	14
1843–45	62	31
1853–55	35	35
1863–65	77	32
1873–75	70	37
1883–85	75	45

Source: État Civil.

119. Bruno, *Le Tour de la France par deux enfants*, p. 161, taken from Bernard Salques, "Écrits et littérature occitans du Vivarais," in *La Langue d'oc en Vivarais et Ardèche, Mémoire d'Ardèche et Temps présent*, 52-I (November 1996), p. 42.

120. *Annuaire du département de l'Ardèche,* year IX, pp. 60–61.

121. Peyrard and Joly, *En Ardèche, notre école,* p. vii.

122. *Annuaire du département de l'Ardèche,* year IX, pp. 60–61.

123. See Chanet, *L'École républicaine et les petites patries.*

124. F17 9322, 1855. Jones, *Politics and Rural Identity,* p. 122. "French suffered an enormous disadvantage in the competition with patois. . . . Only when more peasants spoke French . . . would the balance tip against the vernacular. This did not happen until the 1880s at the very earliest." In Jones's words, the clergy "hovered between the two languages." A survey undertaken in 1864 revealed that in the Ardèche, 13 percent of the population could not speak or write in French. This figure misleads because patois remained the language of everyday life.

125. Reboul, *Moeurs de l'Ardèche au XIXe siècle,* p. 288; MR 1248, "Mémoire sur les environs de Privas et Viviers," 1846; 15M 1, February 28, 1849.

126. Georges Massot, *La Langue d'oc en Vivarais et Ardèche,* in, "Genèse et histoire de la langue occitane et des idioms vivarois." *Mémoire d'Ardèche et Temps présent,* (November 1996), p. 19.

127. See Jones, *Politics and Rural Society,* pp. 127–28, 160–61.

128. See David Bell, *The Cult of the Nation in France: Inventing Nationalism, 1680–1800* (Cambridge, Mass., 2001).

129. Chanet, *L'École républicaine et les petites patries.*

130. F17 10779; ["Sylvestre"], "Le Patois vivarois," *Annales du Vivarais,* 14 (1906), p. 272.

131. BB30 382, PGN, October 11, 1859; F17 9279, rector reports, May 1852 and October and November 1853; V 51, December 24, 1882; 1Z 773, subprefect, December 6, 1853. Some of the parents asked that their children be transported across the river at no charge, but the fee charged for crossing the river in the *bac* was minuscule; Mairie of Balazuc, reports from the 1880s.

132. T 70; Mairie de Balazuc; in September 1844, seven girls were still "at home." During the 1882–83 school year in Balazuc, of 427 half days possible at school, boys were absent 2,828 times of 17,565 possible "presences"; girls did better, 2,748 absences out of 22,842 half days (16 and 12 percent respectively).

133. Peyrard and Joly, *En Ardèche, notre école,* p. xxxxviii.

134. T 209. The girls' teacher took in 200 francs from the municipality and 320 francs paid by parents and hoped for an additional 50 francs as "eventual salary."

135. T 70, inspector, October 23, 1879.

136. F17 9253, July 3, 1877; n.d., 1880; Cholvy, ed., *Histoire du Vivarais,* p. 242; Jean Debard, "Premiers écoliers de Saint-Pons," in *Le Chemin des écoliers: L'Enseignement en Ardèche,* I, in *Mémoire d'Ardèche et Temps présent,* 21 (February 1989), p. 30.

137. T 27.Religious orders taught 477 of the Ardèche's 883 schools (54 percent), and made up 1,246 of the 1,745 teachers in the department (71 percent). In all, the religious orders taught 62 percent of children in school in the Ardèche (33,081 of 53,257).

138. F17 2740, report, June 18, 1884; T 27 and T112. The former school, below in the present *mairie,* was sold in 1911 for six hundred francs. February 28, 1881; architect's plan, May 30, 1880; 2 O 184. An *école normale* for women opened in 1880 with ten students (Cholvy, ed., *Histoire du Vivarais,* p. 243). T 322; V 51; 2 O 184, architect's plan; August 15, 1880.The house was purchased from Antoine Tastevin *dit* Pouchon. Ozil replaced Henri Moulin on October 3, 1881, and was followed by Fournet and then by Aristide Roux. Ozil also briefly taught an adult course with twenty pupils, with the goal of teaching basic aspects of the French language.

139. V 51, 1883.

140. September 3, 1885; T 359, subprefect, October 13, 1885; Pays, October 10, 1885; inspector, November 26, 1885; Cholvy, ed., *Histoire du Vivarais,* pp. 244–45. Laws in 1903 forced the *congréganistes* to leave or to secularize. In the Ardèche in 1887–88, 38.4 percent of male pupils and 69.4 percent of girls still had teachers from the religious orders.

141. November 21, 1897, May 18, and July 13, 1899; 2 O 184, inspectors' reports, August 18, 1885, and March 18, 1898. T 27, note (n.d., 1888); T 97 and T 124, report of July 10, 1899. Some children from Louanes, which had thirty-five residents, and from Couzamas, which by then had fifteen residents, then went to school in Pradons (T 51, February 20, 1887).

142. August 10, 1902.

143. November 1 and December 29 (the third convocation), 1901. The prefect had rejected the first estimate of cost because the population of Balazuc was falling. T 443; 1Z 507; 2 O 184, inspector, October 27, 1899; V 51; T 3375; October 2, 1904; 1Z 779. The land purchased for 1.25 francs per square meter and the cost of construction (28,447 francs) were largely financed by a government subsidy of 18,450 francs and a loan of 10,378 francs. Architect Louis Raphanel claimed Balazuc owed him more money but lost his case. The old girls' school at the Portail d'Été was sold in 1906 (V 51). The municipality had voted to

create a school fund in 1882 (law of June 1, 1878), but it seems never to have existed before 1912, when the prefect insisted that one be created and provided 10 francs' encouragement. Beginning in 1904, a municipal commission (Law of March 28, 1882) came into existence "to oversee and encourage attendance in the schools."

144. T 379 and T 383; architect's plan (Mairie de Balazuc), June 19, 1899.

145. Peyrrard and Joly, *En Ardèche, notre école*, p. 3; V 51. At this time pupils remained in primary school until they were thirteen or fourteen. With the establishment of *collège* (middle school), pupils left after CM2 (U.S. fifth grade) at about age eleven. Those who went to school under the old system sometimes say that someone who earned a *certificat* knew as much as someone with a *brevet* from a *collège*.

146. This and the following draw heavily from the wonderful account of Peyrard and Joly, *En Ardèche, notre école*, pp. 3–67, quotes from pp. 3, 10, 14–15, 29, 39, 46.

147. *Conseils à propos de la vie privée de l'instituteur en 1879.*

148. Mairie de Balazuc; T 71.

Chapter 6

1. Albin Mazon, *Voyage au tour de Valgorge* (Privas, 1879), pp. vi–xvi, 232.

2. Cholvy, ed., *Histoire du Vivarais*, pp. 219–22. The number of Protestants stood at about 12.5 percent, 51,000 in 1861 (p. 224).

3. Jones, *Politics and Rural Society*, p. 143.

4. *Le Républicain des Cévennes*, July 27, 1895. Another tradition, long since disappeared, was festivity surrounding the *tirage au sort*, the drawing to see who would leave the village as military conscripts. For example, in 1894 (*Le Républicain des Cévennes*, February 9, 1894) the young men of the military class of that year presented "their magnificent flag of real value, which they honorably carried at the time of the drawing" for military service.

5. BB18 1244, PG Nîmes, February 8, 1837.

6. Allignol, *Balazuc et le Bas Vivarais*, pp. 397–98. His take on this was that "undesirable elements" had joined and changed the confraternity.

7. The *procureur général* of Nîmes confused Balazuc with the village of Balaruc in the Hérault, knew of no trouble there, and had to be reminded by the minister of justice that Balazuc was in the Ardèche (*procureur général* of Nîmes, February 18, and minister of justice, Feb-

ruary 27, 1837). Peter Jones mentions the incident (*Politics and Rural Society,* p. 143).

8. BB18 1244, PG Nîmes, March 9, 1837. Allignol (*Balazuc et le Bas Vivarais,* pp. 398–99) blames Dours and suggests that some sort of hearing took place in January 1841, bringing together the municipal council and several leading citizens. Dours had resigned and did not show up. The new bishop, Jean-Hippolyte Guibert, insisted that never again would such "superstitious practices" occur on the occasion of the feast day. When Albin Mazon visited Balazuc in 1884, he heard about the event, which had lodged in the collective memory.

9. October 6, 1830: Jean Leyris, a *propriétaire* of modest means, and Antoine Auzas, son of the former mayor from the hamlet of Louanes; 2MP 34, prefect, October 21, 1830.

10. 3M 103; Maire de Balazuc, original list submitted by the mayor. Four years later there were but three (Alexandre Tastevin, Antoine Auzas, Jacques Mollier) and in 1846, Auzas, Leyris *dit* Icard, and Teyssier.

11. March 10, 1832; 3M 150; Mairie de Balazuc, prefect, October 25, 1834. Tastevin, faithful to the Restoration, was conspicuous by his absence from the list. Municipal councils were to meet once in February, May, August, and November in "ordinary session" with the prefect's authorization.

12. 2MP 34, Tastevin, November 14, 1840; subprefect, December 26, 1840; and prefect, February 2, 1841; 3M 266; January 17 and March 14, 1841; 3M 221; 3M 220, subprefect, February 26, 1841. The prefectura council had annulled the elections for the municipal council, and a second election had to be held (prefect, August 7, 1840). Dours resigned as mayor "in favor only of Jean-Antoine Tastevin" (January 11, 1841).

13. The phrase echoes Maurice Agulhon's brilliant *La République au village* (Paris, 1970).

14. Élie Reynier, *La Seconde République dans l'Ardèche* (Privas, 1998; originally published 1948), pp. 35–39.

15. 2M 337, subprefect, May 7, 1849. Because Balazuc's vote was counted with those of Pradons and Ruoms, we do not know what percentage of men voted.

16. Cholvy, ed., *Histoire du Vivarais,* p. 233; Jones, *Politics and Rural Society,* pp. 214–15. Edward Berenson (*Religion and Mass Politics in France* [Princeton, 1984]) has emphasized the links between the Montagnards (democratic Socialists) of the Second Republic (thus "Jesus the Mon-

tagnard"), considering, for example, the impact of religious aspects of utopian socialism, but largely ignores telling regional variations.

17. 2M 337; Reynier, *La Seconde République,* pp. 70–79, 84; 5M 10, sub-prefect of Largentière, September 18 and November 1, 1848; 1Z 250; 2M 273. In the Ardèche, Louis Napoleon Bonaparte received 39,320 votes, Cavaignac 16,495, and Ledru-Rollin 3,719 votes. In Ruoms, Pradons, and Balazuc, Bonaparte garnered 213 votes, Cavaignac 12 votes, and Lamartine a single ballot.

18. On the first ballot 123 men elected Henri Denis Cartoux and Claude Mollier, both members of the previous council, with 79 and 62 votes, respectively. On the second ballot, only 48 men voted, and André Teyssier led with 31 votes, followed by Jean Antoine Tastevin, *rentier,* and Cyprien, both with 29 votes. Mollier, who operated the small boat, and Lapierre, the village baker, were among those elected.

19. 3M 261 and 3M 265; 3M 248, 3M 261, and 3M 265, procès-verbaux, report of December 29, 1848, and August 29, 1848. Jean-Antoine Tastevin became deputy mayor.

20. In his *French Peasants in Revolt,* Ted Margadant has linked the expansion of rural industry during the Restoration (1814–30) and the July Monarchy (1830–48) to the success of the Montagnards during the Second Republic, highlighting the role of small market towns (like Joyeuse, Vallon, and Aubenas) in this process.

21. Reynier, *La Seconde République,* pp. 38–39, 104, 90–97. See Merriman, *The Agony of the Republic: The Repression of the Left in Revolutionary France, 1848–51* (New Haven, 1978). For Balazuc, we have again only the results combined with those of Pradons and Ruoms. On the left, Laurent (de l'Ardèche), the only staunch republican elected in 1848, led the way with 164. In the by-election of 1850, only 144 of the 255 eligible voters took part in Balazuc, casting 82 ballots for Carnot, a republican with a strong family history brought into the Ardèche to run, and 62 for the successful legitimist candidate Latourette (1Z 250).

22. 1Z 285; Mairie de Balazuc, lists of March 1 and July 11, 1850; 2M 341, justice of the peace of Vallon, June 12, 1850; Reynier, *La Seconde République,* p. 121. In the canton of Vallon, the number of voters fell from 3,055 to 2,156, and the department lost a third of its voters.

23. 5M 11, teacher and secretary of Orgnac, July 14, 1851, and March 8, 1851; Mayor Boissin of Grospierres, July 14 and subprefect, July 17, 1851.

24. 5M 11, SPL, March 23, 1851.

25. 5M 10, Vigier, November 11, 1851; undated gendarmerie report; 5M 18, testimony of Joseph Leyris; 5M 11, subprefect, April 18 and May 21, 1851, describing the supposed use of Montagnard carrier pigeons in Chassiers. See John M. Merriman, "On the Loose: The Impact of Rumors and *Mouchards* in the Ardèche during the Second Republic," in Jonathan Sperber, ed., *Europe 1848: Revolution and Reform* (London, 2000).

26. Quoted by Siegfried, *Géographie électorale de l'Ardèche*, p. 36; Jones, *Politics and Rural Society*, p. 153.

27. April 20, 1851; T 212.

28. So much that the subprefect requested the prefect to permit the sale of several kilograms of powder, banned during the state of siege, for hunting, noting that this would be a good political move.

29. 5M 11; October 10, 1851. In 1845 a dam had been constructed above the Pont de Ruoms, which made it impossible for fish below that point to swim back up the river. The council's conclusion was thus that free fishing should be allowed between the Pont d'Aubenas and the dam at Ruoms. The municipality's wish was in the context of a deliberation on the question of whether the river could ever be navigable.

30. Peter McPhee, *The Politics of Rural Life: Political Mobilization in the French Countryside, 1845–1852* (New York, 1992), p. 241.

31. 6M 53, CP Vallon, July 14, 1851.

32. See Margadant, *French Peasants in Revolt*.

33. 5M 18, interrogation of Antoine Fromentin and the extremely damaging testimony of Joseph Leyris. Augustin Nicolas *dit* Rousset, a *cultivateur* from Pradons, stood accused of going to Balazuc at three in the morning to spark resistance. He denied the accusation, saying that he had not been in the village of Balazuc itself (as opposed to the commune) for more than six years and only in the commune twice since the previous August (5M 18, interrogation of Augustin). He was freed.

34. 5M 14, subprefect, December 7, 1851.

35. Reynier, *La Seconde République*, p. 169.

36. BB30 395, *procureur général* of Nîmes, December 6 and 19, 1851; BB30 396, January 4, 1852; 3M 334, prefect, n.d. (December 1851).

37. 5M 14, subprefect of Largentière, December 9, 1851, five in the morning, and December 10, 1851; BB30 395, subprefect, December 8, 1851; BB30 396, *procureur général* of Nîmes, January 27,1852. In the plebiscite of December 1851, there were 504 no votes in the

arrondissement of Largentière, none in Balazuc. In the plebiscite approving the advent of the empire the following year, of 255 eligible voters, 220 voted, with only 4 daring to vote no (1Z 250, 1Z 274, 2M 176 and 3M 231). See Reynier, *La Seconde République,* pp. 186–87.

38. Margadant, *French Peasants in Revolt,* pp. 139–42; 5M 21, report of June 26, 1852. André Encrevé, "Protestantisme et politique: Les Protestants du Midi en Decembre 1851," in *Droite et gauche de 1789 à nos jours* (Montpellier, 1975), pp. 161–95. Twenty-five percent of the population of the canton of Vallon was Protestant.

39. 3M 265 and documents in the *Mairie* de Balazuc.

40. 5M 18, Mayor Tastevin, January 18, 1852, and gendarme report.

41. 5M 18, interrogation of Jean Jullian *oncle.* His father, born in Balazuc in 1776, had been sentenced in August 1830 to five years of hard labor for fraud.

42. 5M 18, interrogation of Antoine Fromentin.

43. 5M 18, interrogation of Claude Mollier, January 22–23.

44. 5M 11, September 16, 1832, authorized Exbrayat to borrow 224 francs, but from whom, we do not know, nor why; May 16, 1847; F15 3992 (the witnesses were Mathieu Gibert, the teacher; Antoine Boyer, Jean Laroche, and Antoine Brun, the latter three *cultivateurs*); 5M 18, interrogation of Exbrayat, who, although saying that he was illiterate, nonetheless could sign the interrogation.

45. F15 3991, dossier Gamel. The witnesses at his marriage had included Mollier, the boatman, and Louis Fromentin, *cultivateur.* Jean and Antoine Vallier, brothers, were let go (5M 18). Louis-Vincent Chaniol, an illiterate farmhand from Uzès, had been arrested when he carried a load of laundry to his mother's house, as the soldiers pursued insurgents. He saw three of the latter turn and shoot at the soldiers on the main road below. He was freed on the word of his master, Mouraret, that he had not left Audon during the night (5M 18, interrogation of Chaniol).

46. 5M 20, Tastevin, April 27, 1852, and gendarmerie report, May 14, 1852; F15 3990, dossier Daumas.

47. 5M 14, ministerial circular, March 21, 1852; *attestation* that he received sixty centimes, April 28, 1852, on the way to Villeneuve-de-Berg (5M 28, Mayor Tastevin, June 18, 1852, and Mollier, mayor, September 15, 1852; monthly report of September 1852; justice of the peace, September 30; gendarmerie commander, September 30, 1852).

48. In the Ardèche, eleven men were condemned to be sent to Cayenne,

seven from the arrondissement of Largentière. From the latter, forty-eight men received deportation to Algeria, with incarceration; fifteen received simple deportation to Algeria; twenty-one were sentenced to imprisonment followed by years of "surveillance"; eleven, to "simple" surveillance; six, to temporary exile outside the Ardèche; four, to permanent expulsion from the region. Twenty-eight were sent to the courts for minor effenses, four to the Conseil de guerre for offenses against gendarmes, and forty-seven were freed (Reynier, *La Seconde République,* p. 175).

49. 5M 21, prefect, April 23, 1852, gendarmerie commander, November 28, 1852, and Mayor Mollier, November 28, 1852; 5M 14, Tastevin, September 24, 1857; 5M 31, "liste des condamnés politiques," March 17, 1858, "Contrôle des enemis du gouvernement," listing Damas [*sic*] as no longer very dangerous or influential, while identifying Queyroche as dangerous by virtue of his "exaltation." Jean Mollier *dit* Prieur was listed as still subject to surveillance by this latter document.

50. 1Z 331, subprefect, June 2, 1857; 5M 21, subprefect May 30, 1857, and police report, May 16, 1857; gendarmerie report, May 11, 1857; justice of the peace, May 28, 1857; F15 3992.

51. F1cIII Ardèche 7, prefect, April 6, June 26, and November 12, 1852.

52. Subprefect, September 26, 1857.

53. 3M 326, Mollier, July 25, 1853; subprefect, January 6,1854. Seven members of the council in May 1851 said that they would not continue their functions if Leyris stayed on.

54. 1Z 276, prefect, August 16, and Constant, November 8, 1855.

55. 1Z 303, Tastevin, August 23, 1856, and November 4, 1858; 3M 307; 3M 327, subprefect, December 21, 1858; 3M 314, 3M 332, subprefect, November 5 and 11, 1865, and Cartoux, n.d. In 1860, 74 of 225 voted, and 62 of 233; August 21, 1864, and August 13, 1865. In 1865, Tastevin was not elected to the council and thus could not be reappointed mayor. The prefect then named Henri Cartoux to serve as mayor, but he quickly resigned, citing other obligations. Cyprien Laroche became mayor. He resigned along with his deputy mayor the following year.

56. They included a relative of Exbrayat, who had been convicted by the Mixed Commission in 1852. On the Ardèche and the Franco-Prussian War, see Jordan Gaspin, *Les Mobilisés de l'Ardèche 1870–71* (Privas, 1996).

57. Jones (*Politics and Rural Society,* p. 221): "Between 1871 and 1884 the battle for the control of the countryside was fought more tenaciously

than at any time since the Revolution." Vincent had married the daughter of the former mayor Laurent Tastevin and lived at Salles.

58. September 4 and October 16, 1870, and June 25, 1871. 1Z 278; F1bII Ardèche 4; 3M 320. Vincent was not among the leading recipients of votes. He was unanimously reelected later in the year.

59. F1bII Ardèche 4, "liste des maires et d'adjoints, nomination en 1871"; 1Z 303, Mayor Vincent, March 5, 1876, and subprefect, July 15, 1876; F1bII Ardèche 7, prefect, September 30, 1878, and note, Ministry of the Interior, October 4, 1878. In the elections for the Conseil Général in October 1871, Balazuc gave 177 votes to the monarchist candidate, Lauriol, and 9 to the republican.

60. 1Z 258.

61. F1b II Ardèche 7, prefect, October 25, 1877, asked for confirmation of a number of suspensions of officials who had openly opposed republican candidates, including Banne, Sampzon, and Malarce; record of hearing held August 11, 1878; F15 3992, minister of the interior, January 24, 1907; Mollier's letter, n.d.

62. 1Z 303, prefect's decree, July 15, 1878; F1b II Ardèche 7, prefect, September 30, November 26; subprefect, August 31 and November 5, 1878, and January 4 and August 20, 1879; minutes of investigation, August 11, 1878; note, Ministry of the Interior, October 4, 1878; Mayor Claron of Vallon, September 7 and October 31, 1878.

63. 1Z 258.

64. V 155, V 204, and V 141, minister of the interior, May 23, prefect, May 23, and subprefect, May 21, 1879, referring to a missing letter of Deputy Mayor Tastevin, May 20. Senator and former Minister of Justice Tailhaud also helped the conservative cause, maintaining influence over the nomination of local magistrates, employees of Ponts-et-Chaussées, and other posts large and small. Bonnet established a reputation as an "ultramontane" bishop, looking across the Alps to Rome for guidance.

65. Jones, *Politics and Rural Society*, p. 268. In Balazuc, the hamlet of Servière has often been identified with the left. Jean-Luc Mayaud (*La Petite Exploitation rurale triomphante*) argues (p. 110) that many peasants associated the republic with the virtues of small-scale farming.

66. 1Z 303, letter of Vincent, January 24, 1881. The council elected Tastevin mayor by six votes to five for Vincent, with one blank, and it took three ballots to select a deputy mayor, Mouraret of Louanes. Several times in 1880 meetings lacked quorums. In 1889, several resi-

dents complained that Tastevin was not only serving as mayor but also collecting the small salary of the village secretary for taking notes at the meetings (subprefect, October 16, 1889). Moreover, Tastevin had the money payable "to one of his creatures."

67. 1Z 303, Tastevin, May 21, 1882 and Brun, May 10, 1882. Jean Boyer relates that Brun in 1885 was arrested for *attentat à la pudeur* involving several girls younger than twelve.

68. Balazuc, *Mémoires de soie,* p. 156.

69. Jean Boyer; Cholvy, ed., *Histoire du Vivarais,* p. 230; in the 1860s, 516 priests, 446 brothers, and 1,759 nuns worked in the Ardèche. Jones, *Politics and Rural Society,* p. 143: "The church exercised a rare monopoly over the opportunities for community self-expression. . . . [T]he clerical character of village sociability led inevitably to clerical involvement in village politics."

70. Jones, *Politics and Rural Society,* p. 120.

71. 1Z 279, subprefect, n.d. (1881). See Sahuc, *Le Fils du pauvre,* pp. 183, 249, 256–57: "[O]ur countryside was not so isolated. Peddlers sold almanacs."

72. Peter Jones emphasizes that "seigneurialism remained lodged in the collective memory of villages in the Vivarais (*Politics and Rural Society,* pp. 160–61). . . . Folk tales of sheaves of corn being carted off to château or monastic granary would continue to excite the apprehension of their grandchildren, even their great-grandchildren. . . . Servile habits of mind lingered on as well. The 'feudalisation' of democratic politics in which votes were traded for favours—the opening of a new road, perhaps, or the gift of a fine picture to hang above the altar—was partly attributable to the shadow of seigneurialism."

73. Ibid., pp. 214–15, 280–81; Balazuc, *Mémoires de soie,* p. 125.

74. Jones, *Politics and Rural Society,* pp. 280 and 308.

75. Nicole Joffre, "La Question scolaire dans l'Ardèche de 1880–1914" (mémoire de maîtrise, Université de Dijon, 1975), p. 38.

76. Vogüé, *Notes sur le Bas-Vivarais,* pp. 91–101; Cholvy, ed., *Histoire du Vivarais,* p. 238. Vogüé himself had come to accept the republic.

77. Peyrard and Joly, *En Ardèche,* pp. xxiii–vii, xlvii; 5M 51, letter of Félix Picaud, October 15, 1885; 5M 43, subprefect, September 24, 1889, and others.

78. Joffre, "La Question scolaire dans l'Ardèche," p. 51.

79. 5M 44, subprefect, September 9, 1889, December 7, 1891, and April 4, 1892; V 155, minister of justice and of religion, October 10, 1890;

T 359, prefect, September 17, 1891, and academic inspector, December 12, 1891.

80. V 186, subprefect, March 14, 1892.

81. 1Z 285; 5M 43; the poster was denounced by a letter of October 9, 1885; 1Z 279, subprefect, October 13, 1894. See Jones, *Politics and Rural Society,* p. 288. In the Ardèche, the municipal elections in 1878, a year after the *coup de seize mai,* had increased the number of councils with a republican majority (1Z 285, prefect, January 30, 1878). See Sahuc, *Le fils du pauvre,* pp. 23–29. In 1885 the right won 40 percent of the vote, to 35 percent for the moderate Opportunists, thus electing six deputies.

82. Siegfried, *Géographie électorale de l'Ardèche,* pp. 101, 104–07, noted that in all, support for the left rose roughly to 44–47 percent of voters and for the right to about 38–40 percent. See also Jones, *Politics and Rural Society,* pp. 288–94, who argues that Siegfried places too much emphasis on property structures and geographic determinism (p. 242).

83. *L'Echo de Largentière,* January 12, 1895; Siegfried, *Géographie électorale de l'Ardèche,* pp. 105–06. Siegfried associates right-wing voting with elevations above nine hundred feet, particularly above twenty-four hundred feet, and left-wing voting with nine hundred feet and below (p. 113).

84. *L'Echo de Largentière,* July 11, 1914; T 119; January 1, 1898, cited in 2MP 50. By 1891–92, of boys between the ages of six and fourteen, 3,195 were in public schools, and 1,197 in private schools (total 4,392), and of girls, 2,908 were in public schools and 1,168 in private schools, for a total of 4,074.

85. Nicole Joffre, "La Question scolaire dans l'Ardèche," p. 63; *Le Républicain des Cévennes,* February 27, 1909. Lay teachers formed an association, the Amicale des Instituteurs et Institutrices de l'Ardèche. The Ligue de l'Enseignement set up a committee of jurisconsuls to help defend teachers against any possible litigation undertaken by "the associations of the fathers of reactionary families."

86. 1Z 258; 1Z 279, mayor of Vallon, January 18, 1881. In Balazuc in 1881, the republican candidate for the Chamber of Deputies, Vaschalade, fell only three votes short of the conservative in the first election; in the electoral runoff he and the conservative Bournet each had 104 votes.

87. November 2 and December 21, 1879; September 24, 1882; Mairie de Balazuc, September 1, 1884; May 13, 1883, January 6, February 27,

and October 5 and 11, 1884; August 15, 1890, prefect, May 15, 1884; June 26, 1880; September 24, 1882. The council made an arrangement with the owner of the mill to create a *canal de décharge* in order to lower the volume of water by six feet. Boiron, the last to hold the right to operate the small boat, had failed to get the price he paid reduced, claiming that the bridges in Vogüé and Ruoms had cut into his business and citing the poor condition of the paths leading to the river. The loan was relatively small, in that an earlier loan of forty-five hundred francs had been approved in 1869 but never used. The requested subsidy was thirty-five thousand francs. Lauriol had defeated Hugon in the election for a seat on the Conseil Général in 1880, but the election was thrown out because of irregularities (including a complaint by three voters in Balazuc), and Hugon was then elected. A tradition says that the deceased should not be brought across the bridge.

87. August 26, 1888; August 14, 1892.

88. Fonds Mazon, Abbé Chareyre to Mazon, September 27, 1884; Jean Boyer.

89. August 26, 1888, and August 14, 1892; Mairie de Balazuc, dossier. Not until 1909 could the municipality afford to improve the path from the bridge down to the river on the village side (November 21, 1909, and February 20, 1910). Jean Boyer notes that one sign of the importance of the new road (as well as the relative decline of the old *quartier* of the now-deconsecrated church) was the transfer in 1900 of the municipal posting board from that *place* to the local near the Portail Neuf and along the new road, where it still stands.

90. July 16, 1871, August 15, 1884; Raymond Chevalier and Michelle Redon-Chevalier, "Centenaire de l'église paroissiale de Balazuc, 1895–1995"), unpublished manuscript, 1996, p. 2.

91. 1Z 802, subprefect, May 15, 1903. The municipal council contributed ten francs to purchase disinfectants for Balazuciens too poor to do so themselves. The chapel is now closed almost all the time, with a Mass said only once a year.

92. July 6, 1890; Chevalier and Redon-Chevalier, p. 5.

93. Chevalier and Redon-Chevalier, "Centenaire de l'église," pp. 2–3. Abbé Chareyre may have suspended a master mason whose work he did not like on July 14, 1891. The date may suggest that the mason, whose skills were required in the enterprise, had made a crack about the French national holiday. Some masons, cabinetmakers, and stonecutters may have received "vouchers that allow them to be paid directly by virtue of the gift of a donor."

94. June 19, 1898.

95. Jean Boyer notes that in 1907 Bishop Bonnet of Viviers chastised the parish of Balazuc for contributing only 270 francs per year, when 90 francs more would have been expected by virtue of its population!

96. Marie-Louise Tastevin, Hippolyte Pays, Casimir Boyer, Philippe Ranchin, Louis Ranchin, Joseph Georges, Charles Soubeyrand, Albert Pays, Isidore Mouraret, the abbé A. Tastevin of Salles, Léa Eldin and Anne Ranchin, Abbé Tastevin "de Balazuc," Abbé Laffont (from Balazuc), the sisters of the Convent of St.-Joseph in Aubenas, and Augustin Thiery, a *peintre verrier* from Lyon who did the image of *Ste. Marie, Reine de la France* along the nave, the gift of the abbé Laffont.

97. The smallest of the three bells was a gift of Madame Despuech in 1821; the second, weighing in at over three hundred pounds, was the gift of another outsider, Léon Desboulets, and given the name Léontine-Eulalie, presumably after his wife or daughter; the third, and largest, cast in Alès, had Marie-Victorine Duffour-Mollier of Louanes as godmother.

98. August 15, 1885. In 1903, on two occasions in 1904, and again in 1911. For lack of a quorum three convocations were required before council meetings could be held.

99. 1Z 303, Tastevin, February 2, 1884. The nomination of a tax receiver had irritated him.

100. Mairie de Balazuc, prefect's approval, July 3, 1886 (yet in the elections of 1885 and 1886, conservatives defeated the republican list by about thirty votes, with 258 eligible voters); 1Z 280, Hugon, May 6, 1884; Mairie de Balazuc, prefect, March 2, 1885. Significant Protestant minorities in Salavas, Labastide-de-Virac, Vallon, and Lagorce had helped move the canton of Vallon, which voted for the right in 1871, 1876, 1877, and 1885, to support the left straight through 1936.

101. August 15 and November 10, 1885, and February 7, 1886; 2 O 185, Pays, August 17, 1885, and petition. The two even voted against the construction of walls for the cemetery on August 14, 1887.

102. 5M 18 bis, prefect, decree of October 1, 1881; dossiers; F15 3990, F15 3991, F15, 3992, including Hugon's letter of April 6, 1881, and that of Claude Mollier, September 28, 1881.

103. F15 3964, prefect, April 11, 1881. Jean Louis Pays also received two hundred francs for having been arrested in 1853 for having denounced the empire. In his letter of July 16, 1881 (F15 3992), he claimed to

have been practically the only person in Balazuc waving the flag of the republic during the crisis of May 16, 1877.

104. F15 3992, Mollier, September 28, 1881.

105. 1Z 234, prefect, October 25 and November 19, 1892, subprefect, April 10, 1893, and August 27, 1897; Mollier, letter of May 25, 1921. One of the pensions paid in 1897 (to Henri Fallot) amounted to only thirteen francs per year. In 1907, not long before his death, Jean Mollier requested an increase in his pension but was informed that the committee that considered such demands had been dissolved in 1883. Following World War I, seventy years after Louis Napoleon's coup d'état, his son began proceedings to have the indemnity shifted to him.

106. 1Z 285; 5M 44, prefect, May 11 and October 12, and subprefect, August 30, 1889; 5M 43, prefect, April 2, 1889; 1Z 259. Blachère, the son of a monarchist deputy, received in Balazuc 132 votes in 1885 and 130 in 1886; the staunch republican Vieilfaure won only 78 and 97 votes respectively. In the 1888 elections, there were 102 to 87 and 131 to 97 votes for candidates on the right, while 226 of 258 elegible voters cast ballots in Balazuc in the 1886 legislative election.

107. 1Z 281, subprefect, June 19, 1888. Tastevin was elected mayor with only seven of twelve votes and had been only tenth in attracting votes to the council. Louis Pays, the republican mayor, died just before the election, thus becoming one of the first to be buried in the new cemetery that he had helped create.

108. T 71, prefect, October 1 and 31, 1888.

109. 1Z 280, Hugon, May 6, 1884; 1Z 281, subprefect, June 19, 1888, and May 28 and 31, 1892; 1Z 281, subprefect, May 28 and 31, 1892; 1Z 282.

110. 1Z 282, *procureur,* June 17, 1896, and subprefect, n.d. Philippe Charousset led the way with 137 votes, but the even political split was revealed by the fact that the next four candidates had between 132 and 136 votes and the next two at 130. Still, the subprefect noted that "political color did not have the greatest role in the choice of the voters; personalities played a great role."

111. 1Z 227, prefect, December 31, 1889, committee letter, n.d., and Conseil Général note, May 28, 1891. The mayor too provided information (June 2, 1891). 1M 321, Mouraret, January 9, 1901. The meeting on Christmas 1900 had for its agenda "republican program, the raw silk question, and the school question."

112. 1Z 279, subprefect, October 13, 1894, and July 10 and October 7, 1897.

113. A Comité Républicain began in Balazuc in 1900 and met on Christmas Day. It changed its name to the Comité Républicain Démocratique the following year.

114. Charousset had late in 1899 turned against the municipal employee and, after having changed his mind once or twice, proposed his dismissal to the prefect, claiming that the guard had even tendered his resignation.

115. 2 O 183, prefect to Deputy Barrot, July 6, 1900; Barrot to prefect, June 5, 1900, Charousset, May 6, 1900; report to prefect, May 18, 1900; prefect, June 2, subprefect, June 20. Charousset, furious over the turn of events in the election, denounced Boyer and Mollier *fils*, but he hired the latter in 1908. Jean Boyer suggests that the small raise in taxes, as well as the previous municipality's decision to force purchasers of commune land to pay back taxes rendered for them by the commune over the past ten years, may have played a role.

116. May 20 and June 16, 1900; Jean Boyer.

117. In 1902: 121 votes to Barrot and 82 to Duclaux-Monteil. In 1906: 105 votes to Vincent and 99 for his conservative rival.

118. *La Républicain des Cévennes,* May 14, October 29, and July 30, 1904. Charousset served as president, Freydier as vice-president.

119. Estimate of Victor Giry, December 18, 1902, February 16 and June 28, 1903, petition of March 17, 1905, and subprefect, April 6 and August 24, 1903, Blachère, May 23 and August 18, 1903, and March 24, 1906. The council argued that "one can surely count on all those who abstained as favorable to the project."

120. Philippe Charousset, August 15, 1903, mayor, August 20, 1903, prefect, May 13, 1905, April 11, 1906. By virtue of the law of April 5, 1884, the commune had to provide the priest with either housing or an indemnity.

121. *L'Echò de Largentière,* June 6, 1903; 1MP 154, prefect, April 1 and May 12, 1904. In all, after the elections 155 communes in the Ardèche with a municipal council favorable by at least a majority to the government, 140 against, and 46 were "doubtful."

122. IZ 283; 1MP 154, prefect, April 1 and May 12, 1904; May 15 and June 12, 1904; *Le Républicain des Cévennes,* April 30, 1904. Radical-Socialists included Charousset, Hippolyte Freydier, Perbost, and Fromentin; simply Radical, Boucher and another Perbost.

123. March 25, 1906, subprefect, May 19, 1906, and April 12, 1908. The separation of church and state gave the municipality full use of the

presbytery, and the council in 1908 decided to rent it out for three
years at thirty francs a year.

124. *L'Echo de Largentière,* January 7 and December 30, 1905. Yet a woman
from Balazuc recalls stories about her great-uncle, a man of the left
who lived near the Tour Carrée, inviting the priest, politically on the
other side, in to drink a good amount of wine when he saw him walking by the house. Relations may have remained cordial, and one must
be cautious not to exaggerate the extent to which these rivalries
impinged on daily life.

125. *L'Echo de Largentière,* May 19, 1906.

126. Ibid., May 5,1906; 1Z 259. Duclaux-Monteil received 13,109 votes
to 11,037 for Vincent in 1906 (though the latter carried the canton of
Vallon, in part because of Protestant votes).

127. *L'Ardèche républicaine,* March 10, 1906.

128. *L'Echo de Largentière,* March 24 and March 31, 1906; *L'Ardèche républicaine,* March 17, 24, and 31, 1906.

129. Jean Boyer. Accounts of this resistance do not appear either in available archives or in the coverage of the events elsewhere by newspapers
on either side. However, since determined opposition occurred in virtually every one of the surrounding communes, it is likely that collective memory has it right. Maurice Allignol claims (*Balazuc et le Bas
Vivarais,* p. 638) that a number of families kept pieces of the broken
door as relics and that the door was not repaired until after World War
II.

130. "Sylvestre," *Un scandale electoral à Balazuc* (Aubenas, 1909), p. 4;
Mairie de Balazuc, mayor, October 12, 1883. Allies included Marius
Mollier, Philippe and Baptiste Tastevin, Marius Guiboudenche (future
mayor), Hippolyte Redon, Jules and Firmin Dufaud, Eugène Auzas,
Marius Laroche of Audon, Boyer (a surveyor), and Auguste and Marius Charousset. Note the duplication of family names on both sides of
politics, for there was more than one branch of several family names,
notably Charousset, Boyer, Redon, and Mollier (and of course, nothing necessarily guaranteed agreement within families).

131. Ibid., pp. 12–15, thus echoing Peter Jones cited in *Politics and Rural
Society.*

132. "Sylvestre" and Z 284, *procès-verbal* of judgment. A letter of protest of
July 23, 1908, included the request that "a municipal administration
that looks after all of the citizens of the commune without distinction"
be named. Charousset and others, August 17, 1908; *L'Echo de Largen-*

tière, April 10, 1909. The newspaper claimed that the *blocards* were trying to intimidate voters by saying that if the right won, no path would ever lead to Audon. Charousset had been elected mayor with eleven votes and one blank ballot, as always.

133. *Le Républicain des Cévennes,* January 11 and December 5, 1908; "Sylvestre," *"Un scandale electoral,"* pp. 12–13.

134. 1Z 285. In pencil at the bottom of the decree someone, probably in the subprefecture, had written "invalid decree . . . no fact of the nature to justify it has occurred in the commune."

135. "Sylvestre," *"Un scandale electoral,"* pp. 9–11; 2 O 183, subprefect, October 13, 1906; petition, cosigned by Charousset, September 20, 1906; and gendarmerie report, September 26, 1906, subprefect, April 5, 1909; 1 Z 304, February 21, 1909; Charousset, February 27, 1909; Mollier, *"devoir horthograph* [*sic*]," February 27, 1909, for which he chose the topic "the citizen" and the duty of obeying the law to keep civilization from "animality." The shepherds, both illiterate, were from the Cévennes.

136. 1Z 284, Charousset, June 14, 1909.

137. 1Z 285.

138. August 28 and September 4, 1909; *La République des Cévennes,* October 9, 1909.

139. 1Z 260 and *L'Echo de Largentière,* May 15, 1910. In the 1910 legislative elections, in Balazuc on the second and telling ballot, Vincent had 103 votes and Duclaux-Monteil 101 votes. On the first ballot Duclaux-Monteil had 94 and Vincent 86 votes, whereas in 1906 it had been Vincent, 105, and Duclaux-Monteil, 99. The Audon 1910 elected in the arrondissement. Vincent made the state one of his campaign promises, another example of deputy patronage.

140. *L'Echo de Largentière,* September 24, 1910, select's res- mayor, Perbost, and Freydier. Z 284, procès-Madame letter of July 18 and appeal of July 23, 1909d voted ignation, August 30, 1910, and subprbmitted Charousset, August 17, 1910. Charousal guard. but added, "I don't remember very usly (Sep- two letters of resignation in 1900 Conserva- The council now elected Guillau tember 18, 1910).

141. 1Z 284, Mayor Perbost, n.d

tives voted as one, each winning candidate receiving between 101 and 107 votes, with the left votes ranging between 90 and 98 votes. Only three councillors lived in the village itself.

142. 1Z 285, May 25, 1911, Vincent, May 8, and prefect, June 8, 1912. Forty-five names were no longer on the electoral list in 1912. The left accused Mouraret and his faction of fraud, a claim rejected by the Conseil de Préfecture.

143. 2M 285; 1Z 344, subprefect, December 7, 1912, and Charousset's undated reply; *L'Echo de Largentière,* May 2, 1914: Duclaux-Monteil, 93, Thomas, 73 votes.

144. April 18 and 25 and May 23, 1914.

Chapter 7

1. F7 12937, prefect, August 6, 7, 8, and 19, 1914; Jean Boyer; *L'Echo de Largentière,* August 14, 1914. Mairie de Balazuc, dossier "Victimes de guerre, 1914–1918." In 1916 the municipality allocated a hundred francs to purchase copies of brochures published by the Ligue du Souvenir, on "Their Crimes," those of "the race of vampires and of bandits," so that "a copy of this pamphlet should be distributed at no cost to every family in the commune."

. August 23 and November 15, 1914, March 21, 1915, and November 24, 1918; 1Z 229; 2 O 191; Mairie de Balazuc, list of those excused om village labor obligations. The council met six times in 1915, en times in 1916, five times in 1917, and five times in 1918.

 200, prefect, February 4, 1916. See Jean-Jacques Becker, *The War and the French People* (Dover, N.H., 1985).

 de Balazuc, mayor's decree of June 1, 1917, following requisiler of October 1, 1916; 2 O 191. In 1917 the municipal counblished the post of rural guard (1Z 303, August 26, 1917, nber 21, 1919), and in 1919 it awarded an extra 410 francs decorated war veteran, for the extra duties imposed on him ar.

 December 28, 1914 and March 24, 1915; Roux, Sep- ; mayor, September 15, 1915; census of 1911. The jus-e turned down her appeal on September 30, 1915. s not alone in petitioning for "funds for the needy called to defend the flag." In 1916, the committee, n appeal, turned down Henri Jullian, a widower who could no longer work, was sixty-five years of age, and received two hundred francs per year because his father had been a victim of the 1851 coup d'état, as well as a tiny pension of about fifty francs per year from his work (R 189, subprefect, January 16, 1916; Jullian, December 24, 1918).

6. May 10, 1915.

7. Mairie de Balazuc, register.

8. Jean Boyer.

9. January 19, 1919.

10. Hippolyte Redon, Joseph Fabregoule, Félix Guérin, Philippe Munier, Henri Gustave, and Eugène Auzas.

11. Fic III 1125, prefect, January 6, 1918, noted that local morale was, "all in all, quite satisfactory after forty-one months of war and patriotic sacrifice."

12. November 24, 1918, and August 31, 1919; Mayor Guibourdenche, October 30, 1919, and plan of architect A. Vergier, October 30, 1919, prefect's approval, October 20, 1920. The municipal council voted 1,000 francs towards the cost of 3,090 francs (November 5, 1919).

13. See Jay Winter, *Sites of Memory, Sites of Mourning* (New York, 1995) and Daniel Sherman, *The Construction of Memory in Interwar France* (Chicago, 1999).

14. Jean Boyer. Marius Guibourdenche, born in Chazeaux in 1874, had married into one of the Mollier families.

15. November 21, 1921.

16. Cholvy, ed., *Histoire du Vivarais*, p. 271.

17. The municipality was eager to create a *caisse municipale* (municipal treasury), none of the funds for which would come from the commune (March 9 and November 5, 1919). The state provided 75 percent, as well as funding at 1.25 francs per person unemployed.

18. January 8, 1920.

19. Michel Huber, *La Population de la France pendant la guerre* (Paris, n.d.), pp. 59, 176, 270–71, 292.

20. Jean-Louis Issartel, "L'Ardèche à la veille du conflit," *L'Ardèche dans la guerre, Mémoire d'Ardèche et Temps présent*, 42 (May 1994), p. 3.

21. Bozon, *L'Ardèche*, p. 64. Only the valley of the Rhône added residents.

22. Jean Boyer. In 1937 there were 3,988 deaths and 2,913 births.

23. The first loan was for 8,785 francs, and another loan, this of 10,000 francs, had to be undertaken from the Crédit Foncier in 1935. The total cost for the project, undertaken by La Grande Combienne, stood at 135,000 francs.

24. May 27, 1928.
25. May 4, September 14, and October 26, 1930, October 14, 1934, and January 6, 1935; August 22, 1937, and July 10, 1938; 2 O 189, prefect, September 1930, approved loan of 135,000 francs for thirty years for electricity.
26. April 8, 1937.
27. Reynier, *Le Pays de Vivarais*, p. 126; Cholvy, ed., *Histoire du Vivarais*, p. 206. In 1918 the production of cocoons in France fell to about 3 million kilograms, with the Gard, Ardèche, and Drôme producing 1 million, 700,000, and 400,000 respectively.

INCUBATION OF EGGS AND NUMBER OF PEOPLE
PRODUCING RAW SILK IN THE ARDÈCHE, 1872–1943

	OUNCES	*Sériculteurs*
1872	278,000	40,300
1902	47,220	23,900
1912	33,750	19,530
1922	17,330	12,000
1943	2,559	3,369

Source: Reynier, p. 208.

28. Reynier, *La Soie en Vivarais*, pp. 1, 2, quoting Daniel Bellet; Bozon, *La Vie rurale*, pp. 376–78.
29. Siegfried, *Géographie électorale*, pp. 31–33.
30. February 20, 1921, and October 15, 1933; 12M 217; 12M 243. In 1931 there were 2,000 quintals of mulberry leaves; Mayor Guibourdenche, December 20, 1929. In France as a whole, only 49,132 *onces* were put into incubation in 1915, 67,136 in 1918, 57,075 in 1919, and 72,826 in 1920; in the Ardèche, 14,557 in 1915, 15,803 in 1918, 15,509 in 1919, and 18,312 in 1920. In the Ardèche, 11,374 people produced raw silk in 1915; 13,014 in 1918 and 13,981 in 1920.
31. Cholvy, ed., *Histoire du Vivarais*, p. 274.
32. *La Belle Lurette*, 8 (Summer 1997), pp. 8–12. Moreover, anytime cutting down a mulberry tree was unavoidable, the *propriétaire* had a legal obligation to replant another.
33. Reynier, *Le Pays de Vivarais*, pp. 122–23. During the same period, hectares under cultivation had remained about the same, 127,000 and 125,000, falling to 95,000 in 1935–40. A hectoliter equals 100 liters.
34. 12M 192, 12M 203, 12M 217, 12M 298. 5M 44, subprefect, August 6, 1936. In 1940 farmers cultivated 326 hectares of land, producing rye, barley, and oats. They planted 104 hectares in vineyards, along

with 2 gardens and fourteen orchards and nurseries. There were then 330 hectares of woods. The rest of the territory of Balazuc consisted of moors and imposing stone cliffs. Balazuc also had a *syndicat agricole,* which had begun before the war; an association of hunters, whose members retained the exclusive right to hunt in Balazuc; and a musical society. In 1923 sixty-six property owners renounced their rights to hunt in the commune for three years; thenceforth "the right to hunt on the territory of the commune will be considered by mutual agreement in the best interests of the commune" (January 21, 1923); Jean Boyer.

35. Guy Boyer, "La Coopération viti-vinicole en Ardèche," in *Villages en Vivarais, Mémoire d'Ardèche et Temps présent,* 1987, pp. 117–18.
36. Issartel, "L'Ardèche à la veille du conflit," pp. 4–5.
37. September 13, 1932, and August 6, 1933; 1M 34, minister of the interior, January 20, 1937.
38. When the roof of the presbytery was repaired in 1929, bids were made with candles burning just as in the sale of the *biens nationaux* during the Revolution (2 O 185, subprefect, September 24, 1929).
39. 2 O 185, subprefect, September 24, 1929; July 10, 1927, and April 5, 1936; Jean Boyer. The budget for 1936 allocated 7,783 francs for the upkeep of village roads and paths (July 7, 1935).
40. January 23, 1921, June 17, 1923, July 6, 1930, and February 7, 1932. In 1932 there was an extra 250 francs for the elderly, 62 francs for new mothers, 2,635 francs for school repairs, 72 francs for *assurances sociales* for the two municipal employees, and 1,200 francs for the purchase of a time switch for the clock. In 1930 the council raised the allocation to *femmes en couches* to 2.50 francs per day. At the same time, the minimum allocation to *vieillards* was 30 francs per month (20 for food, 8 for clothing, and 2 for lodging). Small sums were required by the end of the 1930s to pay for insurance for the few municipal employees.
41. September 20, 1936. In 1937, *femmes en couches* received six francs per day, *familles nombreuses* twenty-five francs a month, and the elderly, ill, and incurably ill, seventy francs a month.
42. 1Z 261; 1Z 344, SPL, January 20 and March 24, 1925; the latter included extracts from *La Croix de l'Ardèche,* March 22, 1925 and *L'Ancien Combattant,* March 29, 1925; Cholvy, ed., *Histoire du Vivarais,* p. 248; *Journal d'Aubenas,* May 2, 1925. The Cartel des Gauches was also attacked as "*Le Cartel de la fausse monnaie.*" Jean Boyer. In 1919, Balazuc gave twenty-two votes to the republican list, fifty to the Social-

ists, and sixty-one to the "liberal" list. Of 183 eligible voters, 135 submitted ballots.

43. 1Z 286. A protest followed this election, seemingly put forward by one of the defeated candidates, Lafont, who corresponded with the subprefect assessing the chances of the left. The Conseil de Préfecture rejected the protest. One commentary: "The parties assume positions at the last moment. Personal rivalries enter the fray. The republicans are often divided and it sometimes is difficult on the second balloting to heal pride wounded on the first."

44. 1Z 287; Jean Boyer; in the legislative elections of 1929, Balazuc gave eighty-one votes to Duclaux-Monteil, twenty-nine to the Socialist candidate, and sixteen to the Communist. In 1932 the candidates of the left emerged with seventy-two votes (forty-two for the Socialists, sixteen for the Radicals, and fourteen for the Communists) to sixty-eight for the right.

45. 5M 44, subprefect, July 21, 1934; 5M 49/1, subprefect, March 24, and December 22, 1934, and prefect, March 26, 1934. The department had only 5,858 foreign residents in 1932 (half Italians, followed by Spanish and Armenians).

46. The list headed by the mayor had seventy-six votes to sixty-five for the left; of 165 eligible voters, 144 voted.

47. Issartel, "L'Ardèche à la veille du conflit," pp. 6, 8; Jean Boyer. The Ardèche elected only one deputy for the Popular Front, returning Vallat, Thibon, and another on the right, as well as a Radical hostile to the Popular Front.

48. Jean Boyer.

49. Cholvy, ed., *Histoire du Vivarais,* p. 301.

50. November 10, 1942. See Brigitte Feret, "Le Ravitaillement en Ardèche," *39–45: L'Ardèche dans la guerre, Mémoire d'Ardèche et Temps présent,* 42 (May 1994), pp. 55–61.

51. See Maurice Boulle, "Les Parlementaires ardéchois et les pleins pouvoirs au maréchal Pétain le 10 juillet 1940," in *39–45: L'Ardèche dans la guerre, Mémoire d'Ardèche et Temps présent,* 42 (May 1994), pp. 19–33; *Le Journal d'Aubenas,* February 1, 1941.

52. *Le Réveil de Largentière,* July 14 and November 21, 1942, and February 12, 1943. One woman said that no one in Balazuc knew anything about concentration camps. Le Chambon-sur-Lignon, a village that saved many Jewish children from Lyon and St.-Etienne by adopting them with false papers into their families, is only a few miles from the Ardèche.

53. Cholvy, ed., *Histoire du Vivarais*, p. 256. The "Chansonnette sur le vin": *"Si ti iya resta à l'oustau, La banno dau biau t'aurio pas fa mau"*/*Si tu était resté à la maison, La corne du boeuf ne t'aurait pas fait mal."*

54. See Maurice Boulle, "Maîtres d'école et maîtres du pouvoir," and Pierre Broué, "Révolutionnaire du premier XXe siècle [Élie Reynier]," *Le Chemin des écoliers*, 2, *Mémoire d'Ardèche et Temps présent*, 22 (May 1989); Eric Darrieux, "Une Génération d'instituteurs Ardéchois dans la crise des années trente," *Mémoire de maîtrise* (Université d'Aix-Marseille, 1995). However, Marie-Hélène, *Balazuc: Mémoires de Pierre: Histoire de Ruoms en Ardèche* (L'Atelier de L'Harmonie, 2000), p. 96, writes that "He was certainly executed by the *milice* who threatened him."

55. Account taken from René Maisonnas, *La Résistance en Ardèche 1940–1944* (Aubenas, 1984), pp. 25–79. The French Forces of the Interior (FFI) set up a headquarters in Antraigues on July 10, 1944.

56. Cholvy, ed., *Histoire du Vivarais*, p. 249.

57. See John Sweets, *Choices in Vichy France* (New York, 1986); Anne-Marie Pouzache, "Résistance et maquis en Ardèche," in *39–45: L'Ardèche dans la guerre: De la Résistance à la Libération, Mémoire d'Ardèche et Temps présent*, 43 (August 1994) pp. 6–11.

58. F1a 3900, including letter of J. Bouniol, n.d., 1942; F1a 4000, police report, January 15, 1944.

59. Maisonnas, *La Résistance en Ardèche*, quote from p. 18. Xavier Vallat was sentenced to ten years in prison following the war.

60. Maurice Boulle, "Sur l'épuration en Ardèche," *Mémoire d'Ardèche et de Temps présent*, 43 (August 1994), p. 62.

61. Jean Boyer adds "after having conferred with Allied headquarters and with officials of the Bridges and Roads Division." One man who heard the explosion recalled that it was widely known that the bridge would be blown up, as ordered by the FFI. Occasionally one still hears comments that the bridge had been blown up to cover up "things that happened during the war."

62. Jean Boyer.

63. There were reprisals elsewhere, most notably in Fons, above Aubenas. Not long ago a journalist who expressed interest in researching the topic changed his mind under the strongest of pressure.

64. August 24, 1944. The members signed the minutes and dutifully sent them along to the new prefect for approval. The original committee included Evesque, Maurice Duffaud, Elie Rossignol, and Julien Fromentin.

65. Jean Boyer.

66. Proclamation of October 10, 1944; May 17, 1945; prefect, telegram of May 7, 1945. Marcel Evesque, Maurice Lathey, Elie Rossignol, Julien Fromentin, Germain Lèbre, Marius Duffaud, Hippolyte Guérin, Emile Boucher, Hippolyte Freydier, Noël Boyer, and Ernest Baron made up the "delegation." The first elected council included Jean Poudevigne, Marius Ranchin, Hippolyte Freydier, François Boyer, Pierre Berre, Hippolyte Guérin, Germain Lèbre, Gabriel Boyer, Raoul Dufaud, and Julien Fromentin.

67. Jean Boyer notes that in the referendum in May 1946, Balazuc did not follow the advice of the right and voted *oui* by 102 votes to 76, while the national result was decidedly *non*.

Chapter 8

1. "D'Alba à Balazuc," *Combat*, August 8, 1949.

2. René Tissot, *Aubenas et ses environs* (Aubenas, 1947), pp. 124–26. In 1946, 75.3 percent of the population resided in the countryside (46.8 percent for France [Bozon, *La Vie rurale*, p. 9]).The nucleated village had a slightly older population than the commune as a whole, with, for example, over 5 percent fewer residents younger than twenty years of age. Balazuc's population in 1946 represented a loss of 17.2 percent from the prewar years. During the previous ten years there had been twice as many deaths as births, seventy-four to thirty-seven.

3. January 20, 1952, and July 18, 1954; Maurice and Elise Boulle, "Survol de l'enseignement en Ardèche en 1988," in *Le Chemin des écoliers, 2, Mémoire d'Ardèche et Temps présent* (May 1989), pp. 35, 37, 68–69.

4. June 30, 1946.

5. January 18 and May 6, 1951, and December 11, 1955.

6. In 1949, in eight villages of the Cévennes, 56 percent of the houses were more than a hundred years old. In Genestelle, 59 of 112 houses had been abandoned by 1961 (Bozon, *La Vie rurale*, pp. 466–67).

7. December 10, 1948; June 3, November 6 and 8, 1949; June 20, 1950; April 9, 1952; April 5, 1959; May 6, 1962; and February 10, 1963. Following Freydier's resignation, Jules Dufaud was elected mayor, but with only five votes out of nine, one left blank.

8. May 31, 1947, June 24, 1951, and December 7, 1952. Thus the budget for 1960 anticipated 35,070 francs in income and expenses, and that of 1969 anticipated 69,469 francs in income and expenses. The

meeting of October 20, 1977, approved a loan of 20,000 francs to be repaid in fifteen years. In 1946 the indemnities paid the mayor and his deputy were increased to keep pace with the postwar inflation to 6,000 and 3,000 francs (June 30, 1956). The mayor earned 916 new francs in 1963.

9. May 10, 1956; November 10, 1957; May 1, 1964; June 25, 1971; August 25, 1973; December 10, 1975; December 10, 1977; July 3 and August 2, 1978.

10. March 11, 1951, February 2, 1953, May 30, 1958, September 13, 1959, November 4, 1962, February 10, 1963, and May 1, 1964. In 1953, the municipal council assumed the cost of burying an indigent woman.

11. April 8, 1951, and June 6, 1953. The length of communal roads has increased from 8.4 to 14 miles.

12. November 1, 1954; July 10, November 22, and December 31, 1959; October 2, 1960; September 4, 1961 (authorizing a loan of 30,000 francs at 5 percent interest); January 28, March 18, and April 15, 1962; July 14, 1963; June 28 and August 9, 1964; August 1, 1965; November 1, 1970; and of April 1, 1980, which requested 120,000 francs to improve the road to Uzer. Work in 1963 was financed by a loan of 30,000 francs and subsidies. Five years later Balazuc again asked that the "path" be reclassified because of its burden on the communal budget. The cantonal committee turned the village down again.

13. Bozon, *La Vie rurale,* pp. 483–84; Jean Boyer; August 13, 1950, January 14, 1951, January 4, March 1, and September 10, 1953, August 30, 1954. Balazuc's part of the loan was 4,021,000 francs, though the latter meeting had Balazuc guaranteeing 2,715,161 (old francs), to be repaid within thirty years.

14. June 4, 1961. That year the tiny salary paid for this service was raised from 360 to 450 francs, in view of the increase in calls for villagers and the fact that some people called upon him to deliver to others in the village "news and to do various errands."

15. March 20, 1960.

16. November 22, 1959.

17. A recent article in *Libération* (July 5, 1999) claims that two million people still can speak some version of Occitan in the south of France (defined by a line north of Bordeaux, extending up to north of Limoges and down south of Lyon), a number that certainly seems inflated.

Former Education Minister Allègre is alleged to have once referred to patois and other minority dialects as the "languages of shepherds."

18. Banks too came to play a greater role. Between the wars, Julien le riche (not to be confused with Julien le pauvre) was known as the banker because he loaned out money.

19. See, among others, Gordon Wright, *Rural Revolution in France;* Henri Mendras, *La Fin des paysans;* Georges Duby, et al., *Histoire de la France rurale.*

20. Ozil, *Magnaneries,* pp. 63–65; *La Belle Lurette,* 8 (Summer 1997), pp. 12–14; Bozon, *La Vie rurale,* pp. 375–77. The high cost of labor was also a factor.

21. Bozon, *La Vie rurale,* p. 398; Guy Boyer, "La coopération viti-vinicole en Ardèche," pp. 117–27. On November 23, 2000, a local paper carried a photo of Guy Boyer and other members of the Confraternity du Cep Ardéchois in Leeds, England, carrying the taste for Ardéchois wines to that country.

22. Sahuc, *Le Fils du pauvre,* pp. 183, 188.

23. Guy Boyer, letter of welcome to the bishop on the occasion of the centenary of the church, n.d., 1995.

24. November 1, 1970, and March 29, 1971.

25. *Des rives de l'Ardèche au Coiron: Journal interparoissial,* no. 22 (Summer 2001): "The Church is at the service of mankind for unity, solidarity, and reconciliation."

26. Weber, *Peasants into Frenchmen.*

27. In 1953 the victorious list won by an average of 118 votes to 95.

28. In 1977 only two members of the old council were held over, including Aimé Mouraret, who became mayor. The Communists received twenty-seven votes in the 1993 legislative elections (15 percent), the Socialist party twenty votes (11 percent, a decline of 16 percent since 1988); the extreme right Front National received only 4 percent of the vote.

29. April 30, 1961. Yet the municipality contributed funds (as was routine, it must be said) to aid victims of flood in the southwest in 1949, of an earthquake in Algeria in 1954, and of another natural disaster in Fréjus in 1959, Balazuc's inhabitants having often been victims of the ravages of nature.

30. March 31 and July 14, 1963.

31. Among those elected to the municipal council in that or subsequent elections, Mollier, Mouraret, Laroche, Boyer, Gamel, Freydier, Redon,

and Thibon also represented families with long histories in Balazuc.

32. Nicole Lélie, followed by Ginette Michalon and Paulette Balazuc in 1989.

33. The people of Balazuc may well have shared the distaste for politics and politicians (*ils,* the government) noted by Laurence Wylie in his study of Roussillon (*Village in the Vaucluse*) and represented in a civics book, "the distaste for politics and for politicians who are often portrayed as men of little morality, of slight merit, incapable of making their way honestly and serving usefully"(p. 208). Thus in postwar elections from 1946 to 1953 the percentages of those eligible to vote and turning up to do so were consistently higher for municipal than for national elections (p. 233).

34. *Le Monde,* March 16, 2001.

35. November 29, 2000.

36. *La Tribune,* February 15, 2001.

37. There were 228 votes cast, and 216 were counted as real ballots.

38. In the second round of the cantonal elections of March 2001, Balazuc once again gave a majority of votes to the conservative candidate, ninety-eight votes to forty-eight for the Socialist. In the first round, the Front National candidate received only ten votes, the Communist candidate eighteen, and the Green candidate thirty-two.

39. October 5, 1989. In 1961, Balazuc joined St.-Maurice-d'Ardèche and Lanas to form an association "to defend the river banks of the Ardèche" River (July 9). See *Le Monde,* February 25–26, 1990.

40. Public meeting, November 24, 2000.

41. February 17 and April 7, 1946; Jean Boyer. That year the municipal council asked that for a school that would serve the residents of the hamlets of Louanes and Cousamas, whose children had to walk almost four miles a day round trip.

42. April 6 and December 7, 1952; May 9, 1954, and May 1, 1955; December 22, 1957; December 28, 1958; September 13, 1959; June 15, 1976. Departmental subsidies: 110 francs in 1973, 137 francs in 1977, and 220 francs in 1980.

43. For example, June 24, 1951, April 6 (84,000 francs for teaching materials), August 24 and December 7, 1952; May 12, October 1, and December 28, 1958; May 8, 1960; April 30 and May 30, 1961; April 23, 1963; May 1, 1964; January 15, 1974; June 15, 1976; December 27, 1977; and December 13, 1980. Expenses included the distribution of milk to pupils less than ten years of age, at least in 1957 and

1958. In addition, the council paid a woman to sweep out the school every Wednesday.

44. March 3, 1979, and October 27, 1989.

45. May 5, 1961, inspector's letter of February 14, 1961.

46. April 5, 1970: "It is unfortunately certain that this figure will not increase during the coming years."

47. Wylie (*Village in the Vaucluse*, p. 63) notes "teachers are especially vulnerable to criticism. Their social prestige and privileges arouse resentment among the villagers who saw that the teachers 'have it easy,' that they are well paid but do not have to work hard, that they have a long summer vacation and many shorter holidays throughout the year, that they have to work in the classrooms only thirty hours a week!" Other than joking comments about the easy life of a *fonctionnaire,* I have not heard this in Balazuc.

48. *Libération,* September 24, 1996. During the 1993–94 school year, the Ardèche was one of the departments that still had between 14 and 22 percent one-room schoolhouses.

49. Deborah Reed-Danahay's recent study, *Education and Identity in Rural France,* of a village in Auvergne emphasizes resistance of parents to the school. Her main argument is that "local schools, even in the centralized system of France, may work to reinforce local identity, as parents and children resist aspects of national culture and state power" (p. 3). That is, parents defend a regional identity by maintaining—or did at least in the early 1980s—Auvergnat patois (to exclude the teachers, viewed in her analysis as inevitable outsiders) and resisting the use of napkins in the lunchroom as a way of maintaining their distance from what she calls urban, bourgeois values. "Families and children in Lavialle use strategies of both resistance and accommodation to shape the role and meaning of schooling. . . . Lavialle's school is a social space within and around which people have found ways to be both Laviallois and French" (p. 208). In contrast, Laurence Wylie in *Village in the Vaucluse* makes the point that families and primary school teachers share similar patterns of authority, so that there is little difference between home and school in this respect, and parents, by implication, are therefore less likely to resist and subvert the authority of the *instituteur.*

50. Parents living in Balazuc who put their children in school in other towns have been criticized.

51. *Bulletin municipal no. 5,* December 1997.

52. June 30, 1946; May 25 and October 14, 1947; March 5, 1950; and January 26, 1952. Balazuc took out yet another loan of 208,000 francs to improve its roads and paths. An additional tax on residents was assessed for the work on January 30, 1949. In 1954, Balazuc was among those communes with fewer than five automobiles per hundred inhabitants, thus only between ten and fifteen cars (Bozon, *La Vie rurale,* p. 485).

53. July 17 and October 30, 1955; the latter approved repairs of the church for 400,000 (old) francs, with winter approaching; the municipality also requested funds from the Ministry of National Education and the Service des Beaux Arts. On November 13, 1955, the council voted to accept thirty thousand and fifty thousand francs respectively from Jean Delsaux, who lived in Paris, and Dr. Pierre Chadourne, Chevilly-la-Rue, Seine.

54. March 31, 1979, followed by a request for a subsidy, June 8, 1980.

55. *Les Plus Beaux Villages de France: Guide official* (Paris, 1997), preface.

56. *Cahiers* made available to me by Abbé Rouveyrol. Dissenting voices included one who complained about the choice of music left playing ("A choice of music from the 17th or 18th century would have been more judicious") and another, who wrote in July 1997, "A pretty church but one must also recall that the greatest cause of mortality has without doubt been wars of religion." More sobering are obviously notes like that signed simply "Me": "When I think of you [Lord], it will be in anger because you took my mother too soon . . . we, her children, still needed her" (July 27, 1999).

57. High in the canton of St.-Martin-de-Valamas, the village of Chanéac, which had had a population of about 1,000 in 1900, had only 227 people in 1960. In 1965 the mayor founded the Association des Amis de Chanéac, the purpose of which was to enrich and save the village. Six years later the mayor, joined by the curé and two young people, began a hunger strike in order to obtain authorization and assistance to begin a *maison de vacances,* which opened in 1976. Little by little, Chanéac has revived, but, besides some young people raising goats and a few remaining farmers, only in the summer, thanks to new secondary residences (CR., "Un village parie sur son avenir," *Coopérateur de France* [June 20, 1981], pp. 42–43).

58. The notebooks left for tourists to sign in the church quickly reveal that about a third of the notes are signed in Dutch/Flemish.

59. Bozon, *L'Ardèche* p. 105; Ozil, *Sériciculture,* vol. III, p. 174.

60. Two academic couples, one British, one American, who visited us on several occasions have since purchased summer houses in Balazuc.

61. Carlat, *Architecture populaire,* pp. 22–25, 102, 128, 151–55, 286–87. Last quote from Roger Ferlet.

62. Balazuc, *Mémoires de soie.* See Harriet Rosenberg's excellent *A Negotiated World.* She considers the politics of tourism in Abriès (Hautes-Alpes) and argues that while villagers in the Ancien Régime enjoyed a surprising access to power through a process of negotiation and lobbying ("peasant diplomacy"), their descendants have no control over decisions made from the outside (pp. 199–203). Her study shows how both the mayor, with positions to award, and government authorities have had a stake in developing tourism and examines some of the ways that tourism remains disconnected from villagers, accentuating the fragmentation of economic and social life.

63. Carlat, *Architecture populaire,* p. 109.

64. "Message à la population et aux Vacanciers," n.d., June 1995.

65. Mayor's letter to "Chers compatriotes," December 22, 1995.

66. "Compte rendu réunion Commissions tourisme et développement environment et cadre de vie," August 23, 1996; *Bulletin Municipale no. 5* (December 1997). The mayor created a Committee on Tourism and the Development of the Environment.

67. Guy Boyer said in his welcome to the bishop of Viviers, n.d. (1995): "Young couples are the source of life, hope, and the future. . . . The quality of rural life is a source of attraction for those who come here, but we run into the difficulty of finding available permanent housing, as well as the precariousness of employment."

68. *Balazuc, bulletin municipal no. 8* (August 1999). This jump represented a gain of 20 percent, compared with the Ardèche as a whole (2.90 percent).

69. The number of people employed in service in the Ardèche increased by about 40 percent just between 1975 and 1982 and has increased ever since.

70. One woman makes a point that people in Balazuc particularly frown on people who are considered proud or arrogant.

71. October 5, 1989. The municipality could have acquired some land to enlarge that small *place* in the early 1950s.

72. *Balazuc, bulletin municipal no. 6* (July 1998).

73. June 19, 1949; December 28, 1958; for example, seven hundred francs allocated to the Comité des Fêtes, December 16, 1980; April 6, 1989.

74. Recently the municipality sold a parcel of land for two hundred thousand francs to earn money. In 2000 a woman who died left some money to the residents of the village but not to the municipality.

75. Mairie de Balazuc, taxes in the village, 1994, population, 282: tax on residency (296 households), 139,325; tax on land with construction, 62,704; tax on property without construction, 71,606; tax on business (23 *enterprises ou commerces*), 18,356—total 291,981 francs.

76. *Balazuc, bulletin municipal no. 8* (August 1999).

77. Carlat, *Architecture populaire*, p. 20.

78. Ibid., p. 21.

79. "Actualités: Les Résultats du recensement de 1999," *Cahiers de Mémoire d'Ardèche et Temps présent*, 68 (November 2000), p. 11, with well less than a fifth of the population under twenty years of age. Sadly, as has been sometimes noted for the region as a whole, Balazuc has of late had more than its share of suicides.

80. Laurence Wylie (*Village in the Vaucluse,* p. 207), remarks that in Roussillon schoolchildren in the early 1950s learned by heart "A good citizen possesses the spirit of cooperation and mutual aid." In 2000 Balazuc raised more than nine thousand francs for charity in the Téléthon, donating money to play boules or cards or to hike or buying lottery tickets.

PRIMARY SOURCES & BIBLIOGRAPHY

Primary Sources

Archives Nationales (AN)
BB30 382, 395–96, 401
C 945
DIV bis 4
F1a 3900 (Ardèche), 4000
F1bII Ardèche 1, 2, 3, 4, 7
F1cIII Ardèche 7, 10, 11, 1125
F7 3652 (2), 9632, 12357, 12396,
  12753, 12936–37
F15 3964, 3990–93
F9 4371
F11 2697
F15 3964, 3990-3993
Series F17, Ministry of Public Instruction
F 17*83, *2598, *2740, *3160,
  3652(1), 3652(2), 9253, 9279, 9306,
  9310, 9313–14, 9317, 9319, 9322,
  9336, 9370, 9374–75, 9580, 9632,
  10259–60, 10286, 10374, 10382,
  10691, 10779, 11140, 11285,
  F20 161

Archives of the Ministry of War
(Vincennes)
MR 1248

Archives Départementales (AD) de
l'Ardèche (Privas)
B 138 (2MI 158), 142 (2MI 76)
C 17–18, 42-43, 54, 81, 656, 672,
  843, 991, 1051, 1063, 1090–91,
  1141, 1150, 1239, 1242, 1254,
  1361, 1511
2E M.L. 631–32, notarial archives,
  Year 13–1806
52 J 134 (Fonds Mazon, manuscript
  Delichères)
8J 6/5 and 6/6
8J 26/10 (Fonds Reynier)

13J 1*

21J 145

J 469

L 252, 267, 269, 544, 559–60, 876,
877, 897, 901, 911, 923, 931, 937,
939, 963, 967–68, 970, 974, 1167,
1212, 1561, 1566, 1572, 1607, 1637

Q 47, 195, 248, 270, 282–83, 316,
486

2M 239, 273–74, 276, 337–38, 341,
524

3M 44–45, 73–74, 78, 84, 88, 96,
103, 150, 210, 220–21, 230–31,
248, 261, 265–68, 307, 314, 320,
326–28, 332, 334

2MP 34

5M 10–11, 14, 18, 18 bis, 19-21, 28,
31–32, 37–38, 40–41, 44–45, 49/1,
53

6M 52–53

10M 28, 51, 71

12M 53–59, 76, 81, 176-77, 179,
181–82, 184, 187, 189, 191–92,
194, 200, 203, 207, 213, 217, 243,
253, 273, 286, 298

15M 1

1MP 34, 154

2MP 34, 50

3P 170, *cadastre*, 1825

O 545

2 O 183–91

R 189

T 27, 43, 69, 70–71, 74, 97–99,
112–13, 115, 119, 124, 175,
209–11, 216, 218, 246, 283, 322,
343, 357, 359, 361, 379, 383, 417,
425, 443, 495, 498, 500, 502, 576,
586, 589, 594, 597, 598, 3285,
3290, 3298, 3375

V 51, 53, 141, 155, 186, 189, 204,
211, 217, 226–34, 245, 247,
249–52, 254, 258–63, 276-87, 298,
303, 305, 311, 321, 331, 344, 438,

458, 507, 520, 526, 528, 531–32,
535, 570, 745, 765–68, 771, 773,
776–77, 779, 801–02, 842

1Z, 186, 227, 229, 233–34, 250,
258–61, 273, 276, 279–85, 287,
303–04, 311, 321, 331, 344, 483,
507, 520, 535, 570, 733, 765, 779,
802

Fonds Mazon, 3, 9, and 13

État Civil (births, marriages, deaths)
5Mi 15, 19, 1668–1789
6 E 23/1*-12*, 421*-422*, État Civil
1792–1902

Archives Départementales (AD) de
l'Hérault (Montpellier)
C 3014, 4019

Archives Départementales (AD) du
Gard (Nîmes) 10T8

Mairie de Balazuc
Registers of deliberations (*procès-ver-
baux*), municipal council of Balazuc,
1809–1990
Censuses, 1804, 1846, 1876, 1911
Nonclassified documents

Bibliothèque Nationale (BN)
Collection Languedoc-Bénédictins
(Salle des Manuscrits)

Newspapers
Le Journal d'Aubenas, 1941
Le Réveil de Largentière, 1942–44
L'Echo de l'Ardèche, 1871
L'Ardèche républicaine, 1905, 1906
L'Echo de Largentière, 1905–06,
1909–10, 1914, 1921
Le Républicain des Cévennes, 1892, 1895,
1896, 1898, 1900, 1904, 1906,
1908, 1909, 1912, 1925, 1935
Le Courrier d'Aubenas, 1895
Courrier de la Drôme et de l'Ardèche,
1851

Secondary Sources

Allignol, Maurice. *Balazuc et le Bas Vivarais.* N.p., 1992.

André, M. "La Visite des paroisses de l'officialité d'Aubenas en 1715." *Revue du Vivarais* (1974–75).

Arché, Guy-Jean. *L'Espoir au coeur, l'insurrection de 1851.* Poët-Laval, 1981.

Balazuc, Marie-Hélène. *Mémoires de soie.* Robiac-Rochessadoule, 1992.

Blain, Charles (Albin Mazon). *Quelques scènes et récits du Vivarais.* Aubenas, 1981.

Blanc, Jean-François. *Paysages et paysans des terrasses de l'Ardèche.* Annonay, 1984.

Boulle, Maurice. *Révoltes et espoirs en Vivarais 1780–1789.* Privas, 1988.

———. "Sur l'épuration en Ardèche" 39–45: L'Ardèche dans la guerre. *Mémoire d'Ardèche et Temps présent,* 43 (August 1994), pp. 6–11.

Bourdin, Louis. *Le Vivarais: Essai de géographie régionale.* Paris, 1898.

Boyer, Jean, "Chronique Balazucaine de la Révolution à nos jours," unpublished manuscript.

———. "Historique de Balazuc," unpublished pamphlet.

Boys, Albert du. *Album du Vivarais.* Grenoble, 1842.

Bozon, Pierre. *L'Ardèche: La Terre et les hommes du Vivarais.* Poët-Laval, 1985.

———. *La Vie rurale en Vivarais.* Valence, 1961.

Brown, Howard G. "Bonaparte's 'Booted Justice' in Bas-Languedoc." *Proceedings of the Annual Meeting of the Western Society for French History,* 24 (1998), pp. 120–30.

———. "From Organic Society to Security State: The War of Brigandage in France, 1797–1802." *Journal of Modern History,* 69 (1997), pp. 661–95.

Caffarelli, Charles Ambroise. *Observations sur l'agriculture du département de l'Ardèche.* Paris, [Year IX].

Carlat, Michel. *Architecture populaire de l'Ardèche.* Poët-Laval, 1984.

———. *Architecture rurale en Vivarais.* Paris, 1982.

———. *L'Ardèche traditionnelle.* Poët-Laval, 1982.

———. *L'Ardèche: La Terre et les hommes du Vivarais.* Poët-Laval, 1985.

———. *L'Ardèche: Les Chemins du coeur.* Voreppe, 1990.

Chambon, André. *Paysans de Vivarais.* Vals-les-Bains, 1985.

Chanet, Jean-François. *L'Ecole républicaine et les petites patries.* Paris, 1996.

Charrié, Pierre. *Dictionnaire topograpique du département de l'Ardèche.* Paris, 1979.

———. *Le Folklore du Bas-Vivarais.* Paris, 1982.

Chevalier, Raymond, and Michelle Redon-Chevalier. "Centenaire de l'église paroissiale de Balazuc, 1895–1995," unpublished manuscript, 1996.

Cheynel, Hélène. *Contes et légendes du Vivarais.* Valence, 1993.

Cheyron, Jean. *L'Acceptation du Second Empire dans l'Ardèche.* Largentière, 1985.

———. *Epidémies du choléra en Ardèche.* Largentière, 1985.

———. *Le Plebiscite du 8 mai 1870 dans l'Ardèche.* Largentière, 1986.

Cholvy, Gérard, ed., *Histoire du Vivarais,* Toulouse,1988.

Cornu, Pierre. *Une Économie rurale dans la débacle: Cévenne vivaraise, 1852–1892.* Paris, 1993.

Darrieux, Eric. "Une génération d'instituteurs Ardéchois dans la crise des années trente." Mémoire de maîtrise. Université Aix-Marseille, 1995.

Feret, Brigitte, "Le Ravitaillement en Ardèche." *39–45: l'Ardèche dans la guerre. Mémoire d'Ardèche et Temps présent,* 42 (May 1994), pp. 55–61.

Ferlet, Roger. *Le Vivarais d'antan.* 2 vols. Valence, 1981-82.

Forot, Charles, and Michel Carlat. *Le Feu sous la cendre: Le Paysan vivarois et sa maison.* St.-Félicien, 1979.

Gardès, Jean-Marc. *Et ils déplacèrent les bornes! Le département de l'Ardèche, héritage de la Révolution française.* Privas, 1989.

Gaspin, Jordan. *Les Mobilisés de l'Ardèche 1870–71.* Privas, 1996.

Gemie, Sharif. " 'A Danger to Society'? Teachers and Authority in France, 1833–1850." *French History,* 2, 3 (September 1988), pp. 264–87.

Gildea, Robert. *Education in Provincial France, 1800–1914: A Study of Three Departments.* New York, 1983.

Gourinard, Pierre, "La Part de l'Ardèche à la mise en valeur de l'Algérie." *Revue du Vivarais,* 73, 2 (April–June, 1969), pp. 91–102.

Gutton, Jean-Pierre. *La Sociabilité villageoise dans la France d'ancien régime.* Paris, 1979.

Harp, Stephen. *Learning to Be Loyal: Primary Schooling as Nation Building in Alsace and Lorraine, 1850–1940.* De Kalb, Ill., 1998.

Issartel, Jean-Louis, "L'Ardèche à la veille du conflit." *39–45: L'Ardèche dans la guerre; Mémoire d'Ardèche et Temps présent,* 42 (May 1994), pp. 39–48.

Joanne, Paul. *Géographie du département de l'Ardèche.* Paris, 1911.

Joffre, Nicole. "La Question scolaire dans l'Ardèche de 1880–1914." Mémoire de maîtrise. Université de Dijon, 1975.

Jolivet, Charles. *Les Chouans du Vivarais.* Taulignan, 1987.

———. *La Révolution en Ardèche (1788–1795).* Challes-les-Eaux, 1988.

Joly, Jean, and J. Peyrard. *En Ardèche, notre école au bon vieux temps.* Lyon, 1993.

Joly, Michel. *L'Architecture des églises romanes du Vivarais.* Paris, 1966.

Jones, Peter, "Common Rights and Agrarian Individualism in the Southern Massif Central 1750–1880." In Gwynn Lewis and Colin Lucas, eds., *Beyond the Terror.* Cambridge, England, 1983.

———. *Politics and Rural Society: The Southern Massif Central, 1750–1880.* Cambridge, 1985.

———. "Towards a Village History of the French Revolution: Some Problems of Method." *French History,* 14, 1 (March 2000), pp. 67–82.

Ladet, Pierre. *Entre Coiron et Tanargue: Aubenas sous le vent de l'histoire.* Privas, 1991.

Lequin, Yves. *Les Ouvriers de la région lyonnaise.* 2 vols. Lyon, 1977.

Le Roy Ladurie, Emannuel. *The Peasants of Languedoc.* Urbana, Ill., 1976.

Maisonnas, René. *La Résistance en Ardèche 1940–1944.* Aubenas, 1984.

Margadant, Ted W. *French Peasants in Revolt: The Insurrection of 1851.* Princeton, 1979.

Massot, Georges. "La Langue d'oc en Vivarais et Ardèche." *Genèse et histoire de la langue occitane et des idioms vivarois. Mémoire d'Ardèche et Temps présent,"* 51-I (November 1996).

Mayaud, Jean-Luc. *La Petite Exploitation rurale triomphante.* Paris, 1999.

Mazon, Albin. *Notice sur Vinezac.* Privas, 1897; reprinted Villeneuve-de-Berg, 1987.

———. *Voyage au tour de Valgorge.* Privas, 1879.

———. *Voyage dans le Midi de l'Ardèche.* Aubenas, 1884.

————. *Voyages le long de la rivière Ardèche*. Aubenas, 1885.

McPhee, Peter. *The Politics of Rural Life: Political Mobilization in the French Countryside, 1845–1852*. New York, 1992.

Merriman, John M. "On the Loose: The Impact of Rumors and *Mouchards* in the Ardèche during the Second Republic." In Jonathan Sperber, ed., *Europe 1848: Revolution and Reform*. London, 2000.

Molinier, Alain. "Les Difficultés de la scolarisation et de l'alphabétisation sous la Restauration: L'Exemple ardéchois." *Annales du Midi* 97, 170, pp. 129–56 (April–June, 1985).

————. *Stagnations et croissance: Le Vivarais aux XVIIe–XVIIIe siècles*. Paris, 1985.

————. "En Vivarais au XVIIIe siècle: Une croissance démographique sans révolution agricole." *Annales du Midi*, 92, 148 (1980) pp. 301–16.

Morel, Yves. "Les Maîtres du fil: Une industrie textile en milieu rural: Le Moulinage ardéchois au XIXe siècle." Doctoral dissertation, Université Lumière-Lyon II, 1999.

Mouly, P. *Le Concordat en Lozère-Ardèche, 1801–1805*. Mende, 1942.

Noir, Michel. *1789, Des faubourgs de Paris aux montagnes d'Ardèche*. Paris, 1988.

Ogden, Philip E. "Industry, Mobility and the Evolution of Rural Society in the Ardèche in the Later Nineteenth and Early Twentieth Centuries." In Philip E. Ogden and Paul E. White, *Migrants in Modern France: Population Mobility in the Later Nineteenth and Twentieth Centuries*. London, 1989.

Ozil, Hervé. *Magnanerie et vers à soie: La Sériciculture en pays vivarois et Cévenol*. Lavilledieu, 1986.

————. "*La Sériciculture en Ardèche:* Survivence d'une production?", Doctoral thesis. Université au Lyon II, 1983. 3 vols.

Peyrard, Jean, and Jules Joly. *En Ardèche, notre école au bon vieux temps*. Lyon, 1993.

Pouzache, Anne-Marie. "Résistance et maquis en Ardèche." *39-45: L'Ardèche dans la guerre: De la Résistance à la Libération*." *Mémoire d'Ardèche et temps présent*, 43 (August 1994), pp. 6–11.

Reboul, Annet. *Moeurs de l'Ardèche au XIXe siècle*. Valence, 1849.

Régné, Jean. *Histoire du Vivarais*. 3 vols. Largentière, 1914.

————. *La Vie économique et sociale dans 150 localités du Vivarais, d'après les Estimes de 1464*. Aubenas, 1926.

————. *La Vie économique et les classes sociales en Vivarais, au lendemain de la guerre de cent ans*. Aubenas, 1925.

Reynier, Élie. *Le Pays de Vivarais*. Vals-les-Bains, 1923.

————. *La Seconde République dans l'Ardèche, 1848–1852*. Privas, 1998; originally published 1948.

————. *La Soie en Vivarais*. Largentière, 1921.

Riou, Michel, "La Vente des biens nationaux dans le département de l'Ardèche." In *Communautés d'oc et Révolution française*, II. Largentière, 1987.

Roudil, Jean-Louis. *Préhistoire de l'Ardèche*. Soubès, 1995.

Rouvière, Michel. "Le Gras de Balazuc, Vinezac, Lanas," unpublished paper, 1998.

————. *Paysages de pierre, paysages de vie*. Chirols, 1991.

Roux, Jacqueline. "L'Enseignement primaire dans l'Ardèche sous la monarchie de juillet: La Contribution des congrégations religieuses à l'enseignement elémentaire." In *Eglises, Pouvoirs et Société en Ardèche (milieu XVIIIème siècle–milieu XIXème siècle)*. Ucel, 1993.

Sabatier, Gérard. "De la révolte de Roure (1670) aux Masques armés (1783): La Mutation du phénomène contestataire en Vivarais." In Jean Nicolas, ed. *Mouvements populaires et conscience sociale, XVIe–XIXe siècles.* Paris, 1985.

Sahuc, Régis. *Le fils du peuple.* Le Pay, 1994.

Salmon, J. H. M. "Peasant Revolt in Vivarais, 1575–1580." *French Historical Studies,* 11, 1 (1979), pp. 1–28.

Siegfried, André. *Géographie électorale de l'Ardèche sous la IIIe République.* Paris, 1949.

Sonenscher, Michael. "Royalists and Patriots: Nîmes and Its Hinterland in the Late Eighteenth Century." Doctoral dissertation. University of Warwick, 1977.

Sudres, Jean-Daniel, and Michel Carlat. *Visages et paysages de l'Ardèche.* Aubenas, 1986.

"Sylvestre" [Paul Gouy]. *Un scandale electoral à Balazuc.* Aubenas, 1909.

Thomas, François, and Marthe Thomas. *Le Vivarais.* Paris, 1947.

Tissot, René, *Aubenas et ses environs.* Aubenas, 1947.

Valgorge, Ovide de. *Souvenirs de l'Ardèche,* vol. II. Paris, 1846.

Védel, Léon (Taveny de Largentière). *A travers le Vivarais: Balazuc et Pons de Balazuc.* Lyon, 1884.

Villard, Eugène. De *la situation des intérêts agricoles dans l'arrondissement de Largentière.* Nîmes,1852.

Vogüé, Eugène-Melchoir de. *Notes sur le Bas-Vivarais.* Paris, 1893.

Volane, Jean. *L'Ardèche pittoresque.* St.-Etienne, 1989, first published, 1899.

Woloch, Isser. *The New Regime: Transformations of the French Civic Order, 1789–1820s.* New York, 1994.

Related Studies

Amann, Peter. *The Corncribs of Buzet: Modernizing Agriculture in the French Southwest.* Princeton, 1990.

Bell, David. *The Cult of the Nation in France: Inventing Nationalism, 1680–1800.* Cambridge, Mass., 2001.

Carles, Emilie. *A Life of Her Own.* New Brunswick, N.J., 1991.

Gemie, Sharif, "'A Danger to Society'? Teachers and Authority in France, 1833–1850." *French History,* 2, 3 (September 1988), pp. 264–87.

Héliaz, Pierre-Jakez. *The Horse of Pride: Life in a Breton Village.* New Haven, 1978.

Higonnet, Patrice. *Pont-de-Montvert: Social Structure and Politics in a French Village, 1700–1914.* Cambridge, Mass., 1971.

McPhee, Peter. *Les Semailles de la République dans les Pyrénées-Orientales, 1846–52.* Perpignan, 1995.

Mendras, Henri. *La Fin des paysans.* Paris, 1970.

Merriman, John M. *The Agony of the Republic: The Repression of the Left in Revolutionary France, 1848–51.* New Haven, 1978.

Meyers, P. "Professionalization and Social Change: Rural Teachers in 19th Century France." *Journal of Social History,* 9 (1976), pp. 542–58.

Reed-Danahay, Deborah. *Education and Identity in Rural France: The Politics of Schooling.* Cambridge, England, 1996.

Rogers, Susan Carol. *Shaping Modern Times in Rural France: The Transformation and Reproduction of an Averyronais Community Village.* Princeton, 1991.

Rosenberg, Harriet G. *A Negotiated World: Three Centuries of Change in a French Alpine Community.* Toronto, 1988.

Serre, Robert. *Grane: Histoire d'un village du Val de Drôme,* vol. 2. Crest, 1993.

Thibault, Roger. *Mon village.* Paris, 1982.

Tindall, Gillian. *Celestine: Voices from a French Village.* New York, 1996.

Van Zanten, Henriot. *L'École et l'espace locale.* Lyon, 1990.

Weber, Eugen. *Peasants into Frenchmen: The Modernization of Rural France 1880–1914.* Stanford, 1976.

Wylie, Laurence, ed. *Chanzeaux, a Village in Anjou.* Cambridge, Mass., 1966.

———. *Village in the Vaucluse.* Cambridge, Mass., 1974, published in 1954.

Zonabend, Françoise. *The Enduring Memory: Time and History in a French Village.* Manchester, England, 1985.

INDEX

Page numbers in *italics* refer to illustrations.

wine *(continued)*
  intercommunal cooperatives for
    production of, 266–67
  military requisitions of, 231
  production levels of, 25, 53,
    112–13, 115, 153, 239, 267
  quality of, 115, 267
  silk industry vs., 96
  in storage cellars, 11
  trade difficulties and, 39, 113,
    142
  vineyard diseases and, 113–14,
    141, 173

wolves, 37
wood supplies, 41
World War I, 229–36, 242
  monument to Balazuc victims of,
    xiii, 235
  silk-industry decline in, 237
World War II, 245–54
  resistance movement in, 246,
    249–52, 254, 257
Wylie, Laurence, xii

Year in Provence, A (Mayle), xii
Young, Arthur, 32, 50, 53